W9-AEY-490

Choosing Democracy
A Practical Guide to Multicultural Education

Duane E. Campbell
California State University, Sacramento

Merrill,
an imprint of Prentice Hall
Englewood Cliffs, New Jersey   Columbus, Ohio

Library of Congress Cataloging-in-Publication Data

Campbell, Duane E.
    Choosing democracy : a practical guide to multicultural education / Duane E.
Campbell.
      p. cm.
    Includes bibliographical references and index.
    ISBN 0-13-351370-X (pbk.)
    1. Multicultural education—United States. 2. Education—Social aspects—United
States. 3. Pluralism (Social sciences)—United States. 4. Racism—United States. 5. United
States—Race relations. 6. Social classes—United States. 7. Sex differences in education—
United States.   I. Title.
    LC1099.3.C36   1996
    370.19'6—dc20

95-7654
CIP

Cover photo: Todd Davidson/The Image Bank
Editor: Debra A. Stollenwerk
Production Editor: Louise N. Sette
Photo Editor: Anne Vega
Text Designer: Ed Horcharik
Design Coordinator: Julia Zonneveld Van Hook
Cover Designer: Tammy Johnson
Production Manager: Deidra M. Schwartz
Electronic Text Management: Marilyn Wilson Phelps, Matthew Williams, Karen L. Bretz,
   Tracey Ward
Illustrations: Jane Lopez

This book was set in Kuenstler 480, Avant Garde, and Swiss 721 by Prentice Hall and
was printed and bound by R.R. Donnelley & Sons Company. The cover was printed by
Phoenix Color Corp.

 © 1996 by Prentice-Hall, Inc.
A Simon & Schuster Company
Englewood Cliffs, New Jersey 07632

Photo credits: AP/Worldwide

Printed in the United States of America

10 9 8 7 6 5 4 3 2 1

ISBN: 0-13-351370-X

Prentice-Hall International (UK) Limited, *London*
Prentice-Hall of Australia Pty. Limited, *Sydney*
Prentice-Hall of Canada, Inc., *Toronto*
Prentice-Hall Hispanoamericana, S. A., *Mexico*
Prentice-Hall of India Private Limited, *New Delhi*
Prentice-Hall of Japan, Inc., *Tokyo*
Simon & Schuster Asia Pte. Ltd., *Singapore*
Editora Prentice-Hall do Brasil, Ltda., *Rio de Janeiro*

To Dolores Delgado-Campbell. Your more than twenty years of instruction from a Chicana feminist perspective informs all that I say and write. You have helped me to cross the borders of culture and to appreciate the dialectics of change.

To Javier Sean Campbell. Your sense of conscience and integrity about your issues re-teaches me to treat young people with dignity and respect. Hay que pensar en el futuro—y el futuro pertenece a su generacíon.

Foreword

By Henry T. Trueba

Over the years the struggle for social justice in California has produced unusual powerful statements that revisit the democratic foundations of America as a free country with justice for all. This book belongs to that category but in a strict sense deserves to be seen as a foundational volume in teacher education for three reasons: (1) it places "multicultural" education as pivotal to retain the democratic fabric of American society; (2) it refocuses on "culture" (without neglecting social class and sociological theories on equity and stratification) as a crucial factor cementing ethnic and racial harmony in our modern pluralistic world; and (3) it addresses the reality of poverty in North America, and especially poverty of school-age children. There are important implications of these three issues for a practical pedagogical approach to "multicultural" education, for educational reform, and for social transformation.

Education is crucial to the realization of the American dream. The reason is that it is primarily through the acquisition of knowledge and skills associated with formal education that immigrant and low-income students become empowered and a part of mainstream America. It is particularly relevant to speak of multicultural education as the kind of education that will permit Americans to become aware of "democracy at work," realize their full potential, and live in harmony. The obstacle to a good education for racial and ethnic minority groups and others who become marginalized is the use of white mainstream culture as a vehicle for classroom instruction; that is, as a mediating tool or agent in the transmission and acquisition of knowledge. The use of white mainstream culture also tends to devalue the cultures of people who have been excluded from educational opportunities. Multicultural education brings us back to understand the democratic philosophy that has permitted all citizens in this country to pursue the goals of freedom and economic prosperity without prejudice, at least, prejudice *de jure*.

I find *Choosing Democracy* to be a very clear, pragmatic, and powerful statement guiding teachers, educators, and scholars to engage in substantive reflection about our educational philosophy, policies, and practices. I find it refreshing and useful. Most of all, I find this book extremely timely. The fact that American democracy is at risk because of the "revivalistic" or "nativistic" tendencies of the 1980s and 1990s (identical to those of a century ago) is not dissimilar to the events faced by this country during the Industrial Revolution and the increasing immigrant waves of the last century. Social unrest, rapid cultural change, economic crises around the world, and cultural confusion about what America is all about have resulted in scapegoating immigrants and attempting to exclude them from the social benefits of this country, in spite of the fact that those immigrants help build the economic strength of America. Some people refer to these historical parallels as "malaise" but others see these cyclical crises as normal reactions and adjustment in American values. This "malaise" is not unique to this country. Indeed, France, Spain, Belgium and Germany have seen their share of anti-immigrant currents now politically strong that have won a good portion of the European populations on issues about exiling non-Europeans, or at least excluding them from receiving employment. Nativism has led to xenophobia and even to hysteria in some countries. Even in California the hysteria about undocumented immigrants and their children has had a serious detrimental impact on many other children of the same ethnic groups who are legal. Su rez-Orozco says that California is not a victim of undocumented workers, but a victim of unfair distribution of federal taxes paid for by undocumented immigrants, a positive balance of some $12 billion (Suarez-Orozco & Suarez-Orozco, in press). This irrational behavior of many Californians has led to cruel and random acts of violence against innocent peoples, often by white youngsters, but also by border patrol agents and vigilantes (Suarez-Orozco & Suarez-Orozco, in press).

In the face of irrational behavior and prejudice, *Choosing Democracy* reaffirms our philosophical position that for this country to remain democratic, it must embrace the principles of multicultural education, including respect and appreciation of languages and cultures of other immigrants. It is not enough to embrace these principles. We must act on these principles as well. What this means is that education is intrinsically a political act that creates awareness of how democracy works and what its fundamental components are. We must start from what Freire (1993) has called the "ontological" need for hope, or the essential commitment to pursue human existence with dignity even in the worst of circumstances:

> Hope is an ontological need. As a program [for action], lack of hope paralyzes us and makes us fall into fatalism where it is impossible to muster the necessary strength in order to fight for the recreation of the world (p. 10).

American society is prey to currents and counter-currents that occur in cycles. In the late nineteenth century with the sentiment against "foreigners," there was a hysteria surrounding the use of languages other than English. In the 1980s there was a hysteria about brown people and the use of Spanish and other "foreign" languages in California, Texas, and Florida. For individuals who were born here and treated like unwanted people, hope must be ontological, essential to existence, in order to pursue democratic ideals. Yet, as Paulo Freire (1993) explains, hope is not enough:

> Hope alone cannot win a struggle, but without hope we will be weak and hesitate in the struggle. We need critical hope, in the same way that a fish needs clean water (ibid.).

The philosophical and theoretical foundations, as well as the actual content of this book, are clearly marked by Freire's critical pedagogy. In fact, there are very few books that have accomplished both: the presentation of a solid theoretical basis for critical pedagogy and the presentation of a content congruent in practice with its theoretical basis. The examples, the approach to the various issues, the suggestions made, the way various audiences are handled (teachers, educators, parents, etc.) respect the principles established by Freire. The author, having recognized the need for critical pedagogy in the schooling of linguistically and culturally diverse student populations, proceeds to teach the content exemplifying the pedagogical principles of respect and appreciation to all groups.

This book not only provides a better idea of what multicultural education is all about, but also an even more profound understanding of how schooling can integrate multicultural education in the curriculum. This book does a great deal, because it

1. Invites serious reflection about the nature of American society and the role of schools.
2. Shows the way to teachers and students to heal from prejudice and racial/ethnic biases.
3. Provides clear guidelines to regain a sense of purpose and resolve ethnic/racial conflicts.
4. Engages teachers and students in more effective classroom organization and meaningful curriculum exercises that will heal the wounds opened by conflict.
5. Suggests the creation of support groups to promote better teaching/learning skills and strategies to enhance human relations.
6. Emphasizes cooperation and integration beyond the "melting pot."
7. Offers a guide for a democratic school reform.

I believe that teacher educators, teachers, and students will find this book extremely useful and a constant companion as they discover the importance of healing from prejudice and of linking democratic ideals with pragmatic school reform. They will find the book written in a clear and simple style, well organized and practical for daily use and for serious reflection. Each chapter has extremely useful references and additional sources for those individuals who want to pursue a more in-depth knowledge of specific subjects. In the end, the main contribution of this book will be to understand better the relationship between our historical past as a democratic society and the politics of culture and education today. The danger in ignoring this relationship is to permit prejudice and cultural hegemony to become pervasive and destructive in schools. In turn, the serious recognition of the need to respect ethnic identities, linguistic and cultural heritages, and the rich variety of contributions by all the groups who form modern America is crucial for the future democracy of our country and its survival as a free and powerful country. Giroux (1994) has clearly pointed out that

> The relationship between history and identity is a complex one and cannot be reduced to unearthing hidden histories that are then mined for positive images. On the contrary, educators need to understand and develop in their pedagogies how identities are produced differently, how they take up narratives of the past through the stories and experiences of the present (p. 50).

Critical pedagogy is indispensable in order to establish an adequate learning environment, congruent with American democratic principles and hence with multicultural education, and one in which ethnic identification of students paves the way for their empowerment in schools, a positive self-image, and the motivation to achieve academically. "Critical pedagogy situates itself in the intersection of language, culture and history—the nexus in which students' subjectivities are formed, contested and played out" (McLaren, 1989, p. 233). Theoretically, we accept the role of critical pedagogy and advocate it. In practice, we are not sure how to pursue it. McLaren (1989) insists that

> The struggle is one that involves their history, their language, and their culture, and the pedagogical implications are such that students are given access to a critical discourse or are conditioned to accept the familiar as the inevitable. Worse still, they are denied a voice with which to be present in the world; they are made invisible to history and rendered powerless to shape it (p. 233).

Ethnic identification and the creation of cultural bridges for students to acquire new knowledge (both cultural and subject-matter related to traditional schooling) are processes intimately related and mutually interdependent. In the end, cultural bridges will be required to live up to our ideal of human solidarity in a society which demands respect for racial, ethnic, linguistic, cultural, and socioeconomic diversity. Duane Campbell makes an important contribution to education and educational reform as he strongly advocates for multicultural education as an expression of critical pedagogy in the service of human solidarity and genuine democracy.

Henry T. Trueba, Ph.D.
University of Houston

References

Suarez-Orozco, Marcelo M., & Suarez-Orozco, Carola. (In press). *Transformations*. Stanford, CA: Stanford University Press.

Giroux, Henry A. (1994). Living dangerously: Identity, politics and the new cultural racism. In H.A. Giroux & P. McLaren (Eds.), *Between borders: Pedagogy and the politics of cultural studies* (pp. 29–55). New York: Routledge.

Foreword

By Cornel West

Duane Campbell is an organic intellectual with a deep commitment to a substantive democratic vision. He understands education as a critical activity that unsettles our presuppositions and unstiffens our prejudices such that we can bond with others to alleviate social misery. His acute sense of history enables him to view schooling within a broad multilayered context in which the harsh realities of race, class, and gender as well as the sweet possibilities of freedom, equality, and democracy loom large.

This magisterial treatment of our contemporary crisis in American society, culture, and education takes us step-by-step through the treacherous terrains that impede our efforts to examine critically and expand effectively democracy in our time. His powerful text is the most comprehensive analysis we have of sharpening the practical strategies for multicultural education in America.

Like the exquisite poetry of Walt Whitman and the exhilarating music of Louis Armstrong, Duane Campbell's empowering pedagogy is shot through with profound democratic sentiments. In our frightening moment of class polarization and racial balkanization, his themes of social reconstruction, cultural innovation, and political transformation—themes that link any talk about diversity to the expansion of Democracy—are refreshing and uplifting. They also present the principal means by which we can link order to justice, civility to mutual respect, and merit to fairness.

His radical democratic analysis and vision is a voice of sanity at a time of irrationality—a voice that understands rage yet transforms bitterness into bonding. This bonding is neither naive nor utopian; rather it is rooted in a candid encounter with the sources of our rage and an unleashing of the best in us for serious democratic engagement that goes far beyond our hostilities.

The best of American life has always been embodied and enacted by courageous figures who chose democracy—from Thomas Paine, Harriet Tubman, César Chávez, Ronald Takaki to Dolores Huerta. Duane Campbell makes it clear what it means to choose democracy in our classrooms, workplaces, homes, and civic life. In short, like James Baldwin, he frightfully reminds us that we either choose democracy now or ultimately witness the fire this time!

Cornel West
Harvard University

Preface

As teachers, readers of this text will participate in the construction of the future of our society. In deciding what future is constructed, I anticipate that substantive school reform, including the development of multicultural education, will be necessary for the preservation of our democratic community. *Choosing Democracy: A Practical Guide to Multicultural Education* seeks to assist future teachers to analyze their own cultural frames of reference and to develop a second, multicultural perspective. It further seeks to ally teachers' commitments to democratic opportunity and to expand that value position to include cultural democracy in school and equal educational opportunity.

Developing A Successful Multicultural Perspective

In the last few years, California State University at Sacramento has become one of the most successful multilingual, multicultural teacher preparation programs in the nation. I believe this is due in part because over the last ten years those of us involved in the California State program have listened to teachers struggling with trying to create successful bilingual and multicultural classrooms. In *Choosing Democracy: A Practical Guide to Multicultural Education* I share these teachers' concerns. Because of this dialogue and the developmental usage of this text material with hundreds of my own students over the years, I am convinced that confrontation strategies such as attacks on a Eurocentric viewpoint, particularly in textbooks, do not usually advance multicultural understanding or provide direction away from an increasingly hostile, divided, and violent society. Rather "a nature of culture" approach, as developed in this text, allows most students to participate in re-conceptualizing their own basic assumptions and frames of reference.

Text Organization

Part One of this text combines a critical analysis of race, class, gender, and poverty as they apply in school. *Chapters 1-5* include research evidence and conclusions about societal crises, culture, economics, racism, and gender discriminations to demonstrate how they impact classrooms, teachers, and schools. Armed with this information teachers can begin to understand how these matters affect their own classrooms.

Part Two of the text then provides practical strategies for teachers to use in responding to problem areas. In *Chapter 6* students will consider the importance of developing quality interpersonal relationships with students and between students; an issue seldom addressed in other texts. It also offers ideas on promoting positive self-esteem, serving as a cultural mediator, and assisting students in conflict resolution.

Chapter 7, "Teaching to Empower Students of Color", has a number of teaching strategies that pursue goal empowerment and the philosophy of social reconstructionism. *Chapters 8–11* present more than five major approaches and one hundred concrete suggestions on how to change the classroom to adapt to our rapidly changing society. These include descriptions of strategies, objectives, and lesson plans on classroom management, guidance and lesson plans to initiate cooperative learning, and theory and practice of bilingual education and second language acquisition.

By *Part Three*, readers will have developed both a theory and practice for multicultural education. They will have the background to examine the controversies and enter the dialogue on school reform. Chapter discussions in Part Three will provide support for these efforts. *Chapter 12* describes the battle of the textbooks in California and New York and offers ideas for curriculum reform. *Chapter 13* analyzes the recent struggle for school reform including Goals 2000, The Educating America Act, efforts toward national standards, the role of teacher's unions, and interactions with parents. It critiques reform efforts for inadequate attention to the problems of the marginalized, students of color and the poor. It concludes with a vision for pluralistic democracy and a description of some of the successful efforts of school reform including "Accelerated Schools" and the Comer model.

Conclusion

We have the skills, abilities, opportunities and the hopes necessary to sustain one of the greatest social experiments in history, a democratic republic where wealth and a high quality of life is shared. It is the hope of this author that

Choosing Democracy: A Practical Guide to Multicultural Education will contribute to teachers' opportunities to create a society where all students receive a quality education to prepare them to produce for the world, to compete in the world economy, to trade with the world, and to build a world with a diverse, democratic community.

Acknowledgments

Choosing Democracy is a product of years of dialogue with my students and former students. They consistently reteach me and remind me to respect the invaluable contributions that teachers make to the nation and to social justice. I have tried to pass on some of their wisdom. Particularly helpful since my last book have been Ed Buendia, Marcella Enriquez, Miguel Hernandez, Wayne Miyao, Melinda Melendez, Drine Ramirez, Enrique Sepulveda, and Marta Rodriguez.

I want to thank Dolores Delgado-Campbell for her co-authorship of Chapter 5, "How Schools Shortchange Girls and Boys." Her Chicana, feminist perspective added wisdom and insight to this important chapter. I also want to thank Manning Marable, Director of the Center on African American Studies at Columbia University, for his co-authorship of Chapter 3. I have been fortunate to work with Manning on a number of projects. This chapter continues a dialogue.

I have also been fortunate to work with and learn from the wisdom, poetry, and art of community intellectuals (Gramsci's organic intellectuals) and former students including Armando Ayala, Olivia Castellano, Jose Montoya, Celina Perez, and particularly the constant inspiration and support of my compadre, Ricardo Torres.

Although I graduated from a fine university, I learned more about the commitment to justice and equality by my own participation in several of the social justice movements of the last two decades. These continuing struggles for economic justice and social democracy provided organic intellectuals as tutors, coaches, guides, and teachers. Particularly important to my own education has been working with César Chávez, Bert Corona, Br. Ed Dunn, Dolores Huerta,

Francis Quinn, and Philip Vera Cruz. Movements are more than the individual names. I owe much of my political education and respect for discipline and the working people to service with CISPES, DSA, and the United Farmworkers of America (AFL-CIO), and opportunities to work with the FSLN (Nicaragua) and the PRD (Mexico).

I am grateful to have worked with and learned from Michael Harrington, Shakoor Aljuwani, Jack Clark, Ben Dobbs, Barbara Ehrenreich, Manning Marable, Mark Levinson, Jose La Luz, Christine Riddiough, Joe Schwartz, and Eric Vega, among others. Their insights and critical reflections are found throughout this book.

I am fortunate to have a position within a community of scholars who have worked together for over a decade and have recently become the Department of Bilingual Multicultural Education at CSU-Sacramento—a people's university. The collective efforts and integrity of this group sustain me and guide me to resist the individualism and to avoid the narcissism and self-indulgence of many university departments. I particularly thank José Cintrón, Thomas P. Carter, Diane Cordero de Noriega, Forrest Davis, Richard Figueroa, Sue Heredia-Arriaga, Victoria Jew, Harold Murai, John McFadden, Betty McEady, Nadeen Ruiz, René Merino, Miguel Martinez, and Leo Maestas for their support at crucial moments, their insights, and their challenges.

A number of other scholars and friends who have helped me, supported me, and encouraged me to refine ideas is too long to mention. But particularly helpful have been Henry T. Trueba of the University of Houston, William Dorman, and Chris Hasagawa. The following individuals reviewed chapters and urged me to clarify important points: Barbara Arnstein, Victoria Jew, Henry T. Trueba, Pia Linquist Wong, Sharon Alexander, and Gloria Ladson-Billings.

I also wish to acknowledge the contributions of the reviewers who offered many helpful suggestions: Wanda Fox, Purdue University; Maureen Gillette, College of St. Rose; Samuel Hinton, Eastern Kentucky University; Marguerite W. Parks, Ripon College; and Elizabeth Quintero, University of Minnesota, Duluth.

The book has benefited from the considerable editorial assistance of Georgia Lyga, Fred Nichols, and Cindy Peck. Michael Pincus helped at an early stage. The book went through several drafts and rewrites, each with the patient assistance of Tricia Springer as typist. I also thank Lilia Ibarra and Katy Romo for their numerous acts of kindness and editorial assistance.

The César E. Chávez Foundation and Marc Grossman assisted me with research, as did Nancy Folbre of the Center for Popular Economics and Norm Gold of the California Department of Education. I wrote substantial portions of an early draft of this work while on a sabbatical leave in the Spring of 1992, funded by the people of California. I respect and appreciate their contribution and fully intend to repay their investment.

Duane E. Campbell

To the Instructor

This book was written, developed, and critiqued over the last 10 years in dialogue with hundreds of teachers in the graduate program and the Department of Bilingual/Multicultural Education at California State University, Sacramento. Each idea has been tested and revised as appropriate, based on teacher experience.

When I use this book with practicing teachers or in the preservice program while students are practice teaching, I often begin with Chapter 10 on cooperative learning and then proceed immediately to Chapter 8 on classroom management. These chapters help readers to get started with practical strategies to resolve immediate classroom issues. After experiencing success with these strategies, readers often are more open to considering the alternative perspectives presented in other chapters.

In working with preservice teachers, I have found that most of them have little preparation in economics, and what they do have is only of limited usefulness, yet economics are central to arguments about school renewal. I have found the work of Nancy Folbre and the Center for Popular Economics particularly helpful in explaining complex economic issues. You will find their graphs used often in this text. These graphs and others as well as economic cartoons are included in an excellent work, *A Field Guide to the U.S. Economy* (1995, Amherst, MA: Center for Popular Economics). I recommend that you get a copy of it so you can photocopy graphs and transfer them to transparencies for use on an overhead projector.

A second excellent source for economics is the publication *Social Stratification in the United States, The American Profile Poster* (1992, New York: The New

Press). The poster of U.S. social class found in this book and the many readable one- to two-page essays explaining aspects of the poster provide excellent preparation for teaching.

At the ends of several chapters, you will find activities for further study of the subject covered in the chapter. These are suggestions drawn from how we teach this material in our basic Introduction to Multicultural Education class. I hope you find these useful.

These activities are followed by teaching strategies, which are written for your students to use as teachers in K through grade 12 classrooms. In Chapters 9, 10, and 11, these strategies include actual lesson plans that are designed to introduce readers to issues such as critical thinking and cooperative learning. I encourage you to add to and amend these lessons. Often in dealing with complex issues such as critical thinking, I find that students agree with the concept in general, but have only a basic understanding of how to implement the strategies in the classsroom. Students better understand the strategies and the need for advance planning of the strategies when they see them applied in lesson plans and lessons.

Contents

4   With Liberty and Justice for Some: Class Relations and Schools   81

5   How Society and Schools Shortchange Girls and Boys   109

Part 2
Teaching Strategies to Promote Democracy and Multicultural Education   **127**

Part 3
The Dialogue Between Democracy and Multicultural Education   277

12   Curriculum and Multicultural Education   279

13 Democratic School Reform: How Do We Get from Here to There?   303

Introduction

May the truth of my tale speak for me.

This book addresses teachers at a remarkable time in this country's history: the dramatic birth and development of a new, more culturally and linguistically diverse society. In the last decade, economic turmoil and unprecedented levels of immigration have filled the public schools of the United States with a rich rainbow of faces. Many classrooms include dozens of cultures, and the use of three, four, or even five languages among students. Few societies have classrooms and schools as diverse as those faced by teachers in the United States each day. Schools and teaching reflect society, but they also participate in the construction of our future society. New forms of knowledge and new approaches to teaching have emerged in response to the turmoil in our economy, in our society and in our schools. Teachers have forged a variety of new strategies to respond to the demands for economic relevancy, democracy, equal opportunity, and this remarkable diversity.

This book shares the insights gained by dozens of teachers working with bilingual and multicultural education as they developed new cross-cultural perspectives, new pedagogies and curriculum, and new strategies and programs to respond to the continuing social crises of our society and the education of their students. Innovative teachers have found ways to validate students' diverse cultures while preparing them to participate in the social, economic, and political mainstream of our society.

Teachers dedicated to multicultural education hope to build on the cultural diversity of our nation to create a new, dynamic, democratic—yet, fair—society not racked by the problems of poverty, homelessness, unemployment, community dislocations, and racial division. It is the teachers and students in our urban centers who feel the fullest brunt of the demographic and economic changes in our society. It is teachers who are developing the strategies to respond to the poverty crisis and the educational crisis in our society.

What are these crises?

1. The difficulty for students and teachers alike in dealing with and responding positively to cultural diversity, cross-cultural and class conflicts, and violence and oppression.

2. The stress students bring to school aggravated by the rapidly changing demographics and declining economic conditions in their communities.

3. The budget cutbacks, lack of resources, fragmentation, and lack of coordination between student programs that paralyze many school districts and prevent school reform.

4. The failure of over one third of all schools in major cities to provide a positive educational environment for an increasing number of poor and racial and ethnic minority students.

Teachers now know a great deal more about teaching in a cross-cultural environment than we knew in the 1970s and 1980s. Effective teaching strategies and programs have been identified, clarified, and developed to take advantage of classroom diversity and to weave a stronger, more united community.

We now know that teachers can make a difference. Dedicated teachers from all racial, ethnic, and cultural backgrounds can learn to be effective cross-cultural teachers and brokers of information that provides students with greater access to economic opportunity and social equality. We know a great deal about teaching. New teachers are fortunate to be able to learn from the experiences of their predecessors.

We now know that schools are not politically neutral. Teachers and schools are situated in a specific economic, political environment. Study and reflection on that reality help teachers to select strategies for the success and empowerment of their students. Studies on the nature of race, class, and gender relations in our society provide teachers with a theoretical framework for selecting and evaluating teaching strategies (see Chapters 1 through 5).

But theoretical analysis of the problems of urban and problem schools is not enough. Teachers—particularly new teachers—need practical strategies for responding to the dozens of problems they face each day in the classroom. There is no one solution to these complex problems. In fact, the complexity of teacher decision making often baffles and, at times, overwhelms new teachers. While working through the problems of critical thinking, for example (see Chapter 8), teachers will also need clear, descriptive assistance on issues such as cooperative learning, classroom management, and helping students to learn English (see Chapters 6 through 11).

To some readers, the challenges of racism, sexism, class bias, and anti-democratic teaching that are presented in this book may be too strongly stated. The directness of the statements and the writing may offend. But, as the spiritual says, "May the truth of my tale speak for me." I seek to share a view of our society as I and my colleagues in the schools have come to know it. We recognize both the hope and the tragedy of our schools.

A Few Words About Words

Language use is constantly changing. Since 1960, the most common term for one group of people has changed from *Negro* to *Black* to *African American*. In the same period, the most common term for another group changed from *Latin* to *Mexican American* to *Chicano* to *Latino*. These changes reflect substantial redefinitions of the problems of race and ethnic conflict occurring in the curriculum, the schools, and the society.

The purpose of language and of books is to communicate. In *Choosing Democracy*, I use terms based on two primary criteria:

1. What terms do the leaders, the intellectuals, and the community itself prefer?
2. What terms most precisely describe the group?

African Americans

I will use the term *African American* for the nation's largest minority group, reflecting the preferred current usage. Ron Daniels, a leading African American political activist, argues that the effort to encourage the use of this term over *Black* goes back to the early 1980s. Jesse Jackson reinvigorated this discussion in 1988.

Black is a racial term that attempts to describe a racial group. Biologists encourage us to avoid use of race because the concept is so imprecise, while sociologists have documented the social importance of race (see Chapter 3).

Race and ethnicity are not the same. In the classic work, *They and We*, the sociologist Peter Rose (1974) states:

> Groups whose members share a unique social and cultural heritage passed on from one generation to the next are known as ethnic groups. Ethnic groups are frequently identified by distinctive patterns of family life, language, recreation, religion and other customs that cause them to be differentiated from others. (p. 13)

The racial term *Black* includes significant new immigrant groups of Haitians, Dominicans, and many Puerto Ricans. These groups share Blackness and are treated as Black by the larger society. They are, however, distinct ethnic groups and cultural groups.

Asian Americans

The term *Asian American* will be used to describe the common experiences of Asian peoples. The enormous differences among the groups in language, culture, and immigration histories lead more often to referring to the specific group—for example, Vietnamese or Korean—rather than an often-misleading generic group. The inclusion of population numbers for the Asian / Pacific Islander subcategory in Chapter 3 illustrates the diversity.

European Americans

This book will use the term *European American* to describe persons commonly referred to as *White*. Like the decision to use *African American* over *Black*, the term *European American* describes the complex cultural heritage of the majority group and macroculture in the United States.

Most European Americans come from a mixture of a variety of cultural and national groups, for example, Italian, Greek, Irish, and English. Members of these groups have been in the United States for generations, and most have little contact with the sending societies. They tend to consider themselves *Americans*. The designation *American* is not used in this text since it implies that the other groups are not American or are less American than the Europeans.

The use of the term *European American* encourages this group to recognize their own ethnicity and cultural roots. The European American culture is substantially derived from the Anglo-Saxon or English culture in language, common law, and Protestant religion. Many immigrant groups, such as Greeks, Poles, Scandinavians, and Irish, have added to the developing common culture.

Native Americans

I have chosen to use the term *Native Americans* and *Indians* interchangeably within the text. Both terms are in popular usage and both have drawbacks. It is most important to recognize the tribal and historical diversity of members of the several native nations. Whenever possible, the text will refer to a group by its tribal name, for example, the Dineh Nation or the Cree Nation.

Latinos

This book will use the term *Latino* to describe people who are descendants of immigrants from Latin American countries and the Caribbean and those persons of Spanish-Indian mixed heritage present in the Southwest when U.S. armies first moved into the area in the 1840s. The U.S. Census and many people use the term *Hispanic* for this group. Neither term is perfect, but *Hispanic* seems to overemphasize the influence of Spain and to deemphasize the major contributions of Native American and African cultures. Preference for the two terms varies by region. In the eastern half of the United States, *Hispanic* is more often used, whereas in the West, *Latino* is more common.

Latinos share some cultural characteristics yet are also widely diverse. Sixty-two and one-third percent of Latinos are descendants of Mexican parentage; 12.7% are Puerto Ricans, 5.3% are descendants of Cubans, and the remaining 19% are from a variety of Latin American and Caribbean nations.

The term *Latino* unfortunately connotes the male gender even when used to describe males and females. When referring to females, the specific term *Latina* or *Chicana* will be used. While most Latinos are of mixed races, the U.S. Census attempts to count Hispanics separately by racial categories: Indian, White, and Black. More details on the variety within Latino culture are described in Chapter 3.

People of Color

In referring to the collective experiences of racial groups in the United States, the text refers to *people of color* rather than minority groups. This deliberate word choice highlights the fact that in many urban and some rural areas such as Texas, Mississippi, and New Mexico, people of color are the majority—not a minority group.

Americans

The term *people of the United States* is deliberately used to refer to our residents and citizens. The common term *American* is a misnomer and seems arrogant to some of the millions of people who live in the Americas. *American* refers to the residents of both North and South America. Thus, Brazilians, Peruvians, Costa Ricans, and Canadians are all Americans. And the many indigenous groups in these nations are all Native Americans.

In spite of this, citizens of the United States of several racial and ethnic groups commonly refer to themselves as Americans. When other authors have used the term *American* to describe U.S. citizens, I have respected their word choice.

The Poor

The United States has a large poverty class. Official statistics number this group around 13%, while more careful studies show that as many as 20% of the U.S. population are poor in any one year. Poverty among children is growing.

When the term *poor* is used, the reference is to the economic income of the people, not to their lifestyles, morals, values, or family stability. The term *low income* hides the gravity and permanence of poverty in our society. The many euphemisms developed to avoid saying "the poor" significantly obscure the magnitude of poverty in influencing school opportunities. At times, authors are so polite that they refuse to name reality.

The Problem of Categories

The formation of categories of people encourages social scientists to fit everyone into a category. Allegedly racial categories are particularly misleading. Peter Rose (1974) described the issue as follows:

> Mexican-Americans are largely the children of Spanish and Indian parentage; Puerto Ricans are the offspring of white and black as well as Indian ancestors; and many people who we call black are very white indeed. (p. 11)

Each person is both an individual and a member of several groups. We may fit into several categories: Latino, Catholic, middle class, and teacher, for example. Each individual's worldview is a complex compilation of diverse influences. Even within a single group such as Guatemalans, there are Indians, Latinos, men, women, children, immigrants, poor, and rich. Categories are necessary for analysis, but they are only transitional starting points for coming to understand the complex varieties of human experience.

Part 1

The Social, Economic, and Cultural Foundations of the Current School Crisis

Chapter 1

The Need for Multicultural Education

It was a simple news story—one that could be written in any major city in the nation (see Figure 1.1).

The Structural Crisis in U.S. Society

Our society and our schools are in crisis. In many areas, crime and street gangs make travel unsafe at night. Funds for basic government services, such as police and fire protection, emergency medical response, public safety, and schools, have been cut. Unemployment and homelessness have continued at recession levels for decades for certain populations. Families are stressed and often destroyed by poverty, crime, and violence.

Though these crises are common throughout our society, they do not affect everyone equally. We live in a three-tiered society. One part of our nation is affluent, comfortable, successful. The well-off have access to cars, the latest technology, exotic foods, and spacious homes. A few miles away lives a second society: the middle-class majority, who pay increasing taxes while their standard of living stagnates and opportunities for their children erode. The third society is that of the chronic poor and those temporarily forced into poverty by loss of jobs, a health crisis, or recurring economic recessions. In this tier, we find levels of poverty, crime, and health hazards that are typical of underdeveloped nations. This society of poverty is growing the fastest, particularly among children.

Figure 1.1 Laura's Story

The Sacramento Bee   Dateline: Monday, November 2, 1987

Tracking a Poor Reader's Stumbling Steps Through School

By Deb Kollars [Bee Staff Writer]

In an unruly classroom at California Middle School, a dark-eyed seventh-grader named Laura Montero sits quietly, day after day, stumbling over simple words like "justice," rarely finishing her work before the bell rings.

She is 13 years old, has average intelligence and reads at a third-grade level. At a time when many junior high students are bracing for algebra, compositions and "Romeo and Juliet," Laura has arrived at a different crossroads. She can barely read, spell, multiply or divide. Her teacher holds little hope she will ever catch up. She doesn't like school much anymore.

"I work as hard as I can, but I feel so behind," she said, looking down at her hands. "I'm scared of high school. I don't think I can do it."

The road Laura will follow is almost assured. She has spent her entire academic life on it and there's no turning back. When she emerges from public school within the next few years, Laura will likely join millions of adults who have serious literacy problems.

Her journey is not unique. California schools are failing to educate at least one-third of all students, according to test results, dropout rates and research by leading educational experts in the state.

Although test scores and graduation requirements indicate schools are doing better these days, many children who are poor, who live in big cities, who are minority members are coming through school without ever learning to read, to write, to understand history or math or science.

Laura's report cards show that year after year she was passed into the next grade at Oak Ridge Elementary School in Sacramento without having adequate reading and language skills for her age. The older she got, the further behind she fell.

Teachers in Laura's past said during interviews that they either didn't realize she was so far behind or did their best and could not do anything more about her low skills because of large class sizes and the serious home problems of many of their students.

Brooks Cassidy, her teacher now, said she probably won't progress much this year, either.

"I have a room full of students who are as far behind as Laura. I'll be lucky if I can raise her reading level by one year," he said. "I have so many behavior problems in this class right now that I just don't have the time to give her the individual help she needs."

Laura is known as a remedial student. She is not alone.

In the Sacramento City Unified School District, 872 of 2,951, or 30 percent of all seventh-graders, are two or more years below grade level in reading. Another 874 eighth-graders are similarly behind. In Los Angeles, 13,000 or 37 percent, of all seventh-graders are two or more years behind. In Oakland, in San Francisco, in San Diego, the story is the same.

These children reach middle school with severely low skills. They can't multiply five by six. They can't spell the names of the states. They can't use a ruler. They don't know what the plot of a story is. They have no idea where Israel lies on a map.

"I get kids who don't know that California is a state and Sacramento is a city," Luther Burbank High School teacher Barbara Johnson said, shaking her head.

'I don't think I can do it,' says Laura, looking ahead to high school.

Note. From "Tracking a Poor Reader's Stumbling Steps Through School" by D. Kollars, November 1987, *The Sacramento Bee*, p. 1. Copyright, The Sacramento Bee, 1994

The extremes of wealth and poverty in our neighborhoods lead directly to unacceptable differences in the quality of schooling offered to our children. Schools on one side of town serve children of the affluent and the middle class, many of whom can look forward to a healthy economic future. In poor neighborhoods, middle-class teachers face overcrowded classrooms filled with children from immigrant groups and from the oppressed African American and Latino communities. The quality of instruction and school experience in the middle-class school varies dramatically from that of the school serving poor and working-class children. As the news story in Figure 1.1 illustrates, school failure is endemic in many poor neighborhoods.

A related problem, and one of the ironies arising from the growing race-class divisions, is that while the affluent and well-educated provide most of the teachers, the poor provide most of the students. In addition, most new teaching positions are in districts and schools filled with poor children from a variety of racial, cultural, national, and linguistic backgrounds, many of whom have no reasonable hope of achieving the same social and economic privileges as the person instructing them. The hard truth is, these children come from a separate economy that exists alongside that of the affluent and the middle class in our society.

In *America: What Went Wrong?* (1992), two reporters for the *Philadelphia Inquirer,* Donald Bartlett and James Steele, described the destruction of economic opportunity for millions of middle-class and formerly middle-class families:

> Worried that you are falling behind, not living as well as you once did? Or expected to?
>
> Worried that the people who represent you in Congress are taking care of themselves and their friends at your expense?
>
> You are right. Keep worrying.
>
> For those people in Congress that wrote the complex tangle of rules by which the economy operates have, over the last twenty years, rigged the game—by design and default—to favor the privileged, the powerful and the influential. At the expense of everyone else.
>
> Seizing the opportunity, an army of business buccaneers began buying and selling and trading companies the way most Americans buy, sell and trade knickknacks at a yard sale. They borrowed money to destroy, not to build. They constructed the financial houses of cards, then vanished before they collapsed.
>
> Caught between the lawmakers in Washington and the dealmakers on Wall Street have been millions of American workers forced to move from jobs that once paid $15 per hour into jobs that now pay $7. If, that is, they aren't already victims of mass layoffs, production halts, shuttered factories and owners who enrich themselves by doing the damage and then walking away.
>
> As a result, the already rich are richer than ever; there has been an explosion in overnight new rich: life for the working class is deteriorating, and those at the bottom are trapped. For the first time in this century, members of the generation entering adulthood will find it impossible to achieve a better lifestyle than their parents. Most will be unable to even match their parents' middle-class status.
>
> Indeed the growth of the middle class—one of the underpinnings of democracy in this country—has been reversed. By government action. (p. 2)

The growth of the low-wage economy contributes to the decline of the U.S. economy for all. The low-wage economy and the economy below it of the marginally employed, the unemployed, and the homeless, burdens and frightens the middle class. In the area of community health, for example, the middle class tends to view the diseases and violence endemic in poverty areas as degrading the quality of health care for the entire community. Tuberculosis and other contagious diseases associated with poverty are on the rise. The chronic health problems of the poor overwhelm emergency health care facilities so the hospitals and clinics cannot respond adequately to accidents, heart attack victims, and other urgent care needs. Uncomfortable with homeless beggars and other increasingly visible signs of poverty, middle-class voters have insisted that tax monies be allocated to increase police power and prison space, while reducing health care, even preventative health care for children.

As the gap between the lower classes and the upper classes grows, our secondary schools, particularly in the cities, are increasingly ineffective in preparing non-college-bound students for entrance into a highly skilled workforce. Some middle-class children have access to higher education, enabling them to move into well-paying professional careers. But the majority of children of the working class will end up in the service sector as fast food employees, service workers, and maintenance personnel earning (using the prevailing wages of today's economy) less than $7 an hour. Unless education gives working-class students access to new careers, knowledge systems, and technology, they will join the working poor.

From the point of view of the unemployed, the underemployed, and the poor, our society is deeply troubled and divided. Presently, over 31 million people are trapped in the lower strata of our economy. As jobs move out of the cities, the poverty and the desperation of these families increase. Their lives become increasingly brutal. Some of the young people turn to crime, violence, and acts of rage that make schools and areas in some cities battlegrounds.

A Day in the Life

The Children's Defense Fund (CDF) has earned a national reputation for its advocacy work. In its work, *A Vision for America's Future* (1989), the CDF describes a day in the life of America's children (see Figure 1.2).

In 1991, the Economic Policy Institute recorded that over 19%[1] of all children come from a family in poverty (Mishel & Frankel, 1991). For African American children, the figure was 43%; for Latinos, 35%. And poverty among the young is rapidly increasing. Impoverishment of the young results from their parents having low-paying jobs, relying on an inadequate and demeaning welfare system, and living in neighborhoods dominated by crime, violence, and drug abuse. The poor are marginalized from economic and political participation in our society and their children attend understaffed, poorly financed schools.

---

[1] These figures vary slightly from the 1989 estimates of the Children's Defense Fund.

Figure 1.2   A Day in the Lives of American Children

Note. From *A Vision for America's Future,* (p. xxxvi), by the Children's Defense Fund, 1989, Washington, DC.

16,833	women get pregnant
2,740	of them are teenagers
1,105	teenagers have abortions
369	teenagers miscarry
1,293	teenagers give birth
676	babies are born to women who have had inadequate prenatal care
700	babies are born at low birthweight (less than 5 lbs., 8 oz.)
125	babies are born at very low birth-weight (less than 3 lbs., 5 oz.)
69	babies die before one month of life
107	babies die before their first birthday
27	children die because of poverty
9	children die from guns
6	teens commit suicide
7,742	teens become sexually active
623	teenagers get syphilis or gonorrhea
1,375	teenagers drop out of high school
1,849	children are abused
3,288	children run away from home
1,629	children are in adult jails
2,407	children are born out of wedlock
2,989	children see their parents divorced
31,003	people lose jobs

Robert Reich (1991), a Harvard economist and current Secretary of Labor, used examples from Massachusetts to demonstrate the results of these divisions in our society as reflected in the schools:

> [I]n Belmont, an affluent suburb of Boston, the average teacher earned $36,100 per year, only 3% of the eighteen-year-olds dropped out of school, and 80% of the seniors chose to go on to college. In nearby Chelsea, a more impoverished town, the average teacher earned $26,200, more than half of the eighteen-year-olds did not graduate, and only 10% planned to attend college. (p. 44)

If you were a parent in Chelsea or one of the hundreds of other poverty areas, would you not resent the lack of opportunity for future success offered your child? When you become a teacher, how will you feel about the differences in pay, working conditions, student attitudes, and your own success rates?

The Emerging Diversity of Students

Cultural diversity is increasing in our society and in our schools (see Figure 1.3). The case of California illustrates the impact of immigration on schools. Since 1977, the number of students who struggle to learn English has increased steadily and sharply. According to Olsen (1988, p. 14), these students now comprise over 15% of the total school population in California. The single largest group of limited-English students is Spanish speaking (73%), followed by Vietnamese (5.4%), Cantonese (3.5%), Cambodian, Filipino, and dozens of other languages including Farsi, Russian, and Polish.

Students from these minority cultures are concentrated in specific school districts and in the elementary grades. While a few benefit from high-quality bilingual education programs, the great majority of teachers who must deal with these students are unprepared to help them. Most immigrant students receive inadequate English instruction and little academic support in their native language.

In the 1970s, 80s, and 90s, the Latino population became the largest of the nation's refugee and immigrant groups. More than one third of all Latino children live in poverty. High school completion rates of Latino youth are falling,

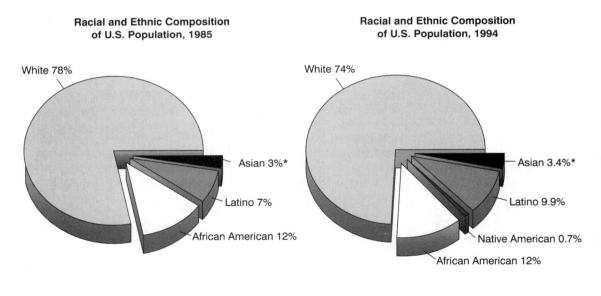

**Racial and Ethnic Composition
of U.S. Population, 1985**

White 78%

Asian 3%*

Latino 7%

African American 12%

*Includes Asian, Pacific Islander, American Indian, Eskimo, Aleut

(a)

**Racial and Ethnic Composition
of U.S. Population, 1994**

White 74%

Asian 3.4%*

Latino 9.9%

Native American 0.7%

African American 12%

*Includes Asian, Pacific Islander, Eskimo, Aleut

(b)

Figure 1.3   U.S. Population by Ethnicity

Note. From *Field Guide to U.S. Economy, 1985–1995* (Fig. 4.1) by Center for Popular Economics, 1994, Amherst, MA. Reprinted with permission.

and Latinos are less likely to attend college than other young people. Latino males have a substantially higher unemployment rate than the national average, while Latinas (Latino women) suffer more of a wage disparity between men's and women's wages than any other group.

In California, Hawaii, New Mexico, and Mississippi, the aggregate of "minority" students will soon constitute a majority of the total student population. In urban areas throughout the country, European Americans are becoming a minority (see Figure 1.4).

The rapid changes in the ethnic and cultural composition of our society worry many adults, particularly those who presently enjoy power, influence, and privilege. In April 1990, *Time* magazine devoted a special issue to what they considered the "crisis" of a changing nation. Its editors wrote:

> In the 21st Century—and that's not far off—racial and ethnic groups in the U.S. will outnumber whites for the first time. The "browning of America" will alter everything in our society, from politics and education, to industry, values, and culture. (p. 28)

The Fire This Time

In the absence of quality educational opportunities and enlightened social policy, increased racial diversity interacts with painful changes in the economy to produce racial polarization and an increase in violence. In 1963, the African American writer James Baldwin published an essay entitled *The Fire Next Time* predicting widespread violence if racial justice was further delayed. In 1965, 1967, and 1968, major U.S. cities were, in fact, rocked by race riots as economic conditions declined in urban areas. In 1985, 1990, and 1992, race disturbances returned to plague our cities, the largest insurrection occurring in Los Angeles from April 29 through May 1, 1992 (see Figures 1.5 and 1.6).

The cost of the 1992 Los Angeles riots? 51 dead, 1,032 injured, 3,000 arrested, $1.5 billion in property damage. The people hurt most by this rebellion and riot were the residents of the neighborhoods where the rioting took place: the people of South Central Los Angeles—a predominantly African American neighborhood—and the people of the Pico Union district—predominantly a Latino immigrant neighborhood.

On Monday, May 4, 1992, Los Angeles' 800,000 students returned to school after the riots and looting left parts of their communities devastated. In many schools, teachers focused on discussion of the events. Students wanted to talk, to discuss, to share their own stories. Some students wrote, some spoke up, some listened. In Compton, near the riot area, a group of parents went to the child care center and protected "their school" from arsonists.

Race had divided neighborhood against neighborhood, African American families against Korean families. The children watched this racial polarization going on around them and on their television screens at night. It frightened and confused them.

Figure 1.4 Map of States with Majority of Minority School-Age Populations

Note. From *Education That Works: An Action Plan for the Education of Minorities* (p. 12) by Washington, DC: U.S. Department of Education.

Figure 1.5 Los Angeles, 1992

Photos: *Time, Newsweek,* and the *Los Angeles Times.*

Figure 1.6 **Selected Race Riots in U.S. History**

Date	Place	Results
1866	Memphis, TN	48 dead
December, 1874	Vicksburg, MS	70 dead
July, 1917	East St. Louis, IL	49 dead
May, 1921	Tulsa, OK	36 dead
June 3, 1943	Los Angeles, CA	Thousands of U.S. sailors attack Mexican youth; fighting lasts for days.
July 23, 1943	Detroit, MI	43 dead
August 11, 1965	Los Angeles, CA	35 dead
July 23, 1967	Detroit, MI	43 dead
April 4, 1968	Pittsburgh, PA Chicago, IL and other U.S. cities	Riots erupt after the assassination of Martin Luther King, Jr.
August 29, 1969	Los Angeles, CA	3 dead; Chicano anti-war march becomes a three-day battle with police.
1980	Miami, FL	15 dead and 743 arrested, mostly African American men. Unemployment among African Americans in the area is 23%, compared to 9% for the nation.
April 28–May 1, 1992	Los Angeles, CA	101 dead

The rebellion in Los Angeles and simultaneous disturbances in Seattle, San Francisco, and Atlanta confirmed that living conditions for many poor, disenfranchised African Americans and Latinos deteriorated in the decades of the 1970s and 1980s. The lesson of the riots is that our society once again is moving toward racial and ethnic polarization. Angry, alienated young people—African Americans, Latinos, and other ethnic groups—cluster and stagnate in our inner cities. The stalled economy does not provide them with entry-level jobs, and the schools have not reached them. They feel abandoned by the economic system and oppressed by police power.

Unlike the substantial response to the riots of the 1960s, there were no national-level investigatory commissions of the 1992 riots, nor was there any funding of substantial new programs to combat poverty, division, and alienation. Outside of Los Angeles, most of the political leadership went back to their old ways of doing business and tried to forget that the riots had occurred, ignoring the root causes of the violence. School leaders and teachers were left to deal with the continuing crises of racial divisions, crime, and poverty.

The Crisis in Our Schools

The citizens of the United States have long believed in education. For over 100 years, parents have trusted the public schools to provide a better future for their children. Today, however, schooling is in crisis, particularly for children living in poverty. At least 13 million children live below the artificially low poverty line set by the U.S. government. More realistic figures show that at least 20 million children are poor (see Figure 1.7). Most of the 43% of all African American children, the 35% of all Latino children, the 17% of all Asian children, and the 12.5% of all European American children living below the official poverty line attend underfunded, poverty-stricken schools.

A debate on educational reform raged during the 1980s, but there was widespread disagreement on the cause of the education crisis. Conservatives, led by Reagan administration Secretary of Education Bill Bennett, criticized schools for mediocrity and focused school reform on issues of promoting excellence.

In 1983, the U.S. Department of Education published *A Nation at Risk,* a report that dramatically warned:

> Our nation is at risk. Our once-unchallenged preeminence in commerce, industry, science, and technological innovation is being overtaken by competitors throughout the world. . . . The educational foundations of our society are presently being eroded by a rising tide of mediocrity that threatens our very future as a nation and a people. (p. 5)

Since the publication of *A Nation at Risk,* over 100 books and a countless number of articles have been written and hundreds of conferences and symposiums have been held about the crisis in our schools, emphasizing the need to encourage excellence. Several states have discussed dramatic program changes. However, by the most basic measures, school achievement remains the same as 20 years ago (see Figure 1.8).

From the conservative Republican point of view, the problem was mediocrity. But from the point of view of advocates for the poor and those monitoring the

Figure 1.7 A Child's Chances of Being Poor in the United States

Note. From *A Vision for America's Future* (p. xlvi) by Children's Defense Fund, 1989, Washington, DC.

If White	1 in 6
If Black	4 in 9
If Hispanic	4 in 10
School age (6–17)	2 in 10

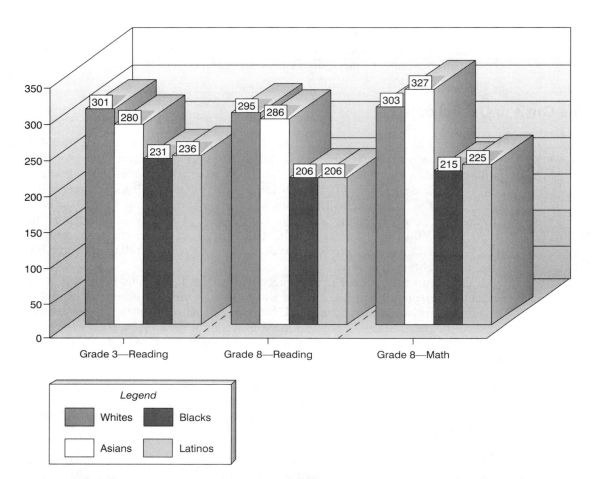

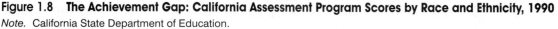

Figure 1.8   The Achievement Gap: California Assessment Program Scores by Race and Ethnicity, 1990
Note. California State Department of Education.

growing urban crisis, the source of the problem was quite different. In the 1985 book *Choosing Equality,* Bastian and her colleagues reviewed all the major arguments about the source of the crisis in education. They described the problem in these terms:

> There is, however, a far more fundamental crisis in our schools. It is located where it has always been, in the bottom layers of a multitiered system, in our failure to provide even minimal levels of quality to the school population that is working class and poor. This crisis can be measured in some stark statistics: 50–80% of all inner-city teenagers drop out of high school, 1 million teenagers cannot read above the third-grade level, 13% of all seventeen-year-olds are functionally illiterate, 28% of all students do not get high school diplomas. (p. 26)

Many Latino, African American, and other minority children are concentrated in de facto segregated schools where low expectations are the norm. A 1984 report by the National Commission on Secondary Education for Hispanics noted:

> Over two-thirds of all Hispanics attend schools with student bodies that are more than 50% minority. Schools that Hispanics attend usually are overcrowded, or poorly equipped, or have lower per pupil budgets than other schools in adjacent areas. (p. 10)

The problems of elementary schools become crises in middle schools and high schools. Dropout rates soar. The gap in the quality of curriculum and school retention between schools serving the rich and middle class and schools serving the poor increases. School tracking by alleged "ability groups" and at times hostile teacher attitudes deprive many young people of an enriched, relevant, and motivating school experience. The chaos and destruction of life in certain areas of our cities make it difficult for students to study and to learn in school.

For some of our young people, the results are catastrophic. A young African American child born in the United States is as likely to go to prison as to college. The percentage of African American males who are in prison in the United States is greater than that of Black Africans incarcerated under apartheid in the Republic of South Africa. Economic and educational opportunities for many Latinos and Native Americans are similarly bleak.

In some schools, teaching and learning conditions are an outright scandal. In Los Angeles, California, schools cannot hire enough credentialed teachers to face classrooms already overcrowded with more than 35 students per class. More than 800 teachers lack minimal teaching credentials. On any Monday or Friday, up to 30% of the faculty are substitutes or persons with limited training and no personal knowledge of the students. In 1993, the Los Angeles School Board proposed that teachers accept a 10% pay cut to respond to California's state budget crisis.

Such schools do not provide a safe or productive environment for learning. Teaching and learning conditions in these schools, like those described earlier in Figure 1.1, clearly indicate that society accepts the failure of these children. Although many dedicated teachers continue to struggle against the scandal of urban public schooling, individual efforts are not enough. Substantial and effective reform is needed.

Schools and Democracy

This book argues that multicultural education is a part of the effort to create a more democratic society. We must then define democracy. Robert Dahl, a leading political scientist, lists the following criteria to describe the democratic process:

1. Equal votes,
2. Effective participation,
3. Enlightened understanding,

4. Final control of the agenda by the people, and

5. Inclusiveness. (Dahl, 1985, pp. 59–60)

A democratic society encourages the widest possible participation in political decision making, respects the rule of the majority and protects the rights of minorities. Fundamental values of our constitutional form of democracy include justice, equality, protection of individual rights, and the promotion of the public good.

Public schools were created in part to promote these democratic ideals. John Dewey, the preeminent U.S. philosopher of education (1859–1952), described in the "Democratic Conception of Education" the relationship between schools and democracy as follows:

> A society which makes provisions for participation in its good of all its members on equal terms and which secures flexible readjustment of its institutions through interaction of the different forms of associated life is in so far democratic. Such a society must have a type of education which gives individuals a personal interest in social relationships and control, and the habits of mind which secure social changes without introducing disorder. (Dewey, 1916/1966, p. 90)

Civitas: A Framework for Civic Education (1991), prepared by the Center for Civic Education, elaborates on the U.S. constitutional heritage and applies the democratic heritage to teaching. *Civitas* argues that schools must prepare all citizens for equal participation and responsibility in society. Schools, as public institutions, must also provide equal preparation and equal opportunity for entrance into a prosperous economic life. Despite these democratic goals, however, inequities among schools are a reality. Extreme inequalities in public funding and quality of schooling exist and are described well by Jonathan Kozol in *Savage Inequalities: Children in America's Schools* (1991). These inequalities deny, thwart, and obstruct democratic opportunity in our society.

The preservation of prosperity and democracy depends on a system of education that prepares all children—majority and minority—with an equal opportunity for high standards of success in the basic skills of reading, writing, arithmetic, and the motivation to participate in rebuilding a democratic community. Democracy requires excellence in education for all, not just for a favored few.

Today, groups that have been historically excluded (African Americans, Latinos, Native Americans, immigrants) seek equal opportunity throughout society in jobs, housing, health, and schools. Their struggle for these basic rights focuses most immediately on the schools because, although these parents realize they cannot undo the hardship and deprivation of their own lives, they insist on equal opportunity for their children.

Democracies are characterized by a formal equality of political power for each citizen. In landmark court cases in 1896, *(Plessy vs. Ferguson)* and 1954 *(Brown vs. Board of Education)*, the U.S. Supreme Court decided that schools, as public institutions financed by tax dollars, have an obligation to provide *equal* opportunity for all students. For a democracy to achieve its promise, schools must provide an arena where students receive equal preparation for full participation in the economic and political life of society. We have yet to achieve these goals.

Schools can be used to promote inequality or equality. Unfortunately, the present system often promotes inequality. The 1984 report, *Excellence for Whom?* states:

> [T]here is considerable evidence that our system denies minority youngsters an education of the same quality as that provided to other youngsters. When predominantly minority schools are compared to predominantly white schools, certain systematic differences begin to appear. By virtually every measure of quality, predominantly minority schools are the losers: teacher quality, staffing ratios, college prep classes, overcrowding, and instructional materials. (Brown & Haycock, p. 8)

One way in which inequality is promoted in the schools is through unequal government spending. States differ widely in the amount of financial support they provide for their schools. For example, one of the points of comparison in a study by the California Legislative Analysts Office (nonpartisan) in 1994 was expenditures per pupil. The results of this comparison in five states, shown in Table 1.1, reveal expenditures per student as low as $4,451 (in California) and as high as $8,452 (in New York).

Student achievement also varies significantly by state (see Table 1.2).

While the suburban and rural students in selected states perform very similarly, the *California K–12 Report Card* shows that disadvantaged students do much more poorly in some states than others (see Figure 1.9).

Studies done at the liberal, Washington-based, Economic Policy Institute show that, in per capita funds spent on public education for grades K–12, the United States ranks fourteenth out of sixteen modern industrialized nations (Rasell & Mishel, 1990). Underfunded schools cannot provide equal opportunity within an unequal society. They cannot prepare workers for the high-tech industries of the future or for full participation in a political or economic democracy.

Table 1.1 Measures of Diversity in Five States

	CA	AZ	FL	NY	TX	National Average
Home language other than English	31.5%	20.8%	17.3%	23.3%	25.4%	13.8%
Nonwhite students	46.3	37.8	34.6	31.6	49.0	30.0
Adults without a high school degree	23.8	21.3	25.6	25.2	27.9	24.8
Children living in poverty	18.2	22.0	18.7	19.1	24.3	18.3
Expenditures per pupil	$4,451	$4,625	$5,280	$8,452	$4,457	$5,241

Note. Data from *California K–12 Report Card* (p. 14) by Elizabeth E. Hall, February, 1994, California Legislative Analyst's Office.

Table 1.2   California's Scores on the 1992 NAEP (National Assessment of Educational Progress) Are Lower Than Scores of Comparison States.

	CA	AZ	FL	NY	TX	National Average
Fourth-grade mathematics	207	214	212	217	217	217
• Difference from California	—	7	5	10	10	10
Fourth-grade reading	203	210	209	216	214	216
• Difference from California	—	7	6	13	11	13
Eighth-grade mathematics	260	265	259	266	264	266
• Difference from California	—	5	−1	6	4	6

Note. Data from *California K–12 Report Card* (p. 4), by Elizabeth E. Hall, February, 1994, California Legislative Analyst's Office.

School Reform

In the 1970s and 1980s, Ron Edmonds and others located, described, and analyzed so-called "effective schools." They found that approximately 2% of schools in low socioeconomic areas function well. Even though the percentage is low, it shows that effective schools are at least possible in poor areas. Students in these schools learn basic skills and enjoy academic enrichment. The schools work in spite of the economic chaos in the surrounding neighborhoods. Graduates of these schools are as well prepared for college and our new information-based economy as are graduates of suburban schools (Carter & Chatfield, 1986; Olsen, 1986).

We know how to improve our schools. The report, "Making Schools Work for Children in Poverty," prepared by the Commission on Chapter 1 (1993), states:

> The fact is that we know how to educate poor and minority children of all kinds— racial, ethnic, and language—to high levels. Some teachers and entire schools do it every day, year in and year out with outstanding results. But the nation as a whole has not yet acted on that knowledge, even though we need each and every one of our young people to master high-level knowledge and skills.
>
> Instead, to those who need the best our education system has to offer, we give the least. The least well-trained teachers. The lowest level curriculum. The oldest books. The least instructional time. Our lowest expectations. Less, indeed, of everything we believe makes a difference.
>
> Of course these children perform less well on standardized tests; the whole system conspires to teach them less. But when the results come in, we are only too happy to excuse ourselves, and turn around to blame the children and their parents. (pp. 46–47)

There are several keys to quality schools and quality teaching. Critical elements include high expectations for all students (eliminating tracking), protection of academic learning time, a high degree of direct instruction and on-task behavior, and maintenance of a safe and orderly learning environment. Latinos

Disadvantaged urban fourth graders score far below comparison students

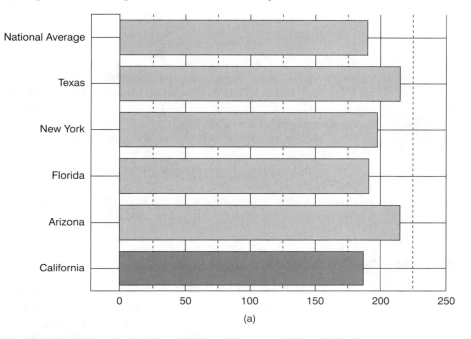

(a)

Suburban/rural fourth graders score a little lower than comparison students

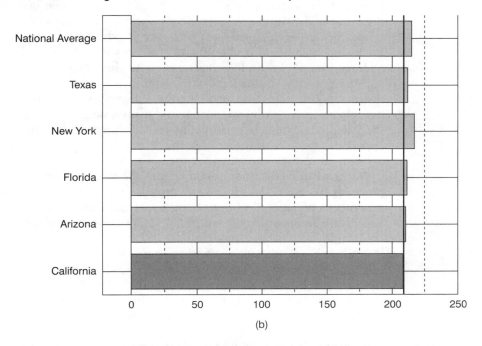

(b)

Figure 1.9   Comparisons of Scores of Disadvantaged Versus Suburban / Rural Fourth Graders on the 1992 NAEP (National Assessment of Educational Progress)

Note. Data from *California K–12 Report Card* (p.8), by Elizabeth E. Hall, February, 1994, California Legislative Analyst's Office.

19

attending many Catholic parochial schools have enjoyed these advantages for years. Non-Catholic, African American families often are fleeing public schools and paying over $1,000 a year in tuition to send their children to Catholic schools and other religious schools in search of a safe and productive learning environment. In other areas, such as the Central Park East complex in Harlem of New York City, public schools provide an environment where academic success and personal support are integral parts of the curriculum for cultural and linguistic minorities. Research and practices described in *The Good Common School* (National Association of Advocates for Children, 1992) demonstrate that well-run, orderly schools with an academic focus, higher expectations, and high achievement levels make a difference in the lives of children.

Teachers Touch the Future

We need multicultural educational reform to improve the quality of school life for all of our children. Multicultural school reform is directly linked to the pursuit of democratic opportunities. Developing democratic dispositions in students is a formidable task in a society like ours, divided by inequality and loss of economic security. But democratic practices and economic behaviors are learned, not inherited. Middle-class students—around whose needs the present public school system is designed—learn to exercise their democratic rights and assume their responsibilities. It should come as no surprise, then, that the perspectives and agendas of the middle class dominate the schools. While maintaining this domination may be satisfactory to some, it is not healthy for society as a whole. If our working class and poor become convinced that they are not expected to participate in the political, social, and economic processes that run our society, then democracy itself becomes at-risk. Improving the quality of educational opportunity for these students is the central task of multicultural education and is essential to the survival of our society as a democracy.

Multicultural education assumes that the future of our society is pluralistic. It proposes to restore and fulfill the promise made in the establishment of public schools: to prepare all of our young people for full participation in the economy and in the democratic community. It also proposes to validate the humanity and cultural life of diverse people.

Multicultural education assumes that teachers want all their students to succeed and that they are looking for positive and effective democratic responses to the economic crisis and the demographic changes taking place in our classrooms. Twenty-five percent of the U.S. labor force for the next decade will pass through our urban schools. These generations of citizens must be prepared to work, investigate, explore, and decide on public policy that will benefit the entire community. If the schools fail, even if only the urban schools continue to fail, then the U.S. economy will fail. Linda Wong of California Tomorrow, a research group committed to educational reform and supportive of racial and ethnic diversity, invokes the frequently used lifeboat analogy to describe our choices:

California—eventually the nation, if the demographic projections are correct—is a life boat. If the boat is springing leaks because of inadequate and poor quality education, because of deepening poverty . . . the people who are sitting in the boat are going to figure out some ways of plugging those leaks and working together if they value their lives. (Njeri, 1991, p. E9)

The debate and dialogue in our society over justice, freedom, and equality continue. A new wave of immigrants is adding to the populations of historically dominated cultures and ethnic groups. Faith and hope in democratic opportunity are currently on trial in the public schools.

Multicultural Education—A Definition

Multicultural education was developed to assist teachers who are trying to solve the diverse problems imposed on their classrooms by the rapidly changing and, at times, decaying society.

Today, teachers in most urban areas face students from a variety of social classes and cultural and language groups. Often, European American children are a minority group. In many rural areas, such as the Rio Grande Valley of Texas, the central valleys of California, Arizona, New Mexico, Georgia, and Mississippi, and the Appalachian region, the majority of the students do not share the middle-class, European American culture common to college-educated teachers.

Substantial school reforms are needed to give these diverse students an equal chance in school, in the job market, and in contributing to the building of healthy communities. James Banks (1989), one of the leaders in the field of multicultural education, offers this definition:

> Multicultural education is at least three things: an idea or concept, an educational reform movement, and a process. Multicultural education incorporates the idea that all students—regardless of their gender and social class, and their ethnic, racial, and cultural characteristics—should have an equal opportunity to learn in school . . .
>
> Multicultural education is also a reform movement that is trying to change schools and other educational institutions so that students from all social class, gender, racial, and cultural groups will have an equal opportunity to learn. (pp. 2–3)

This preliminary definition will be elaborated in subsequent chapters. Teachers, as they work with and motivate the young, must serve as community leaders who observe reality and recognize the gap between the stated ideals of society and actual living conditions. Democratic citizens respect the rights of their neighbors, including language and cultural rights. In our roles as teachers, we participate in the struggle to extend democracy to students from populations and cultures previously excluded. We must not allow the growing poverty, violence, and anarchy in our streets to overcome our schools and destroy their contribution to the American dream.

Multicultural education builds on democratic theory to argue for the dignity of the individual, the possibility of human progress, and the fundamental equality of all people. Teachers have a responsibility to both teach and reflect these values. We already know how to improve the schools. Effective school reform begins with you, the teacher. We need to end tracking, hold high expectations for all students, promote success and self-esteem, and empower students.

An elaborated and extended definition of multicultural education is developed in the following chapters. Sleeter and Grant, in *Making Choices for Multicultural Education* (1988), described their version of five approaches: teaching for cultural diversity, human relations, single-group studies, multicultural education, and multicultural education that is social reconstructionist. Each of these approaches is described in the following chapters with a somewhat different emphasis. The categories created by Sleeter and Grant—and earlier by Margaret Gibson—were important, but no longer adequately encompass the rapidly emerging field. Chapter 2 begins with a focus on "The Nature of Culture," a current and more useful version of the prior cultural diversity / cultural deficit approach. Chapters 3 and 5 draw on the major developments of African American Studies, Latino Studies, Ethnic Studies, and Women's Studies representing the single-group studies approach. Chapter 6 describes and advocates the human relations approach, which is particularly useful in grades K–4 but is also an element of multicultural education at all age levels. Chapters 4 and 11 describe important elements of the multicultural education approach. Chapters 7, 11, and 13 bring each of these analytical frameworks together as a basis for a multicultural education that is social reconstructionist—an approach most often found in middle schools and high schools, although specific strategies are also applicable in the elementary grades.

Our multicultural society requires multicultural education. Students from all cultural and racial groups must learn to get along and to respect our several cultural traditions. Schools must change. They must recognize and draw on the background knowledge and languages of all of our children. Both the teachers and the curriculum must validate the home and community knowledge that all children bring to school. To do this, teachers must respect and draw strength from diverse cultural traditions of our society. Teachers must adopt new strategies so that African Americans, Latinos, Asians / Pacific Islanders, Native Americans, Appalachian whites, and others achieve equal opportunity in our schools.

Schools did not create, and they cannot resolve, the political / economic crises of our times or its racial, class, and gender divisions (Greider, 1992). But schools and teachers can and do affect individual students' lives every day. Chapters 2 through 6 introduce the concepts of culture, race, gender, and class essential to developing a practical teacher philosophy of multicultural education. Multicultural teaching strategies, like those described in Chapters 7 through 11, provide planned, organized, and direct teaching of self-respect, mutual respect, democracy, and equal opportunity. Several approaches to multicultural education have been developed and will be described in the following chapters. The first is the Nature of Culture approach defined in Chapter 2.

Questions Over the Chapter

1. Compare the ethnic and gender composition of the students in your own teacher preparation program with the population of your region. How do you explain the differences?
2. Some people consider the disturbances of April 29 through May 1, 1992, in Los Angeles a riot; others describe what occurred as a rebellion. What are the differences in point of view between these two positions?
3. Study Figure 1.7. How do you explain the differences in poverty rates by race among children?

4. Define the following concepts as they pertain to schools:
   a. Economic crisis
   b. Ethnic diversity
   c. Language diversity
   d. Mediocrity
   e. Equal opportunity
   f. Democratic responsibility

References

Banks, J. A. (1989). Multicultural education: Characteristics and goals. In J. A. Banks & C. A. McGee Banks (Eds.), *Multicultural education: Issues and perspectives* (pp. 2–3). Newtown, MA: Allyn & Bacon.

Banks, J. (1994). *An introduction to multicultural education*. Newton, MA: Allyn & Bacon.

Bartlett, D. L., & Steele, J. B. (1992). *America: What went wrong?* Kansas City, MO: Andrews & McMeel.

Bastian, A., Fruchter, N., Gittell, M., Greer, C., & Hoskins, K. (1985). *Choosing equality: The case for democratic schooling*. Philadelphia: Temple University Press.

Brown, P. A., & Haycock, K. (1984). *Excellence for whom? A report of the planning committee for the Achievement Council*. Oakland, CA: The Achievement Council.

Carter, T. P., & Chatfield, M. L. (1986, November). Effective bilingual schools: Implications for policy and practice. *American Journal of Education*, pp. 210–233.

The Center for Civic Education. (1991). *Civitas: A framework for civic education*. Calabasas, CA: Author.

Children's Defense Fund. (1989). *A vision for America's future*. Washington, DC: Author.

Commission on Chapter 1. (1993, January 13). Making schools work for our children. *Education Week*, pp. 47–51.

Cotton, K. (1989). *Expectations and student outcomes*. Portland, OR: Northwest Regional Laboratory.

Dahl, R. (1985). *A preface to economic democracy*. Berkeley: University of California Press.

Dewey, J. (1916/1966). *Democracy and education: An introduction to the philosophy of education*. New York: The Free Press & Macmillan.

Greider, W. (1992). *Who will tell the people? The betrayal of American democracy*. New York: Simon & Schuster.

Hall, E. E. (1994, February). *California K–12 Report Card*. California Legislative Analyst Office.

Kollars, D. (1987, November). Tracking a poor reader's stumbling steps through school. *The Sacramento Bee*, p. 1.

Kozol, J. (1991). *Savage inequalities: Children in America's schools*. New York: Crowne.

Mishel, L., & Frankel, D. M. (1991). *The state of working America, 1990–1991, Economic Policy Institute*. Armonk, NY: M. E. Sharpe Inc.

Mullis, I. V. S., Owen, E. H., & Phillips, G. W. (1990, September). *America's challenge:*

Accelerating academic achievement, A summary of the findings from 20 years of the NAEP. National Assessment of Education Progress, U.S. Department of Education.

National Association of Advocates for Children. (1992). *The good common school.* Boston, MA: Author.

National Commission on Excellence in Education. (1983). *A nation at risk.* U.S. Government Printing Office.

National Commission on Secondary Schooling for Hispanics. (1984). *Make something happen: Hispanics and urban high school reform.* U.S. Government Printing Office.

Njeri, I. (1991, January 13). Beyond the melting pot. *Los Angeles Times,* E1, E8, E9.

Olsen, L. (1986, January). Effective schools. *Education Week,* 11.

Olsen, L. (1988). *Crossing the schoolhouse border: Immigrant students and the California public schools.* San Francisco, CA: California Tomorrow.

Rasell, M. E., & Mishel, L. (1990). *Shortchanging education: How U.S. spending on grades K–12 lags behind other industrialized nations.* Armonk, NY: Economic Policy Institute.

Reich, R. B. (1991, January). Secession of the successful. *New York Times Magazine,* p. 44.

Sleeter, C., & Grant, C. (1988). *Making choices for multicultural education: Five approaches to race, class, and gender.* Englewood Cliffs, NJ: Merrill / Prentice Hall.

Chapter 2

Culture and Schooling

Political changes, changing immigration patterns, and the growth of minority student populations have led to renewed interest in multicultural education and bilingualism. In fact, these populations have changed so much that most of the students in urban classrooms share histories and experiences that differ dramatically from those represented in the curriculum or lived by the teacher. As a result of these differences, teachers and schools are struggling to find ways to bring success to new and diverse populations.

When properly understood, the concept of culture explains a great deal about school success and failure for both students and teachers. Unfortunately, many teachers and teacher preparation programs deal with the concept of culture in ways that are not useful and, in some cases, even harmful. Cultures are often presented as fixed, static, homogeneous; they are not. Nor are cultures sufficiently understood by looking at artifacts, eating tortillas, or by participating in idealized dances.

This chapter seeks to help you to recognize, understand, and evaluate the concept of culture—your own culture and the cultures of your students. The perspectives of this chapter have been developed from the field of anthropology, particularly the works of Henry Trueba, George and Louis Spindler, and others.

Your active reading and working toward a sophisticated comprehension of culture will provide you with the foundation you will need for developing new teaching strategies and understanding the process of school change.

The Nature of Culture

Over 100 years ago, Edward Tylor (1871) provided a preliminary working definition of **culture:** "that complex whole which includes knowledge, belief, art, morals, law, custom, and any other capabilities and habits acquired by man as a member of society" (p. 7). Culture is a complex web of information and experiences that serves as a basis for each person's observations and interpretation of events. James Banks (1984), an authority in the field of multicultural education, describes culture as "the behavior patterns, symbols, institutions, values, and other human made components of society" (p. 52). For further elaboration, see Valentine (1968).

All human beings learn a culture. All parents teach a culture to their children. Culture is also learned and transmitted through the organizations and institutions of a society. That is, cultures are not individuals. Individuals experience and transmit culture uniquely, but culture itself transcends individual experience. Individuals within a culture participate in a vision of social life that is interactive, shared, and learned.

A culture is the way of life of a group of people. Explicitly and implicitly, a culture teaches its members how to organize their experience. To learn a culture is to learn how to perceive, judge, and act in ways that are recognizable, predictable, and understandable to others in the same community.

Children bring these cultural values—including language—with them when they enter school, where they may suddenly find themselves in an entirely new community with new values and perhaps even a new language.

The School Culture

In U.S. society, the job of training children to participate in the **macroculture—** the central, dominant culture of the society—has been assigned to the schools. The Spindlers (1991) write, "As a teacher, a student, a delinquent, a superlatively good student, or a miserably inept student, we are all caught up in a cultural process" (p. 1). They identify the school system as a "mandated cultural process" and the teacher as a "cultural agent" (p. 1).

The multicultural environment of most urban schools is a culture in its own right; the authority structure of teachers and administrators, the sealed-off quality of the campus, the grade-by-grade hierarchy of the students, as well as the rich mix of ethnic home cultures, create a unique cultural arena. Entering a public school for a minority culture child is similar to being thrust suddenly into a foreign country. Even if the child knows the native language (and many don't), the habits, rules, customs, and expectations encountered at school can all be dramatically different from those learned at home.

The teacher who has developed a critical comprehension of the role of culture can assist students of diverse cultures as they grapple with the public school experience. The teacher can guide and be an advocate for these students as they adapt to the school culture and begin to learn the dimensions of the macroculture beyond. From a multicultural perspective, the task of a teacher is to respect the culture the child brings from home, to guide the student's learning of the basic skills and attitudes of the dominant culture, and to nourish each student's self-esteem.

To be a guide to culture, the teacher must be able to communicate with students. The most appropriate and effective means of guiding children is to build on what they already know. Effective teachers use the concepts and strategies the children have acquired at home to teach them new concepts and new strategies. The need to build on knowledge acquired at home before a student starts school is most apparent in language acquisition. Languages are central to cultures. When teaching a child a second language such as English, the effective teacher communicates with the child and provides instruction the child can comprehend. When the teacher can use the home language of the child, the lesson is more comprehensible.

Few issues in education are more controversial than bilingual education and English-language acquisition by non-English-speaking students. These issues, along with useful teaching strategies, are explored in detail in Chapter 10.

Students have a need and a right to learn about their own culture as well as the dominant culture. For students from minority status cultures, studying their own culture can empower them to make important life choices, such as to complete high school or college. Studying the culture and historical experience of their people validates minority students' background knowledge and converts it into an accessible base for further learning activities. The incorporation of this background information into the official school curriculum gives status to the students' parents and community.

With the security and self-confidence provided by self-knowledge, students can begin to learn about the school culture and the macroculture, which they must do to gain entry into the political and economic institutions of the larger society. However, if the macroculture is simply imposed with little recognition or use of the student's home culture, the student may become confused, frustrated, hostile, resistant, and frequently, an educational casualty.

Imagine a young boy who enters kindergarten knowing how to read. This student delights in reading, in discovering new stories in books. What would happen to him if the teacher began presenting prereading skills without acknowledging the unique skills the child had brought from home? He would feel that his own skills were being devalued, and he would be bored and frustrated with the material being presented to him.

Many children from Latino, African American, and other minority cultures experience such devaluation of their cultures. Some schools insist that children must immediately integrate into the school culture. But this has been proven to be counterproductive. To pull children (or adults) from one culture and place them in another, produces anxiety, frustration, and culture shock; it seldom produces learning. Children respond in a number of ways to this rejection of their home culture. They often withdraw and become passive; others engage in open power struggles against the teachers and the school.

Students from microcultures are more successful in learning and adapting to the school culture when their own home culture is recognized and used as a basis for instruction. Strategies that build on the child's own prior knowledge and culture are empowering and improve the child's skills, abilities, and sense of self-worth. If a teacher can speak in the child's home language, the teacher can access even more of the child's background information and cultural preferences.

Worldview

All people develop a worldview as a part of learning their culture. A **worldview** is the set of *a priori* judgments and expectations with which we perceive other people, history, our own culture, other cultures, and daily events. Components of our worldview are taught to us by our parents, family, friends, and later, teachers.

We also have unique individual experiences that shape our worldview. For example, the oldest child in a family will experience some aspects of childhood differently than the youngest child. The oldest child cannot look to older siblings for guidance, while the youngest child will not have younger siblings on whom to practice parenting behavior.

Our worldview is composed of all the things we have learned, all of our previous experiences. Our culture defines and directs the ways in which we interpret this information and thus how we may react to new experiences. For example, some cultures view racial differences as extremely important while others view racial differences as less important.

To clarify this point, imagine a family gathering at which a 9-year-old child contradicts the statement of a grandparent. In one culture, this might be interpreted as an expression of self-confidence and independence. The child is learning facts in school that the grandparent does not have. In another culture, however, the same event is seen as disrespectful, as a lack of education (the child has not yet learned respect for the wisdom of the elderly). The significance of the same event can be different depending on the worldview and the culture of those involved.

This process of learning a worldview also applies to the school experience. Different cultural groups develop their own analysis of schools and education. U.S. schools have been based on the cultural practices of the dominant European American culture. Rules, strategies, curricula, methods of evaluation, and systems of discipline derive primarily from this culture. Students reared in the macroculture take these school rules for granted. To them, our school patterns seem natural, normal, and logical. The pressure to compete for grades and attention is viewed as part of universal human experience.

However, if we view schools through the experiences and perceptions of some urban ghetto residents, a different analysis of schools emerges. The real experience of generations of African Americans, particularly those from the lower classes in urban ghettos, is that school is a place of frustration and failure. Over 50% of these students do not complete high school. Many of those who do complete school have a difficult time finding a secure job.

Many African American families have experienced school as a place where their child is measured, tested, and found to be inadequate. Hard work in school does not always lead to success. In spite of the nation's formal commitment to democracy in schools, the experience of a lower class, African American child is likely to be significantly different from the ideal. School may be a frightening, cold, intrusion into the child's life. Or it might even be a zone of safety from the violence in many neighborhoods.[1]

John U. Ogbu (1978), an anthropologist from the University of California at Berkeley, has argued that some students from subjugated minority groups may believe that teachers and successful students in the school promote "acting white" (pp. 278–282). (Also, see Fordham, 1988.) Such students may perceive that the teachers criticize the homes and families of the children for not monitoring homework or for not attending back-to-school nights. Children who are already defensive and uncertain about their home culture receive these school messages with anxiety and often amplify and distort them into negative judgments about themselves, their families, and their communities. Such cultural conflict between the macroculture and subjugated cultures extends to many rural Appalachian areas where European American students often suffer educational neglect similar to that of racial and ethnic minority groups (Eller-Powell, 1994).

The conflict between cultures and worldviews begins when children from a minority culture enter school—a process that may continue throughout the years of schooling. These students learn the macroculture's values at school. But they continue to learn their home culture's often-conflicting values and views. Their culture is reconstructed and redefined based on their school experience. For example, the parent may teach "go to school, get a good education, get a good job." But the lived experience of many young people may be that school is an alienating, struggle-filled scene of conflict and even degradation. The student learns a different view of school than that intended by the parent or the teacher. As they mature, students may enter a youth culture with values and views that conflict with both the home culture and the macroculture. This continuing cultural conflict has a cumulative eroding effect on the student's confidence and ability to focus on school tasks.

Many young African American and Latino students experience failure and frustration in school, falling behind in basic study skills. Persistent failure breaks down the student's self-esteem until some failing students begin to believe that they cannot learn, that school failure is normal and inevitable for children like them. Once a negative attitude is internalized, the pattern of school failure repeats itself. Students who doubt their own capacity will not learn well. They become in-school casualties or they leave.

---

[1] The above sketch of the worldview of a group called "the underclass" has been simplified for illustration. The actual acquisition of a worldview for an individual of any culture is far more complex and interactive than the illustration presented. Chapter 4 includes a detailed discussion of the "underclass" thesis.

The Macroculture and U.S. Schools

The dominant worldview in U.S. society, and therefore, U.S. schools, has been defined by the values, attitudes, beliefs, and folkways of the European American majority.[2] These patterns of communication and life are used as criteria by which to judge right and wrong behavior. In the classroom, this cultural domination is reinforced by the preponderance of middle-class, European American teachers who unconsciously use their cultural values to judge their students' work and behavior.

Students from minority cultures and from the working class are generally respected and accepted by the school culture to the degree that they imitate the cultural traits of the macroculture, particularly its middle-class language and customs. That is, they become assimilated. They learn that the middle-class, European American culture represents the preferred way of living, working, and learning.

In the early 1900s, a view that schools should promote Eurocentric assimilation was popularized in educational literature through the concept of the "melting pot." It was believed that in a few generations all of the differences between immigrant people would merge into one common culture. Advocates of the melting pot viewpoint assumed that all people could melt into one common culture, and they assumed that all people wanted to be like the European American view of an "ideal American."

Common observation demonstrates that the melting pot has not worked for many groups, particularly those visibly identifiable "racial" groups. People have not melted into one "model American." In fact, the melting pot viewpoint was often damaging to students from minority cultures in schools. Dramatic achievement gaps emerged between students from the dominant group and minority students, as shown in Figure 1.8. Members of certain racially visible minority cultures could not easily assimilate. Their performance in school suffered; to some, this lower achievement was proof of the inferiority of the racial and cultural origins of these students.

Even though racial integration became a national goal and ultimately the law of the land in the 1960s, today's schools are in many ways more isolated, more segregated, and more unequal than those of previous generations (Network of Regional Desegregation Centers, 1989). Both schools and society are moving methodically away from equality. Today schools prepare African Americans, Latinos, and Native Americans for unequal, lower-status positions in the economy. Far from melting into one common culture, U.S. society is rapidly dividing into multiple racial, ethnic, cultural groups who increasingly regard each other with suspicion and hostility.

---

[2] The dominant culture in the United States, referred to as "European American," is a product of numerous contributions. A relatively common culture has developed in modern urban society. Several ethnic cultural groups contributed to this culture (e.g., Italians, Irish, and Greek). At times, the culture is referred to as Anglo or Anglo European because that group's language, laws, religion, and customs came to dominate the culture.

Cultural Democracy

By the late 1960s, a new theory had emerged to contend with the melting pot theory. Termed **cultural democracy,** this new approach drew from different perspectives on our nation's history, developments in the social sciences, and a different analysis of the educational process.

Cultural democracy argues that our society consists of several cultures. In this multicultural society, each culture has its own child-rearing practices, languages, learning styles, and emotional support systems. These cultures contribute to and participate in a common culture (the macroculture), which includes such features as a commitment to a democratic political system and a public school system. Groups may have different views on specific issues, such as secular versus religious schooling, but schooling itself is seldom questioned.

The change from a melting pot view to a culturally democratic view involves a major conceptual shift for the majority of persons becoming teachers—particularly for those who are part of the dominant European American culture. The worldview they were taught while growing up no longer adequately frames our society. More precisely, the melting pot view failed to explain the persistent lack of school success by children from dominated cultures. As the explanatory power of the melting pot view declines, the fundamental ideas about schools that were based on this view including curriculum practices, teaching strategies, teacher recruitment, measurement, and motivational assumptions require reexamination.

In the new multicultural worldview, cultures and cultural values are analyzed relatively. That is, they are investigated by considering the group's own vantage point. Adopting a multicultural perspective is not to argue for the extreme position of value neutrality or relativity, however. For example, an immigrant cultural group from Afghanistan may have practiced the forced subordination of women, but when a young girl enters school in our society, she has a right to equal treatment and respect. While developing a cross-cultural perspective does not presume ethical relativism, it does require that teachers become precise observers of cultures. Rejecting both the past practices of melting pot cultural domination and the hands-off, *laissez faire* value-neutrality approach, democratic teachers become **cultural mediators** and present models of ethical leadership that encourage equality and respect.

Teachers and the Concept of Culture

Helping teachers understand the nature of culture provides a direct way to help them diminish the effects of prejudice in the classroom. An understanding of the complexity of culture helps teachers to work against ethnocentrism and provides a central strategy for reform of schools. Most of us are so immersed in our own cultures that we fail to recognize how much of our behavior derives from cultural patterns. Teachers need to understand how their own cultures affect their lives, their teaching strategies, and the lives of their students.

Persons learn a series of strategies, perceptions, and responses during their childhood. Culture, gender, and socioeconomic class overlap within the home to produce behavior patterns, attitudes, and values. For example, some children are reared with a great deal of criticism, others with little criticism but a great deal of modeling, and still others with little or no direction at all. These patterns, learned before the age of 4, provide a subconscious framework for much of what the child will learn later.

Cultural patterns are not absolute but do produce tendencies toward certain behaviors or beliefs within a group. For example, Mexican Americans tend to speak both English and Spanish. Some members of the group speak Spanish almost exclusively, some speak a balance of English and Spanish, and some speak almost no Spanish. A few Mexican Americans also speak German or other languages. A cultural pattern then is a possibility—a probability—but not a certainty. Individuals within each group also have their own histories and experiences.

Latino, Hispanic, Chicano, or Cultural Diversity?

It is important for teachers to be aware of the variations of experiences within cultural groups and not assume that all members of a group have similar background experiences. An explanation of the complexity of the Latino cultural heritage will illustrate this point.

Latinos comprise all of those people who are descendants of immigrants from Latin American countries and those persons of Spanish-Indian heritage present in the Southwest when the U.S. Army arrived in the 1830s and 1840s. As Figure 2.1 shows, there is wide diversity within the Latino (also called Hispanic) culture.

The largest component (60.4%) of the Latino population in the United States are descendants of Mexican parents (for a historical timeline, see Appendix B). In the Southwestern United States, descendants of Mexicans predominate, making up over 80% of the Latino population. In Northern New Mexico, this population arrived before Mexico was established as an independent nation, and therefore they often describe themselves as "Hispanos," a term that retains some sense of historical linkage with the European-Spanish culture.

The Mexican American population in the United States is very diverse. Some lived as Indians on what is now U.S. territory before the Spaniards and the United States arrived to conquer the land. Others immigrated during the several major periods of migration: 1911–1924, 1945–1954, and 1965–present. Some of the most recent immigrants are bringing modern urban Mexican cultural traditions, while others continue the rural traditions. In recent years, large numbers of Mixtec Indians from the southern Mexican state of Oaxaca have arrived to perform farm labor.

Puerto Ricans constitute another part of the Latino population (12.2%). Puerto Rico's Indian population was decimated by the Spanish invasion and colonization prior to 1800. They were replaced with African slave laborers who,

Composition of the Hispanic Population

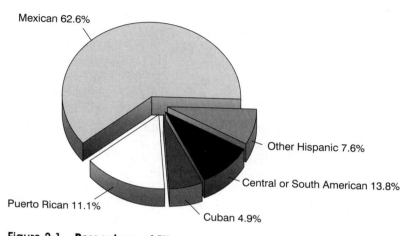

Mexican 62.6%

Other Hispanic 7.6%

Central or South American 13.8%

Puerto Rican 11.1%

Cuban 4.9%

Figure 2.1   Percentage of Ethnic Groups Within Latino Population in the United States, 1990

Note. From "The Hispanic Population of the United States" by the Bureau of the Census, March 1991.

after abolition, were integrated into the society. The United States conquered the islands of Puerto Rico in 1898 and gave it Commonwealth status in 1924. However, in the early 1950s, new "economic development" plans drove many Puerto Rican families from their farms. As a result, millions migrated to the U.S. mainland in search of work, often settling in cities along the East Coast.

A third part of the Latino population in the United States is the Cuban Americans. The one million Cuban Americans living in Florida have become a powerful social and political force in that state. They make up about 4.7% of the total Latino population in the country. Their genetic heritage is similar to that of the Puerto Ricans, but their history is quite different. After the War of 1898, Cuba achieved a limited independence. Unlike Puerto Rico, it was not integrated as a part of the United States. Governed by a series of U.S.-supported military dictators, Cuba in the 1950s was in a state of economic and social crisis. Gambling, poverty, prostitution, and underdevelopment were severe. In 1959, a nationalist guerrilla group led by Fidel Castro seized power in a war, they turned to the former Soviet Union for support and assistance, and adopted communism as their economic and political system.

A large segment of educated middle-class Cubans fled the island at the time of the 1959 revolution. With U.S. government assistance, they established an effective Cuban American community in Florida that later supported subsequent immigrants fleeing Cuba. While Mexican Americans and Puerto Rican families experienced decades of economic hardships in the United States, many Cubans were able to move into successful businesses within a single generation. Eventually they established majority status in the economy and government in parts of Florida. Thus, though the decades of Cuban immigration were difficult, they did not last for generations and suffer the cultural disruption experienced by both Mexican Americans and Puerto Ricans. Assimilation was the major experience for Cuban Americans, while domination by the host culture was the major experience for Mexicans and Puerto Ricans (Crawford, 1992; Llanes, 1982).

In the 1980s and 1990s, a large number of immigrants arrived from El Salvador, Nicaragua, Guatemala, and Peru, fleeing the deteriorating economy and extended wars in these areas. The 2.2 million recent immigrants from Latin America make up only 11.5% of the total Latino population in the United States, but they add even more diversity to the Latino population. Some areas of Latin America (Costa Rica, Uruguay, and Argentina) were so thoroughly shaped by Spanish and European cultures that little of their native cultures or native peoples remains. Other areas (Mexico, Guatemala, El Salvador, and Peru) had such strong Indian cultures and so few Spanish immigrants (and these mostly male) that areas of their societies remain substantially Indian even today.

Recently hundreds of thousands of Latinos from the Dominican Republic, Haiti, Cuba, and other islands have been landing on the East Coast of the United States, fleeing the political and economic chaos of their countries. They bring yet another distinct cultural heritage.

As these communities live in the United States and adapt to the social and economic conditions they find here, they often metamorphose into another kind of cultural group, one neither native to their country of origin nor imitative of the European American macroculture. Second- and third-generation descendants of Mexicans and Puerto Ricans tend to speak only English. For some, their formative years were spent in communities and schools where being perceived as Latino put them at a social disadvantage. Others lived in barrios and attended de facto segregated schools where, despite being the majority in their own neighborhoods, they were still regarded as a second-class minority by government and school authorities. These groups have developed new cultural experiences based on their lives in the United States. Unlike recent immigrants, who tend to view the school system as a vehicle for assimilation into U.S. life, Chicano (descendants of Mexican Americans) and Puerto Rican students may see their schools as run-down and shabby, symbols of their oppression and second-class status in U.S. society. These dominated cultural groups have developed new cultural traits such as bilingualism and dramatic new poetry and art in the process of creating a culture of resistance to domination.

For many parents, the schools were the sites of disempowerment. In response, anti-school or alternative views of schooling developed. Often the conflict between home and school produced alienation, at other times, failure. The culture of the Latino communities is currently in transition as a result of this ongoing struggle.

The current Latino culture emerged from the people's experiences and the diverse communities' responses. For example, some Latinos have turned to Catholic schools to guard their children from urban violence. Another portion of the community has turned to Evangelical religious experiences, while a third group has been overwhelmed by failing schools, gangs, and street violence. Each of these and other experiences have continually reconstructed the Latino culture.

All of these diverse elements make up the groups that the U.S. Census Bureau calls "Hispanics" (1988). Similar diversity exists within most cultures, be it Asian, Native American, or African American. Teachers who pursue a cross-cultural perspective take years to learn the complexities of interaction within this cultural diversity. Often by the time one group is familiar, a new group will arrive (for example, Rumanians and Russians).

Because culture is constantly changing, teachers need to be cautious about all generalizations concerning Latinos and other groups. Most generalizations apply to only one part of the population and many are overdrawn, including popular media generalizations about the underclass and learning styles. For example, some Latinos are Catholic, have large families and large weddings, and speak Spanish. Others are Protestants, atheist, speak only English, and prefer to be called Hispanic.

While teachers should not generalize, they should learn to observe, listen, and learn. Teachers need to be aware of the differences between ideal and real (lived) culture and foster mutual respect in the classroom. Teachers help students navigate the troublesome terrain between their home culture, with all of its changes and complexities, and the macroculture's traumas, including gangs, crime, poverty, and social dissolution.

The multiple perspectives on culture useful for teachers working in multicultural education have been well summarized in Figure 2.2.

Cultural Politics and Cultural Ethics

Like most modern societies, we in the United States have chosen to use schools to introduce students to dominant cultural patterns. Our mainly European American political leaders have decided that all students should learn a common civic culture and that schools should teach that culture. Schools are therefore a primary site of cultural transmission. In the process of transmitting the cultural patterns—through both formal and informal curriculum—the U.S. macroculture itself is redefined. But in California, New York, Illinois, Florida, New Mexico, and Texas, total English dominance can no longer be assumed. In many border and urban areas, the bilingual high school graduate has an advantage for business and educational success.

Even European Americans continually reevaluate and reinterpret their culture. The dominant European American culture is being forced to change by the pressures of economic transitions and several urban crises. The melting pot model assumed that over time and with proper instruction people from diverse cultures could be molded into an approximation of an "ideal American." The characteristics and values of that ideal person were derived from the European American macroculture.

Figure 2.2   Perspectives on Culture for Teachers

What Culture Is
- Dynamic, neither fixed nor static.
- A continuous and cumulative process.
- Learned and shared by a people.
- Behavior and values exhibited by a people.
- Creative and meaningful to our lives.
- Symbolically represented through language and people interacting.
- A guide to people in their thinking, feeling, and acting.

What Culture Is Not
- Artifacts or material used by a people.
- A "laundry list" of traits and facts.
- Biological traits such as race.
- The ideal and romantic heritage of a people as seen through music, dance, holidays, etc.
- Higher class status derived from a knowledge of the arts, manners, literature, etc.
- Something to be bought, sold, or passed out.

Why It Is Important To Know About Culture
- Culture is a means of survival.
- All people are cultural beings and need to be aware of how culture affects peoples' behavior.
- Culture is at work in every classroom.
- Culture affects how learning is organized, how school rules and curriculum are developed, and how teaching methods and evaluation procedures are implemented.
- Schools can prepare students for effective participation in dealing with the cultures of the world.
- Understanding cultural differences can help solve problems and conflicts in the school and in the community.

A Multicultural Worldview

In place of the single idealized "American," the worldview of the multicultural education movement sees a society in which members of several different cultures are all equally valued and respected. Most people are not even aware they have a worldview. They assume that all people see reality through a perspective similar to their own. The Persians (Iranians) have a saying for this myopia: "It is difficult for the fish to see the stream." In schools, the assumption that "my way is the right way" is revealed when teachers state, "I just want to get beyond this ethnic divisiveness. I treat everyone as an individual. I am tired of having to deal with this ethnic, cultural thing."

Developing a Crosscultural Perspective:
Becoming Aware of Culture in Ourselves

- Involves perception or knowledge gained through our senses and interpreted internally.
- Helps in understanding and avoiding areas of unnecessary conflict and allows us to learn through contrast.
- Calls attention to value positions and value hierarchies of our culture which may be different from the value structures of other cultures.

Becoming Aware of Culture in Others

- Involves a certain degree of ethnocentrism, which is the belief that our own cultural ways are correct and superior to others. Ethnocentrism is natural and occurs in each of us.
- While ethnocentrism helps to develop pride and a positive self-image, it can also be harmful if carried to the extreme of developing an intolerance for people of other cultures.
- Is, in part, based upon the value of cultural relativity, the belief that there are many cultural ways that are correct, each in its own location and context.
- Analyses based on cultural relativity are essential to building respect for cultural differences and appreciation for cultural similarities.
- Cultural relativity as an analytical system is not the same as ethical neutrality in teaching.

Note. Reprinted with permission of the Cross Cultural Resource Center, California State University—Sacramento, n.d.

Persons making this choice fail to recognize that denying the significance of ethnicity and cultural differences is a privilege reserved primarily for members of the dominant group. In our society, the primacy of the individual's rights and needs ("I've got to do what's right for me") derives from cultural patterns rooted in the Protestant tradition of European American culture. In this tradition, individuals—not groups—are the significant elements of a society, and the individual's primary responsibility is to seek personal salvation. Of course, achieving salvation means obeying certain laws and carrying out certain social admonitions such as those found in the Bible's Ten Commandments. But the focus is on the private and personal relationship between an individual and God. Thus, admiration for strong individualism is an attribute of the dominant culture in our society, but it is only a culturally specific choice, not a human universal.

Multicultural educators believe that teachers do not have the right to insist that students from other cultural traditions abandon their less individualistic, more communal values. For example, a young Mexican American child may be taught from an early age to respect the family first, then La Raza (cultural identity), and then humanity. Rural Irish children are taught a roughly similar hierarchy of values based on their shared rural, Catholic culture. African American teenagers may well have learned to stick together to defend their neighborhood friends against the intrusion of dope sellers, police, social workers, landlords, and the political powers of a city.

These students have learned a less individualistic value structure, and the teacher using a culturally democratic approach will recognize and respect these values. The teacher, as a cultural mediator who reduces conflict and helps children succeed in school, can help students to better comprehend both their own cultures and the demands of the macroculture.

Teaching About Culture

Students first learn about culture at home. Lessons about families and roles in the primary grades help students to draw on their home experiences. We know that the very young are often aware of ethnic differences. Students can be empowered by studying the groups and institutions closest to them, including family and school. Studies of concepts including kinship, education, health, leadership, and community help young children to understand the more general concept of culture.

Children at very young ages can begin to analyze the facets of culture that they have learned from the family. Later, after ages 10 to 12, when peer groups become more important, students can begin to analyze the differences between the values that their parents taught them and the new values encouraged and advocated by their peer group.

Beginning in about fourth grade, children can study themselves in the context of their cultural patterns. Children can begin to see that they have *learned* to be who they are. They can study the process of learning and the traits and languages taught at home. It is very important for children to see that they are active participants in the learning process of acquiring their culture. For example, a young Chicano boy should understand that in the home he is a product of the Chicano culture. Yet the same child deserves to know that he is also being trained to be a part of the dominant European American culture in the school. Some conflict about this is unavoidable, but in a culturally democratic classroom it can be discussed and analyzed and become the source of new insight. If unexamined, cultural conflict creates anxiety which, once internalized, hardens into dysfunctional responses such as a chronic expectation of failure.

For example, U.S.-born children of Mexican descent (Chicanos or Mexican Americans) and U.S.-born Puerto Rican children frequently do not perform well in English or in reading. Bilingual education has served immigrant students well but has done little to resolve the cultural conflict of English-speaking Chicano, Puerto Rican, Hawaiian, or Filipino students. Drill and practice alone will not change the pattern of school failure, not even when the drill is presented by a computer. The difficulty with English and the difficulty in acquiring reading skills are frequently related to the student's conflicts of existing in two cultures—one dominant and one subordinate. Some students attempt to overcome this conflict by abandoning their native culture and totally adopting the dominant European American culture. This cultural abandonment strategy has proven to be disastrous for many. It leads to an achievement gap, withdrawal, passivity, a high rate of school failure, and leaving school before graduation.

Rather than accept failure, students can study those aspects of their culture that determined their language acquisition patterns and try to understand how those patterns conflict with the job of mastering American English (Trueba, 1989).

Cultural conflict is an important subject of study in the multicultural classroom. Students need to be aware that they have learned many cultural patterns from their family and other cultural patterns from their formal education. Students also need to see themselves not only as products of the decisions of others but also as competent individuals who are in charge of the direction of their lives. When students learn that they can analyze and overcome educational problems, their self-confidence and self-control are increased. By studying the school culture and the student's role in the school, teachers can encourage students to assume a position of being responsible for and in control of their future.

Schools can offer students the unique opportunity to study themselves and their classmates in the safe context of the classroom. Problems that emerge in the classroom, such as weakness in reading and math, can be treated as obstacles for the student to overcome. When children experience failure, the study of cultural conflict may help them to analyze the difficulties and to select ways to overcome educational problems. They will be able to overcome some obstacles by individual effort, such as acquiring new learning skills; other problems may require group work. The experience of being part of a team that successfully completes a project can help a student develop the courage and confidence to overcome educational and psychological barriers.

Keeping Up with Culture

All cultures are dynamic. As students learn about their culture, the culture itself is changing. Some approaches to multicultural education completely fail to consider this. For example, primary teachers have frequently approached multicultural education by introducing young children to a variety of culturally specific foods. Such an approach teaches that variety exists and little else. Many units on teaching the culture of Mexican children present idealized pictures of people eating tortillas, tamales, and similar traditional foods. Studies of Chinese Americans focus on the use of chopsticks, rice, and fortune cookies. However, if students actually looked at the most frequently eaten food of young Mexican or Chinese American students, they would probably find it is a McDonald's hamburger—cultures are dynamic!

Even the dominant culture is changing—forced to adapt to the pressures of economic transitions and the several urban crises including crime, drugs, violence, technological change, and dislocation. One portion of the Evangelical Christian Right guard their children from these changes, neoconservative scholars of the 1980s used the textbooks to assert their views of cultural literacy, and teachers facing an increasingly diverse and undisciplined student population assert their views. At the 1992 Republican convention, conservative candidate Patrick Buchanan described this process of trying to defend the dominant culture against change as "cultural wars."

Many students in a macroculture-run school system are not only in the process of learning how to operate in the dominant culture, but they are also adapting to continuing change within their own home culture. Acquiring new patterns does not necessarily mean abandoning the home culture; acculturation can be an additive process. Engaging in and studying this process under the guidance of a teacher skilled in multicultural education help students to make sense of what is happening to them. Understanding cultural conflict empowers students to make effective choices about how to pursue their education, their careers, and ultimately, their lives. When schools do not help students sort out this conflict, street gangs and the criminal justice system offer more violent alternatives.

Glossary

Accommodation: When people of two or more cultures living in an area learn from and adapt to each other. For example, members of a minority culture might accept some cultural change in this process. For example, they might accept bilingual transactions for business and medicine.

Acculturation: The process of learning a new culture and adapting to that culture. This involves the exchange of cultural elements leading to a change in both groups. For example, an immigrant might learn to use English and to communicate in English.

Assimilation: When one cultural group learns and accepts the cultural behaviors and values of a second group and gives up some elements of their home culture. For example, when an immigrant totally accepts and adapts to the macroculture.

Biculturalism: The process of learning to function successfully in two cultures. All teachers can become bicultural by learning the culture of their students. In some cases, biculturalism requires bilingualism, the learning of a second language.

Pluralism: When two or more groups learn to accept and to respect each other's culture. Members of each group have equal opportunities for success. Within pluralism, each group may retain elements of home culture such as religion, language, and traditions. The cultural differences of each group are respected.

Activities[3] for Further Study of Culture

1. Conduct a life history or ethnocultural interview of a person from a major culture other than your own. You are to interview a male or female adult or student from one of the major cultural groups found in your state. Choose specifically from one of the following groups:
   a. Asian: Chinese American, Japanese American, or Korean American
   b. Black/African American/Afro American

---

[3] Activities 1 and 3 were adapted from assignments drafted by Dr. José Cintrón, California State University at Sacramento, 1994.

c. Southeast Asian: Vietnamese, Cambodian, Laotian, Hmong, Thai, or Mien

d. South Pacific Islander: Filipino, Samoan, or Tongan

e. Appalachian Anglo Saxon: European American

f. Indian / American Indian / Native American / Indigenous Peoples

g. Cajun

h. Latino / Hispanic: Mexican, Mexican American, Chicano, Cuban American, Puerto Rican, Central American, or South American

Do not interview spouses, fiancés, boyfriends, girlfriends, or close relatives.

The interviews should be approximately 1 hour in length; however, be prepared for a longer duration. If possible, you might want to record the interview for later analysis and convenience, but be sure to ask the person you are interviewing for permission to do so. Recording also allows for a more natural dialogue between you and the interviewee.

The interview should include a brief biography and proceed through a series of questions that highlight the person's cultural views and perspectives. Your goal is to gain an understanding of how this person's specific cultural "lenses" help to determine how he or she perceives society. You are to probe for information and not hesitate to ask what you might think of as "dumb" or embarrassing questions; these are often the most insightful. As you probe, it is likely that the interviewee will guide the direction of the interview, which is appropriate. Record this interview and bring it to class for discussion.

Typical probing questions might include the following:

a. To what ethnic or minority group (such as Hispanic or African American) would you describe yourself as belonging? Why do you identify yourself as being part of this group?

b. When did you or your family first arrive in the United States? If you are a recent arrival to this country, how would you describe your first impressions of the dominant U.S. culture?

c. Describe your current worldview about this society and how you perceive your role or place in it.

2. Share the results of your interview with other students in the class.

3. Please observe the general school and classroom surroundings at a school site. After the observation, answer the following questions.

a. Describe the grounds. Are they clean and well maintained? Are they paved or grass? Is the playground equipment safe and operable?

b. Is the school fenced or open? What type of security is provided? Are the windows and the doors barricaded?

c. How does the inside of the school appear? Are the hallways and walls clean and well-lighted?

d. What does the neighborhood community look like? Does it appear to be an affluent, middle income, or poor neighborhood? Be specific. What criteria do you use for middle income?

e. How would you describe the classroom supplies? Are they missing, adequate, abundant? Do the teachers have to pay for many of their own supplies? What is the condition of the books and other materials? Are computers available for students?

f. How would you describe the general mood, morale, and noise level of the school? Are the faculty and staff friendly to you? Are they friendly to students at the school?

g. Are parents visible? What kinds of jobs do parents and volunteers perform? What is the mood of the parents you observe?

h. How would you describe the mood and morale of the children? Are they happy and engaged? What levels of conflicts do you see among the students? How are conflicts dealt with?

At the end of this task, share your observations with students who have observed another school.

4. Play BAFA-BAFA, a cross-cultural simulation.
5. Since you are entering the profession of teaching, consider teachers as a cultural group. What are the norms of this culture? How are they enforced? What sanctions are available?

Teaching Strategies

1. Recognize that schooling is only one form of education. Plan lessons that incorporate and build on the informal educational systems of the home and the community.
2. In teaching new concepts, use concepts, strategies, and language the students already know.
3. Study the nature of culture and of cultural conflict.
4. Study both positive and negative cultural conflict.
5. Study the concepts of kinship, education, health, leadership, language, beliefs, and community prior to the concept of culture.
6. Study and analyze the learning process in school and in the home.
7. Do not assume that students accept your management rules. Use direct instruction to teach school-appropriate behavior.

References

Banks, J. A. (1984). *Teaching strategies for ethnic studies* (3rd ed.). Boston, MA: Allyn & Bacon, Inc.

Cintrón, J. (1994). *Life history interview.* California State University at Sacramento.

Crawford, J. (1992). *Hold your tongue: Bilingualism and the politics of "English Only."* Reading, MA: Addison-Wesley.

Eller-Powell, R. (1994). Teaching for change in Appalachia. In E. R. Hollins, J. E. King, & W. G. Hayman (Eds.), *Teaching diverse populations: Formulating a knowledge base.* Albany, NY: State University of New York Press.

Fordham, S. (1988, February). Racelessness as a factor in Black students' success: Pragmatic strategy or Pyrrhic victory? *Harvard Education Review,* pp. 54–84.

Law school performance as an adaptation: The case of Blacks in Stockton, Calif. (1991). In M. A. Gibson, & J. U. Ogbu. *Minority status and schooling* (pp. 278–282). New York: Garland Publishing.

Llanes, J. (1982). *Cuban Americans: Masters of survival.* Cambridge: Abbott Books.

Network of Regional Desegregation Centers. (1989). *Resegregation of public schools: The third generation.* Washington, DC: Author.

Ogbu, J. U. (1978). *Minority education and caste: The American system in cross cultural perspective.* New York: Academic Press.

Spindler, G., & Spindler, L. (1991). The process of culture and person: Multicultural classrooms and cultural therapy. *Cultural therapy.* Stanford, CA: Stanford University School of Education.

Trueba, H. T. (1989). *Raising silent voices: Educating linguistic minorities for the 21st century.* Rowley, MA: Newbury House.

Tylor, E. B. (1958). *Primitive culture.* New York: Harper Torchbooks. (Original work published 1871). Cited in Bennet, C. (1986). *Comprehensive multicultural education: Theory and practice.* Boston, MA: Allyn & Bacon, Inc.

U.S. Census Bureau. (1988, March). *The Hispanic population in the United States.* Advance report.

Valentine, C. A. (1968). *Culture and poverty: Critique and counter-proposals.* Chicago: University of Chicago Press.

Chapter 3

Racism and Schools [1]

We find ourselves threatened by hordes of Yankee emigrants . . . whose progress we cannot arrest.

—Jose Sepulveda, last Mexican Governor of California, 1846
San Francisco Examiner, (February 23, 1986)

The New Majorities

You may well encounter in your classroom the growing cultural, racial, and ethnic diversity of our society. Until 1990, the majority of people in the United States were European Americans. In most of our major urban areas, however, a new majority is emerging—a majority of people of color: African Americans, Latinos, Asian/Pacific Islanders, and many others.

Who is this emerging new majority? It includes the 31 million African Americans, many of them descendants of slaves, who today must struggle against segregation, ghettoization, poverty, high rates of unemployment, and police brutality.

It includes the Latino population, which is now projected to reach 35 million by the year 2000, more than double the 1980 Census figure. Nearly two thirds

[1] This chapter was written by **Duane Campbell** and **Manning Marable**.

45

of the Latino population is Chicano (that is, U.S.-born persons who are descendants of Mexican heritage). Like African Americans, Latinos experience systemic racial and class oppression. In 1990, 25% of all Latino households were below the federal government's poverty line, compared to just 9% for European Americans. While the average annual family income for European Americans was $35,975 in 1990, the average annual family income for Chicano families was only $22,200 and for Puerto Rican households, $19,900 per year. Latinos and African Americans also suffered double the rate of unemployment and triple the rate of homelessness experienced by European Americans.

The new majority includes the Asian / Pacific-American population, which has doubled in size over the past decade to more than 6 million people. Though portions of this community are economically less disadvantaged than other people of color, Asian Americans have had to endure their full share of exploitation and oppression by the European American macroculture. In 1942, rumor, hysteria, and profit seeking convinced the majority of Americans to support the arrest and incarceration of Japanese Americans on the West coast. In 1992, Japanese Americans and other Asians were targeted for racial hate crimes in California, Oregon, New York, and Michigan. The continuing ethnic harassment of Asian people throughout the country and efforts to undercut their educational opportunities link their struggle with that of African Americans and Latinos.

The new majority also includes approximately 3.5 million Arab American citizens who are subjected to political harassment, media abuse, and ethnic discrimination and over 2 million Native Americans who have survived genocide and cultural domination for more than 200 years. The struggle of Native Americans is simultaneously political, cultural, and spiritual. It is a struggle for national self-determination, for the reclamation of land, and for the renewal of the strength and vision of a people (Marable, 1992).

A look at the six cities in Table 3.1 illustrates how demographic changes have increased the national diversity.

The emerging majority is also evident in small towns and rural areas of the South and Southwest where Mexican Americans, African Americans, or Native Americans often constitute a majority population within their communities. Chapter 2 described some of the diversity within the group identified as "Hispanic" by the U.S. Census. A similar diversity exists within the Census Bureau's Asian or Pacific Islander category. Table 3.2 presents data from the Los Angeles metropolitan area that illustrate the complexity that exists within these two broad census categories.

The emerging diversity is even more pronounced among young people and students. The 1990 U.S. Census revealed that in New York City, whites made up 40% of the population, blacks 28.7%, Hispanic 24.4%, Asian / Pacific Islander 7%, and Native American 0.4%. However, in 1990 the New York City schools served a student population that was 38% black, 35% Hispanic, 19% white, and 7.9% Asian / Pacific Islander. Thus, in New York City, African American, Latino, and Asian students each represent a higher percentage of the student population than the same groups in the total population.

Table 3.1 National Diversity in Six U.S. Cities, 1990

				Racial Origin							
	White	Black	%	American Indian, Eskimo, or Aleut	%	Asian or Pac. Islanders	%	Other Race	Hispanic Origin	%
Chicago, IL	1,263,524	1,087,711	39.1	7,064	0.3	104,118	3.7	321,309	545,852	19.6
Los Angeles, CA	1,841,182	487,674	14.0	16,379	0.5	341,807	9.8	798,356	1,391,411	39.9
Sacramento, CA	221,963	56,521	15.3	4,561	1.2	55,426	15.0	30,894	60,007	16.2
Seattle, WA	388,858	51,948	10.1	7,326	1.4	60,819	11.8	7,308	18,349	3.6
Honolulu, HI	97,527	4,821	1.3	1,126	0.3	257,552	70.5	4,246	16,704	4.6
New York, NY	3,827,088	2,102,512	28.7	27,531	0.4	512,719	7.0	852,714	1,783,511	24.4

Note: % = percent of total population

Note. From the U.S. Census, 1990.

Table 3.2 Racial Diversity in
Los Angeles, California, 1990

Detailed Race	Population
White	1,841,182
Black	487,674
American Indian, Eskimo, or Aleut:	
• American Indian	15,641
• Eskimo	299
• Aleut	439
Asian or Pacific Islander:	
• Asian	
• Chinese	67,196
• Filipino	87,625
• Japanese	45,370
• Asian Indian	17,227
• Korean	72,970
• Vietnamese	18,674
• Cambodian	4,257
• Hmong	30
• Laotian	1,083
• Thai	9,270
• Other Asian	10,672
• Pacific Islander	
• Polynesian	
Hawaiian	2,635
Samoan	1,790
Tongan	225
Other Polynesian	155
• Micronesian	
Guamanian	2,140
Other Micronesian	32
• Melanesian	301
• Pacific Islander, not specified	155
Other Race	798,356
Hispanic Origin:	
• Not of Hispanic Origin	2,093,987
• Hispanic Origin	
• Mexican	936,507
• Puerto Rican	14,367
• Cuban	15,225
• Other Hispanic	425,312

Note. From the U.S. Census, 1990. By U.S. Census definition, those of Hispanic origin may be of any race. Figures shown here do add to 100% of the U.S. population.

In many states and school districts, the increased diversity of the student population has resulted in the districts' having no single majority group. *All* cultural groups including European Americans are minorities. Since there is no majority group, the term *minority* loses much of its meaning. As a means of addressing the new reality of the diverse populations in their towns and cities, community activists often refer to African Americans, Asians, Latinos, and Native Americans collectively as "people of color."

Race and Racism

Race is the term used to describe a large group of people with a somewhat similar genetic history. Many observers believe that they can describe a racial group based on hair color and texture, skin color, eye color, and body type. Chapter 2 explained that we learn culture but we inherit race. **Racial prejudice** is the *prejudgment* by others that the members of a race are in some way inferior, dangerous, or repugnant.

Most biologists and physical anthropologists recognize the futility of previous attempts to "scientifically" define race and believe that there are no pure races on earth. In popular discussion, persons often incorrectly refer to national groups (such as Mexicans) or cultural or language groups as races.

Race is more of a social category than a reliable biological classification. Racial categories have been used to describe a group, a culture, or an ethnic group or even to genetically link racial groups. These social definitions have changed over time often based on the relative power of the group. In early Greece and Rome, for example, it was important to be a Greek citizen or Roman citizen because these people were accorded the privileges of a superior group. Genetic lineage was of little importance. In ancient Egypt as well, skin color seems not to have been a major issue, a historical finding that causes confusion today in the debate over the alleged African roots of the Egyptian and Greek cultures. The attempt to create racial definitions based on observed physical characteristics became important in the European-dominated part of the world between 1490 and 1850.

Racism

The danger to our democracy is not race, but **racism,** the oppression of a group of people based on their perceived race. Racism is both a belief system and the domination of a people based on these beliefs. As Europeans conquered, enslaved, and dominated coastal areas in Africa and certain population centers in the Americas, Christian religious leaders wrestled with the question of whether Africans and "Indians" were human. After a furious debate, the Catholic hierarchy decided that both groups had souls and could become Christians. This theology-based decision had important consequences in shaping the nature of conquest and slavery in the Americas.

In contrast to Catholic (Spanish and Portuguese) law, primarily Protestant European settlers moving west in the territory of the present United States justified their murder of Native Americans (including women and children) and their enslavement of Africans by declaring them to be a separate species—not really human. In the 1840s, the press and the dominant political groups in the United States actually believed that the Irish were a separate, substandard race. During the early 1900s, the first IQ tests, administered in English and allegedly "scientific," were used to demonstrate that immigrant Jews, Slavs, and people from Eastern Europe were a racial group of inferior intellectual stock. In the 1930s, a California court ruled that Mexicans could not be assigned to segregated schools since they were legally Caucasians, while other courts permitted segregation of black, Native American, and Asian children on allegedly racial grounds.

Racism has produced a tortuous history in the U.S. intellectual community. Approaches allegedly based on a "science" of race developed theories of superiority that found not only African Americans inferior, but at various times allegedly proved the inferiority of women, the Irish, Jews, Italians, and Slavs. The theories, derived from distorted Darwinism, sought to demonstrate the historical inevitability and moral superiority of European Americans as a race. These purportedly scientific theories of race argued for genetic explanations of African American and Native American behavior while ignoring the violence and terrorism of slavery, genocide, and imperialism as causal factors (Omi & Winant, 1986).

Although racial definitions are vague and imprecise, racism continues to divide our society and our schools. Racism is the systematic oppression of a person or persons based on the perception that they belong to a race. Difficult as it may be for scientists to agree on a definition of race, for a racist nothing could be easier. A race is "them," "those people"—that is, any group the racist hates and fears. At times, racism is directed at nationality groups (such as Irish, Mexicans, Uzebeks, and Armenians), language groups (such as Spanish, Creole, and Hawaiian), and cultural groups (such as "hillbillies"). Racism uses the power and authority of a dominant group to enforce prejudice and to prevent the subjugated group from gaining equal access to employment, quality housing, health care, and education.

Racism and Schools

As shown in the graphs in Chapter 2, groups of students identified as racial groups (that is, Latinos, Asians, Native Americans, African Americans, and European Americans) succeed and fail at dramatically different rates in our schools.

The reason for this is relatively straightforward: Schools for poor children and children of color are inadequately funded. Economic choices—the unequal and inadequate funding of schools—produce most of the differences in achievement that are used as evidence of racial superiority and inferiority. Jonathan Kozol, in his book *Savage Inequalities: Children in America's Schools* (1991), describes some school conditions that would never be accepted in European American schools.

"We work under difficult circumstances. The school was built to hold one thousand students. We have 1,550. We are badly overcrowded. We need smaller classes, but to do this, we would need more space. I can't add five teachers. I would have no place to put them," says a principal of a New York City school.

"I can't set up a computer lab. I have no room. I had to put a class into the library. I have no librarian. There are two gymnasiums upstairs, but they cannot be used for sports. We hold more classes there. It's unfair to measure us against the suburbs. They have 17–20 children in a class. Average class size at this school is thirty."

"We have no science room. The science teachers carry their equipment with them."[2]

Kozol (1991) describes one of the schools he visited:

The school is 29% black, 70% Hispanic . . . We sit and talk in the nurse's room. The window is broken. There are two holes in the ceiling. About a quarter of the ceiling has been patched and covered with a plastic garbage bag.

"Will these children ever get what white kids in the suburbs take for granted? I don't think so," says the principal. "If you ask me why, I'd have to speak of race and social class. I don't think that the powers that be in New York City (with an African-American mayor) understand, or want to understand, that if they do not give these children a sufficient education to lead healthy, productive lives, we will be their victims later on. We'll pay the price someday—in violence, in economic costs." (p. 89)

Our country's history of race relations has been mired in tragedy, including the enslavement of Africans, the murder of Native Americans, and the seizing of two thirds of Mexico's arable land in addition to all of Puerto Rico and Hawaii, making these people domestic, conquered, minority groups. We must recognize that, despite decades of resistance and struggle, only limited progress has been made toward ending racial stratification and oppression. Martin Luther King, Jr., a major campaigner for human rights and recipient of the Nobel Peace Prize, commented on the centrality of the struggle against racism in his "Beyond Vietnam" speech:

We must rapidly begin the shift from a "thing-oriented" to a person-oriented society. When machines and computers, profit motives and property rights are considered more important than people, then the giant triplets of racism, materialism, and militarism are incapable of being conquered. (King, 1967)

Racism and Privilege

As we shall explore in detail in Chapter 4, a poor African American or Latino faces oppression, both as a poor person and as a member of an ethnic group. These two forms of oppression interact and reinforce each other. Families who live in poverty belong to a social class. Class relationships influence and affect the status of racial groups.

[2] *Note.* From *Savage Inequalities* (p. 89) by Jonathan Kozol, 1991, New York: Crowne Publishers. Reprinted with permission.

Racism interacts with class, gender, and other variables to construct a complex fabric of intergroup relations. For example, while the African American middle class has achieved significant advancement in the last two decades, the African American lower class suffers increased poverty and unemployment. Robert Reich, currently the U.S. Secretary of Labor, writes in his book, *The Work of Nations* (1991):

> [B]etween 1977 and 1990 the average income of the poorest fifth of Americans declined by about five percent, while the richest fifth became about nine percent wealthier. During these years, the average income of the poorest fifth of American families declined by about seven percent, while the average income of the richest fifth of American families increased by 15 percent . . .
>
> Among blacks, whose earnings at all levels continued to trail whites, the gap is wider still. Between 1978 and 1988, the average income of the lowest fifth of black families declined by 24%, while that of the top five percent of black families received 47% of total black income, compared with 42.9% of total white income received by the top five percent of white families . . . (p. 197)

Affirmative Action

Racism produces privileges for some and oppression for others. The beneficiaries of racism often are taught not to recognize their personal participation in an unjust system. Take the example of a European American teacher candidate in California. Let us call her Jane and place her in a teacher education program at a publicly financed university. Racism provides Jane with an easy admission to the program. Nearly 50% of all African American, Latino, and Native American students dropped out of high school. Of those who graduated, another 50% decided not to go on to college or were tracked to a nonacademic program in community college. Jane received admission to the teacher preparation program without recognizing the privileges granted to her (and withheld from others) by a tracking system in high school.

Jane notices that there are only a few Latinos, African Americans, Native Americans, and Asians in the teacher preparation program, even though over 50% of the students in the schools where she completes her teacher training are from these cultural groups. She relies on folk knowledge to explain this gap. Jane does not recognize that her own admission to the program benefited from a quality high school education that others were denied. Instead, she assumes that her admission to the teacher preparation program was the result of a fair and equitable system based on merit. (In California, it would be college grade-point average or a passing score on the National Teachers Exam.) She also is taught to assume that her college preparation provides her with the appropriate knowledge needed to teach and motivate all children. During student teaching, she will be puzzled and confused when some students from diverse cultures do not respond enthusiastically to the Eurocentric viewpoint she took for granted in college.

When Jane completes the teacher preparation program, she looks for a job. The first districts she applies to are seeking minority applicants. Jane feels she worked hard to earn her degree and her teaching credential, and she did. Affirmative action programs that recruit bilingual teachers and members of cultural minorities seem to give them an unfair advantage. Many job seekers resent these programs. Her own job search convinces Jane that many minorities are given preferential treatment that they do not deserve. She may even assume, without evidence, that she is better prepared for teaching than the minority person who gets the job.

Rather than recognize her own privileges (quality public schools, low-cost public universities), Jane resents minorities and assumes they are less qualified. She believes that good test scores and good grades obtained within the European American-centered university system are proof of superior preparation—an ideological position now challenged by affirmative action policies. The truth is, Jane may be well prepared to present the curriculum, but she is poorly prepared to teach children whose cultures and communication styles are different from her own.

Jane's privileges and her consequent problems reflect the experiences and fears of many prospective teachers. Public employment and publicly funded employment, such as teaching, now operate under the scrutiny of affirmative action programs as a counterbalance to the racial privileges granted to European Americans. Affirmative action programs designed to remedy historical social problems sound just in the abstract, but individuals such as Jane end up paying the price and experiencing the frustration of employment insecurity. These frustrated job seekers begin to resent programs that benefit minorities and to blame minorities for the loss of economic opportunity. A growing majority of European Americans oppose affirmative action policies and refer to affirmative action programs as "reverse discrimination."

An additional problem is that affirmative action programs, while helpful, have primarily benefited ethnic minorities and middle-class or professional women. They have benefited working-class minorities less. A second example clarifies this point. A Latino candidate we will call Joe comes from a middle-class home, benefits from quality public schooling, and is admitted to the university. Because of the recognized shortage of Latino teachers, Joe receives priority treatment in admission to the teacher preparation program. After the program, he receives numerous employment offers. Yet Joe fails to recognize the *class* privileges he receives. His preferential admission and preferred position in interviews were produced because there were few Latinos graduating. The massive failure of working-class Latinos to excel in schools, the more than 50% dropout rate of Latinos in high school, and the only 9.2% college completion rate place Joe at an advantage. He competes from a sharply reduced pool of applicants.

Twenty-five applicants sought the teaching position in which Jane and Joe were interested. However, neither Jane nor Joe get the job; Carmen does. Carmen was born and raised in Arizona. Her home language was Spanish. No bilingual education was available in her school in the 1960s. At age 16, she left school and married. Carmen raised three children who are now grown. She and her family performed back-breaking labor in the lettuce, grape, and tomato fields for over 15 years. Finally, because of a death in the family, the family settled in Sacramento, California.

Carmen began to attend community college at age 36. She studied very hard while continuing to raise her children. Learning to read and write English at a college level was difficult. Most of her communication for the previous 15 years had been in Spanish. After six years of study, she finally received her B.A. degree and was admitted to the teacher preparation program. Carmen speaks English and Spanish well, but her college grades were lower than Jane's.

Carmen was an outstanding student teacher. She drew on her skills and competence as a mother, her maturity, and her bilingualism. The school district was under pressure from Mexican American parents to improve the poor quality of education for their children. The teacher selection committee consisted of a principal and one bilingual teacher. They selected Carmen because 50% of the children in grades 1 through 3 speak Spanish as their first language.

Twenty-one of the 25 applicants for the teaching position now believe that they were passed over because of preferential hiring. They each assume that they were superior to Carmen. But clearly there was only one job opening. If a European American female (Jane) had received the job, the other 24 would still be left out and injured by California's low funding of schools and large class sizes.

If California reduced its per-pupil ratio (not class size) from 24 students to 1 teacher to the national average of 17 to 1, this action would create a need for over 30,000 new teachers.[3] But the state's elected officials do not allot such funds, resulting in overcrowded classrooms. These political and budgetary decisions make finding teaching positions difficult. Many applicants accept these decisions as natural and inaccurately blame minorities and affirmative action programs for their personal difficulty in finding a job.

A growing political movement, primarily European American, angrily opposes "affirmative action." They believe that less-qualified females and persons of color are receiving privileges in hiring. How would you judge the case of Carmen? Was the hiring committee correct or practicing "reverse discrimination"? How realistic is this case to your own teacher preparation program?

Institutional Racism

As these composite examples illustrate, racism, poverty, and gender discrimination are interactive, complex, and often misunderstood. During the 1980s, racial hate groups increased in number and size, and more incidents of racially moti-

---

[3] Per-pupil ratios are arrived at by dividing the total number of teachers by the total number of students. Because many teachers, such as those in special education, work in small special classes, per-pupil ratios do not reflect actual class size. While California's pupil to teacher ratio was 25 to 1 in elementary schools in 1993, its average class size was actually 29.5 students to 1 teacher (*Fact Book*, 1994–1995).

vated violence were reported. But racism is much more than acts of violence, expressions of individual prejudice, and the preservation of demeaning stereotypes. Racism does its greatest damage in our institutions, where well-meaning people preserve a seldom-examined social structure that benefits some people while frequently harming others. Current discrimination in wages, schooling, health care, housing, and employment opportunities continue the historical pattern of racism into the present. In these areas, institutions such as schools reinforce and recreate racism.

Our educational institutions work for some students and don't work for others. Schools for middle-class European American, Latino, and African American children fundamentally fulfill their purposes. But schools for poor African American, Latino, and European American children often fail. While this institutional failure harms all poor children, it disproportionately affects the children of ethnic minorities. Figures for 1989 from the National Center for Children in Poverty (1991) show that 50% of all African American children and 40% of all Latino children are poor, while only 14% of all white children are poor (see Figure 3.1).

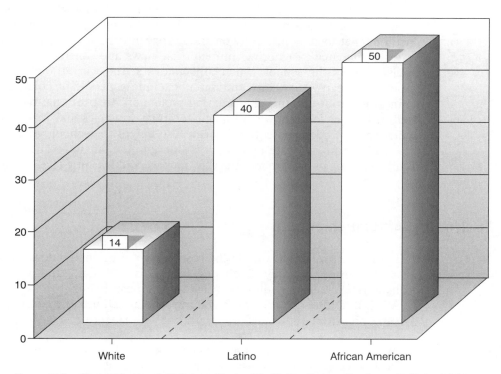

Figure 3.1   Percentage of Children Under Six Living Below the Poverty Line, 1989

The differences in income and poverty levels among racial and cultural groups are not accidental. They are a result of our economic, social, and educational system. Extreme poverty is a direct result of a lack of employment skills. Educational discrimination and failure in one generation often lead to poverty and school crises in the next. These are cycles that a functioning democracy ought to be able to interrupt and remedy.

Low-quality education in prior generations led to a concentration of African American and Latino workers in the low-skilled industrial labor fields. From the 1970s through the mid-1990s, however, as the U.S. economy began to shift from a reliance on these low-skilled jobs to a demand for more technical and highly skilled jobs, millions of industrial jobs in steel, auto, and other heavy industry were eliminated. As a result, even workers who once had secure and relatively high-paying industrial jobs were at risk. Today, the children of these endangered workers are in school. They must either prepare for new jobs in knowledge-based industries or suffer the poverty of the working poor in low-skilled service industries.

As a result of decades of poverty within minority communities, forms of racist behavior became embedded in our institutions. African American and Latino children in urban areas have few teachers who understand their cultural reality. They attend overcrowded and understaffed schools, and immigrant children are measured by standardized tests biased against persons who speak more than one language.

Institutional racism seeps into the schools through unequal funding and a curriculum that focuses primarily on the European American view of history, literature, and language—ignoring multicultural views and contributions. Institutional racism enters the schools when universities select over 90% of future teachers from European American candidates, excluding people of color and language minorities from entering the teaching profession. Institutional racism is embedded in teacher folk knowledge about teaching strategies and inaccurate assumptions about student potential. Racism also enters the school when teachers and the curriculum validate and support one group's language and learning styles while ignoring or even repressing the language and learning styles of other groups.

Racism and African Americans

The African American story is the best known of the many devastating histories of racism in our country. The work of DuBois, Douglass, and others provides a substantial scholarly tradition of African American history.

W. E. B. DuBois (1975) was a leading scholar-activist in the African American community from 1890 until his death in 1963. He wrote:

We can no longer regard Western Europe and North America as the world for which civilization exists; nor can we look upon European culture as the norm for all peoples. Henceforth the majority of the inhabitants of the earth, who happen for the most part to be colored, must be regarded as having the right and the capacity to share in human progress and to become copartners in that democracy which alone can ensure peace among men, by the abolition of poverty, the education of the masses, protection from disease, and the scientific treatment of crime . . . [So long as] the majority of men can be regarded mainly as sources of profit for Europe and North America . . . we are planning not peace but war, not democracy but the continued oligarchical control of civilization by the white race. (p. 249)

An accurate inclusion of the African American contribution to U.S. history provides a substantial alternative interpretation of much of the United States' past. Africa, prior to the slave trade, had rich and diverse cultures, major cities, and advanced civilizations. Slavery existed in other societies, including Greek, Egyptian, Roman, and several Arab and African societies. But the British and American slave trade assumed a particularly brutal racial context. Slave traders used their superior firepower to capture, rape, and murder Africans. Many Africans brought to the United States as slaves came from advanced, sophisticated societies, yet they were treated like animals. This war against African cultures was followed by the horrors of the slave ships where as many as half of the human cargo died in passage. The African American experience of slavery—the breaking up of families, the erasure of African culture and history, the forced labor, two and a half centuries of being regarded as less than human—gives a dimension to their suffering different than that of any other immigrant group.

The domination by the slave-owning class in the southern part of the United States created a slave culture. Slave practitioners developed ideologies of racial superiority, and their apologists defended and extended their brutal system. Institutional structures of slave holding, selling, law, and punishment reduced humans to chattel. Combined with the European immigrants' genocidal assault on the native populations, the institution of slavery established the racial foundations of present U.S. society.

The Civil War and the end of slavery did not end the terror of racism against African American people. Legal segregation, inadequate schooling, ideologies of racism, lynching, and other forms of open terrorism prevented African Americans from achieving equal opportunity until well into the 1960s. The struggle to maintain white supremacy has shaped and distorted the labor movement, the populist movement, our political parties, and our economic system.

Manning Marable, in *Black American Politics* (1985), argues that although the United States prides itself on having a two-party system, African Americans faced a one-party system in the South well into the 1960s. The black Civil Rights Movement of the 1950s and 1960s grew up outside of the traditional political parties. The movement broke the monopoly of power held by European American Democrats in the South and finally brought a two-party system to the region. When blacks gained new power in the Democratic Party, large numbers of European Americans became Republicans.

The growth of a Republican voting majority in the southern congressional districts, along with major transformations of the Southern economy, helped Republicans gain control of the U.S. presidency from 1968 until 1992, except for the period from 1976 to 1980. In 1994, Republicans won half of all congressional seats in the South, a major change in the politics of the region (DeWitt, 1994).

The Civil Rights Movement also produced major changes in the relationship between African Americans and the dominant society. Michael Omi and Howard Winant argue in *Racial Formation in the United States from the 1960s to the 1980s* (1986) that the Civil Rights Movement produced a change in African American self-perception from an earlier colonized view to a recognition that the poverty and powerlessness of African Americans were the products of systems of oppression. This change of viewpoint produced some improvements in race relationships, and the dominant culture lost its ideological power to define the boundaries of race relations.

The political ideology, behavior, and cultural consciousness of several generations of African Americans evolved into the idealism of the Civil Rights Movement. Marable argues that the worldview of most African American leaders, with the exception of the Black Power period of the late 1960s and early 1970s, could be termed *integrationist*. Integrationists called for the elimination of structural barriers that prohibited African Americans from full participation in the mainstream of American life. The goal was the achievement of a "color-blind society," which in the words of Martin Luther King, Jr., would mean that blacks "will not be judged by the color of their skin but by the content of their character."

Integrationists had an implicit faith in U.S. democracy. The political system could be made to work, they believed, if only people of color and others victimized by discrimination and poverty were brought to the table as full partners. This could be realized by expanding the number of African Americans, Latinos, women, low-income people, and others into positions of authority within the existing structures of power in business, labor, government, and the media. When one encountered resistance, the integrationist strategy relied heavily on the intervention of a "benevolent" federal judiciary, which could be counted on to defend civil rights and civil liberties.

Politically, integrationists in the period between 1954 and 1988 largely accepted the premise that the electoral system was both rational and inherently fair. Political inequities existed only when certain classes of voters were arbitrarily barred from exercising their right to vote or were prohibited from running for office. With the passage of the Voting Rights Act of 1965 and other civil rights legislation—the result of a sustained campaign of nonviolent direct action—all members of society supposedly had equal access to the process of democratic decision making.

Though notably successful in the political and legal arenas, the integrationist strategy lacked a method for advancing democracy against the many ways that economic power can dominate and thwart electoral participation. Leaders in both major political parties had a vested interest in "managing," if not eliminating, the electoral participation of African Americans, along with the unemployed and low-income workers. Two thirds of all European Americans and three fourths of all upper-class European Americans voted for Ronald Reagan in 1984. The Republicans saw few advantages in encouraging the electoral participation of constituencies of people of color because they were inclined to vote Democratic. But the Democrats also had problems with African American and low-income voters. Increased electoral participation by African Americans would translate into organizational influence within the Democratic Party's structure. Most European American Democratic officials, as shown in the organizational development of the Democratic Leadership Council led by Bill Clinton, were convinced that the Democrats had to become more conservative and incorporate elements of the Reagan agenda into their own programs. They also believed that they had to overcome the perception that the Democratic Party was too influenced by African American leaders.

New forms of racism developed during the 1980s. In the wake of the Civil Rights Movement, it was no longer possible or viable for European American elected officials, administrators, and corporate executives to attack "niggers" openly. The Ku Klux Klan and other racist vigilante groups still existed, but did not represent a mass movement among European Americans.

Instead, many racists developed a new strategy that attributed the source of racial tensions to the actions of people of color. For example, David Duke, former Nazi and Klan leader, received the majority of European American votes in his Senatorial race in Louisiana by arguing that "affirmative action" programs discriminated unfairly against innocent European Americans. African American college students were attacked as "racists" for advocating the adoption of African American studies academic programs or the creation of African American cultural centers. African American workers were accused of racism for supporting special efforts to train people of color in supervisory and administrative positions.

African American political leaders had to defend themselves against charges of "reverse racism." In this context, *racism* had begun to be defined by some European Americans as any behavior by individuals or groups that empowered Latinos, African Americans, or other people of color, or an agenda that took away long-held privileges of European American elites. Many conservatives promoted a theory of "reverse discrimination." Many European Americans were frustrated by being caught on a "treadmill" economy that ensured prosperity primarily to the upper 20% of the society but delivered increased economic frustration and even failure to working people (Joint Economic Committee, 1992; Tate, 1992). Frustrated workers often blamed affirmative action programs, special admissions, and other remedial programs for their loss of educational and economic opportunity.

Of course, the concept of "reverse discrimination" could exist on an institutional level only if African Americans, Native Americans, Latinos, and other people of color actually controlled the institutional resources that could affect European Americans' life chances and opportunities. If people of color owned the banks and financial institutions, the systems of transportation, communication, housing and health services, even in numbers commensurate with their percentages in the population, then one might theoretically perceive a pattern of institutional prejudice aimed at European Americans.

In spite of affirmative action programs, institutional racism, discrimination, and prejudice continue to be present within the economy and the schools. Far from implementing a policy of reverse discrimination, affirmative action plans and programs have barely influenced the entrenched patterns of power and privilege that continue today.

While many European Americans in the United States say that they believe that racism and the connected violence have declined and that great progress has been made, articulate leaders in the African American, Latino, and Native American communities regularly state the opposite. Speakers who testify to the continued violence of institutional racism are often dismissed or marginalized by the media and in educational institutions.

Derrick Bell, a prominent African American professor of law, states in *Faces at the Bottom of the Well* (1992):

> But the fact of slavery refuses to fade, along with the deeply imbedded personal attitudes and public policy assumptions that supported it for so long. Indeed, the racism that made slavery feasible is far from dead in the last decade of the 20th Century America . . .
>
> What we now call the "inner city" is, in fact, the American equivalent of the South African homelands . . .
>
> [I]n this last decade of the 20th Century, color determines the social and economic status of all African-Americans, both those who have been highly successful and their poverty-bound brethren whose lives are grounded in misery and despair. We rise and fall less as a result of our efforts than in response to the needs of a white society that condemns all blacks to quasi-citizenship as surely as it segregated our parents and enslaved their forebears. The fact is that, despite what we designate as progress wrought through struggle over many generations, we remain what we were in the beginning: a dark and foreign presence, always the designated "other." Tolerated in good times, despised when things go wrong, as a people we are scapegoated and sacrificed as distraction or catalyst for compromise to facilitate resolution of political differences or relieve economic adversity.[4]

By the 1980s, a profound social crisis—a deep sense of fragmentation and collective doubt—had developed within the African American community. The symptoms of this internal crisis were the widespread drug epidemic, black-against-black violence, the growth of urban youth gangs, and the destruction of black social institutions (West, 1993). By the late 1980s, about 12,000 African Americans were being murdered annually. For young African American males in their twenties, the murder rate was more than 1 in 20.

Violence inevitably influenced community relationships. People concerned with street violence, robbery, or death were reluctant to attend neighborhood political meetings after dark. Black-owned businesses in the central cities lost patrons and support, making it even harder for small entrepreneurs to survive. Churches and community centers located in drug-infested areas found it difficult to attract many

---

[4] *Note.* From *Faces at the Bottom of the Well* (p. 10) by Derrick Bell, 1992, New York: HarperCollins. Reprinted with permission.

middle-class African Americans. Large sections of major cities such as Detroit, Newark, and Chicago were depopulated as hundreds of thousands of African American working-class and middle-income people fled to the suburbs.

The internal crisis within contemporary African American life was aggravated by corporate and governmental decisions. In the 1970s, many corporations, searching for higher profits, abandoned their plants in the central cities and relocated to non-unionized, low-wage states and countries. This development greatly speeded the collapse of the economic infrastructure in America's urban centers. The hands-off, "free-market" policies of the conservative government administrations since the 1970s and 1980s allowed corporations to make private decisions that devastated communities. The refusal of the federal government to initiate economic reconstruction programs opened many new neighborhoods to the illegal economies of crack and crime.

Somewhat paradoxically, at the same time that the economic crisis has grown, the political empowerment of African American leaders has continued to grow. Elected officials now commonly incorporate an African American agenda in political programs. In 1989, Virginia became the first state to have an African American governor. African American mayors lead several major U.S. cities. In 1992, an African American woman, Carol Mosely Braun, was elected to the U.S. Senate from Illinois, and the Black Caucus of the House, including both women and men, reached 27 members.

In June 1994, Ben Chavis, then leader of the NAACP (National Association for the Advancement of Colored People), assembled over 100 African American leaders from such diverse traditions as Harvard philosopher and author, Cornel West, to the Minister L. Farrakhan of the Nation of Islam. African American leaders established a series of dialogues to develop a common agenda in response to the social, economic, and moral crises within the African American communities.

Racism and Ethnic Conflict in a Nation of Immigrants

Since its founding in 1776, the United States has been a pluralistic society—a society of immigrants. In spite of this diversity, members of the majority culture have often held somewhat xenophobic attitudes toward foreigners, persons who speak other languages, and the native peoples. A brief history of U.S. immigration patterns provides a context for understanding how successive immigrant populations entered and transformed a racially stratified U.S. society. The specific historical experiences of each group (supplemented in Appendices A through F) describe a part of our present racial divisiveness.

The present territory of the United States was first colonized by the Spanish (St. Augustine, Florida in 1565, and Santa Fe, New Mexico in 1610), English settlers (New England in 1620, Jamestown in 1619), Germans, Swedes, and Dutch (the Middle Colonies from 1624–1640), the French (Louisiana in 1800), and Spanish-Indian Mestizos (the Southwest from 1610–1784).

Immigration from Europe

From 1840–1920, there was an enormous influx of immigrants from Europe to the United States. They came in hopes of building a new, more prosperous life. Poor, hungry, adventurous, and at times desperate, they fled European poverty, wars, and oppression. They settled in Canada, the United States, Mexico, and throughout the Americas. Between 1860 and 1920, 28.5 million people arrived, 74.1% of them from Europe. During this same period, the Native American population in the United States was decimated from over 4 million to less than 1 million and Chinese immigration was banned, first by terrorism and then by law.

From 1840–1870, the European migration consisted mainly of English, Scotch-Irish, Irish, and later, German settlers. The European immigrants entered primarily through the East Coast ports, spoke a variety of languages, and became the working class for an emerging U.S. industry as well as farmers in the Midwest. In the 1880s and 1890s, thousands of Swedes, Norwegians, and Finns arrived, most often settling in the upper Midwest.

The first two decades of the twentieth century produced the largest immigration wave in U.S. history. Between 1860 and 1900, the total number of immigrants was 14 million, but between 1900 and 1915 alone, another 14.5 million arrived. This massive influx set off waves of fear and concern about immigration similar in many ways to the present. The anxiety of U.S.-born citizens was intensified by the varied cultural character of immigrants arriving after 1890. By the 1890s, large numbers of immigrants were pouring into the country from Southern and Eastern Europe: Poles, Italians, Greeks, and Slavs. Unlike the previous immigrants who generally assimilated quickly into the U.S. population, these latter groups created ethnic enclaves in the major cities and across the farming areas of the upper Midwest. These "new immigrants" from Southern and Eastern Europe were Catholic, in desperate economic straits, and often poorly educated. An anti-immigrant or nativist movement grew to stop the influx of immigrants and to maintain the "European American" lifestyle. Power, politics, cultural suppression, and the schools were used to create a myth that all "Americans" were white, Anglo Saxon, and Protestant.

The immigration of Europeans into the eastern United States led to sharp ethnic, economic, and cultural conflicts. However, after two or three generations, the children of these immigrants generally assimilated into the dominant culture while maintaining a few characteristics of their immigrant experience (for example, Catholicism and special meals and holidays).

Migration and Immigration from Mexico

Florida and Louisiana were once territories of Spain. Texas was a territory of Mexico prior to 1835 when Anglo-American immigrants rebelled and created the Texas Republic. Parts of the present states of Utah, Colorado, California, New

Mexico, and Nevada were seized from Mexico in 1848. The Mestizo peoples in this area did not emigrate from Mexico but they were living in the Southwest when the U.S. army arrived.

The border between the United States and Mexico was neither defended nor restricted from 1850 to 1924. Persons of Mexican and Native American ancestry moved freely back and forth. Major cities in the Southwest such as Los Angeles were often predominantly Mexican in population well into the 1870s (Acuna, 1972; Grisold del Castillo, 1979).

From 1850 to 1870, a large, land-holding population of Mexican, Native American and Spanish immigrant communities existed in California, Texas, and New Mexico. After the area was seized in the War of 1848, the Land Law of 1851 forced this population off its lands and into manual labor. Mexicans worked as miners, ranch hands, and on the railroads. A few assimilated into the dominant European American society through marriage.

The Mexican Revolution of 1911–1917 became a bloody, extended civil war. Under the leadership of the brothers Enrique and Ricardo Flores-Magon a significant movement in support of the revolutionaries was organized in the U.S. Southwest. Mexican people residing in the Southwest raised funds and protected family members who fled from Mexico into the United States. Thousands of Mexicans working in the United States contributed time, money, and organizational skills to the revolutionaries.

These refugees fleeing civil and economic unrest in Mexico dramatically increased the size of the Mexican populations in the Southwest, creating large population centers in El Paso, Los Angeles, and South Texas. The European American immigrants had only recently managed to dominate the area, and they perceived the rapidly increasing Mexican population as a threat. In an effort to control these groups, some law enforcement organizations, such as the Texas Rangers, became notorious for eliminating "Indians" and "keeping Mexicans in their place" (Limerick, 1988; Weber, 1973). In the Southwest, many Ku Klux Klan chapters focused on the Mexican "problem."

Resistance to European American (also called "Anglo" or "Norteamericano") occupation of the area was a constant aspect of Southwest history prior to 1890. By the 1930s, Mexican and Chicano workers actively formed their own unions in mining and agriculture to protect their rights under expanding corporate capitalism. The companies and the press accused many of these union leaders of being communists as a means to defeat their organizing efforts. In the 1950s, a program of deportations known as "Operation Wetback" arrested and deported hundreds of local Mexican and Mexican American leaders, terrorizing the community and depriving many areas of effective local leaders for over a decade. Local community organizations, the training ground for political empowerment, were decimated (Garcia, 1994).

From 1952 to 1962, the political progress of the Mexican and Chicano communities was set back. No single, notable national leader emerged. Well over six major attempts were made to organize the largely Mexican, Mexican American, and Filipino population of agricultural workers. Finally in 1964, these efforts unified in the United Farmworkers Union (AFL-CIO) under the leadership of Cesar Chavez, Dolores Huerta, Philip Vera Cruz, and others. The African American civil rights struggle occurring at the same time gave renewed hope to Mexicano and Chicano organizing.

In 1968, conditions in schools in Los Angeles and other cities led thousands of Mexican American students to walk out and strike. The Chicano student movement was born in these walkouts. This movement quickly spread to several locations: Crystal City, Texas; Denver, Colorado; Los Angeles, California; and others.

Chicano/Latino civil rights struggles developed in a highly dispersed manner. Union organizing and educational struggles were major focuses of activity. By 1972, Chicana/Latinas were asserting their own distinct demands for gender equality within the movement. In the 1980s, Chicano/Latino efforts began to merge with Puerto Rican and other "Hispanic" efforts in the Midwest and East.

Until the 1970s, Latinos lacked the benefits of a system of their own colleges, with Latino leadership, dedicated to producing Hispanic professional leaders. Latino and Hispanic efforts at political organization suffered until well into the 1980s from the lack of attention in colleges and universities on Latino issues. The traditionally black colleges in the South had provided this important support to the African American movement. Consequently, the growth of Latino and Hispanic power has been slower. African Americans far outnumber Latino elected officials, even when the two communities have roughly equal voting populations. By 1992, there were 34 African Americans in Congress and only 17 Latino/Hispanic representatives. As the Latino population grows in urban areas, community activists are at times placed in competition with African Americans for elected positions of leadership. (For more specific information, please see the timelines provided in Appendices A through F.)

Chinese and Japanese Immigration

The Chinese—and later, other Asians—had yet a different and distinct experience of immigration. The Chinese began coming to California while it was still a part of Mexico in the 1840s, primarily because of economic hardships and violence in China. California's vast riches were taken from Mexico and incorporated into the United States in the War of 1848. By 1850, when California became a state, there were some 25,000 Chinese working in the gold mines and providing basic laundry and cooking services to the rapidly growing immigrant population rushing to the gold fields of Northern California. Exploited with the xenophobic cruelty rooted in the racial ideology of the times, the Chinese workers quickly learned to live in defensive enclaves, separate from the mining communities.

Anti-Chinese campaigns grew as the gold rush ended. The Chinese, who comprised 10% of California's population, became the target of political hate campaigns, terrorism, murder, and violence. These anti-Asian pressures culminated in 1882 when the U.S. Congress passed the first openly racial restriction on immigration—the Chinese Exclusion Act. While immigration from Europe was open and encouraged at this time, immigration from China was made illegal.

Between 1885 and 1894, the Japanese government supported emigration to Hawaii, sending over 29,000 workers to labor on sugar cane plantations. The Japanese workers were followed by Filipinos. Many of these workers soon moved on to the U.S. mainland. By 1910, there were over 72,000 (mostly male) Japanese working, often under brutal conditions, in California, Oregon, Washington, and Alaska.

Japanese workers saved money and bought land to begin farming. They imported brides from Japan and established families and family farms. The economic success of the Japanese, in spite of severe prejudice and discrimination, led to increased hostility from the European American majority population. When the United States and Japan went to war in 1941, anti-Japanese hostility became so intense that all Japanese Americans on the West coast were arrested and placed in detention camps for the duration of the war. Of all racial and ethnic groups, only Japanese and Native Americans have faced this kind of forced incarceration.

As Ronald Takaki describes in *Strangers from a Different Shore* (1989), anti-Asian discrimination climaxed during World War II and slowly receded. Asian groups who had joined the United States in the war, Chinese, and Filipinos achieved more acceptance in U.S. society after the war. According to the U.S. Census (1980), Filipinos (1,052,000), Koreans (357,000), Asian / Pacific Islanders (260,000), Vietnamese (250,000), and numerous other groups have moved to the United States in the last 40 years, often in connection with our military installations and operations in the Pacific (see Figure 3.2).

Figure 3.2   Who are Asians and Pacific Islanders? (Resident population by separated ethnic categories, 1990.)
Note. From the U.S. Census, 1990.

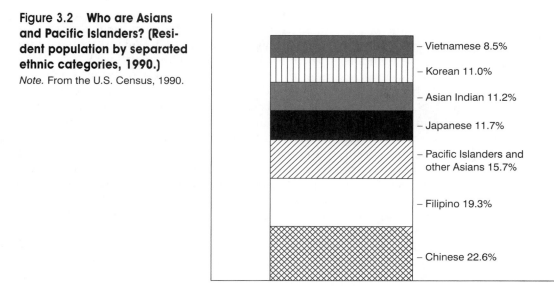

- Vietnamese 8.5%
- Korean 11.0%
- Asian Indian 11.2%
- Japanese 11.7%
- Pacific Islanders and other Asians 15.7%
- Filipino 19.3%
- Chinese 22.6%

Asian/Pacific Islanders

While some Japanese Americans, Chinese Americans, Koreans, Filipinos, and the first wave of Vietnamese refugees have achieved economic prosperity, Takaki shows that other Asian / Pacific immigrants and their children continue to face hostility and discrimination. The stereotype of a "model minority" hides the poverty inflicted on many. Anti-Asian attacks, discrimination, even murders, have grown as Japan has become a major economic competitor with the United States in the 1980s and 1990s. The May 1992, racial rebellion and looting in Los Angeles particularly focused attacks on Korean immigrant store owners by African American youths.

The Hmong and the Mien

Beginning in 1976, the first of over 145,000 Hmong refugees came to the United States. The great numbers came under the Indochina Migration and Refugee Assistance Act of 1975 (P.L. 9423). The thousands of Hmong had acted as special guerilla units, mostly in Laos, helping the United States in the war in Vietnam and Laos. The Hmong became particular targets of repression after the Communists won control of Laos and Vietnam.

The first Hmong to arrive were refugees from war. Thousands suffered incredible terror and hardship, with entire families being killed, in trying to reach refugee camps in Thailand. Many had to stay in the camps for up to six years. The extended and brutal terror, along with the extended periods spent in refugee camps, divided families and broke up traditional family support systems.

As refugees, Hmong received several kinds of financial support and assistance denied to other immigrants. The Hmong and the Mien suffered more cultural dislocation in coming to the United States than did Vietnamese and most other immigrants. Some of the Hmong were from a tribal, almost preliterate society. One refugee described the experience as getting on an airplane in the sixteenth century and then landing in the twentieth century. Others received up to three years of education in Laos prior to leaving. The current generation is the first generation where literacy and formal education serve as indicators of status.

Many U.S. teachers had as their first Asian students the more successful, school-oriented, middle-class Vietnamese refugees of the 1975 immigration wave. These teachers were shocked when the Hmong began to arrive. The languages and cultures of these groups are distinctly different. In part because of the extreme cultural incongruities and the lack of bilingual assistants, Hmong and Mien students in U.S. schools often began with difficult transitions. And the Hmong families often experienced extreme forms of culture shock. Hmong aids and community assistants provide important cultural brokers and should be consulted by school authorities.

The Hmong came to many parts of the United States often sponsored by U.S. church groups and charitable organizations. After their original settlement, many moved a second time to be near other Hmong. The largest groups moved to the

Central Valley of California, and currently over 47,000 Hmong finally have settled in California. Such large Hmong migrations heavily affected a few schools in a short period of time, at times causing stress to these school systems.

Hmong families tend to have many children. The children born in the United States are U.S. citizens, entitled to all of the rights of citizens but not to the special assistance given to refugees.

The current Hmong and Mien girls in school have usually been in the United States for a number of years. Years of acculturation and assimilation have produced conflicts within the Hmong families. While in Laos, Hmong young women might be involved in marriage contracts and early marriages. However, these patterns are changing. School authorities have been drawn into several disputes between young people adjusting to the U.S. system and families wishing to maintain older systems of respect and family loyalty (Bliatout et al., 1988).

Anti-Immigrant Politics

As each immigrant group grew, so did fear, strong prejudice, and hostility in the majority European American population. Irish, Jewish, Chinese, and Japanese immigrants were each described at one time with stereotypes characterizing them as dirty, uneducated, secretive, and subversive. Racial stereotyping, scapegoating, and violence have continued as a sustained theme in U.S. history, often encouraged by the press and so-called "fraternal organizations."

The U.S. economy passed through a difficult recession and stagnation from 1991 to 1993, and the nation faces a prolonged period of economic restructuring and transformation for the next decade. Historically, immigrants have often become targets and scapegoats during recessions and depressions, and the 1990s repeated that pattern (see Figure 3.3).

In the early 1990s, a conservative group known as the Federation for American Immigration Reform (FAIR) became an advisor to the Republican governor of California on population growth and immigration issues. In August 1993, California Governor Pete Wilson, a former U.S. Senator, sent a public letter to President Clinton insisting on strong federal action to stop "massive illegal immigration." Wilson argued that millions of immigrants have come to California illegally and "millions more will follow drawn by the giant magnet of federal incentives." Wilson specifically criticized the provision of education to young immigrant children and the U.S. citizens who were children of immigrants even though the U.S. Supreme Court in *Plyler vs. Doe* required states to provide schooling for immigrant children. The letter was a part of a broad-based campaign of over 30 California legislative proposals and over 20 proposals in the U.S. Congress to punish immigrants.

By the summer of 1993, a recession plagued the economy, and government cutbacks combined to make Governor Wilson the most unpopular governor in recent history. He was able to recover and win election with over 56% of the vote in 1994 by attacking immigrants and blaming the federal government for the state's prob-

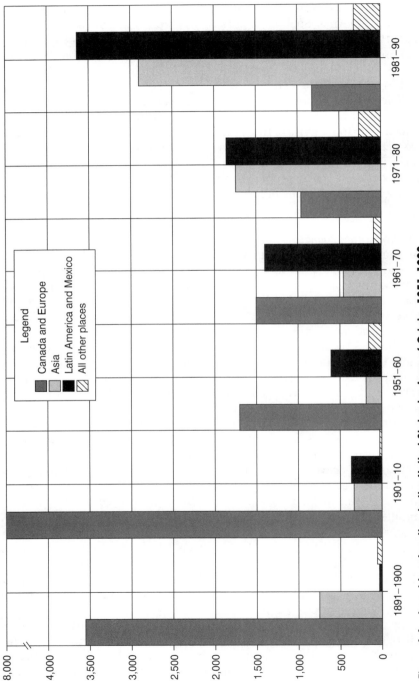

Figure 3.3 Legal Immigration in the United States by Area of Origin, 1851–1990

Note. Numbers are expressed in thousands. From *A Field Guide to the U.S. Economy, 1985–1995* (graph 4.4) by Center for Popular Economics, 1995, Amherst, MA. Reprinted with permission.

lems. Wilson won in large part by using a hostile, divisive campaign that blamed the state's economic woes on the Mexican and Mexican American population.

European Americans make up only 56.3% of the population but represented over 80% of the voters in the 1994 elections. Latinos, on the other hand, make up 26.3% of the population but only about 9% of the voters. Californians voted 62% to 38% in favor of Proposition 187, an initiative to punish illegal immigrants, and in favor of Governor Wilson, who campaigned for the initiative. Voter exit polls revealed that the electorate was polarized along ethnic lines: Latinos opposed the initiative 3 to 1, African Americans and Asians split about 50% to 50%, and European Americans supported the measure by over 64%.

This election demonstrated that anti-immigrant campaigns can mobilize angry voters. Such campaigns have quickly spread to a number of border states, increasing anti-immigrant sentiments in the country. In several border states, immigrants were inaccurately blamed for economic problems, even though numerous studies demonstrate that immigrants contribute far more to the economy in taxes and productivity than the alleged costs of human services such as education for children. But scapegoating campaigns are not about facts; they are about seeking a temporary political advantage at the cost of a weaker group. In this case, political extremists created and capitalized on misinformation and commonly accepted stereotypes to blame immigrant school children for the problems of a rapidly changing economy. European, Asian, Latino, and Caribbean immigrants learn the macroculture and acquire English at remarkably similar rates. Contrary to media-generated stereotypes, Latinos and Asians are not holding on to their home cultures and languages longer than did earlier Italian, German, and European immigrants.

At the same time, many racially identifiable immigrants (for example, Mexicans, Koreans, and Filipinos), their children, and their grandchildren continue to be denied equal access to high-status occupations. The political, economic, and educational systems continue to exclude large numbers of racially identifiable descendants of immigrants from full participation in U.S. society.

Native Americans

By 1840, the U.S. government had driven Native American tribes from most of the arable lands east of the Mississippi, but the native peoples of the Southwest and Florida resisted domination well into the twentieth century. The growing Spanish and Mexican population of the Southwest intermingled with Native Americans to establish cities and some farming areas, but Native Americans continued to dominate large areas of land. The Navajo (Dineh), the largest remaining tribe, survives in regions of Arizona and New Mexico. The 19 Pueblo tribes have maintained their culture and civilization despite Spanish, Mexican, and European American attempts to defeat them. The Cherokee, who had been driven from their lands in the East, settled in Oklahoma, beside the Kiowa. The Lakotah Sioux maintain established societies and cultures in the Dakotas. A host of other tribes maintain their societies in the intermountain region. Along the coast in California and Oregon, Native American peoples such as the Chumash and Miwok were virtually eliminated (see Figure 3.4).

One by one, the diverse Native American (Indian) societies signed treaties and became domestic dependent nations. They signed these treaties to protect the limited land and water rights assigned to them, but few of these rights have been honored by the states or the U.S. government. For decades, European Americans maintained a continual military presence on or near the reservations and ignored terrorism against and exploitation of this population.

Gradually, political control of the Native American nations was established and maintained through the Bureau of Indian Affairs. The Bureau penetrated the tribes by control of schooling, allocation of "missionary" rights, and through deliberate policies aimed at terminating tribes, or confining them to reservations on unproductive land.

Today approximately 38% of Native American people live on reservations. With few exceptions, they live in extreme economic poverty. Reservation economies and standards of living often resemble the economies of the most exploited regions of the world.

A few tribal nations, the Cherokee, the Navajo, some of the Pueblos, and the Cree, have successfully pursued economic development through education and extended legal struggles to control and profit from the vast mineral resources (oil, coal, uranium) located on their reservations. Recently, other tribes have

Figure 3.4   Who Are Native Americans? (Resident population by separated ethnic categories, 1990.)

Note. From *A Field Guide to the U.S. Economy, 1985–1995* (chart 4.3) by Center for Popular Economics, 1995, Amherst, MA. Reprinted with permission.

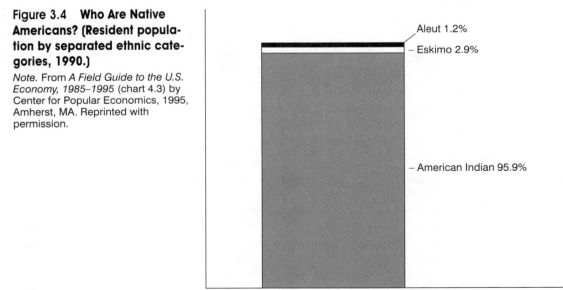

Aleut 1.2%

Eskimo 2.9%

American Indian 95.9%

Native Americans

sought economic opportunity by operating gambling casinos on their land. Their struggle for economic development continues in dozens of Native American nations, at times assisted by and coordinated with urban Native Americans through organizations such as the Inter-Tribal Council. Nevertheless, for many Native American children, extreme poverty, degradation, disease, and both cultural and physical suicide are the legacy of the conquest of their people by the European American culture.

Public schooling, whether on or off the reservation, often serves a contradictory function in Native American communities. Clearly, schooling provides opportunities to enter the macroculture and to seek economic progress. But even more than other subjugated groups (for example, African Americans and Chicanos), the several Native American societies continue to experience cultural repression in the public school system. Many schools have imposed a colonized perspective among young Native American children, with all of the attendant cultural conflicts and problems. Only in the last 20 years have some tribes achieved control over their own schools, providing needed cross-cultural educational experiences.

Multicultural Education and Racial Ideology

The specific and diverse historical experiences of each group (supplemented in Appendices A through F) explain a part of our present racial divisiveness and crisis. Although seldom recorded in public school history books and university courses, popular struggles against racism and toward cultural democracy have also occurred throughout our history. An accurate and comprehensive understanding of history and current race relations will help teachers and this generation of students to build a more appropriate curriculum and more supportive classroom relationships.

Schools teach ideas. Systems of ideas are called *ideologies.* Teachers model either an ideology of racism or pluralism, an ideology of equality or inequality. The dominant ideology in our society supports the present social structure and the resulting stratification of opportunity. Most school curriculums reinforce ideas that legitimize the present distribution of power and money. Since present U.S. society is stratified by race, gender, and class, schools tend to legitimize the present racial divisions as normal and natural, even logical and scientific. But logic and science are not responsible for the low quality of education that children from poor and minority neighborhoods receive. These children, who most need education, are often assigned to attend underfinanced, poorly equipped, and often rundown schools. Only a few of them will be able to overcome the economic consequences of a poorly funded education. Power and money—not logic, not science—determine that some students receive a quality education and others a poor education. Multicultural education is a school reform process that challenges the continuing domination of inherited privilege.

Multicultural education offers an alternative worldview, an alternative ideology. It argues that schools, along with church and family, are potential sources of knowledge and thus sources of power in a democratic society. Schools should promote the growth and extension of democracy rather than maintain the status quo. Advocates of multicultural education emphasize the values inherent and unique to democratic societies: citizenship participation, liberty, and equality of opportunity. We recognize that developing a democratic worldview of mutual respect and shared opportunity is difficult in a society divided by race and class. Yet, limited as it is, the school system is one of the few vehicles we presently have that permit us to work toward political, economic, social, and cultural democracy.

Our once resource-based economy is evolving into a knowledge-based economy that is becoming increasingly dependent on international trade. As economic changes accelerate, people who have knowledge will gain financial and political power. Children who acquire knowledge and skills in school will get ahead. Children who suffer in low-quality schools and receive a low-quality education will suffer permanent underemployment and limited economic opportunities.

The European American ideological bias in the present curriculum maintains inappropriate privileges for European American children. Children from all ethnic and cultural backgrounds deserve to see themselves and their families represented in the curriculum in order to see schooling as a path toward a prosperous future. Many young African American and Latino students experience failure and frustration in school; they fall behind in basic study skills. Omission from the curriculum and consistent school failure lead to an erosion of the students' self-esteem. Many students of color internalize the opinion that they can't learn, that failure is their fault. Thus, a cycle of failure begins. Students who doubt their own capacity do not learn well. Their anxiety and frustration as they constantly face failure reinforces self-doubt and soon leads them to question the value of staying in school. The persistent academic failure of African Americans, Latinos, and Native Americans leads some of these students to conclude that schools are negative, intrusive institutions rather than gateways out of poverty and discrimination.

As the economic crisis continues to cause neighborhoods to decline and schools to deteriorate, some students are increasingly turning to resistance. They respond to school failure with open hostility. They have developed a youth culture of resistance to school authority, rebelling against the school's negative view of themselves. Sometimes resistance is necessary and positive, such as in the development of a Chicano identity distinct from a Mexican identity. Unfortunately, many of these young people are choosing destructive forms of resistance such as gangs, violence, and drugs. Schools become war zones. Gangs and resistance culture make instruction difficult in many urban schools, depriving all students of their future economic opportunities.

Each individual and family experiences school domination or empowerment in their own manner. The ethnic and racial experiences of African Americans are substantially different from those of Latinos. The experiences of racial and minorities such as African Americans, Chicanos, and Puerto Ricans can be significantly different from the experiences of immigrant minorities from Latin America or Asia such as the Japanese, Chinese, and Vietnamese (Ogbu, 1978).

As a consequence of the increasing hostility, divisiveness, and racial conflict in our society, schools, when not segregated, become cauldrons of individual and intergroup conflict, sometimes leading to positive outcomes, sometimes leading to negative outcomes. Figure 3.5 illustrates the complex interrelationships between race, class, gender, culture, and personal histories.

The struggle against racism and for multicultural education calls on teachers and schools to participate in the painful birth of a new, more democratic society. Democratic teachers seek to claim the promise of the American dream of equal opportunity for all. In part, the struggle calls for a change in worldview. The view of cultural democracy and pluralism presented in this chapter replaces stereotypes of racial ideology and challenges Eurocentric views of history.

The United States is and has been a pluralistic society. The current struggle for multicultural education is one more step in the 200-year-old effort to build a more democratic society. Multicultural education poses this challenge: Will teachers and schools recognize that we are a pluralistic, multilingual society in curriculum, testing, ability grouping, and hiring? Will teachers choose to empower children from all communities, races, and sexes? Or will schools continue to deliver

Figure 3.5   Interrelationships Between Race, Class, Gender, Culture, and Personal Histories

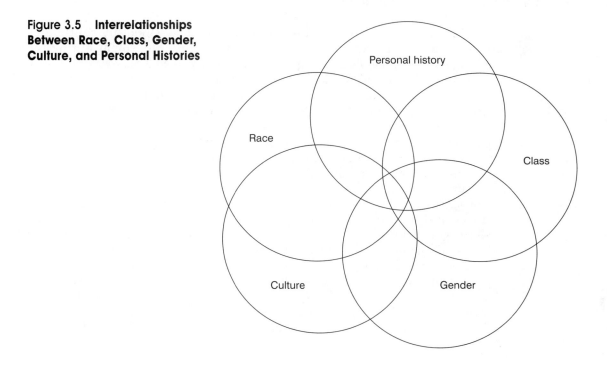

knowledge, power, and privilege primarily to members of the European American dominant culture at the expense of students from other cultures?

When students study the ideals of the Declaration of Independence and the U.S. Constitution, they learn a worldview that includes a commitment to democratic opportunity. They are taught an ideology of the "American creed." Multicultural education insists that schools serve as an arena where we achieve the promises of the Declaration of Independence:

> We hold these truths to be self evident, That all men are created equal and are endowed by their creator with certain unalienable rights, that among these rights are life, liberty and the pursuit of happiness. . . .

Throughout the nation's history, citizens have faced conflicts between our ideals and our national reality. Important battles have been won, such as the fight to end slavery and the campaign to recognize women's right to vote. Some of the battles have been lost, such as the survival of several diverse Native American nations. But the struggle to create a democratic society continues, and the manner in which we instruct our young people is crucial to that struggle.

The Attacks on Multicultural Education

Achieving political change toward democracy is not a smoothly continuous process. After the advances made by the Civil Rights Movement during the 1960s and 1970s, including an emphasis on more equal educational opportunity and the development of multicultural education, the end of the civil rights era brought attacks on these advances in the 1970s and 1980s. As conservatives gained political power in the 1980s and 1990s at national, state, and local levels, they began to advance their social agenda.

An ideology of conservative educational "reform" emerged from 1982 to 1992 emphasizing excellence and pushing aside discussions of equality. Public support for funding education to advance equal opportunity declined. Public education itself came under attack from the political right.

Conservatives labeled the crisis in public education as a crisis of mediocrity. The federal document, *A Nation at Risk* (1983), described the crisis of school mediocrity as equivalent to a war. The schools were blamed for not preparing students adequately for the rapidly changing economy. President Ronald Reagan and his second Secretary of Education, William Bennett, signaled their long-range goals by attacking bilingual education. *Education Week* journalist, James Crawford, described their efforts: "William J. Bennett had never set foot in a bilingual classroom on September 26, 1985, the day he launched a broadside against two decades of federal policy on language-minority children" (Crawford,

1991, p. 70). Bennett and Reagan isolated bilingual programs for budget cutting. In California and other states, new Republican governors vetoed bilingual education laws. Business and corporate interests, faced with new international business competition, blamed the schools for failing to prepare workers adequately.

The national economic crisis of business failure, enormous federal deficits, corruption, and loss of competitiveness was disingenuously represented as an educational crisis. Nine billion dollars were plundered in the savings-and-loan scandals, leaving the U.S. government with over $21 billion in bad debts and overpriced real estate. Three hundred and fifty bank executives were prosecuted for misuse of funds, and (as of this writing) 297 were convicted. Five U.S. senators were indicted for their participation in the scandal.

The Reagan and Bush administrations borrowed heavily to avoid raising taxes to pay for the economic policies they imposed, increasing the percentage of the national budget used to pay for interest on the debt from 6% in 1959 to 14% in 1992. The interest paid each year on the debt alone amounted to more dollars than the federal government provided for schools.

In times of economic crisis, some people have often turned to racial scapegoating. Racism, stereotyping, and scapegoating are often still used to explain economic and school failure. Stressed European American voters accepted false explanations and campaign slogans that affirmative action, ethnic minority rights, bilingual education, and eventually, multicultural education were leading to the decline of schools and the decline of order in the society.

As a result of the conservative political climate of the 1980s and 1990s, funding for public schooling and other social services remained stagnant while student enrollment climbed. Already underfunded schools in poverty areas were devastated by budget cuts. The federal government transferred substantial costs for immigrants, health care, and education to the states to save money for the defense budget (Sawicky, 1991). Low-income schools, school districts, and even some cities went bankrupt.

As economic conditions continued to worsen, many teachers' salaries and school budgets were cut back. By 1987, in response to weaknesses in their own reform strategies, conservatives began to blame the multicultural education movement for declining student performance, an attack that began with Allan Bloom's *The Closing of the American Mind* (1987) and continues to the present in works such as Arthur Schlesinger's *The Disuniting of America* (1992).

Conservatives at the university level (in think tanks and advocacy groups such as the Educational Excellence Network, the Bradley Commission on History in the Schools, the *Social Studies Review*, the Olin Foundation, and the American Textbook Council), in the media, and among textbook authors attack and distort efforts at multicultural education in an effort to regain control of the discussion about race, racism, schools, and democracy (Adler, 1982; California State Dept. of Instruction, 1987; Ravitch, 1990; Schlesinger, 1992). The current efforts of multicultural education challenge the conservatives' hegemony of ideas and power.

The Way Ahead

The long struggle against racism and cultural oppression continues today. Multicultural education is a part of that struggle. Neoconservative educational leaders including Alan Bloom, E. C. Hirsch, Dianne Ravitch, Chester Finn, Bill Honig, Bill Bennett, Al Shanker, and others resist the change to a more inclusive curriculum. They assert that multicultural education is political and divisive. Other conservatives like Shelby Steele, Linda Chavez, Richard Rodrigues, and Thomas Sowell demonstrate that persons of all races can favor the traditional curriculum.

This time attacks against the idea of equal educational opportunity will fail. The demographics of a rapidly changing population assure us that students will be more diverse. These students will speak more languages, not fewer. All of the students in our schools need to study diversity to understand and to participate in this rapidly changing society. Multicultural education is an ideological project to move the schools toward cultural democracy. It reasserts the traditional role of the common school to provide economic opportunity for all. This effort necessarily operates within the current contested and disputed worldview of the appropriate role and functions of public schools in a democratic society.

Control of schools and the curriculum is central to the effort of neoconservatives to maintain a dominance of the European American agenda against the demands for cultural pluralism. Operating out of fear of losing their privileged positions and leadership, these critics argue that national unity requires the reassertion of dated, European American-centered culture (Ravitch, 1990; Schlesinger, 1992). Multicultural education advocates respond that national unity comes from respecting our diversity and developing a free, democratic allegiance to a common nationhood (Ladson-Billings, 1992).

The election of Bill Clinton to President in 1992 began the process of pushing back conservative political control on a national level, including conservative dominance of school reform efforts. Political debate and school debate have moved back and forth since 1992. The neoconservative agenda produced its own problems. Businesses need well-trained workers—not high school dropouts. Unless education improves its ability to prepare many more students, including students from diverse cultures, the economy will suffer a skills shortage. School failure reinforces institutionalized racism and deepens the divisions in our society. Meanwhile the welfare system and the penal system are increasingly expensive and overloaded. Without quality educational opportunities for all, there will be no economic justice. Without economic justice, there will be no social peace. Multicultural education offers a positive alternative to current divisions in our society by preparing all students for productive employment and democratic participation.

Summary

U.S. public school classrooms commonly encompass a cultural, linguistic, and ethnic diversity found in few nations. The United States has suffered a long and troubled history of racial conflicts and oppressions. The diverse historical experiences of African Americans, Latinos, Asians, Native Americans, and European Americans explain a part of our present racial divisiveness and crises.

A racist ideology emerged from the cauldron of expansion, settlement, slavery, displacement, migration, and immigration. This racial ideology permeates our society and distorts efforts at school reform. Multicultural education is a part of the 200-year-old struggle to foster democratic opportunity in this society. Multicultural education combats racist ideology with an ideology of cultural pluralism and equal educational opportunity.

Questions Over the Chapter

1. Define the difference between race and culture.
2. Define racism.
3. Give three examples of racial inequality in schools.
4. In what ways did Jane, the teacher in our case study on p. 52, receive privilege?
5. How is institutionalized racism different from prejudice?
6. How did racism impact the U.S. tradition of a two-party political system?
7. Explain factors that contributed to social fragmentation in the African American political leadership in the 1980s.
8. List four ways that public schools reflect the macroculture.
9. List three educational settings where culture is learned.
10. Give two examples of how your own culture is changing.

Activities for Further Study of Race and Racism

1. Compare the ethnic and gender makeup of your own teacher preparation program with the population of the region and with the student populations in local schools. Explain the differences.
2. If you have not already done so, play the simulation game BaFa BaFa (see "Activities," Chapter 2) or Star Power.
3. In cooperative groups, describe your most vivid memory of racial or ethnic differences. Who was the "other" group? What were their characteristics? Who was the source of information about this "other"?
4. In cooperative groups, describe a time when you were separated into racial, ethnic, class, ability, or gender groups. Describe your memory of that event.
5. In a group or individually, assume the points of view of the following different Native American tribes: (a) a Plains tribe (Sioux, Crow, etc.), (b) a Pueblo tribe, or (c) a Cherokee tribe. Describe the arrival and settlement of European Americans into the territory of each group.
6. Several of the figures in this chapter are from *A Field Guide to the U.S. Economy, 1985–1995*, which provides nearly 100 clearly drawn graphs and explanations of the economy. They can be readily converted into transparencies for classroom use. Using infor-

mation from the graphs you select from the guide, prepare a short written presentation on the patterns of immigration from 1950 to 1990. (The guide is available in bookstores or can be obtained by writing to Center for Popular Economics, Box 785, Amherst, MA 01004. Phone: (413) 545-0743.)

Teaching Strategies

1. Present accurate, truthful information on the role of race and the separate role of class in determining school and economic opportunity.
2. Teach students necessary school knowledge as an addition to, not in place of, community knowledge.
3. Study racism and the forces that sustain racial privilege.
4. Plan strategies to develop pro-democratic values of equality and the dignity of each individual.
5. Reorganize history and the social studies to present a multiethnic point of view.
6. Help students to analyze the interactive and complex nature of race, gender, and class oppressions.
7. Provide all students with instruction in a language they comprehend.

References

Acuna, R. (1972). *Occupied America: The Chicano's struggle toward liberation.* San Francisco: Canfield Press.

Adler, M. (1982). *The paideia proposals.* New York: Macmillan.

Bell, D. (1992). *Faces at the bottom of the well.* New York: HarperCollins.

Bliatout, B. T., Downing, B. T., Lewis, J., & Yang, D. (1988). *Handbook for teaching Hmong-speaking students.* Folsom, CA: Southeast Asia Community Resource Center, Folsom Cordova Unified School District.

Bloom, A. (1987). *The closing of the American mind: How higher education has failed democracy and impoverished the souls of today's students.* New York: Simon & Schuster.

California State Department of Instruction. (1987). *California history-social science framework.*

Center for Popular Economics. (1995) *A field guide to the U.S. economy, 1985–1995.* Amherst, MA: Author.

Crawford, J. (1991). *Bilingual education: History, politics, theory and practice* (2nd ed.). Trenton, NJ: Crane Publishing.

DeWitt, K. (1994, December 19). Have suburbs, especially in the South, become the source of American political power? *New York Times.*

DuBois, W. E. B. (1975). *Color and democracy: Colonies and peace.* Millwood, NY: Kraus-Thompson.

Fact Book. (1994–1995). Sacramento, CA: California Department of Education.

Garcia, M. T. (1994). *Memories of Chicano history: The life and narrative of Bert Corona.* University of California Press.

Grisold del Castillo, R. (1979). *The Los Angeles barrio: 1860–1890, A social history.* University of California Press.

Joint Economic Committee. (1992). *Families on a treadmill: Work and income in the 1980s.* Washington, DC: U.S. Congress.

King, M. L., Jr. (1967, April 4). Speech to clergy and laity concerned. In J. Washington (Ed.), *A testament of hope.* San Francisco: Harper.

Kozol, J. (1991). *Savage inequalities: Children in America's schools.* New York: Crown Publishing.

Ladson-Billings, G. (1992, September). The multicultural mission: Unity and diversity. *Social Education,* pp. 308–311. Washington, DC: National Council for the Social Studies.

Limerick, P. N. (1988). *The legacy of conquest: The unbroken past of the American West.* New York: W. W. Norton.

Marable, M. (1992). Multicultural democracy: The emerging majority for justice and peace. *The crisis of color and democracy: Essays on race, class and power* (pp. 249–251). Monroe, ME: Common Courage Press.

National Center for Children in Poverty. (1991, Fall). *News and issues.* New York: Columbia University School of Public Health.

National Commission of Excellence in Education. (1983). *A nation at risk: The imperative for educational reform.* Washington, DC: U.S. Department of Education.

Ogbu, J. U. (1978). *Minority education and caste: The American system in cross-cultural perspective.* New York: Academic Press.

Omi, M., & Winant, H. (1986). *Racial formation in the United States: From the 1960s to the 1980s.* New York & London: Routledge & Kegan Paul.

Ravitch, D. (1990, Spring). Diversity and democracy: Multicultural education in America. *American Educator,* pp. 16–48.

Reich, R. B. (1991). *The Work of Nations: Preparing ourselves for 21st century capitalism.* New York: Alfred A. Knopf.

Sawicky, M. B. (1991). *The roots of the public sector fiscal crisis.* Washington, DC: Economic Policy Institute.

Schlesinger, A. M., Jr. (1992). *The disuniting of America.* New York: W. W. Norton.

Takaki, R. (1989). *Strangers from a different shore: A history of Asian Americans.* Boston: Little, Brown.

Tate, K. (1992, Winter). Invisible woman. *The American prospect, (8),* pp. 74–81.

U.S. Bureau of Census. *1980 Census.*

Weber, D. J. (1973). *Foreigners in their native lands: The historical roots of the Mexican Americans.* Albuquerque, NM: University of New Mexico Press.

West, C. (1993). *Race matters.* Boston: Beacon Press.

Chapter 4

With Liberty and Justice for Some: Class Relations and Schools

The Crisis of Poverty

In *The Work of Nations* (1991), U.S. Secretary of Labor Robert Reich demonstrates that our society is increasingly divided along economic lines. The wealthy live in luxury housing in affluent neighborhoods, professional workers live in comfortable middle-class suburbs, and working-class and poverty-stricken people make do with deteriorating and substandard housing in the central cities and many rural areas. By the mid-1980s, federal policy toward low-income housing had changed. Most forms of subsidy were eliminated, and now at least 3 million people have no homes at all.

More than one out of five children in the United States live in poverty—a higher rate than that tolerated by other industrialized nations. Despite our idealism about equal educational opportunity, poor children generally attend poor schools. This is because schools frequently mirror the neighborhoods around them. After detailed studies of five large metropolitan areas, Harvard political scientist Gary Orefield and Carol Ashkinage (1991) concluded that because poor neighborhoods usually have poorly financed schools, class is a major determinant of educational opportunity.

Yet working people have a faith in education. They have been among the primary supporters of public education since the growth of state-supported schools in the 1840s. Through good times and economic crises, working people have insisted on improving public schools. They expect the schools to teach their children how to participate in a democracy, prepare them for employment, and show them how they can improve the quality of their lives. They expect equal opportunity for their children.

But our schools are not living up to these expectations, especially for children of the poor. Thirty-nine percent of African American children, 32% of Latino children, 17% of Asian children, and 12.5% of European American children live in poverty (National Center for Children in Poverty, 1991). Too many of them attend inadequate and even failing schools.

Four social crises have devastated teachers and schools particularly in urban America during the last decade. As described in Chapter 1, an economic crisis began developing in 1972 as the U.S. economy lost its domination of world markets. Confusing cause and effect, business leaders blamed this crisis on the schools. The economic policies of the 1980s created a second crisis in which public financial support for all social programs, including schools, was severely cut. Studies conducted by Max Sawicky of the Economic Policy Institute (1991) show that tax cuts increased the profits of our major corporations.

A third crisis was the societal abandonment of responsibility to care for and guide our children. Adults without children pursued their own wealth. They demanded tax reductions while increasing their own public benefits. Reversing a 100-year pattern, voters refused to pay taxes to fund the schools sufficiently. The voting majority of the adult population and their political leaders abandoned the schools, children, and the future in favor of buying a new car, a new home, or a new missile system. The financial and physical condition of urban schools sank into a state of chronic crisis. At the same time, many parents, squeezed by a slow, hidden economic decline of working-class incomes between 1970 and 1990, were working more hours and consequently shifting more of the responsibility for child rearing onto the schools. Poverty continues to grow. Increases in poverty particularly affect women heads of households and their families, as shown in Figures 4.1 and 4.2. How do you explain the massive increase in poor families headed by women?

Barbara Ehrenreich, in *Fear of Falling* (1989), summarizes decades of research to describe a fourth crisis produced by these social changes: the abandonment of the cities by the middle class. With the rapid growth in the ranks of the poor and consequent increases in homelessness, street gangs, drug abuse, and prostitution, many middle-class professionals no longer find the cities a safe and congenial environment. They may have to work in the city, but increasingly they choose to live in the suburbs. The cities, with their declining tax base and decaying school systems, are being left to the working poor (white, black, and Latino) (Jargowsky & Bane, 1991).

These crises in society have produced crises in the schools. Today's parents are working more hours and earning less money. More than ever they are looking to

Figure 4.1 Women's Income as a Percentage of Men's in the United States, 1967–1986

Note. From *A Field Guide to the U.S. Economy, 1985–1995* by Center for Popular Economics, 1995, Amherst, MA. Reprinted with permission.

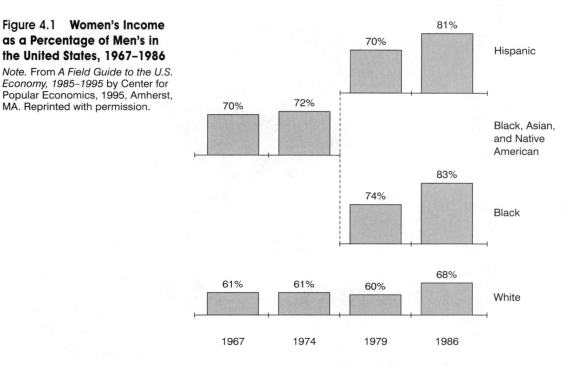

the schools to bring up the next generation of children. But schools have been unable to respond to these momentous changes in the economy and the society. With shrinking budgets, decaying physical facilities, and a deteriorating social environment, the schools are falling behind. The burden of this failure weighs most heavily on the children of people of color because their parents can escape neither the public school system nor the cities where the problem is most acute.

Social Class as an Analytical Concept

The racial and cultural analyses of school achievement described in prior chapters reveal only part of the story. Social class and gender interact with race and culture to influence each individual child's school achievement.

Social class is a *concept,* a mental tool that helps us to categorize, store, and retrieve information. In Chapter 2, we used the concept of culture to organize a wide variety of information about how groups of people live. We may not remember all of the particulars of a group of people, but we recognize the general concept of culture. Having learned this concept, we can approach learning about new groups of people using the same organizing principle.

Another attribute of concepts is that they shape the thinking of their users. Thomas Kuhn, in his landmark work *The Structure of Scientific Revolutions* (1970), described how the selection of basic concepts for research strongly influ-

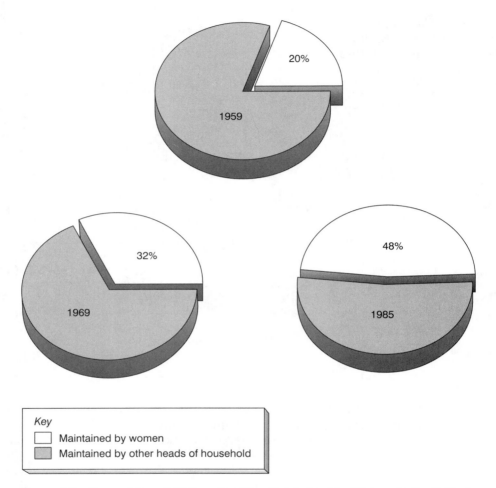

Figure 4.2   Percentage of All Poor Families Maintained by Women in the United States, 1959–1985

Note. From *A Field Guide to the U.S. Economy, 1985–1995* by Center for Popular Economics, 1995, Amherst, MA. Reprinted with permission.

ences researchers' methodologies and results. For example, a researcher who sought explanations for school failure by examining the concept of social class (usually a sociologist or economist) would pay attention to different evidence than a researcher who looked at failure through the concepts of psychology or the neo-conservative philosophies of the 1982 through 1992 school reform movement.

As a result of their personal histories and the worldviews and cultures of most professional educators and many U.S. sociologists and psychologists, the litera-ture in education pays only limited attention to class issues or avoids discussing class.[1] Instead researchers refer to *socioeconomic status (SES)*. The social status approach, commonly taught in university sociology courses, follows the tradition of W. Lloyd Warner (1898–1970). Socioeconomic status blends both economic issues of jobs and income (or lack of them) with status issues of role relationships, consumption patterns, and implied values to determine a prescribed socioeconomic status. Educational research usually follows the Warner tradition and uses the concept of SES rather than the concept of social class to describe differences among families, neighborhoods, and schools. While SES studies explain some issues, the concept as Kuhn (1970) noted, also shapes the perceptions of social scientists and teachers.

The use of SES as an analytical tool emphasizes the role of the individual in determining success or failure. SES can be improved, for example, by getting more education or earning a big promotion at one's workplace. Researchers using SES as an organizational concept usually assume that people improve their position in society primarily by individual effort and that schools serve as vehicles for economic and social advancement. The SES approach rarely challenges the inequality of the system. The use of the concept of status leads to seeking incremental improvements in the schools to benefit those students who appear to be willing to try harder.

The assumptions behind status research reinforce the position that it is individuals who need to change, not the schools. Decades of educational research and policy development from this perspective have described the deterioration of educational opportunities for at-risk students without leading to the development of democratic alternatives for teachers and students.

Research organized around the concept of social class works from substantially different assumptions. From a class perspective, our society is made up of an upper class that includes the owners and managers of businesses and corporations; a middle or working class that includes a professional stratum, many service workers, and blue collar workers; and a lower class characterized by social isolation, often irregular employment, welfare, and family disruption.

Some of the difficulties that result from using the idea of SES rather than class are revealed in the common use of the term middle class. The press and people in casual conversation use the term to mean a wide variety of living situations. Stephen Rose, in his excellent work *Social Stratification in the United States* (1992), gives examples of two people who would probably be considered middle class.

> The term *middle class* is widely used—most Americans consider themselves part of it—but rarely defined. People usually reject the alternative categorizations, lower or upper class, because no one wants to be poor and few consider themselves wealthy enough to be classified as rich.

[1] The complexity of definitions of social class in the United States and the rapid changes in professional jobs in the middle class lead some researchers to avoid class issues. But the difficulty of arriving at a clear definition of class is not an adequate reason to avoid using class as an analytical concept (Ehrenreich & Ehrenreich, 1979; Parker, 1972; Walker, 1979).

Consider the following two families. In the first, the family income is $22,000: the husband works as a forklift operator at an assembly plant while the wife stays at home caring for their two children. The other family is a suburban couple, a dentist and psychologist, with a combined income of $110,000; they own a $250,000 house and three cars, one child is in college, and another attends a local private school. Both families might describe themselves as being "strapped" for money and as having little left over for frills. Both would probably consider themselves part of the middle class—though, the first family might add the adjective "lower" and the second add "upper."

In other words, "middle class" has become a nearly all-inclusive category, one so broad that it not only blurs real distinctions in income, lifestyle, and well-being but often clouds public discussion as well.

In Figure 4.3, middle class (including both professional employees and blue and pink collar workers) would include all families making over $20,000 per year (the federal low budget line) and less than $85,000 per year.

Most people in this society work for someone else. Managers direct workers and owners control the jobs. Over 50% of all U.S. families depend on wages for their income. The jobs, the income, and the class position of the parents of students largely determine where the student will live and the quality of the school the student will attend.

Bowles & Gintis (1976), Carnoy & Levin (1985), and others whose research is based on a social-class perspective argue that our economic system produces social classes and that these classes are group phenomena, not individual choices. Changes in class composition occur as a result of changes in the economic system. The structural changes presently occurring in our economy are having this effect. Good paying union jobs in auto, steel, electronics and other industries are being transferred to other countries and are being replaced by low-paying service jobs. These are class changes—not individual changes.

Attention to social class rather than SES yields additional insights into the functions of schooling in our racially and class-polarized society. Scholars, teachers, and researchers interested in promoting equality in schooling use the concept of social class to explain how the gaps in school achievement among students from the upper, middle, working, and poor classes reproduce and maintain inequality in society. According to Bowles & Gintis (1976), only when we grasp the role of class in our educational system can we begin to counteract its effects:

> Understanding the dynamics of class relationships is essential to an adequate appreciation of the connection between economics and education. For the institutions of economic life (including schools) do not work mechanistically and mindlessly to produce social outcomes, but rather change and develop through the types of class relationships to which they give rise. The educational system is involved in reproducing and changing these class relationships and cannot be understood by simply "adding up" the effects of schooling on each individual to arrive at a total social impact. (p. 67)

Researchers such as Gary Orefield (1991) and William Jules Wilson (1978, 1987, 1988) who pay attention to class issues, view the way in which education

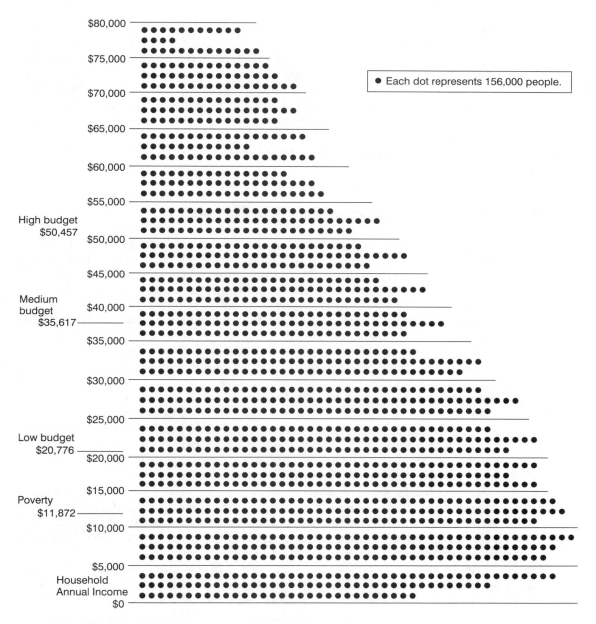

Figure 4.3   Distribution of Income in the United States, 1990

Note. Instructors can order the entire chart in a 30″ × 60″ format for classroom use. From *Social Stratification in the United States* by Stephen Rose, 1992, New York: New Press. Reprinted with permission.

is presently dispensed as a part of the system of maintaining class relationships. Tracking, ability grouping, teacher expectations, counseling services, and inequitable school expenditures reinforce already existing social class differences (Carnoy & Levin, 1985). Researchers who approach these problems from the perspective of social class usually have different goals for schools than those using a status-based approach. They argue that democratic schools should produce more equality rather than advance a few individuals within the present unequal system. This viewpoint regards schools as a product of public policy and as an institution that is subject to change based on the democratic demands of the majority.

An American Dilemma: Poor Children in Poor Schools

There often exists a direct relationship between poverty and school failure. Under our present structure of schooling, poor kids fail more often than kids from middle-income families. The number of poor people in our society is growing. We can therefore predict that a growing number of children will fail in school. *Why* they are failing is a more complex question.

To understand the crisis of poor children in urban and rural schools, we need more information about the growth of poverty in our society and how poverty, schools, and cultural minority groups interact to produce school failure.

As described in Chapter 1, substantial economic transformations are causing rapid changes in our society and our schools. The U.S. economy has lost its dominant position in the world. Bartlett & Steele (1992), in *America: What Went Wrong?* demonstrate that the Reagan-Bush economics of the 1980s resulted in the decline in the standard of living and job opportunities of many young people from the working class. Present trends described by Bartlett and Steele indicate that both the absolute and relative size of the poverty class will grow. As poverty increases, school problems increase.

During the 1960s, as a result of economic growth and government programs known as "the war on poverty," there was an overall decline in poverty in the United States. In the 1970s, the poverty rate stopped declining, but remained stable despite the fact that the poverty level increased with each recession and decreased in each recovery.

As the economy entered the current period of structural change, poverty levels have increased in recessions and remained high during recoveries. Clearly, some segments of society do not benefit significantly from current economic recoveries.

According to the U.S. Census Bureau (DeParle, 1994), the total number of people living below the official poverty line, with an annual income of $14,763 for a family of four, climbed beyond 39 million in 1993. Over 15% of the total population lives below this index of poverty. Poverty levels in the United States are higher than they have been at any time since 1961 (see Figures 4.4 through 4.7).

In Figure 4.4, notice that the percentage of both African American and Hispanic children exceeds the percentages of African American and Hispanic adults by large numbers (over 10% each). Use this information to predict the percentage of children in poverty in 1993 based on Figure 4.5.

A study by the Center on Budget Priorities shows that between 1978 and 1987, the poverty rate for Latinos climbed from 21.6% to 28.2%, while the poverty rate for whites increased from 8.5% to 10.5%, and for African Americans from 30.6% to 33.1%. Poverty rates for all three groups climbed sharply during the recession of the early 1980s and again in the recession of the early 1990s (Center on Budget and Policy Priorities, 1988). And poverty is still increasing. In 1970, 15% of children in the United States lived in poverty, while in 1990, 20% lived in such severe poverty that their basic needs for nutrition, health, and housing were not reliably met (UNESCO, 1993).

Federal tax changes and budget cuts enacted by the Reagan and Bush administrations (1980–1992) significantly increased the presence of poverty. In 1979, a

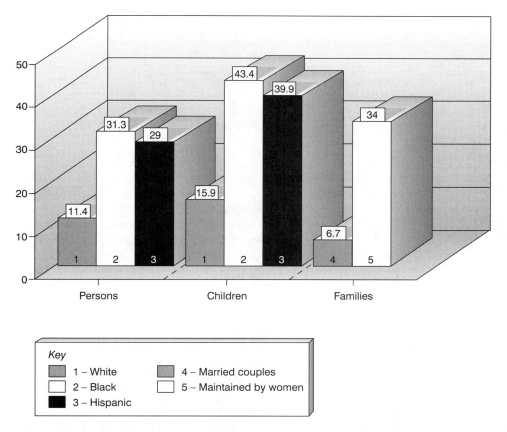

Figure 4.4   Percentages of U.S. Individuals and Households with Incomes Below the Poverty Level, 1985

Note. From *A Vision for America's Future* (pp. 70–71), by the Children's Defense Fund, 1989, Washington, DC: Author. Copyright 1989 by the Children's Defense Fund. Reprinted with permission.

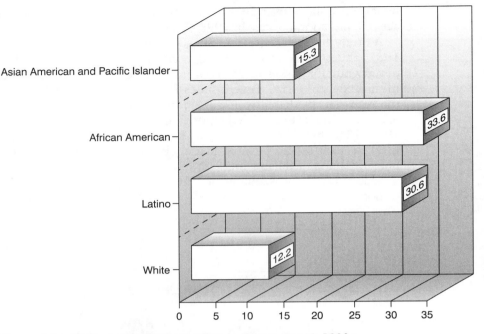

Figure 4.5   Percentages of Persons Below Poverty Level, 1993
U.S. Census Bureau, 1993.

combination of federal, state, and local programs assisted more than one of every eight poor Latino families out of poverty. The Reagan administration, however, dramatically cut these programs. By 1987, only one of every 14 poor Latino families was being lifted out of poverty by government assistance (Jargowsky & Bane, 1991). Since 1982, structural changes in the economy and the removal of government social support programs have produced a growing semipermanent class of poor families with children. Our society does not have a policy to prevent poverty or to help families escape from poverty. Instead, we pay the enormous social and human costs of a poverty class. In 1994 and 1995, the new Republican majority in Congress passed elements of their program, "A Contract with America," which included substantial budget cuts and limited spending for programs providing economic assistance to poor families and children, such as school lunch programs.

One of the very real human costs is that poverty affects whether children live or die. San Francisco, California, for example, has an infant mortality rate of 7 per 1,000 births—the same as Norway or Switzerland. The rate in Detroit, Michigan, on the other hand, with its higher percentage of urban poor, ranks below that of Cuba, and Washington, DC, has the same infant mortality rate as Jamaica. When infant mortality is compared by race, white infant mortality is 8 per 1,000 births—one of the best in the world. Black infant mortality in the United States is 18 per 1,000—higher than that of Bulgaria, Poland, or Cuba.

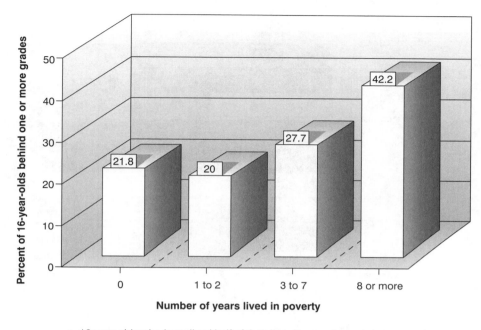

- 16-year-olds who have lived half of their lives in poverty are twice as likely as those who have never been poor to be behind in school.

Figure 4.6   Percentages of 16-Year-Olds Who Have Fallen Behind in School by Years in Poverty, 1986

Note. From *A Vision for America's Future* (p. xxxvi), by the Children's Defense Fund, 1989, Washington, DC: Author. Copyright 1989 by the Children's Defense Fund. Reprinted with permission.

Changes in employment statistics alone are not accurate enough to measure economic progress in our society. The declining unemployment rate during the economic recovery of the 1980s revealed improved employment for some. But other workers were forced into marginal jobs. Wages paid to Latino and African American workers eroded in relation to the rising cost of living (Jargowsky & Bane, 1991). And a 1993 survey by the *Wall Street Journal* (Sharp, 1993) demonstrated that black workers suffered a net loss of jobs from 1990 through 1991, while other racial groups all gained.

One fact that official unemployment statistics often do not reveal is that most of the poor work. *The State of Working America* (Mishel & Frankel, 1990–1991), shows that between 1979 and 1987, the number of poor who worked yet remained poor grew from 6.5 million to 8.5 million people. Hard work does not necessarily keep families out of poverty. The exceptions are the disabled, elderly, and single parents of small children. About two thirds of all other poor people work fulltime or parttime. Many parttime workers would prefer to work fulltime but are unable to find jobs.

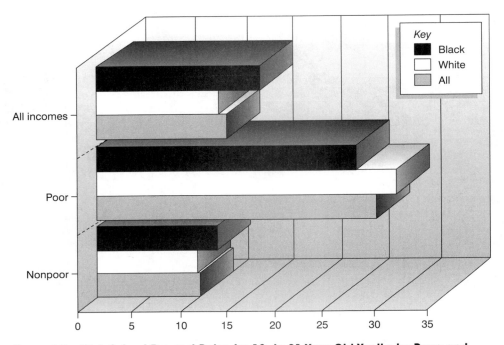

Figure 4.7   High School Dropout Rates for 18- to 21-Year-Old Youths by Race and Poverty, 1987

Note. From *Shortchanged: Recent Developments in Hispanic poverty, income and employment* by the Center on Budget and Policy Priorities, 1988, Washington, DC: Author. Copyright by the Center on Budget and Policy Priorities. Reprinted with permission.

Between 1979 and 1988, real family income for the poorest fifth of our people declined by 4.5% while that of the richest fifth increased by 14%. In 1994, the U.S. Census Bureau reported that the percentage of people working fulltime but earning less than the poverty level—about $13,000 for a family of four—has risen by over 50% in the last 13 years (New York Times, 1994). But it is not just the poorest who are in trouble. According to Marshall and Tuker (1992),

The middle class, the key to social stability in the United States, is also in difficulty. Overall, the top 30 percent of our people in terms of income distribution are getting richer while the bottom 70 percent are getting poorer. (p. xv–xvi)

Poor Children in the Classroom

When a child comes to school from a middle-class family, that child already has learned at home values that closely match the school values advocated by teachers. The child knows much of the culture of the school upon entering. Further, middle-class children have social skills, behaviors, and attitudes that teachers find appropriate. The children are similar to the teachers' own children in most respects. Because the middle-class child's culture is similar to the teacher's culture, most teachers react positively to their middle-class students, and supportive bonds develop between them. In elementary school most of the teachers are female, producing particularly supportive bonds for girls.

A child from a poor, marginalized family is more likely to enter school with a different set of behaviors and attitudes. While the school expects children to know the themes of mainstream children's literature—Cinderella, the Pied Piper of Hamelin, and other European folktales—some children come from homes where few people read. Other children's language skills may be extensive in Spanish or Vietnamese, but limited in English. Yet the school culture expects performance in English. The punishment and reward systems used by schools are often confusing and different from those familiar to the child.

Some children arrive at school from homes where poverty or divorce has disrupted stable living arrangements, although disruption and disorganization of home life are not unique or universal to families living in poverty. Middle-class families frequently experience disruption and are made dysfunctional by divorce, alcoholism, drug abuse, and physical or psychological abuse.

Poor but stable families often prepare their children well for school success. The safety and security of a stable home environment enhance the child's ability to view the new environment of school without undue fear. Getting a good start in school in a safe, protected environment helps children learn the culture of school and the new ways of doing things. Children who fail to learn these new behaviors and values required for school success may encounter conflict at school.

The high rate of children moving from school to school in poor neighborhoods also degrades the quality of their school experience. Poor people often lose their jobs and their apartments. Poverty, health, and economic crises require them to move. Some even become homeless. For children, frequent moving produces a pattern of health problems and school disruption with a constant array of new teachers, new classmates, and new curriculum.

The truly poor have severe financial problems simply getting through the month. A doctor's appointment can require two days of waiting for service at a public health clinic. For recipients of Aid to Families with Dependent Children (AFDC), contacts with governmental institutions are intrusive, overwhelming, and full of dangers. In poor neighborhoods, a simple school request for family information may cause fear and alarm at home. Parents may fear that yet another social worker is going show up to reduce their already inadequate benefits.

In spite of the problems of poverty, most poor parents still look to school as the best hope for their children's future economic opportunity. They believe in the ideals of our school system. They recognize schooling as the best available route to ending their own cycle of poverty. These parents sacrifice for their children. Many low-income Latino and African American parents make enormous financial sacrifices to place their children in Catholic and other tuition-based schools, many paying over $1,500 each year to have their children in safe and orderly classrooms. In middle-class neighborhoods, children typically receive a comparable education in tax-supported schools.

When poor children come to school, too often they encounter frustration and failure. Large urban school districts with bureaucratic authoritarian structures and intrusive cultural demands seldom ensure success for poor children. Not one of the major cities provides a quality education to all of its students. Up to 50% real dropout rates are common. Over 30% of the schools in these urban areas fail to educate these children even to basic levels of literacy (California Commission on Educational Quality, 1988; Orefield & Ashkinage, 1991). The children fail to learn the rules of the school and find it difficult to meet the school's expectations. Middle-class psychologists and educators may label the students "bad" or "unmotivated."

Even in "difficult" neighborhoods, most of the parents are struggling to achieve an education for their children. These efforts are sometimes counteracted by overworked and burned-out school staff workers whose main focus is to maintain control of the school campus. Tired school staff too often hold low expectations for the children, routinely practice tracking, and ultimately blame the children, their parents, and their communities for the problems. The parents blame the schools and the schools blame the parents. Neither approach helps the children. Rather than continue this fruitless cycle, teachers need to accept their responsibility to work with parents to educate children and to maintain high standards for all children.

A damaging piece of folk knowledge that may circulate among teachers preserves the belief that the learning problems of poor children are personal failures or cultural group characteristics. In the face of such prejudice, families can lose hope and confidence in themselves and in schools. Other families, who recognize the violence happening to their children and see their own dreams of opportunity fade, become defensive or hostile toward the schools. They vote for tax limitation plans and "choice" or voucher plans that reduce school funding. Some frustrated parents avoid the school. Others, angry at a society that seems to have abandoned their children, encourage students to engage in open conflict with school authorities.

Society's Obligations to the Children

The interaction between poverty and schooling is complex and changing. Teachers have always needed to control and redirect a few children in each class who fail in their schoolwork or who refuse to adjust to reasonable standards for social behavior. In many poverty neighborhoods today, however, matters are much worse than in prior years. While a teacher in the 1950s might have faced two disruptive children per class, today's teacher may face eight or, in some classes, up to 20.

Two worldviews of society's obligations to its children are contending for support. Voters and taxpayers have long insisted that our democratic society promote the common good. Our federal constitution and most state constitutions assign the government the task of promoting the "general welfare." One view holds that a society needs to arrange itself so that children are cared for, their health protected, and their education provided. This view has been the mainstream opinion since at least the 1850s and provides the justification for establishing schools as a public responsibility.

A "theory of the common good" recognizes that if a society stops caring for its children, all parts of society suffer. Even a family that is responsible, protective, and nurturing can lose children to the war zones found in some urban neighborhoods. Society as a whole loses when a child is shot in random gang violence, killed as a bystander at school, or kidnapped by a person who ought to be receiving mental health care and perhaps hospitalization. Parents in at-risk neighborhoods recognize the danger to their families, and they resent the refusal of political leaders to respond to their children's most basic needs of security and educational opportunity.

Unfortunately for children, the ideology of the conservative political activists of the 1980s promoted an alternative view of society. Conservatives convinced a majority of voters that by saving money and not paying taxes they would be promoting the common good. This was a reversal of traditional conservative thinking. As Robert Reich describes in *The Work of Nations* (1991), the wealthy secede from the cities, buy beautiful homes in suburbs, wall off their neighborhoods, hire private security forces, and richly fund their children's schools. They promote their individual wealth rather than the public good. They try to blame the deterioration of life in poverty areas on welfare recipients, immigrants, and minorities. Their flight from poverty into walled enclosures replaced concern for the common good.

Yet no part of society remains healthy when the other parts are sick. Violence and drug abuse in one part of the community endanger us all. Even in the suburbs, runaway and suicide rates of teens have reached epidemic proportions. The conservative strategy of withdrawing into the suburbs worked only until gangs, violence, and drug abuse appeared there, too.

In the bottom tier of our society—the rapidly growing poverty areas—the decline in good-paying jobs has substantially damaged family life. Families are divided and some are destroyed by crime, drugs, health crises, divorce, abandonment, and permanent underemployment.

These are not crises that most people choose to acknowledge. Bartlett and Steele, in *America: What Went Wrong?* (1992), describe how unemployment, economic decay, and the de-industrialization of society rob the lower tier of hope and economic opportunity. We have already read in Chapter 3 Jonathan Kozol's description, in *Savage Inequalities* (1991), of how teachers, schools, and police departments in the heart of this social deterioration struggle to cope. Neither the schools nor the police are adequately funded or prepared to handle this growing crisis.

Savage Inequalities records how children bring their crises to school each day. Poor and middle-class children mix in some schools. The deterioration of life opportunities among the poor adds to a deterioration of schools. Some students bring to school the same disorder, crime, and gang violence they see in their neighborhoods. Dealing with these problems inevitably takes away from instructional time. Tax cuts and the demand to spend extra funds on school security, plus the need for remediation of basic skills, make many school budgets inadequate.

Only major increases in public spending will improve the schools and promote the common good. But the rich and most corporations paid a higher percentage of taxes in the 1960s than they do today. As a result of the Reagan-Bush tax cuts in the 1980s, the corporate tax burden was shifted instead to the middle class. The rich, the middle class, and the elderly are assiduous voters and as a group have fewer children in public schools than do the poor and working class. The economically privileged tend to vote to limit taxes and to cut school spending, and elected officials respond to their demands. The poor seldom vote and the children cannot vote. Consequently, the needs of poor children have low priority among elected officials, who place little value on arguments for promoting the public good when aroused voters are demanding tax reductions.

Opposing political forces have reached a stalemate on the issue of providing sufficient funds to maintain a positive learning environment in schools. Teachers and their unions argue for smaller class sizes. Yet many conservatives respond that Japanese schools and Catholic schools have even larger class sizes and the students learn more. In an orderly, achievement-oriented society, large class sizes could be tolerated. However, in the present reality of most U.S. poverty-stricken communities, large class sizes increase student failure and teacher burnout.

Interaction of Race, Class, and Poverty

Research on race, class, and poverty in the United States and their cumulative effect on schools is notoriously inadequate. Media descriptions of poverty with their emphasis on sensationalism produce distorted images of poor inner-city youth and minorities. The isolation of teachers (many of whom live in the suburbs) from the communities surrounding their schools combines with a lack of parental participation to produce misunderstandings and the perpetuation of harmful stereotypes.

Multiple experiences and race, class, gender, age, and ethnicity factors combine to create an individual's cultural perspective. Psychologists have sought to measure a variety of characteristics such as motivation. For example, members of some social groups demonstrate a high motivation to succeed in school while members of others do not. Careless psychologists have attempted to ascribe these findings to ethnic and racial factors. They have described what they believed to be characteristics of Japanese American (positive), African American (negative), and Latino families (dependent) based on the observations of the motivation of the children of each group in school settings.

The subjects of stereotyping are not limited to racial and ethnic groups. There is class stereotyping as well. Michael Harrington (1928–1990) spent much of his life studying the poor and wrote dozens of books and articles on the subject. In 1962, he wrote *The Other America,* a landmark work on poverty in the United States. His research led directly to the war on poverty of the 1960s. In a lecture at Haverford College in 1988, Harrington reviewed decades of research on poverty and pointed out that the average poor family is white and headed by a person working fulltime at a low-paying job. Many of the poor are former middle-class women and children whose poverty is due primarily to divorce or spousal neglect to pay child support (Harrington, 1989). Feminist author, Barbara Ehrenreich, continued this research in her important book, *Fear of Falling: The Inner Life of the Middle Class* (1989).

One particularly large portion of the poor studied by Harrington was the people of Appalachia and other rural areas. Rural poverty is often not considered when considering social class. Yet, according to the U.S. Census Bureau, the states with the highest levels of poverty in 1993 were usually rural, beginning with Louisiana at 26.4%, Mississippi at 24.7%, West Virginia at 22.2%, Kentucky at 20.4%, and Arkansas at 20%. Other states with large rural areas followed closely, including Tennessee at 19.6%, Oklahoma at 19.9%, and New Mexico at 17.4%.

Appalachian children, among the most Anglo-Saxon heritage in our nation, also have a distinct culture that at times clashes with school expectations. The example of an "Appalachian" culture reveals the interaction of culture and class. A leader of the Urban Appalachian Council in Cincinnati, Ohio, describes the history of the group as follows:

> Over half a century ago the mechanization of the coal mining industry caused a mass migration from Kentucky, West Virginia, and other Appalachian states. Coal miners, farmers, and railroad men came with their families to nearby industrial cities to look for work. In the early years, work was easy to find. But the labor market was soon saturated with people who had little more to offer than willing hands and strong backs. Nonetheless, migrants continued to pour into the cities, drawn by the hope of a better life. For many families, the move to the cities proved permanent. Their children now have grandchildren, most of whom have no knowledge of life in the hills. Yet they, along with their parents and other more recent migrants, make up a distinct, but not easily defined cultural group.
>
> Urban Appalachians are called the "Invisible Minority" because, by such socio-economic measures as educational attainment, occupational status, income, and housing, Appalachians in urban areas are a distinct group that researchers have found to be significantly less advantaged than members of the majority community. But they are not easily identifiable as a minority, since race, sex, or surname in and of themselves do not set urban Appalachians apart from others. (Sullivan & Miller, 1990, p. 106–122)

Race and Class

Misunderstandings about the causal factors of school achievement occur because in our society there is a strong congruence between race and class. Educational failure by members of the lower class is often reported as a racial problem. But school failure is, in fact, a race-class problem. We collect clear data on race and confusing, indirect data on class. The Economic Policy Institute, in *The State of Working America* (Mishel & Frankel, 1990–1991), provides data on the interaction between poverty and race.

Middle-class, African American students and Chicano students succeed remarkably like their middle-class, European American peers. Meanwhile poor, downtrodden European American students fail remarkably like their poor, African American, and Chicano peers (MacLeod, 1987; Mehan, 1992).

Decades of research reveal the significance and complexity of the interactions between race, class, gender, and culture. For example, young children learn much of their culture at home, but in our society, teenagers learn an additional teen culture from their peers and from television. Race, class, gender, and age variables influence both the home and peer environments.

The secret of motivation is that its arousal depends both on the situation—with all of its components of culture, family, social class, and ethnic background—and the previous experiences of the individual. The complexity of factors makes it difficult to predict where the spark of motivation may appear. A student may lack motivation in science class and still respond competitively on the soccer field. For some students, lack of motivation is often a logical response to the student's own experiences of failure in school. A teacher who possesses and includes a cross-cultural perspective listens to youths and observes their culture. Observation and listening, not cultural and psychological stereotypes, assist the teacher in recognizing patterns and problems.

The Theories of a "Culture of Poverty" and the "Underclass"

In the 1960s, efforts to explain school failure among poor and minority children resulted in a theory termed "the culture of poverty." The less objectionable parts of this theory reemerged between 1976 and 1990 in a new controversial theory termed the "underclass."

Anthropologist Oscar Lewis (1968) originally developed the culture of poverty thesis to explain the relationship between economic conditions and cultural resistance patterns. Lewis noted that culture was the product of a specific historical situation and the dynamic interaction between families and their environment. He argued that living in extreme and chronic poverty produces defensive behaviors such as distrust of schools and government agencies. In Lewis' studies, these defensive, apathetic, or hostile behaviors were not a product of a specific cultural heritage but were learned in the interactions between families living in poverty and social institutions, including schools.

Middle-class educational researchers, not well-grounded in the context-specific nature of Lewis' anthropological perspective, sought immediate policy applications based on the thesis of a culture of poverty. Ideas about culture that were vague and inaccurate to begin with were overgeneralized to justify a series of compensatory educational programs. Researchers and policy advocates created harmful myths of cultural and language deprivation to explain the school failure of some children (Labov, 1970). The cultural and language deprivation theses became incorporated into teacher folk knowledge and curriculum plans.

A few of the reforms that emerged from the debates of the 1960s were successful, notably early childhood education. Compensatory education program services based on the culture of poverty thesis continue as important elements in school curriculum today through a federal program known as Chapter 1. But three decades of these programs have made only marginal improvements in the achievement gap between middle-class students and students living in poverty. The programs have never been adequately funded, but an additional problem is conceptual. Compensatory education programs and the culture of poverty thesis—as interpreted by a generation of mainly European American, mainly middle-class educational theorists—often worked from the unexamined assumption that there must be something wrong with poor people or they wouldn't be poor. The researchers of the 1960s studied the students and found fault with their cultures. They did not study the structures of schooling and therefore did not identify school practices as contributing to student failure. They failed to challenge fundamental practices within the educational system such as tracking and low teacher expectations that tend to restrict poor students to a school life of low aspirations and few opportunities.

In 1976, the sociologist William Jules Wilson began using the term *underclass* to describe the reality he saw in urban African American communities in inner-city Chicago. A serious scholar, he avoided the earlier misuses of the concept of a culture of poverty. Wilson's work, which is controversial, argues that class divisions are increasing between middle-class African Americans, working poor African Americans, and a very poor, marginalized, and isolated stratum of some African Americans in urban ghettos—the group to which the term *underclass* properly applies (Raymond, 1991; Wilson, 1987).

In Wilson's view, the Civil Rights Movement of the 1960s and the governmental policies that followed resulted mainly in the strengthening of the black middle class. The Civil Rights Movement secured political equality, and new government policies assisted some African Americans in leaving poor neighborhoods and finding good jobs, housing, and schooling. The African American middle class grew as a result of these gains. New opportunities were created in government, in education, and later in private industry for well-educated African Americans. Unfortunately, the African American lower class did not share in this prosperity. The rural farmer moving North from Georgia, the marginally employed resident of Harlem, Chicago, Gary, or Los Angeles gained the right to vote, but not economic opportunity.

Wilson's emphasis on the importance of economics in race relations followed the lead of Dr. Martin Luther King, Jr. Early on, King recognized the need for a broad, inclusive movement to promote economic justice as well as racial equality. The Southern Christian Leadership Conference (SCLC), along with others, promoted a multiracial struggle for economic justice with the Poor People's Campaign of 1967 through 1968. King and the SCLC developed their movement based in part on a critical awareness of the relationship between economic justice and political equality. King united the struggle for civil rights with union struggles and other efforts to end class oppression. Unfortunately, King was assassinated on April 4, 1968, before the Poor People's Campaign could organize a sustainable movement for economic justice.

In the 1970s, the U.S. economy changed. Major corporations closed their plants in the industrialized and unionized Northeastern United States, depriving hundreds of thousands of working-class African Americans and Latinos of good jobs and steady income. Plants moved to the South, the Southwest, and to Third World nations, devastating the economic base of the African American and Latino communities. Working-class union families lost their jobs or were pushed into marginal employment in low-paying service industries. The economic crisis of the 1970s devastated many African American families. Wilson describes the consequences of this economic shift in urban areas in his second major book, *The Truly Disadvantaged: The Inner City, The Underclass and Public Policy* (1987). The author meticulously explains how race and class interact to create an underclass among some African Americans.

Wilson contends that in the 1970s and 1980s the deterioration of central cities and the loss of union-wage jobs to the South and to Sunbelt regions and foreign competition left a marginally employed underclass behind in urban ghettos (Wilson, 1987). He argues that the flight of the middle class from Chicago left behind weakened neighborhood institutions and schools. A portion of society was set aside—apartheid style—as an area where drugs, crime, and neglect were considered normal and were tolerated. Today, children from these areas attend inferior schools and enjoy few opportunities for success.

Wilson's work offers an explanation of how race, class, and lack of government policy of economic growth work together to reinforce school failure. He recommends government policies to promote economic growth and change for the entire lower class. In his view, general programs for the poor, such as jobs and quality education, are preferable to racially specific programs, such as affirmative action.

Wilson does not argue that race is unimportant, only that the race-class variables interact. However, conservative ideologues have distorted Wilson's thesis to argue that the Civil Rights Movement and Black Power were to blame for poverty—a totally unsubstantiated assertion. As a result of such misinterpretations of the "underclass" thesis, Wilson has now argued for avoiding the use of the term.

The overextension and misuse of the concept of a "culture of poverty" and cultural deprivations indulged in earlier by educators in the 1960s should lead to caution in the use of the concept of the underclass. Unfortunately, educational researchers and the media have a long history of oversimplifying and rushing to apply new ideas. Predictably, the discussion of the underclass has not remained focused on the precise group described by Wilson. For example, researchers should—but often don't—distinguish between the working poor and members of the marginally employed underclass who, at times, find intermittent work in an illegal economy of theft, prostitution, and drugs. The two are separate groups; they are not all a part of a single "underclass" and their children have distinct educational experiences.

Even more damaging is the way the press has misrepresented the idea of an underclass to characterize all poor, urban African American families. Andrew Hacker, in *Two Nations, Black and White, Separate, Hostile, Unequal* (1992), more accurately describes the diversity among today's black families. He notes that over 40% of African American children live in a family with both parents. Both the growth of the black middle class and the continuation of the poor, but stable African American family challenge stereotypic notions of the underclass.

Further reading about the underclass in areas like Chicago, New York, Boston, Philadelphia, and Los Angeles does not tell teachers much about the life experiences of a child in mid-size cities like Sacramento, Portland, Seattle, or Denver. Nor does the concept of underclass adequately describe the experiences of Atlanta, Birmingham, New Orleans, and the other large cities of the South.

As constructed by Wilson, the underclass thesis describes conditions in large, northern urban ghettos where social institutions have failed and where some communities are dominated by gangs and the drug culture. Even in these devastated areas, not all of the families have lost the battle to guide their children. For these reasons, it is important that teachers avoid stereotypes about the underclass. Descriptions of family life need to be tested to see if they match the reality of an actual neighborhood served by an actual school.

For over two decades, distortions and errors harmful to children's lives have occurred when anthropologists, economists, educators, sociologists, and particularly psychologists, have attempted to describe students in poverty (for example, see McCarthy & Yencey, 1971; McDermott, 1974; Reidford, 1972). Most researchers are unaware of their class biases and the limits of their Eurocentric training. In the 1960s, some research claimed to find a "negative self-concept" in many African American children. Educational writers then assumed a negative self-concept existed in Mexican American children too. After all, it was argued, the two groups had similar school success rates. Drawing conclusions in such a simplistic and wholesale manner does real harm to the people affected. Such overextension is inaccurate, not helpful, and unfair. Psychological attributions of culturally specific information have often been abusive. Minimally, teachers should be wary of conclusions drawn about child-rearing behavior in one cultural group when these conclusions are based on the observations of a distinctly different cultural group.

Joan Moore (1988), in a paper on Hispanic poverty, demonstrated that Wilson's findings about urban black families should *not* be extended to describe urban Hispanics. While Latino poverty has grown substantially—and Latino family poverty is as acute as African American family poverty—the characteristics of community dissolution that are part of the underclass model are not present in most Latino families and neighborhoods (Moore, 1988; Tienda & Stier, 1991).

Hispanics include such diverse groups that it is impossible to formulate one accurate description of Hispanic family poverty (see Chapter 3). Both Mexican American and Puerto Rican families have suffered severe stress since the 1982 recession and are disproportionately suffering in the current economic restructuring (Moore, 1988; Pastor, 1993). But while Wilson noted that the flight of the black middle class left the largest urban ghettos with few supporting institutions intact, Moore observed that the family and community institutions in most Latino communities have not crumbled. Mexican and Mexican American family life, for example, is comparatively unified, stable, and supportive of education. The Catholic church has remained in the barrios and at times has become an immigrant church influenced by and receptive to Latino cultures. The steady flow of new immigrants with their folk culture and expectations of success has also positively influenced the Mexican American community. Moore (1988) concluded that the thesis of the "underclass" does not adequately describe poverty in the Hispanic community. In a similar manner, the responses of the predominantly Puerto Rican neighborhoods in New York, Newark, Chicago, and Milwaukee are not necessarily similar to the Mexican American experiences in San Antonio, El Paso, Los Angeles, San Diego, and Oakland.

School Responses to Poverty

As a response to the dramatic growth of poverty among children in the past 15 years, teachers need to improve on present school curriculum and work closely with community institutions. Classrooms need fewer disruptions. Teachers need more time to work with children. Special compensatory education programs must not interrupt the normal flow of classroom instruction. Children need a safe and orderly environment in order to learn basic skills (Institute for Puerto Rican Policy, 1991; Olson, 1987; Quality Education Project, 1990; U.S. Dept. of Education, 1987). Current supplementary federal and state programs designed to teach basic skills to poor children are underfunded and inadequate to meet the crisis of the rapidly growing population of the poor. Legislators and school administrators fail when they create new programs instead of using their resources to improve the teaching conditions. This endless parade of "experimental" programs wastes money by employing well-meaning bureaucrats and administrators instead of taking concrete steps, such as reducing class size, that would improve classroom conditions.

It is harmful and inaccurate to assume that children in poverty-stricken neighborhoods or from poor families have "characteristic" problems in school. Living in a poor neighborhood does not necessarily affect reading and math, although living in a violent and disruptive family or attending a violent and disruptive school might. A wide variety of people and families live in poverty. Some are chronically unemployed, low skilled, and even criminals. Most are not. The children of these families require extra counseling and support services not presently available. Most poor families have parenting skills and goals very similar to the middle class; they simply have less money.

Summary

A growing crisis of poverty, particularly among children, contributes to many of the failures in our school system. Multicultural education uses the concept of social class along with race, ethnicity, culture, and gender in describing, designing, and improving schools.

Schools serving poor communities are underfunded, staffed with less experienced teachers, and frequently practice tracking by presumed ability. These school practices, not the individual characteristics of children, provide unequal educational opportunity and produce failure. Federally funded and directed compensatory education programs have not remedied the problems of our failing schools in poverty areas. A multicultural perspective helps to design new strategies to attack these continuing problems.

Questions Over the Chapter

1. List factors that contributed to the significant increase in the number of children living in poverty in the 1970s and 1980s.
2. What are differences between the concepts of *social class* and *socioeconomic status?*
3. List three recommendations for school improvement from each conceptual scheme:

Socioeconomic Status
a.
b.
c.

Social Class
a.
b.
c.

4. Explain the differences in poverty rates for African American, Latino, and European American children. How do these differences occur?
5. From 1967 to 1968, Dr. Martin Luther King, Jr., and the Southern Christian Leadership Council expanded their emphasis from civil rights to include economic justice.

a. What were the important elements of an economic justice agenda in the 1960s?

b. Describe the elements of an economic justice agenda today.

6. What are the differences in policy between a racial analysis and a race-class analysis of school achievement?

7. What can schools and teachers do to respond to the rise in poverty among children?

Activities for Further Study of Class Relationships in Schools

1. Observe and document the broad spectrum of diversity found in a classroom, such as culture, ethnicity, gender, social class, gifted and talented.
   a. What are the different groups in the class?
   b. How many of each?
   c. Does the teacher devote more time to certain students or groups?
   d. Are certain students singled out for criticism and punishment?
   e. Are any groups of students treated in a different manner? Are female students treated differently than males? How? Are fast or slow learners treated differently? How?

2. Conduct observations of classes at several school sites. Using the following criteria, work in groups to compare your observations of middle-class schools and schools in poverty areas.
   a. Teacher optimism / teacher stress
   b. School facilities
   c. Discipline systems used
   d. Parent participation, parent respect

3. Take a walking tour of the immediate neighborhood of the school in which you are working. Record your impressions and share them with your classmates.

4. Describe your own current social class position. Compare this position to that of your family.

5. Compare the social class positions of students in your teacher preparation program with those of the school children you serve.

List some class differences between teachers and students—for example, attitudes toward fighting, manners, and other differences.

6. Identify and describe problems of economic achievement that are related to social class.

7. Find references to the "underclass" in educational periodicals and the press. What other terms are used for this social group? How do writers define the underclass?

8. What assumptions are made about the race of members of the underclass?

9. Ask a sociologist or an ethnic studies professor to describe the differences in race-class interactions in various regions of the country.

10. Investigate the class connotations of using the term *Hispanic* rather than *Puerto Rican, Mexican,* or another term. How do persons who use each term see their own class position?

11. Conduct research on the educational success and conflicts of poor, European American children from the Appalachian regions of our country. See the *Foxfire* books edited by Eliot Wigginton.

12. Define a culture of poverty. Describe a group and location where European Americans live in the culture of poverty.

13. Thirty-nine percent of all recipients of Aid to Families with Dependent Children (AFDC) are European Americans, 37% are African American, and 18% are Latinos, yet the stereotype of a welfare recipient is a woman of color. Explain this misperception. What role do the media play in forming our stereotypes?

Teaching Strategies

1. Find literature, music, and videos that begin in the students' own experiences and reach to universal themes and skills.
2. Validate the students' own language and culture.
3. Integrate reading, oral, and written language instruction and skills into several subject-matter areas.
4. Include hands-on learning activities whenever possible.
5. Plan and teach specific study skills as a part of the curriculum. Begin at the students' actual skill level. Teach the use of texts, paragraph writing, and other necessary skills.
6. Maintain the goal of reading and writing at the skill level of the middle-class, suburban schools (or state standards). Do not lower your expectations for achievement. (See Chapter 9.)
7. Teach standard appropriate academic English as a valuable system of communication in addition to the students' vernacular expressions.
8. Use cooperative learning strategies and encourage student-to-student dialogue. (See Chapter 10.)
9. Build a classroom climate of safety, trust, and community building.
10. Study and encourage pro-school values.

References

Bartlett and Steele. (1992). *America: What went wrong?* Kansas City, KS: Andrews & McMeel.

Bowles, S., & Gintis, H. (1976). *Schooling in capitalist America: Educational reform and the contradictions of economic life.* New York: Basic Books.

California Commission on Educational Quality (The Christopher Commission). (1988, June). *A strategy for high performance education in California.* Sacramento: Author.

Carnoy, M., & Levin, H. (1985). *Schooling and work in the democratic state.* Stanford, CA: Stanford University Press.

Center on Budget and Policy Priorities. (1988). *Shortchanged: Recent developments in Hispanic poverty, income and employment.* Washington, DC: Author.

The Center for Popular Economics. (1987). *A field guide to the U.S. economy.* New York: Pantheon Books.

Children's Defense Fund. (1989). *A vision for America's future.* Washington, DC: Author.

DeParle, J. (1994, March 31). Sharp increases along borders of poverty. *New York Times,* A-18.

Ehrenreich, B. (1989). *Fear of falling: The inner life of the middle class.* New York: Pantheon.

Ehrenreich, B., & Ehrenreich, J. (1979). The professional-managerial class. In Pat Walker (Ed.). *Between Labor and Capital* (pp. 5–45). Boston: South End Press.

Hacker, A. (1992). *Two nations: Black and white, separate, hostile, unequal.* New York: Charles Scribner's Sons.

Harrington, M. (1964). *The other America: Poverty in the United States.* New York: Macmillan.

Harrington, M. (1989). "The new American poverty." Lecture delivered at Haverford College, Haverford, PA.

Institute for Puerto Rican Policy. (1991). *The Puerto Rican exception: Persistent poverty and the conservative social policy of Linda Chavez.* New York: Author.

Jargowsky, P. A., & Bane, M. J. (1991). Ghetto poverty in the U.S., 1970–1980. In *The Urban Underclass* (pp. 235–273). Washington, DC: The Brookings Institutions.

Kozol, J. (1991). *Savage inequalities: Children in America's schools.* New York: Crown Publishing.

Kuhn, T. S. (1970). *The structure of scientific revolutions* (2nd ed.). Chicago: University of Chicago Press.

Labov, W. (1970). *The study of nonstandard English.* Champaign, IL: National Council of Teachers of English.

Lewis, O. (1968). Culture of poverty. *Scientific American, 215*(4), 19–24.

MacLeod, J. (1987). *Ain't no making it: Leveled aspirations in a low-income neighborhood.* Boulder, CO: Westview Press.

Marshall, R., & Tuker, M. (1992). *Thinking for a living: Education and the wealth of nations.* New York: Basic Books.

McCarthy, J. D., Yencey, W. L. (1971, January). Uncle Tom and Mr. Charlie: Metaphysical pathos in the study of racism and personal disorganization. *American Institute of Sociology, 76,* 648–672.

McDermott, R. P. (1974). Achieving school failure: An anthropological approach to illiteracy and school stratification. In G. Spindler (Ed.), *Education and Cultural Process* (pp. 173–209). New York: Holt.

Mehan, H. (1992, January). Understanding inequality in schools: The contributions of interpretive studies. *Sociology of Education, 65,* 1–20.

Mishel, L., & Frankel, M. (1990–1991). *The state of waking America.* Armonk, NY: Economic Policy Institute.

Moore, J. (1988, April). *An assessment of Hispanic poverty: Is there an Hispanic underclass?* San Antonio, TX: Thomas Rivera Center.

National Center for Children in Poverty. (1991, Fall). *News and issues.* New York: Columbia University Press.

Olson, L. *Crossing the schoolhouse border: Immigrant students and the California public schools.* San Francisco: A California Tomorrow Policy Research Report.

Orefield, G., & Ashkinage, C. (1991). *The closing door: Conservative policy and black opportunity.* Chicago: University of Chicago Press.

Parker, R. (1972). *The myth of the middle class.* New York & San Francisco: Harper & Row.

Pastor, M. (1993). *Latinos and the Los Angeles uprising: The economic context.* Claremont, CA: Thomas Rivera Center.

Pickney, A. (1990). *The myth of black progress.* Cambridge, MA: Cambridge University Press.

Quality Education Project. (1990). *Education that works: An action plan for the education of minorities.* Cambridge, MA: MIT.

Raymond, C. (1991, October 30). Results from a Chicago project lead social scientists to a rethinking of the urban underclass. *Chronicle of Higher Education,* p. A9.

Reich, R. B. (1991). *The work of nations: Preparing ourselves for 21st century capitalism.* New York: Alfred A. Knopf.

Reidford, R. (1972). Educational research. In C. Weinberg (Ed.), *Humanistic foundations of education* (pp. 257–280). New York: Prentice-Hall.

Rose, S. (1992). *Social stratification in the United States: The American profile poster* (rev.). New York: New Press.

Sawicky, M. B. (1991). *The roots of the public sector fiscal crisis.* Washington, DC: Economic Policy Institute.

Sharp, R. (1993, September 14). Losing ground: In latest recession only Blacks suffered net employment loss. *Wall Street Journal,* pp. A1, 12, 13.

Sullivan, M., & Miller, D. (1990, February). Cincinnati's Urban Appalachian Council and Appalachian identity. *Harvard Educational Review,* pp. 105–124.

Tienda, M., & Stier, H. (1991). Joblessness and shiftlessness: Labor force activity in Chicago's inner city. In C. Jenks & P. E. Peterson, (Eds.), *The Urban Underclass* (pp. 135–154). Washington, DC: The Brookings Institutions.

UNESCO. (1993). *The progress of nations.* New York: United Nations.

U.S. Department of Education. (1987). *Schools that work: Educating disadvantaged children.*

Walker, P. (Ed.). (1979). *Between Labor and Capital.* Boston: South End Press.

Warner, W. L. (1949). *Democracy in Jonesville: A study in quality and inequality.* New York: Harper & Brothers.

Wilson, W. J. (1978). *The declining significance of race.* Chicago: Univeristy of Chicago Press.

Wilson, W. J. (1987). *The truly disadvantaged: The inner city, the underclass and public policy.* Chicago: University of Chicago Press.

Wilson, W. J. (1988, May / June). The ghetto underclass and the social transformation of the inner city. *The Black Scholar,* pp. 10–17.

Wilson, W. J. (1988). The black community in the 1980s: Questions of race, class and public policy.

Wilson, W. J. (1991). Public policy research and the truly disadvantaged. In C. Jenks & P. E. Peterson (Eds.), *The Urban Underclass.* Washington, DC: The Brookings Institutions.

Chapter 5

How Society and Schools Shortchange Girls and Boys[1]

There are strong similarities between sexism and racism. Both are oppressions. Both teach role relationships that leave one group in a subordinate position. Both are primarily expressed through institutional arrangements of privilege for some and oppression for others. Both are forms of violence: individual and collective, psychological and physical. Just as previous chapters described how African Americans, Latinos, and Native Americans, among others, are harmed by low expectations, being female also leads to subtle forms of tracking—even by female teachers.

In *Race, Gender and Work* (1991), Teresa Amott and Jule Matthaei argue that gender, like race, is as much a social as a biological category:

> [G]ender differences in the social lives of men and women are based on, but not the same thing as, biological differences between the sexes. Gender is rooted in societies' beliefs that the sexes are naturally distinct and opposed social beings. These beliefs are turned into self-fulfilling prophecies through sex-role socialization; the biological sexes are assigned distinct and often unequal work and political positions, and turned into distinct genders. (p. 13)

[1] This chapter was written by **Duane Campbell** and **Dolores Delgado Campbell**.

The school site is a stage on which gender roles are developed in our society, and thus schools contribute to the assignment of unequal status and work opportunity in our rapidly changing economy. Schools serve as "gatekeepers" providing opportunity to some, but not to all.

Between 1983 and 1992, the press, elected officials, and corporate advocacy groups conducted a national debate, loosely called the "educational reform movement," concerning the role and future of public education in the United States. The leading "experts" in this debate avoided discussions of race, class, and gender issues whenever possible. In 1992, the American Association of University Women (AAUW) issued a report, *How Schools Shortchange Girls*, that responded to the avoidance of gender issues:

> The absence of attention to girls in the current educational debate suggests that girls and boys have identical educational experiences in schools. Nothing could be further from the truth. Whether one looks at achievement scores, curriculum design, self-esteem levels, or staffing patterns, it is clear that sex and gender make a difference in the nation's public elementary and secondary schools. There is clear evidence that the educational system is not meeting girls' needs. Girls and boys enter school roughly equal in measured ability. In some measures of school readiness, such as fine motor control, girls are ahead of boys. Twelve years later, girls have fallen behind their male classmates in key areas such as higher-level mathematics and measures of self-esteem. (p. 2)

Tracking Female Students

For girls, especially middle-class, European American girls, attending school in the United States means getting a head start in the early grades only to be held back or diverted into less-challenging fields in the higher grades, a system called *tracking*.

Tracking occurs in our schools despite the fact that the schools are predominantly female turf. For example, women now constitute a majority of all college students and 73% of all teachers, concentrated particularly at the elementary school level. In California, the primary schools are basically female-dominated institutions. In Los Angeles, for example, over 70% of the teachers and over half of the administrators in K–6 elementary schools are female (Los Angeles County, 1991).

The women in charge of these schools are usually European American. In most elementary schools, girls are not systematically disparaged and criticized for being girls, although they may be disparaged for being lower class Latinas, African Americans, or Asians. The emotions and turmoil of middle-class European American girls are sympathetically understood by elementary school authorities, both teachers and principals. The female-dominated institution produces female success during the critical early years when the child is defining her own identity and her relationship to learning and schooling (NEA, 1990; Sadker, Sadker, & Long, 1989).

Self-Esteem

Although racism and sexism both have damaging effects on the oppressed and the oppressor, their manifestations in the early years of school are often quite different from their adult forms. While the excellent AAUW report argues that positive cross-sex relationships may be more difficult than cross-race relationships, in elementary schools the problem is more complex. This is because families and schools generally are much better at giving young children positive cross-gender experiences than they are at giving them positive cross-racial experiences. Several examples of these positive cross-gender experiences can be seen in the home.

Children develop a view of self in their very early years, usually in the intimate and nurturing surroundings of the home. Evidence indicates that children learn both about themselves and about others by at least age 4. Generally most of this learning of "appropriate" role relationships takes place under the guidance of females, either in the home or in child care.

When children or adults work in an intimate relationship with another person in a positive environment, they learn to like and respect that person. This equal status interaction teaches mutual respect (Buteyn, 1989; NEA, 1990; Sadker et al., 1989). Almost all little boys have an intimate, trust-building relationship or an equal-status relationship with at least one female—usually their mother. In the early formative years, most boys learn to respect and love their mother or some other female caregiver, such as a grandmother or aunt. Few young boys learn to dominate their mothers. This early relationship should provide a basis for future learning of mutual respect and cooperation in relationships with women.

Of course, this picture does not match the experience of all children. In a home with an abusive or dominating male, the child may learn abusive and dominating patterns. In homes with a single female head of household, a boy could still learn a respectful relationship. In some such homes, however, a boy may fail to experience positive relationships with males. He then may get his guidance from television and the streets—both inadequate substitutes for a caring family. However, generally speaking, prior to age 6, most young boys and girls learn to interact with their peers without male dominance. Their early experience of respect and cooperation provides a basis for future equality-based relationships.

While our families provide opportunities for cross-gender respect, they seldom provide opportunities for cross-racial respect. Our neighborhoods, cities, and families are segregated by race and culture. Most of our cities are more racially segregated in 1990 than they were in 1960. Too many of our young children do not develop an intimate, loving, caring relationship with persons of other races.

Like our neighborhoods, the teaching profession is increasingly female and racially segregated. As a result, too few young students have a positive relationship with a teacher from a minority culture. The lack of this intimate, perception-shaping experience makes the learning of mutual respect and cooperation in cross-cultural relationships more difficult. Children learn to fear the other, the outsider. This fear establishes a basis for future learning of prejudice.

The lack of cultural diversity in the upbringing and schooling of young children hits the children of minority cultures hardest. When African American, Vietnamese, or Latina girls enter school, they enter a new culture, often one where they are regarded as "other," different, and inferior. The shock may be profound. Some of these children may suddenly feel uncertain about themselves and become withdrawn or defensive. Their ability to learn also suffers. Too often failure and frustration in school attacks the student's self-image and distorts the student's view of her home culture (Au & Kawakami, 1994; Foster, 1994). Young girls (and boys) of color first experience an inferior, caste-like status in their neighborhood school.

Entering school is a major, traumatic event in the lives of many girls (and boys) from these cultures. The average African American or Latina student enters school a few months behind their middle-class counterparts in skill development. They fall progressively behind for the next 12 years. Although schools may not be the primary source of this society's oppressions, they are the institutions where the tracking, labeling, and failing first occur.

The work of Jeannie Oakes (1988) documents the negative results of tracking African American and Latina youths away from college-bound classes and into general classes, homemaking, and business courses. New evidence indicates that Catholic schools track Latinas less than do public schools (Oakes, 1985).

Research on European American Girls

School failure and intrusion are substantially different for European American girls than for racial and linguistic minorities. The studies by Sadker et al. (1989) and others (which focus mainly on European American girls) show that gender-based bias in school is significant and powerful. Some schools still track girls to mothering roles and boys to college. By high school, girls score lower than boys on some math and science measures. Since these courses are prerequisites for entrance into traditionally male, well-paying careers, these differences in scores are not acceptable.

In the primary grades, the oppression of girls takes different forms. The average girl enters school academically ahead of boys her age and remains ahead (as measured by grades and test scores) through the elementary grades. The research collected by the AAUW is excellent, but the recommendations are limited substantially to European American girls. The major problems of school achievement for these girls occur after they leave the female turf of elementary schools. A multiracial perspective on gender and student achievement leads to quite different conclusions for girls and boys of color.

Unlike students of color, young European American girls do not come to school and encounter a new environment run by "others." These girls go from a usually female-centered home culture to a female-centered school culture.

Schools and teachers have positive expectations for them. Young, middle-class, European American girls do not encounter the substantially destructive attacks on their gender that young minority children (male or female) encounter on their culture. When students share class, race, and gender with the teacher or the counselor, they are usually encouraged to "become the best they can be." When the female student is from a minority culture, she often encounters the oppression of race and class in school.

Fortunately, gender-role stereotyping in schools is decreasing, but it remains a problem (AAUW, 1992). The efforts to reduce gender stereotyping among teachers create new questions about school achievement across cultural groups.

It is boys who lack role models for the first six years of schooling, particularly African American, Latino, and Asian boys. While young, European American girls benefit from their female-centered primary school experience, children of color—particularly boys—fail. It is boys who encounter the most conflicts and receive the most punishments in school and most often get placed in special education and remedial programs.

The positive school experiences of girls begin to change in adolescence. The teenage years in our society are a time of redefining self and roles. Young girls and boys who were once self-confident, now search for new identities. Earlier self-definitions shift. For many teenagers, belonging to a group becomes a major goal. Young people look to their peers for guidance through these difficult and troubling years.

School girls, at least those European American girls studied, suffer significant declines in self-esteem as they move from childhood to adolescence. The report, *How Schools Shortchange Girls*, (1992) states:

> A nation-wide study commissioned by the A.A.U.W. in 1990 found that on average 69 percent of elementary school boys and 60 percent of elementary school girls reported that they were "happy the way I am"; among high school students the percentages were 46 percent for boys and only 29 percent for girls.
>
> The A.A.U.W. survey revealed sharp differences in self-esteem among girls from different racial and ethnic groups. Among elementary school girls, 55 percent of white girls, 65 percent of black girls, and 68 percent of Hispanic girls reported being "happy the way I am." But in high school, agreement statements came from only 22 percent of white girls and 30 percent of Hispanic girls, compared to 58 percent of black girls. However, these black girls did not have high levels of self-esteem in areas related to school. . . . Obviously, self-esteem is a complex construct, and further study of the various strengths and perspectives of girls from many different backgrounds is needed in order to design educational programs that benefit all girls. (pp. 12–13)

Young girls who excelled in elementary school may begin to falter as they enter the middle grades (6 through 8). Particular concern has been expressed by teachers over the falling grades of girls in science and math (AAUW, 1992). One apparent reason is that young boys are often more assertive than girls are in classes. They receive more teacher attention, both positive and negative. Carol Gilligan's groundbreaking work *In a Different Voice* (1982) developed a hypothesis that many girls acquire feminine ways of learning and relating to others that are distinctly different from the behavior described as universal to boys and girls by psychologists. Gilligan, in critiquing prominent theories of moral behavior, says "While the truths of psychological theory have blinded psychologists to the truth of women's experience, that experience illuminates a world psychologists have found hard to trace" (p. 62). Another researcher, Deborah Tannen, in *You Just Don't Understand* (1990), describes differences in communication styles learned by boys and girls.

The writing and research of feminist authors also provide important insights in classroom differences. Carol Tavris, in *The Mismeasure of Woman: Why Women Are Not the Better Sex, the Inferior Sex, or the Opposite Sex* (1992), systematically examines the research on differences between males and females and finds many assumptions and assertions to be overgeneralized beyond the available evidence. *The Mismeasure of Woman* provides an excellent analysis of over-interpretation from limited data, criticizing work in learning styles, brain activity, as well as Carol Gilligan's assumptions about value orientations and relationships. We must assume, until proven otherwise, that female and male differences do not explain and do not cause the differences in school achievement; The differences can be attributed to how the teachers and the schools treat the children (Tannen, 1990; Tavris, 1992).

Research by Carol Dweck and her associates (1977) suggests that girls may learn "helplessness" in math based in part on teacher expectations and the way a teacher responds to and evaluates the student's work. Teachers of either gender could unknowingly concentrate their responses to girls in a way that discourages intellectual effort, particularly in math (Dweck, 1977).

By high school, girls begin to make career choices. Influenced in part by the ideology of movies, television, teen magazines, and popular culture, some young women learn to prefer nonacademic and nonrigorous classes. They come to regard intellectually challenging classes as "unfeminine." This assault on feminism is described by Susan Faludi in *Backlash: The Undeclared War Against American Women* (1991). In her book, Faludi argues that some current counseling practices continue to track girls to become nurses rather than doctors, legal secretaries rather than lawyers, elementary school teachers rather than college professors. In their immaturity, some young women dream they can escape work by becoming models or movie stars. The AAUW reports that between 40% and 50% of female dropouts leave school because they are pregnant. Their child care responsibilities sharply limit their future economic opportunities. Later, deprived of a quality education, they will find themselves laboring long hours doing unfulfilling work for low pay in a gender-stratified workforce.

The Lure of the Beauty Myth

Many girls and young women become preoccupied with their personal image and their relationships with others. Later, by high school, this becomes the "beauty and romance" myth. Television and popular media teach that a girl can achieve success, defined as marriage and wealth, by becoming beautiful and shrewdly using her sexual powers.

In *The Beauty Myth: How Images of Beauty Are Used Against Women* (1991), Naomi Wolf describes some of the destructive effects of the beauty industry and its ideology. As Wolf describes, the myth is that girls do not need to prepare for a career; they can just be beautiful and become a model, a star, or at least a mother. The male equivalent of this myth is to plan to become a major league baseball player or basketball star and make millions of dollars.

This belief in a magic alternative to hard work misleads both young women and men, but the beauty industry is built on it. Our communications media—especially television and popular magazines—are saturated with the consumer pitch that beauty, popularity, and acceptance can be bought. Girls who succumb to this myth feel secure only when they have a date or when they establish their value in relationship to a boy. In *The Beauty Myth*, Wolf argues that girls' self-esteem may be predicated on being admired by boys, usually for their physical beauty or sexual availability. Many young girls work hard and diet hard in pursuit of physical beauty. Powerful advertising sells the myths of beauty and romance. Television also sells a current culture of assertive, at times irresponsible, sexuality that successfully competes with school culture. Television, consumerism, and teen magazines shape teenage girls' worldview more than does their school experience. For many, the shopping mall is the campus of choice.

Limited Choices for Non-College-Bound Women

Unfortunately, the typical U.S. high school has little to offer non-college-bound female students in the way of technical and professional preparation. Business courses, for example, offer little more than secretarial training.

The conservative school reform movement (1982–1992) sought to reestablish a common academic curriculum for all students in high school. Schools concentrated their time, energy, and funds on improving academic programs. Opportunities for college-bound students improved. But in their emphasis on academic excellence, these reformers neglected vocational preparation—a critical omission at a time when job opportunities and the skills needed to take advantage of them were rapidly changing. Thus the post-high school opportunities of non-college-bound students became more restricted than ever (Weis, 1988, 1990).

In some states, young women may receive quality technical preparation in public community college programs. Overall, however, young women suffer from the society's failure to recognize the need for high-skilled, non-college preparatory programs. The development of high technology career preparation programs, such as proposed by President Bill Clinton, may offer improved opportunities in the future.

Teachers can assist students in taking advantage of school opportunities by sharing their own life histories and by encouraging young women to get a good education. Young women, 16- to 18-years old, often look and dress in an adult manner. Many even engage in adult sexual behavior. Yet their consciousness of the reality of the working world remains underdeveloped. Young women, including those on the beauty track, need to be encouraged to pursue a well-rounded, rigorous education. When female teachers share experiences from their own lives, this sharing validates the experiences of the younger women. Sharing adds a mature view to questions of career choices and sexual roles.

Feminist scholarship argues that girls benefit in school from assistance in developing self-confidence, rather than relying on beauty images. Girls should receive praise for their intellectual work, not for their conformity and obedience to marketed images of women. Further suggestions and strategies on developing positive self-esteem are found in Chapter 6.

Female teachers can gain insight into the complex and changing needs of girls in school by reflecting on their own lives. After a day of teaching, they return home to do over 80% of the housework, cooking, cleaning, shopping, and child rearing. The economy profits from women's work without providing rewards, support (such as child care), or even simple recognition for the extraordinary effort required of successful women in our society.

Gender, Race, and Class

The importance of gender issues can change from one generation to the next and is specific to different cultures. It is often difficult or impossible to separate race, class, and gender discrimination since the oppressions interact with each other. Research on the school behavior of girls and young women of color was notably absent, even in the AAUW report. Most researchers have assumed that young girls have similar experiences across cultures.

Women of color have gained university positions and political leadership in recent decades and have turned their research skills to documenting the conflicts faced by African American, Latina, and working-class girls in schools. Michele Fine has documented some of the ways young women face and react to sex education in high schools. In *Beyond Silenced Voices: Class, Race, and Gender in United States Schools* (1993), Fine and coeditor Lois Weis have collected several powerful essays that begin to move beyond the more restricted early research boundaries of European American women.

A particular concern has been voiced concerning the destructive impact on African American children, particularly boys, of common public school practices usually carried out in elementary schools by female European American teachers. Joyce King, Michele Foster, and Gloria Ladson-Billings, among others, have documented several of the most basic issues facing African American girls and boys in classrooms in *Teaching Diverse Populations: Formulating a Knowledge Base* (Hollins, King, & Hayman, 1994). And they have suggested some characteristics and tendencies in the African American culture that teachers can use as background information to reduce the cultural conflicts in the classroom and to improve student achievement.

The predominantly European American teaching profession needs research like that listed to begin to understand the diverse classroom roles of girls and boys within specific cultures. For example, young Latinas who succeed often have supportive parents, particularly their mothers (Gandara, 1982). These insights support the importance of schools offering programs to develop parental support for education and for attending college. For example, successful programs of uniting mothers and daughters have developed in San Antonio, Texas, and in the *Adelante Latina* conferences in California.

One persistent social myth is that women do most of the work in the home and men do most of the work outside the home. In *Race, Gender and Work,* Amott and Matthaei (1991) provide a multicultural history of how farm and working-class women have labored for wages in increasing numbers since the beginning of the Industrial Revolution in the 1840s. The great historical and social events of the twentieth century—the Great Depression (1929–1939), the shift from a rural to an urban society, and the worker shortages caused by World War II—brought even more women into the paid labor force. More recently the economic stagnation that began in the 1970s has produced a dramatic increase in the numbers of middle-class women entering the paid workforce. While over 50% of all women of color have been in the paid labor force since the 1950s, since the 1970s over 50% of *all* women over age 16 have worked for wages. See Figures 5.1 and 5.2 (Amott & Matthaei, 1991).

In the United States, many women of color must assume extra responsibilities to protect and advance their community's interests. African American women, for example, are often looked to as the centers of strength and the source of leadership within their communities. Because they are regarded by the macroculture as less threatening than African American men, African American women may be less impeded and more accepted as they assume positions of responsibility in their communities or seek career advancement in the professional world. Cornel West (1993) describes the fear of black men and the acceptance of African American women as in part a result of "psychosexual racist logic." Yet many African American women are well prepared for their role as economic providers. Many African societies had strong female leadership. Slavery forced a matrifocal family structure on the African American community. The women of many African American families have drawn strength from this long tradition of female leadership.

Latinas share many of the racially based economic burdens of African American women, including the responsibility to care for the elderly and extended families. Strong female leadership was also common in many Meso American societies prior to the Spanish conquest. Currently, matrifocal family structures have developed in Mexico in response to the migration of millions of male farm workers to labor in U.S. agricultural fields. Most Mexican American and Latino families in the United States remain patriarchal, similar to those in the dominant European American society. Girls and young women have paid a price for

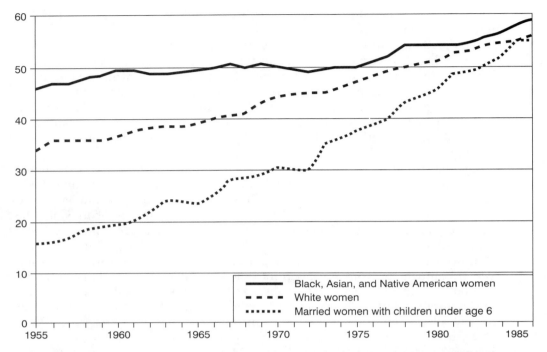

Figure 5.1   Labor Force Participation Rates for Women in the United States, 1955–1985

Note. The rates reported are for women age 16 and older. From *A Field Guide to the U.S. Economy, 1985–1995* (p. 3.1) by Center for Popular Economics, Amherst, MA. Reprinted with permission.

Figure 5.2   Percentages of U.S. Families with Incomes Below the Poverty Level, 1992

Note. From *A Field Guide to the U.S. Economy, 1985–1995* (p. 6.4) by Center for Popular Economics, Amherst, MA. Reprinted with permission.

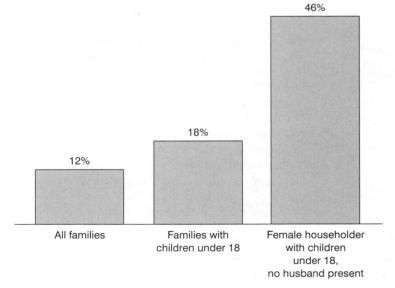

this continued patriarchy, lagging behind African American women in entrance into college and professional schools until the 1990s.

The oppression of African American and Latina women and some rural European American women has taught them to work in cooperative communities. Families take care of the elderly, care for children troubled by divorce and abandonment, and take extended family members (cousins, aunts, etc.) into their homes. In these communities, women serve on the school-parent advisory councils and keep the churches functioning. Women are the primary social service providers in these communities.

School curriculum should acknowledge and recognize the extensive contributions of women to the community's health. The female-centered home and community provide a rich and extensive breadth of background knowledge on which to build an educational curriculum. In *Community Knowledge and Classroom Practice: Combining Resources for Literacy Instruction,* Luis Moll and his colleagues (1992) assert that when classrooms draw on this community knowledge and use it to advance literacy instruction, the children gain. Curriculum and literacy efforts should give more emphasis to women's contributions to provide role models for female students and to counterbalance the devaluation of women by the media and the patriarchal traditions of the macroculture.

While European American women have attended colleges since the 1840s and African American women have had access to the traditionally black colleges that rose up in the South after Reconstruction, substantial numbers of other women of color did not gain access to higher education until the 1970s. The development of both ethnic studies and women's studies on campuses has opened new doors of scholarship and expression. In a pioneering book, *This Bridge Called My Back* (Moraga & Anzaldúa, 1981), women of color spoke eloquently about the nature of male / female roles and the issue of male domination within their respective communities. Gloria Anzaldúa, in *Borderlands / La Frontera: The New Mestiza* (1987), testifies in verse and prose about her own interconnected struggles of race, class, gender, culture, and sexual preference.

An outpouring of African American, Latina, Native American, and Asian women writers has redefined women's sphere in the United States to include women of color. Amy Tan, Gloria Anzaldúa, Maya Angelou, bell hooks, Olivia Castellano, Paula Gunn Allen, Wilma Mankiller, Marian Wright Edelman, and others provide insights into the diverse voices and insights of the many peoples of our nation.

Currently, college-bound students are benefiting from changing work opportunities and the victories of the feminist movement. Title IX victories, apprenticeship programs, mentoring, and women's studies have opened important new opportunities. Title IX (1972) describes the federal commitment to equal gender treatment in matters of federal assistance:

> No person . . . shall, on the basis of sex, be denied the benefits of, or be subjected to, discrimination under any education program or activity receiving federal financial assistance. . . .

Special programs provide additional counseling and encouragement for Latinas and African American women to attend college. Well-educated young women are choosing careers as doctors, attorneys, and politicians.

As yet, however, the benefits and advantages of the feminist revolution of the 1970s are seldom apparent in the school lives and career opportunities of the 50% of women high school graduates who do not go on to college.

Women's Story in the Textbooks

Although feminist scholarship has made strides in the university, this progress is only beginning to have a significant impact on public school textbooks. Mary Kay Thompson Tetreault, Cherrie Moraga, and Gloria Anzaldúa have written about the invisibility and fragmentation of women's history, particularly women of color, in literature and text illustrations (Moraga & Anzaldúa, 1981; Tetreault, 1989).

Some progress is being made. Publishers have started to delete linguistic bias and to use gender-neutral terms. States are requiring that texts move beyond depicting women in stereotypic roles. The National Women's History Project has developed excellent new materials to overcome invisibility.

Students seem to develop self-esteem and a sense of being socially centered when they see their role models in books and other educational materials. Women's literature, history, and sociology assist female students in evaluating their own experiences and traumas. Readings in these areas can help young women gain perspective on the pressures of surrendering self and goals for temporary status and temporary relationships. Social history and popular histories record the extensive participation of women in building our communities, our public schools, and social institutions. Readings from the eras in which the "cult of true womanhood" was promoted (1800–1860) help students to reflect on how public images and role models can promote profit-seeking rather than developing human potential. Readings from the Progressive Era (1890–1920) help students to see how immigrant women organized unions and (European American) women made significant advances in attending colleges and entering the professions.

The curriculum should be authentic, realistic, and inspirational. Reform requires more than adding a few new heroines to existing textbooks. The writings and speeches of Dolores Huerta, Fannie Lou Hamer, Shirley Chisholm, and others are important additions to the curriculum.

Women students can keep journals to reflect on their own lives. Recording a journal helps young girls through times of doubt and insecurity, as does developing friendships. Teenage girls can learn to accept themselves as they are and build a positive future instead of dreaming of cosmetic makeovers.

Young women also gain from learning about the leadership and activism of women in their communities. Working-class women and women of color have raised families and survived. They have created a positive life for their children. Presenting guest speakers from the community teaches that average, normal people run unions, institutions, and essential community organizations. Guest speakers bridge the gap between the school and adult reality. The curriculum empowers and motivates students when it presents hope and optimism without presenting a superwoman model of accomplishment.

In the American Association of University Women report (1992), curriculum researcher Gretchen Wilbur states that a gender-fair curriculum has six attributes:

1. *Variation,* that is, similarities and differences among and within groups of people;
2. *Inclusive,* allowing both females and males to find and identify positively with messages about themselves;
3. *Accurate,* presenting information that is data-based, verifiable, and able to withstand critical analysis;
4. *Affirmative,* acknowledging and valuing the worth of individuals and groups;
5. *Representative,* balancing multiple perspectives; and
6. *Integrated,* weaving together the experiences, needs, and interests of both males and females. (p. 64)

Wilbur and the AAUW report argue that so far no major curriculum reform efforts have explicitly used gender-fair approaches.

The AAUW report offers a list of over 40 action items for change. The following 13 items from the list can be pursued by teachers:

1. Teachers must help girls develop positive views of themselves and their futures, as well as an understanding of the obstacles women must overcome in a society where their options and opportunities are still limited by gender stereotypes and assumptions.
2. The formal school curriculum must include the experiences of women and men from all walks of life. Girls and boys must see women and girls reflected and valued in the materials they study.
3. School curricula should deal directly with issues of power, gender politics, and violence against women. Better-informed girls are better equipped to make decisions about their futures. Girls and young women who have a strong sense of themselves are better able to confront violence and abuse in their lives.
4. Curricula for young children must not perpetuate gender stereotypes and should reflect sensitivity to different learning styles.
5. Girls must be educated and encouraged to understand that mathematics and the sciences are important and relevant to their lives. Girls must be actively supported in pursuing education and employment in these areas.
6. Existing equity guidelines should be effectively implemented in all programs supported by the local, state, and federal governments. Specific attention must be directed toward including women on planning committees and focusing on girls and women in the goals, instructional strategies, teacher training, and research components of these programs.
7. Local schools and communities must encourage and support girls studying science and mathematics by showcasing women role models in scientific and technologi-

cal fields, disseminating career information, and offering "hands-on" experiences and work groups in science and math classes.

8. Continued attention to gender equity in vocational education programs must be a high priority at every level of educational governance and administration. Have students discuss how gender roles are changing in their own generation.

9. Testing and assessment must serve as stepping-stones, not stop signs. New tests and testing techniques must accurately reflect the abilities of both girls and boys.

10. Girls and women must play a central role in educational reform. The experiences, strengths, and needs of girls from every race and social class must be considered in order to provide excellence and equity for all our nation's students.

11. A critical goal of education reform must be to enable students to deal effectively with the realities of their lives, particularly in areas such as sexuality and health.

12. Federal and state funding should be used to promote partnerships between schools and community groups, including social service agencies, youth-serving organizations, medical facilities, and local businesses. The needs of students, particularly as highlighted by pregnant teens and teen mothers, require a multi-institutional response.

13. Child care for the children of teen mothers must be an integral part of all programs designed to encourage young women to pursue or complete educational programs. (p. 64)

Unfortunately, despite the efforts of feminist scholars, educators, and some textbook publishers, self-image and role stereotyping problems for girls continue. Clearly, schools and textbooks are less powerful in their influence than the commercial marketplace is. They are no match for television programs and multimedia advertising campaigns aimed at the youth culture. We are unlikely to make much progress on this front until large companies and the advertising agencies they hire cease to exploit gender stereotyping for profit.

In 1994, Congress passed the revisions of the Elementary and Secondary Education Act (ESEA), the two basic federal programs for schools. The decades of feminist scholarship—particularly the work of the AAUW—led to efforts to strengthen the gender equity provisions of ESEA by allocating some $3 million in new money for gender equity activities. A counterattack was launched by Diane S. Ravitch, former Undersecretary of Education during the Reagan and Bush Administrations, and other critics of feminist and gender-based research. Ravitch claimed that the proposed allocation "takes as findings of Congress that all these flawed research claims were true" (Schmidt, 1994). Senator Nancy Kassebaum argued against the legislation, saying that the gender inequity claims were "supported only by a small body of research which has questionable findings" (Schmidt, 1994). And Professor Joseph Adelson of the University of Michigan called the AAUW studies "a propaganda machine that does not seem to respond to any contrary evidence" (Schmidt, 1994).

The counterattack against claims of gender-based failure in school is growing. Like the attacks on multicultural education (see Chapter 3), the critics accuse advocates of gender equity of promoting an ideology. The role of ideology in shaping research perspectives and educational philosophies will be discussed in the following two chapters.

This chapter concludes the social-political foundations underlying multicultural education. The emphasis in Part 2 shifts from the foundations of multicultural theory to concrete teaching strategies that will help empower all cultural groups to seek cultural democracy. Establishing a positive, trusting, encouraging relationship with your students is the first step, and this is the subject of the next chapter.

Questions Over the Chapter

1. Define "gender role socialization."
2. How does gender affect the learning of a culture?
3. Girls tend to be more successful in school in grades K through 6. Some girls encounter difficulties above grade 7. What factors contribute to this change?
4. List some ways schools may track girls. Why is this practice damaging?
5. What are the arguments in favor of all-male or all-female schools?
6. What is the "beauty myth?" How does it negatively impact girls?
7. List at least four attributes of gender-fair curriculum.
8. List four teaching strategies that lead to gender fairness.
9. What is the name of the primary federal legislation requiring gender-fair school policies?
10. What evidence supports the thesis that elementary schools are primarily female "turf"?
11. What are some of the effects of female dominance in elementary schools?
12. What factors contribute to a "crisis of self-esteem" in middle schools and high schools?
13. Describe your own development of self-identity as you recall your adolescent years.
14. List three strategies to support positive self-esteem among girls.
15. What are careers for women that do not require a college education? What high school classes or subjects prepare students for these careers?
16. List jobs you have held (including parttime). What high school study prepared you for these jobs?
17. How does the absence of strong female role models from textbooks and curriculum affect girls?
18. Name three major female authors.
19. Name two major African American female authors.
20. How has sexual responsibility changed in the last decade?
21. What behaviors are prohibited by Title IX?

Activities for Further Study of Gender Relationships

1. View the film *Union Maids* about class and gender relationships during the period from 1930 to 1945. Compare these relationships to present-day relations.
2. In a small group of students, summarize the effect of gender relationships on schooling. Then report as a team to the class.

3. Invite a guest speaker from the Women's Studies Department at your local college campus to speak. Compare these ideas to the presentation in this chapter.

4. Invite a Chicana feminist or African American feminist to speak on the relationship between ethnic struggles and the feminist struggles.

5. In small groups of students, describe recent experiences in which you were treated unfairly based on your gender or race. Then each group should share its stories with the entire class.

6. Complete a life history interview with a female over age 40. Share your observations with the class.

7. Compare racism and sexism. How are they similar? How are they different? How does socioeconomic class affect each?

8. In class discussion, predict five major changes in gender role relationships that will take place in the next decade. Discuss how these changes will affect schools.

9. Interview another student. If that student is not going into teaching, what other profes-

sion would he or she select? Look for patterns in the student's choices. Ask your partner what influences might encourage him or her to select teaching.

10. Read the entire report *How Schools Shortchange Girls*. Select three recommendations for change. Discuss these suggestions with the director of your campus Women's Studies Program or the Teacher Preparation Program.

11. Make a chart of your own grade-point averages (GPA) in grades 1 through 12. What patterns can you detect? Your instructor may want to hand out a table of the class's GPAs arranged by race and gender.

12. Bring four advertisements from women's magazines that promote "the beauty myth." What messages are the ads sending to readers?

13. Ask students in your class who are mothers or fathers to describe the financial difficulties of graduating from college.

14. Describe the reasons for your choice to become a teacher. How did the female domination of the profession affect your schooling and your career choices? Share your views with other classmates.

Teaching Strategies

1. Include the study of power and gender equity in the curriculum.

2. Use self-esteem-building lessons for girls and boys to combat the destructive messages of the commercial media.

3. Study the stereotyping presented in commercial media. What values are being advocated?

4. Make the curriculum inclusive, including showing women in areas of math and sciences.

5. Use a nonracial definition of women's achievements. Include the contributions of women of color.

6. Write for and use the excellent materials of the National Women's History Project.

7. Praise and encourage girls for their academic excellence and skills in addition to areas such as neatness and compliance.

8. Teach students to recognize and oppose gender stereotyping.

9. Use role playing and role reversal strategies to resist stereotyping.

References

American Association of University Women. (1992). *How schools shortchange girls.* Washington, DC: AAUW.

Amott, T. L., & Matthaei, J. A. (1991). *Race, gender and work: A multicultural economic history of women in the United States.* Boston: South End Press.

Anzaldúa, G. (1987). *Borderlands / La Frontera: The new Mestiza.* San Francisco: Spinsters / Aunt Lute.

Au, K. H., & Kawakami, A. (1994). Cultural congruence in instruction. In E. R. Hollins, J. King, & W. Hayman. (Eds.), *Teaching diverse populations: Formulating a knowledge base* (pp. 5–23). Albany: State University of New York Press.

Buteyn, R. J. (1989). *Gender and academic achievement in education.* (Report No. 313103). Washington, DC: U.S. Department of Education. (ERIC Document Reproduction Service No. ED 313 103)

Butler, J. E. (1989). Transforming the curriculum: Teaching about women of color. In J. Banks & C. M. H. Banks (Eds.), *Multicultural education: Issues and practices.* Newton, MA: Allyn & Bacon.

Dweck, C. (1977). Learned helplessness and negative evaluation. *Educator, 19* (2), 44–49.

Faludi, S. (1991). *Backlash: The undeclared war against American Women.* New York: Crown Publishers.

Foster, M. (1994). Effective black teachers: A literature review. In E. R. Hollins, J. King, & W. Hayman. (Eds.), *Teaching diverse populations: Formulating a knowledge base* (pp. 225–241). Albany: State University of New York Press.

Gandara, P. (1982). Passing through the eye of the needle: High-achieving Chicanas. *Hispanic Journal of Behavioral Sciences, 4*(2), 167–179.

Gilligan, C. (1982). *In a different voice.* Cambridge: Harvard University Press.

Hollins, E. R., King, J. E., & Haymen, W. C. (Eds.). (1994). *Teaching diverse populations: Formulating a knowledge base.* Albany: State University of New York Press.

Los Angeles County Office of Education. (1991). *The condition of public education in Los Angeles County, 1990–1991.* Los Angeles County Schools.

Moll, L. C., Vélez-Ibañez, C., & Greenberg, J. (1992). *Community knowledge and classroom practice: Combining resources for literacy instruction: A handbook for teachers and planners.* Arlington, VA: Development Associates, Inc.

Moraga, C., & Anzaldúa, G. (Eds.). (1981). *This bridge called my back.* New York: Kitchen Table, Women of Color Press.

National Education Association. (1990). *Tracking: Report of the NEA Executive Committee on academic tracking.* Washington, DC: Author.

Oakes, J. (1985). *Keeping track: How schools structure inequality.* New Haven, CT: Yale University Press.

Oakes, J. (1988). Tracking in mathematics and science education: A structural contribution to unequal schooling. In L. Weis (Ed.), *Class, race and gender in American education* (pp. 106–125). Albany: State University of New York Press.

Sadker, M., Sadker, D., & Long, L. (1989). Gender and educational equality. In J. Banks and C. H. M. Banks. *Multicultural education: Issues and perspectives* (pp. 106–123). Newton, MA: Allyn & Bacon.

Schmidt, P. (1994, September 28). Idea of "gender gap" in schools under attack. *Education Week* pp. 1, 16.

Tannen, D. (1990). *You just don't understand: Women and men in conversation.* New York: Ballantine Books.

Tavris, C. (1992). *The mismeasure of woman: Why women are not the better sex, the inferior sex, or the opposite sex.* New York: Simon & Schuster.

Tetreault, M. K. T. (1989). Integrating content about women and gender into the curriculum. In J. Banks & C. H. M. Banks, (Eds.), *Multicultural education: Issues and perspectives* (pp. 124–144). Newton, MA: Allyn & Bacon.

Weis, L. (1988). High school girls in a de-industrializing economy. In L. Weis (Ed.), *Class, race and gender in American education* (pp. 183–208). Albany: State University of New York Press.

Weis, L. (1990). *Working class without work.* New York: Routledge.

Weis, L., & Fine, M. (Ed.). (1993). *Beyond silenced voices: Class, race and gender in United States schools.* Albany: State University of New York Press.

West, C. (1993). *Race matters.* Boston: Beacon Press.

Wilbur, G. (1991, August). Gender-fair curriculum. Research report prepared for Wellesley College Research on Women. *How schools shortchange girls* (p. 64). Washington, DC: AAUW.

Wolf, N. (1991). *The beauty myth: How images of beauty are used against women.* New York: Doubleday.

Part 2

Teaching Strategies to Promote Democracy and Multicultural Education

Chapter 6

Human Relations and Multicultural Education

Good teachers make a difference. Each year schools, districts, individual states, the President, and corporations recognize a few of the many excellent teachers working in schools all around the country. The stories of Marva Collins in Chicago and Jaime Escalante in Los Angeles and Sacramento have inspired books and movies. Excellent teachers illustrate the truism that the quality of interactions between teachers and students is the single most important element in schools. Quality teaching and coaching occur even in underfunded and racially segregated or isolated schools. Quality teaching depends on creating trusting and supportive relationships between students and their teachers.

This chapter will introduce five major issues in promoting positive human relations:

1. Serving as a cultural mediator,
2. Teaching social skills,
3. Promoting positive self-esteem,
4. Conflict resolution, and
5. Building supportive relationships.

Underlying Assumptions of Human Relations

We are, of course, all humans—both teachers and students. Humans are much more alike than they are different, and many teachers begin their approaches to multicultural education by affirming our common humanity. Some teachers welcome human relations lessons but regard other approaches to multicultural education, such as ethnic studies and women's studies, as divisive since they acknowledge and some say emphasize, uncomfortable differences. Discussions, particularly of race, make many new teachers uncomfortable. They would rather affirm our common humanity, putting aside the histories of race, class, and gender oppressions described in prior chapters. Certainly many students in your teacher preparation program hold this worldview.

The **human relations approach** to multicultural education emphasizes our common humanity—the enormous similarities in physical, psychological, and social patterns among humans—and builds lessons to emphasize human similarity. For example, we can see differences in skin color, but well over 90% of all human biology is identical to all other humans (e.g., we all have hearts, kidneys, toes, eyes, etc.).

The human relations approach traces its intellectual roots to efforts during World War II to understand the Holocaust. Scholars and activists sought to develop lessons that schools could use to promote an end to prejudice and discrimination in U.S. society. Other important work was done for the U.S. military to assist them with the desegregation of military units ordered by President Truman.

Applications of human relations research are currently commonplace in the public schools, with human relations being the dominant form of multicultural education in grades K through 4 along with bilingual education. Such approaches remain an important aspect of multicultural education throughout high school and college.

Human relations provide a good place for new teachers to begin pursuing democracy and equal opportunity in the curriculum. The human relations approach is the least controversial of several approaches to multicultural education and the one that requires the least change of worldview on the part of teachers. New teachers, like yourselves, enter the profession believing in the positive possibilities of children; they look for strategies to build on the children's humanness.

At the same time, human relations theory provides the psychological and sociological basis for the democratic claim that schools should promote equal opportunity. Once accepted, the concept of equal opportunity suggests a need for fundamental changes in schools.

Current conditions in our streets make the learning of positive self-esteem and positive teaching strategies all the more important. In human relations lessons, all students are treated as individuals; the same teaching strategies are suggested for diverse racial, ethnic, cultural, language, class, and gender groups.

The central insight of the human relations approach is that the creation of positive human relationships between teachers and students and between students is among the most important issues of school improvement. Young people do not learn math, reading, or English well if they are intimidated, defensive, and fearful.

Violence and the Urban Crisis

From 1980 until 1992, the Reagan-Bush budget cuts and the abandonment of cities to crime, poverty, and decay included the abandonment of students in inner-city schools. The visible decay of the urban infrastructure teaches hopelessness and helplessness to many children. Violence, shootings, and even death plague some of our schools. Teachers are expected to control increasing numbers of students who have serious physical and emotional problems. Young people are bringing weapons to school to protect themselves and to intimidate others.

The poor suffer the most from cutbacks in police, education, fire, health, and nutritional services. The Children's Defense Fund says that one out of five children in the United States lives in poverty—over 50% of African American children and 43% of Latino children. The children live in decaying communities stressed by racism, class and gender prejudice, job loss, crime, and poverty. These conditions create conflict and violence in the community and in schools. Virtually abandoned by the society, some children learn violent responses to the violence they endure. And they bring the violence with them to school.

George McKenna, III (1992), an African American school district superintendent of Inglewood, California, and a former high school principal, described his experience as follows:

> In my 30 years in working in inner-city schools, I have witnessed a decline in student behavior that mirrors the rise of violence in society—the increase in violent assaults on campus, gang involvement, drug use, sexual activity, suicide and other acts that, besides bringing great harm to those involved, leave others in the school community feeling helpless, powerless—and even more disadvantaged than before.
>
> Typically, the schools' response is greater reliance on the police and other campus security agencies. I propose that educators give education a chance: that we teach values and respect for human life through a comprehensive school-based program centered on a nonviolence curriculum at all grade levels. Some of the key ingredients would be . . . parent involvement . . . a nonviolence curriculum . . . peer counseling and community service . . . and antigang education. (p. A-11)

Teachers, social workers, and police cannot stop the violence in the society. But the schools have an obligation to provide safety and security to the children in school. Schools must become islands of safety in the urban landscape. The teacher's difficult task is to organize the curriculum and respond to the students in a positive, nurturing, and constructive manner that encourages the learning of respect and nonviolence. The political leaders of the society—presidents, governors, legislators, mayors, and school administrators from school board to principal—have the responsibility to keep the school grounds safe and clean and to keep drugs, gangs and violence off campus. They have often failed.

To reform the schools toward multicultural democracy, teachers must improve the quality of respect and interchange in the classroom. Teachers create positive environments by their decisions, choices, expectations, and interactions with students. The converse is also true. Students do not learn in stressful, failure-filled environments where their physical and emotional safety is threatened. Research summaries in effective teaching for Hispanic (Latino) students indicate that the quality of the personal relationship between teacher and students is one of the most important issues in motivating students to learn (Garcia, 1994).

The Limiting Effects of Educational Research on Our Views of Students and Schools

Unfortunately, present practices in psychology and the social sciences provide only limited insights into the growing crisis of urban decay and in describing and explaining teacher-student relationships and interaction. The dominant approaches in the social sciences generally accept the present impersonal and control-oriented structures of schools as natural, as the result of "scientific planning." As you have read in prior chapters, multicultural education challenges these basic assumptions, asserting that present school practices are often unequal, discriminatory on gender issues, and stratified by race and class.

To understand the problem of accepting an impersonal and, at times, unjust and violent school structure as natural, we must look at the philosophy of **positivism** that provides the basis for most educational and social science research. Most scholars and teachers in the United States have been educated within the positivist viewpoint. We learn to assume that natural laws of human behavior can be discovered by use of the "scientific method." The philosophy of positivism developed during the Age of Enlightenment (1600–1860). Early scientists such as Newton and Descartes developed a scientific method based on a philosophy of realism and sought to isolate variables for study. Early scientists such as Galileo, created experimental processes to look for natural causes for events. The landmark research of Louis Pasteur and Charles Darwin based on experimentation and observation was admired and copied by others.

The social sciences emerged in the late 1800s following the earlier dramatic developments in the natural sciences. Early social scientists hoped to discover natural laws about human society similar to those laws discovered in the natural sciences by Pasteur, Mendel, Newton, and others. They searched for universal law-like statements and predictive explanations. The early social scientists hoped to move beyond the moral philosophy of their time by applying a "modern," scientific approach to human behavior. Currently, this "modern" scientific approach dominates educational research and writing. This work, based on positivist assumptions, is described in contemporary social science and education literature as behaviorism or reductionism.

The Reliance of the Social Sciences on Positivism

Efforts to develop the scientific methods in human matters were frustrated by the complexity of human experience. Human institutions—like economic systems, school systems, and cultures—are so complex that it is often impossible to create quality experimental designs and to isolate variables. In response to frustration, social scientists continually refined their "scientific methods," their proof processes, and statistical processes. Social scientists who depended on the philosophy of positivism adopted a faith that improved methodology would lead to truth, as it seemed to have done in the natural sciences.

In pursuit of objectivity, psychologists and other social scientists developed more and more precise methods of controlling variables. They limited and restricted what they considered appropriate topics for study.

Over time social scientists developed their separate disciplines of geography, economics, political science, and sociology. Each of these disciplines developed on the basis of the positivist origins. Most of the practitioners in these disciplines sought objectivity and believed in a view that the scientific method and processes offered methodological neutrality. Researchers working within the assumptions of positivism presumed that if they continued to refine their research methods they would eventually achieve their goals of developing universal laws and predictive explanations.

The philosophical limitations of positivism have been examined by Giroux (1979). He argues that the culture of positivism seeks to put aside the normative, value-laden issues, the issues of supreme importance to the teacher. These value-laden issues are central to an effort to reconstruct schools in a democratic manner that would empower minority students.

Behaviorism

Social scientific research based on positivist assumptions emphasizes work that is quantified, measurable, and verifiable. By the 1960s, the so-called "behaviorist" school of social sciences developed. The researchers in this tradition seek to monitor behavior that is observed and measurable. They tend to ignore or cast aside idealism, consciousness, ethics, and faith because they cannot be measured. Behaviorism became the dominant trend in educational psychology and sociology in the 1970s. Applications of behaviorism in education include behavioral objectives, audio-lingual approaches to language acquisition, and the Madeline Hunter model of Direct Teaching. [1]

Behaviorism and cognitive psychology both provide hypotheses about how students learn basic skills. Some students learn basic skills when teachers use these behaviorist strategies. Behaviorist research and behavioral psychology serve reasonably well to describe how a rat or a pigeon learns (Weinberg & Reidford, 1972). However, you may notice that you have never met a rat or a pigeon that could speak a language or do mathematics. Behaviorism also describes strategies to socialize mostly middle-class students to a culturally congruent classroom. But behaviorism can do little to teach students to succeed in the chaotic, decaying social structure of inner-city schools and neighborhoods. Behaviorism also does not serve democracy well since a preference for democracy is not reducible to isolated parts. Behaviorism offers few insights for the oppressed. It fails to convince students from the lower classes to use the schools as vehicles for their own advancement and their communities' health.

Reductionism

Clearly the scientific methods in the natural sciences led to great advancements in modern society. However, in the social and behavioral sciences, one version of the scientific method developed a tendency termed objectivism, or reductionism. **Reductionism** distorts comprehensive observation and limits both the analytical and explanatory powers of much school research. The conceptual framework or research paradigms of objectivists, behaviorists, and to a lesser degree, cognitive psychologists, led them to isolate variables and to study learning behavior out of the real context of schools.

In the pursuit of objectivity, behaviorist and reductionist research has ignored vast amounts of important information on the purposes and intents of learning as well as on the importance of quality relationships between students and teachers. At present, behaviorist and reductionist experimental designs reveal few new useful insights into learning behavior. The effort to be objective, to be empirical rather than normative, directed these research designs away from important issues of power. The pursuit of objectivity and methodological precision distorted and limited research in education and the social sciences. As a consequence, the present unequal distribution of wealth, power, and opportunity

---

[1] For more on this complex topic see the following sources: Bowers, C. A., & Glinders, D. J. (1990). *Responsive Teaching: An Ecological Approach to Classroom Patterns of Language, Culture and Thought.* New York: Teachers College Press; Hartoonian, H. M. (1991). The role of philosophy in the education of democratic citizens. In R. E. Gross & T. L. Dynneson (Eds.), *Social Science Perspectives on Citizenship Education* (pp. 195–219). New York: Teachers College Press; Kaplan, A. (1968). Positivism. In *The International Encyclopedia of the Social Sciences.* New York: The Macmillan Company; and West, C. (1991). *The Ethical Dimensions of Marxist Thought.* New York: Monthly Review Press.

in our society and in our schools was usually not considered an appropriate subject of study by researchers committed to procedural objectivity and neutrality.

Objectivist and reductionist psychologies, restricted by positivist assumptions, avoid questions of oppression and domination as research topics in explaining school failure of students of color. Giroux (1979) described the problem as follows:

> [W]rapped in the logic of fragmentation and specialization, positivist rationality divorces fact from its social context and ends up glorifying scientific methodology at the expense of more rational modes of thinking . . . more important, it leaves unquestioned those economic and social structures that shape our daily lives. (p. 271)

In particular, these research efforts left unquestioned cultural domination and race and gender bias in teaching, learning, and curriculum.

Objectivists' and behaviorists' thought processes dominated most educational research in education well into the 1980s. The behaviorists' view of learning produced reductionist forms of teaching and curriculum, particularly in compensatory programs for children from poverty-stricken neighborhoods. The conservative school reform effort and their faith in allegedly objective testing and a test-driven curriculum are direct results of this narrow and restricted view of research (Valdes & Figueroa, 1994). Behaviorism and reductionism also conveniently reinforce the status quo of power and economic distribution in our society.

Alternatives to Reductionism

A countervailing tradition of reporting and analysis has developed in three arenas: clinical psychology and counseling, the politically informed movements of empowerment, and in the research process of ethnography. Gestalt therapy and Rogerian counseling contributed to the understanding of interpersonal relations and communication styles. Anthropological researchers have developed the skills of ethnography to develop extended and contextually situated observations of classroom interactions.

Gestalt and humanistic psychology and Rogerian counseling therapy have developed new alternative ways of understanding human psychology, emotions, and behavior that do not draw all of their conceptual framework from positivism. Aspects of this psychology will be introduced throughout this chapter, including the work of Abraham Maslow and concerns for self, self-concept, self-esteem, and belonging. These important concepts provide a conceptual framework for human relations teaching strategies (Weinberg & Reidford, 1972).

Over the last decade, many educational anthropologists have developed ethnographic approaches to describe in detail the sociocultural and linguistic context of classroom teaching and learning. In contrast to positivist psychologists who, following the research formats of traditional scientific methods, usually sought to isolate variables for study, ethnologists discovered new insights by focusing on the dynamic, complex, and often subtle nuances found in diverse classrooms (Trueba, 1989).

Rather than look for improvement in student achievement as a result of a single intervention, such as the use of a new curriculum or teaching strategy, educational ethnographers incorporate "classic" anthropological research tools to examine the day to day phenomena unfolding in schools and classrooms. Foremost among these tools is the use of extended participant observation (often over several years) and informant interviews (usually teachers, administrators, staff, parents, and at times, even students). Other data collected come also from the analysis of archival information.

In a recent ethnographic effort, Trueba, Rodriguez, Zou, and Cintrón (1993) studied a Northern California rural school district and a specific school therein to describe the rise to political power of a Chicano community and how this affected school language policies and practices at a local elementary Spanish immersion school. In seeking to describe the development of excellence in bilingual school reform at Beamer Park Elementary School, Cintrón (1993) analyzed the more established quantitative measures employed by the school and then extended the analysis by using ethnographic research methods. The qualitative approach revealed a myriad of interesting findings, including the following: the significance and type of teacher preparation at the school; the inherent reward systems within the school culture; faculty self-identity; immersion teacher relationships with non-immersion colleagues, administration, and students; and parental attitudes toward the school and immersion program in particular. This broader, contextual framework provides a more accurate and richer description of school realities than the limited reductionist approach common in prior educational research.

In addition to these two major new directions and the work of Paulo Freire and others to develop a new educational dialogue based in part on political commitment to democratization of education rather than a commitment to "scientific" neutrality (described in Chapter 7), each separate movement called attention to the importance of an analysis of consciousness and self-knowledge (Freire, 1972).

Consciousness is an awareness of one's own existence and of the environment. Both philosophy and experience demonstrate that consciousness exists. Gestalt psychology argues that consciousness is centrally important to understanding human behavior. Studies of the feminist movement and the struggles of people of color testify to the importance of consciousness raising. Behaviorist educational researchers are unable to measure the role of consciousness. Because they cannot quantify or measure consciousness, they fail to use this important concept in developing educational programs. But failures of measurement do not deny the importance of awareness, consciousness, and self-knowledge.

On the contrary, the best strategies designed for empowering students depend on an understanding of consciousness. The teacher's choice to promote either equality or inequality in the classroom is a product of the teacher's awareness and consciousness. Positivist, reductionist, and objectivist research designs that cannot explain issues of context, classroom ecology and social relations, and consciousness, among other topics, are too limited and unrealistic to provide a basis for developing multicultural education (Bowers & Flanders, 1990).

Human relations theory (Gestalt) provides important insight into the process of whether teachers motivate students or alienate and discourage them. Teachers promote either equality or inequality through their interaction with the students. Some teachers are supportive, motivating, and demanding while others are tentative, distant, disengaged, and at times, oppressive. These different interaction styles significantly influence student motivation and achievement.

Differences between interaction styles are substantially a result of the human qualities and cultural competence of the teacher. Interaction styles are subject to study and improvement. Ethnographic studies add significant power to educational research by focusing on the interaction, context, and the characteristics and the consciousness of both the teacher and the students (Trueba, 1989).

Interaction styles and communication between teachers and students are far more than words and sentences. Communication is improved when teachers and students respect each other, when they know each other's realities, when they can "read" each other's body language, tones, and assumptions. Communication styles differ between cultures and genders. Ethnographic research points to women and Latino teachers and researchers placing more importance on the quality of relationships between teachers and students, while researchers trained in the positivist tradition were satisfied with measuring the number of questions, the nature of the questions asked, and the frequency of responses. For example, the educational effect of the manner in which a teacher responds to an Appalachian or Mexican accent, or the status of the teacher's own accent, is concealed by positivist, quantitative research methodologies.

A growing body of research based on observations of classrooms and of clients in therapy contends against positivism to better describe the complexity of human learning. The observations produce a new paradigm of learning to help teachers understand classroom interaction (see Figure 6.1).

Students' classroom experience improves when teachers design their instruction and interaction using insights from both of the models, or paradigms, in Figure 6.1. Exclusive use of the information in paradigm A may result in improvements in instructional technology, but it will not inform or significantly assist in student human relation empowerment. Paradigm B works from the hypothesis that, for some students, the quality of student-teacher relationships is as important to student achievement as the instructional materials, texts, and teaching strategies. In fact, the quality of the student-teacher relationship may be even more important.

In the humanist and constructivist model (B), teachers are concerned with the quality of their interactions with the students. Both teachers and students enter the classroom with motivational styles that are, in part, culturally influenced (Ramirez & Casteñeda, 1974). For example, research summarized by Eugene Garcia asserts that, while many children achieve well in our increasingly formal-

Figure 6.1 Models of Classroom Interaction

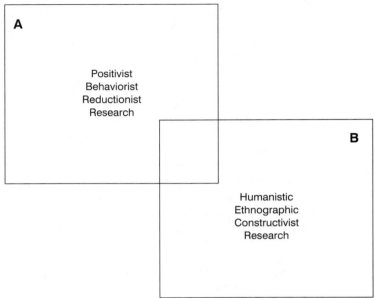

ized, depersonalized classrooms, young Latino children learn more when the teacher provides a positive, supportive, human interaction (Garcia, 1994). Research summarized by Christine Bennet, asserts that African American children tend to learn better in an oral-interactive environment rather than in situations in which they individually read a text and write answers to worksheets (Bennet, 1986; Ladson-Billings, 1994). Native American children may learn more in cooperative settings and where observation and listening are respected. When teachers use communication and motivation styles that respect the students, the relationship is improved. To recognize and participate in multiple communication styles require cultural competence on the part of the teacher.

Teachers as Cultural Mediators

The role of teachers in society varies across cultures. Immigrant children from Latin America and Southeast Asia and migrant students from the South and Southwest come from societies where teachers usually receive respect from the working people. Many immigrant students are confused—and at times, appalled—at much of the disrespectful student behavior in our schools. Some immigrant students from Eastern Europe, on the other hand, frequently have learned an oppositional relationship to teachers.

In our own country, some members of dominated cultural groups (such as African Americans, Puerto Ricans, Chicanos, Native Americans) have learned to perceive teachers as outsiders. They recognize teachers as people who dominate and enforce the rules of a school system in which family members and friends have been failed. As young people, these students are subjected to teacher authority as a price for staying in school. By adolescence, some of these students become rebellious and engage in a struggle for self-worth and identity. They refuse to accept teacher authority, and they struggle against norms expected by the school and usually enforced by teachers.

Schools reward compliance with a promise of future success. This promise is too remote and often unrealistic for many children. Neither our consumer culture nor students' life experiences prepare them to work for long-term educational goals (West, 1993). The students vaguely sense that African American males who graduate from college earn less money than European American high school graduates. When the teacher's role is primarily one of domination, older students (grades 6 through 12) will respond by struggling for their own arenas of power such as in gangs, sports teams, bathrooms, and play areas.

Quality interpersonal relations between teachers and students are particularly problematic in marginalized neighborhoods. Too few teachers live in the neighborhood of the school and participate in the cultures of the students. The teaching profession and teacher preparation programs remain predominantly centered on the European American experience. A cultural and communication gap exists between many teachers and the several communities of color.

When communities suffer economic distress, students' stress levels require even more supportive teacher-student relationships. Quality schools in marginalized neighborhoods must provide a positive alternative to the decaying urban social order. In the primary grades, teachers establish positive relationships with their students by directly teaching appropriate role behavior and communication systems. The social skills of being a productive student are taught rather than assumed. Effective teachers repeatedly encourage rather than demand cooperation between the student, the home, and the school.

Improving the quality of teacher-student relationships and reducing depersonalization are essential to school reform, particularly in middle schools and high schools. Teachers facilitate a democratic relationship by respecting students' rights and by encouraging them to display responsible behavior. At the same time, teachers need to discourage and prevent abusive and disrespectful behavior. The environment of the classroom—not lectures on good intentions—teaches these important lessons. (Additional strategies for positive classroom management are detailed in Chapter 8.)

Schools in low-income areas are brimming with students in crisis. Successful teachers serve as cultural mediators or even cultural therapists for these students (Spindler & Spindler, 1991). They assist students in their painful transitions from a home culture to effective participation in the economy and the society. Many students are at risk and suffer from the crisis of poverty and oppression. Confronted by the society and by failure in school, many students respond with adolescent—at times, destructive—rebellion.

The several crises in our society make students more and more isolated and alienated. They blame themselves, other ethnic groups, and politicians for their loss of equal opportunity. As the authority and legitimacy of government officials and institutional leaders decline, a growing portion of students adopt a cynical, even nihilistic, worldview clearly revealed in some popular music (West, 1993). At the same time, schools and the knowledge and credentials they control are ever more important to students. Alienation from school is ever more damaging to the economic future of the students. Teachers committed to democracy must help the students to fashion a way out of this growing cynicism and defeat.

Schools are transitional institutions where society insists that students adjust to the social stratification of the emerging economy. For many oppressed communities, this emerging economy offers poverty, drugs, underemployment, crime, and alienation or a low-level, poorly paid job with little future. The teacher as a mediator must help students identify and work toward more positive alternatives.

When curriculum by omission or commission attacks the student's culture or gender, it attacks the student's self. In particular, invisibility, intimidation, and failure in the school attack the student's "enduring self" (Spindler & Spindler, 1991). Democratic teachers recognize the root cultural conflicts involved in school failure and assist students in fashioning positive alternative strategies.

Students need to learn effective resistance to economic and racial oppression rather than ineffective resistance. Students best succeed when they understand the changing society and how to pursue individual and community progress. They succeed when they understand their own culture and the forces of assimilation and when they know how to choose new strategies and when to rely on their own culture. Effective teachers help, coach, and guide students through this turmoil.

By middle school, the curriculum should study issues of youth alienation and cultural and racial conflict. Studying these conflicts helps students to comprehend and validate their own reality and to fashion productive responses. Teachers as mediators encourage students to find alternatives. Cultural mediation and cultural therapy help students draw on their own cultures and experiences as resources, as sources of knowledge for developing strategies to overcome the barriers of an often hostile society.

Teachers who are emotionally well adjusted and comfortable with themselves are able to establish a healthy classroom environment that promotes quality relationships among students and promotes quality teaching. Being well adjusted in an urban school includes being comfortable with one's own ethnicity and the complexity of one's own culture. Well-adjusted teachers are not overstressed by fear of others or guilt. Teachers are not responsible for the general societal oppressions of people of color or for the inadequate funding of most urban schools. Teachers *are* responsible for promoting high achievement and educational opportunity for the students in their class.

Teachers help most by encouraging students. Self-reflection about your own school experiences may help you determine how best to assist your students.

Who encouraged you to consider going on to college? How did your favorite teachers encourage you to perform quality work? Were there any teachers you could talk with and confide in?

Human relations theory is helpful for teachers. Teachers must concern themselves with their own mental health, biases, and perceptions. Teachers need to view themselves and their students in generally positive ways if they are to establish positive relationships. Both teachers and students need to consider each other as being successful and able persons with dignity.

Maria Delgado—A Teacher Serving as a Cultural Mediator

The case of Maria Delgado, a high school teacher in Texas, illustrates the importance of positive social relationships between teachers and students. Because her presence at the school establishes the idea that Chicanas can go to college and become teachers, Maria serves as a positive role model to young Chicanas. She can be particularly helpful and sensitive to other Mexican American (Chicana) students.

Maria makes close personal contact with some of her students. She looks for opportunities to talk privately and supportively with her students. She uses a little Spanish, the endearment "Mija," and some friendly advice to establish a safe environment between herself and her female students. Expressions of empathy and understanding as well as active listening skills serve her well. Students often need to talk and explore ideas and emotions with adults other than their parents. When a safe, student-friendly environment is established, many students approach the teacher for advice.

As a female teacher talking to girls, Maria is perceived as a woman who "understands" the daily turmoil and conflicts important to the girls—dress, looks, boyfriends, parents, rules—all are critical issues. Most of these conflicts are personal rather than academic. Maria's own training as a counselor taught her to use active listening skills to establish empathy. With over 160 students per day, each week three or four students need help. She can put her arms around a young girl and give her a hug and reassurance. She can provide the young girls with important information on crisis intervention, dating, birth control clinics, and counseling support for family crises.

It helps that Maria is a Chicana, but teachers do not have to be Chicano to encourage Chicano students or African American to encourage African American students. Many students report that the most active supporting behavior may come from a Japanese or European American. Interviews of college students reveal that the teacher who motivated and encouraged them was often from a different culture than their own.

Support behavior, both verbal and nonverbal, is often culturally specific and precise. Family supervision styles often vary across cultures and are changing. A female European American may lose contact with some of her Mexican American students if she fails to comprehend or respect traditional Mexican American values of close family supervision or Catholic values on birth control. A European American female teacher could provide most of the support that Maria provides. Indeed, it was a European American teacher—not a Mexican American—who first encouraged Maria to go to college.

Some teachers from other cultures learn about Chicano culture, work closely with the Mexican American community for years, and become a part of the community. They are seen in the neighborhoods and get invited to family rituals such as baptisms, first communions, and weddings. They become a friendly and supportive aunt or uncle, padrino or madrina—a significant and accepted member of the community. These teachers and many teacher assistants provide desperately needed guidance for students and important communication between home and school (Garcia, 1994).

Being Chicana is not a guarantee of empathy with Chicana students, nor is being Black a guarantee of support for African American students. Some Mexican American teachers choose to remain apart, uninvolved in their students' lives. The teachers' personal goals and the major differences within the culture, between generations, language usage, and degrees of assimilation divide some students and teachers.

The lack of male role models in elementary school produces a particular problem for young boys of several cultures. By the middle school years, coaches and a few male teachers provide an additional support system and guidance for boys. Female teachers and principals may extend themselves to assist boys, but the gender difference creates barriers that only the more self-assured or more desperate male students will cross.

The increased incidence of harassment charges and actual sexual molestations makes it more difficult today for teachers to use hugs and physical comforting with students of the opposite sex. Racism, racial fears about sexuality, and homophobia frighten many teachers. Lawsuits, abuse charges, and many district policies prohibit teachers from using even small amounts of physical force to direct a child (such as holding onto a child's arm while scolding him or physically breaking up a fight). What seems a simple, obvious, and supportive touch to you as the teacher, may cause concern among a small number of parents. Some children, and unfortunately some teachers, are immature and prone to exaggerate. Children often have little comprehension or concern for the consequences of their accusations. As a new teacher, particularly if you are a male teacher in elementary or middle school, you should exercise care while learning the professional and safety guidelines for touch in your particular school district.

There is cause for professional caution. Sexual abuse, molestation, and unprofessional conduct charges against a very few teachers have frightened others. In addition to a few abusive adults, young children and teenagers in times of crisis develop vivid imaginations. Too few counselors are available. Not all parents are reasonable, rational, and supportive. In our society, where many children need more attention, more comforting, and even more encouraging touch, new guidelines and reasonable procedures have yet to be developed.

Strategies for Human Relations

Psychologist Abraham Maslow provided a framework for understanding the need for human relations in the classroom. He described a hierarchy of needs as illustrated in Figure 6.2. Needs lower on the chart, such as physical and safety needs, must be met before a student will consider higher level needs.

This hierarchy explains important components of behavior, including school behavior. Teachers often assume that the physical security and the safety needs of their students are assured, but in many schools they are not. Increasing numbers of homes and schools are unable to provide simple safety. When physical security and safety are challenged, the students will use most of their time, energy, and creativity simply trying to survive. The struggle for safety and security interferes with learning.

Belonging needs are often strong in school. Children need to know they are a welcomed part of the class. The teacher cannot allow derogatory name calling and other forms of isolation and exclusion to dominate the classroom. These peer-group relations substantially influence school success. It is difficult to learn in hostile, conflict-filled classrooms and schools. Classroom planning and curriculum, such as cooperative learning and peer-group mediation can help convert the classroom environment to one of support and belonging.

Maslow did not consider the hierarchy of needs as rigid. Students will partially fulfill some needs, and thus become prepared to consider higher level

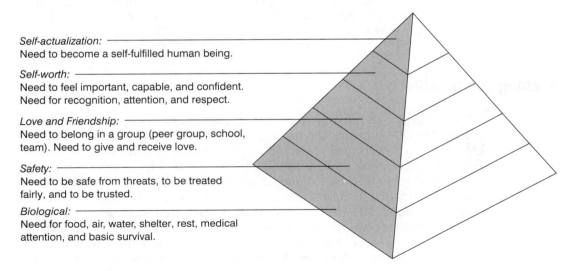

Self-actualization:
Need to become a self-fulfilled human being.

Self-worth:
Need to feel important, capable, and confident.
Need for recognition, attention, and respect.

Love and Friendship:
Need to belong in a group (peer group, school, team). Need to give and receive love.

Safety:
Need to be safe from threats, to be treated fairly, and to be trusted.

Biological:
Need for food, air, water, shelter, rest, medical attention, and basic survival.

Figure 6.2 Maslow's Hierarchy of Needs

Note. Adapted from "Hierarchy of Needs" from *Motivation and Personality* (3rd ed.), by Abraham H. Maslow. Revised by Robert Frager et al., Harper & Row Publishers, Inc., 1954, 1987.

needs. The highest level, self-actualization, is a theoretical position described by Maslow as a goal, usually for adults. Self-actualization is, at most, a goal advocated by practitioners of Gestalt therapy—not a cross-cultural, universal human experience. Teachers can help students learn to meet their own safety needs, the love and friendship needs, and to recognize their own self-worth. These basic needs must be met before education can take place in the classroom.

Responding to these basic needs is particularly problematic when the schools are the primary location for ethnic integration. Neighborhoods and cities are increasingly segregated by race and class. Many urban school districts and the courts seek to integrate children in schools.

In 1991, Selma, Alabama, was rocked by school conflict when an African American superintendent tried to end school tracking that maintained de-facto segregation. Kansas City has long been under a court order to provide equal opportunity in its schools. In 1994, District Court Justice Stanley Roskowski ordered Rockford, Illinois, to integrate its schools even though the district had been officially integrated for over 20 years. And the federal courts found the San Jose, California, school district used tracking to maintain rigid segregation and unequal opportunity for over a decade.

As these and other districts desegregate and de-track, children and adolescents need to be taught to work together cooperatively and to respect one another. These goals are not attained unless they are taught and promoted by specific teaching strategies. It is a major error for districts to desegregate without formally teaching the faculty and the students to improve their human relations skills. School districts can use a variety of strategies including parental involvement, curriculum change, and conflict resolution teams to create a positive nonviolent school climate.

Teaching Social Skills

For kindergarten and first grade, social skill development is a normal part of the curriculum that provides the basis for human relations lessons. Teaching role behavior, social skills, and respectful positive communication styles is an important component of cooperative learning (as described in Chapter 9). Such instruction should begin at least by grade 2 and continue thereafter. In classes with a mix of cultures and in areas with a great deal of inter-ethnic conflict, social skills, human relations, and the study of conflict resolution strategies help teachers achieve a positive classroom environment and improve school social climate.

As a result of social decay, the crises in our cities and families, and the drug crisis, many young students are dysfunctional in the classroom. They do not use respectful communication processes with the teacher or with other students. Skills and attitudes promoting positive communication and positive human relationships must be taught. Strategies for teaching positive social skills are described in Chapter 8.

Some older students do not use respectful communication because their life and school experiences have not taught them to value the use of positive communications. An increasing number of young people have not accepted their role as students and have not learned to interact positively with schools and teachers. Meanwhile, their peer-group experiences on the streets reinforce aggression, competition, and disdain and disrespect for many school norms. [2]

These same students are clearly able to learn under certain conditions. Gangs are, in themselves, schools that teach role relationships and communication styles, albeit negative ones. If the school and family do not offer positive alternatives, the street culture in many cities offers incentives, communication, and motivation styles that are opposed to school success. The economic results of student alienation from school have already reached crisis proportions. The crime results are staggering.

Teachers using human relations help students to work together and to assist one another in the classroom. Social skill lessons teach respect, cooperative social behavior, and problem-solving techniques. Teachers can use assigned roles in cooperative learning groups to help all students to belong to positive social groups in the classroom. Human relations lessons focus on improving self-esteem and encouraging the sharing of positive feelings among the students. The direct teaching of social skills is common in elementary schools and needs to be extended into middle schools and high schools. Additional human relation lessons may deal with stereotyping and scapegoating—long identified as problems that contribute to inter-ethnic conflict.

Teachers present a model of positive human relations when they treat students with dignity and respect and when they insist that the students treat each other with dignity and respect. By the middle school years, an adolescent's alienation and nihilism often dominate peer-group exchanges. Human relations lessons teach students how to develop positive communication and supportive relationships.

Promoting Positive Self-Esteem

Safety and Security

In their classroom, students need a strong sense of comfort and safety from both physical and emotional abuse and criticism. Teachers need to have enough order that students do not intimidate, insult, or overly criticize each other. This sense of positive order is achieved by teaching and developing positive social skills.

---

[2] It is important to not overgeneralize. Many students have learned appropriate role behavior at home, and they may also have learned aggressiveness and rebellion at school. This conflict is not unique to disenfranchised or students of color.

Students do well when they believe that they can depend on the teacher and their classmates. This comfort is achieved by rules and regulations in the classroom that are sensible and consistently enforced (more on classroom management in Chapter 8). Teachers build a trusting relationship by helping and encouraging students and by stopping inappropriate behavior such as racial and gender harassment.

At all ages, students are very sensitive to what they perceive as unequal treatment. When students believe that some students are favored over others, conflict grows in the classroom and their trust in the teacher declines.

In secondary schools, teachers have more students and therefore know them less well. Secondary teachers place more emphasis on teaching a subject matter and tend to place less emphasis on serving as a coach, mentor, counselor, and cultural mediator. The lack of opportunity to develop personal relationships and the wide variety of teacher and student personalities create disharmony. Students want to be listened to and respected as human beings with wants, desires, fears, and emotions.

Over the years, students need to develop a strong sense of security, and they should have the opportunity to develop a trusting personal relationship with some teachers and students. Teams, clubs, and student government projects contribute to this important sense of belonging. Each student should encounter at least one teacher who is interesting and motivating each day. If this does not occur, the school will lose the student. Without positive, personal relationships, schools become warehouses for students rather than learning centers.

Teachers and students without a sense of security develop symptoms of stress and anxiety. They resist change. When schools are full of inter-ethnic conflict or sexual harassment, the violent environment prevents many students from learning. The emerging multicultural classroom is often frustrating and fear-filled for these students and teachers. Human relations lessons and strategies such as those found in *A World of Difference* curriculum help to build a classroom where students feel safe and comfortable. Published by B'nai B'rith, *A World of Difference* offers over 100 lessons emphasizing positive human relations strategies.

Teachers and counselors can identify students who are suffering from undue stress. Insecure people become aggressive and challenge any change in the schedule. Young students may express undue fear by nail biting, teeth grinding, or crying without reason. Older students express stress by withdrawing, avoiding situations where they have to talk to other students or the teacher, and becoming hostile when the school program seeks to involve them.

Self-Worth

When schools serve students well, students develop a sense of self-worth and competence and come to expect to succeed at classroom and social projects. By adolescence, students can recognize their own strengths and develop plans to overcome their weaknesses. The curriculum should be planned and presented so that all students succeed. Reductionism and much of compensatory education impede the development of a strong sense of self-worth.

Teachers can promote a positive sense of self by providing continuous opportunities to succeed in classroom work. Middle-grade students (grades 4 through 8) can learn to set immediate, accomplishable goals. These goals and the clear measurement of success in achieving the goals should be shared with all. With clear goals and lessons, students can recognize and improve their study skills and interpersonal skills. Teachers can plan lessons to demonstrate how to evaluate weaknesses and to plan to learn and profit from mistakes. Quality literature and guest speakers can regularly place positive lifestyle choices in front of the students.

Students who believe themselves competent become more willing to take risks. They generally feel successful at important tasks and school subjects. Such students are willing to share their ideas and opinions and to recognize the accomplishments of other students. Too often teachers use theories of motivation based on the competitive nature of the macroculture and poorly informed teacher folk knowledge about testing, measurement, and curve grading. Overreliance on competition obstructs the goal of developing a positive sense of self-worth for all students. When teachers notice students are dependent, frustrated, or withdrawn, a change of assessment systems is needed.

Students in supportive environments develop a positive sense of self. Violence, drug use, and alienation among teenagers indicate that the schools or the society is failing them. During adolescence, many students struggle with *individuation*, or the becoming of an individual. Adolescents try on many roles and traverse many role changes. Developing an accurate and realistic view of their self is important for students, even as that self changes frequently (Elkind, 1988; Gordon, 1991). Students bridging two or more cultures and identities suffer increased stress and conflict. Literature and lessons about teen conflicts, challenges, and successes offer opportunities for support.

Troubled students overuse negative statements in describing themselves and others and are uncomfortable with praise. Students who overconform and always try to please adults may be displaying a lack of a positive sense of self. Schools with adequate counseling staffs establish programs to supplement the classroom in helping students to question and redefine their identity. Budget cuts that reduce counseling support leave students even more reliant on an often negative peer culture. Peer culture may at times be positive, but it certainly should be supplemented by adult direction.

The sense of self is highly dependent on cultural frames of reference and individual family situations. Descriptions of "normal" behavior and "normal" rebellion should always be tested from within the cultural viewpoint. The ideas of students studying the nature of culture as provided in Chapter 2 provide important cautions to the assumed universality of many theories of self (Spindler & Spindler, 1992).

Sense of Belonging

Students at all ages have a strong need to belong to groups. The desire to fit in provides a major source of motivation—and, at times—challenges to school rules (see Chapter 8). Students may feel conflicting desires to belong to an ethnic or cultural group, girls or boys, an athletic team, or any one of a number of other groups. Learning to work positively within a social group is important to maturity.

Students strengthen their sense of self-worth when they receive recognition, approval, appreciation, and respect from their peers. A human relations approach to multicultural education uses lessons to promote inclusion and acceptance of all students. Teachers can promote these important feelings in the classroom by using cooperative and collaborative learning and classroom projects. Lessons should draw on the wide diversity of languages and skills students bring to school. Leaders, authors, scientists, literature, and teachers from all cultural groups should be recognized.

Deliberately developing peer support groups and recognizing the wide diversity of talents—for example, linguistic, musical, social-leadership—help students to develop a sense of belonging to one or more of the groups in school. If students do not belong to a positive group, many of them will establish a negative group affiliation.

By adolescence, group affiliation can at times contest against school rules and norms. Teen culture, like African American, Latino, or teacher culture, must be respected. If schools set themselves against teenage culture, the conflict will destroy many students. Only negative aspects of teen culture such as drugs, violence, or theft should be opposed. In the many classrooms and schools that seek to impose a Euro-centered culture and also seek to defeat teen culture, conflict and opposition by students can reach destructive levels. Students resist the imposition of a dominating culture in a number of ways. Some forms of resistance such as developing their own styles of dress, their own music, and their own humor are not cause for concern. But many young people join gangs. Others turn to drugs and alcohol. In many neighborhoods, gangs have become the dominant culture, forcing students to either join or fear them. Other students withdraw from school and peers; they become isolated and lonely.

Unfortunately, many public schools must now use desperately short funds to offer programs to assist students to leave the gang and drug cultures dominating many schools and neighborhoods. Principals have turned to peer conflict resolution and gang and narcotics units of police departments to augment the inadequate resources available. Students need to be recruited and encouraged to support the positive aspects of school through clubs, team building, conflict resolution, and leadership development programs.

The school must become a student-friendly, student-safe environment. To achieve this goal, the cultures of students must be respected and celebrated. Peer coaching, peer counseling, and tutoring programs help individual students deal with the many conflicts of adolescence.

A Sense of Direction

While young students often accept the direction of their parents and the school, by adolescence many students are redefining their roles and their choices. Some students need repeated lessons on goal setting and establishing their own sense of responsibility and direction. Students can learn to make decisions and identify consequences. Experiential education programs and outdoor programs help students with goal setting and motivation. Coaching and counseling by teachers can help students make preliminary career and college choices. Teachers serving as advisors to clubs—such as MECHA, MAYA, African American, Ski clubs, teams, and journalism—often play important roles in helping students to define and to select their future. Conversations and support in interest areas often help students develop their own sense of self and become self-fulfilled students.

A Sense of Purpose

Students succeed more when they have a sense of purpose to their school life. Essentially, success at school is their job. School needs to prove its worth to the students. Students benefit from lessons and experiences of decision making and cooperative problem solving. By middle grades and throughout high school, students benefit from lessons on goal setting and accepting their own responsibilities and consequences. These lessons can be taught in combination with study skills lessons or with peer support groups, drug education, and sex education programs.

Teachers encourage positive self-esteem when they recognize, validate, and respect students' own cultures. Curriculum decisions and teaching strategies that take advantage of multiple abilities, such as most cooperative learning approaches, encourage many students to succeed.

The teaching of democratic participation and decision making encourages positive self-esteem. Students can participate in making important decisions about classroom rules. Lessons teach students to give each other guidance and support in lieu of the all-too-prevalent and damaging insults (see Chapter 8).

Cooperative learning and other human relations strategies teach students positive interdependence and how to create and maintain a cooperative group working environment. Students may learn shared responsibility and cooperation. These lessons help to create a classroom environment that is safe and supportive where students can achieve recognition of their self-worth and validate other students as capable, worthy, and confident (see Chapter 10).

Many students need this validation of their self-worth, particularly during adolescence. Some schools are experimenting with all-girl math classes to overcome the recognized loss of self-confidence among middle-school girls in math. Other school districts, where de-facto segregation creates all African American schools, have created all-male primary schools to promote positive self-esteem for endangered black males in school (African American Male Task Force, 1990).

Teachers make decisions to structure their classrooms in ways that encourage learning and cooperation, or they make decisions that produce anxiety, frustration, competition, failure and disruption. Teacher decisions on classroom design are at least as important as planning how to "cover" material in a text.

In particular, a highly competitive classroom environment discourages trust and cooperation. Some students always lose, and these students legitimately feel alienated and angry. When teachers rely on grades and punishment to control students, they reveal their own failure to motivate. Students must come to trust that the teacher has their own best interests at heart, even in difficult times. Teachers achieve this goal by telling the students of their concerns and by demonstrating their respect for the fundamental dignity and worth of each student.

Stopping Demeaning Comments

Too often, particularly in grades 4 through 10, classrooms are the scene of intolerance and demeaning comments between students. Teachers need to work against this intolerance by presenting lessons and activities on tolerance and respect and lessons opposing scapegoating. These positive social values are required first steps in instruction for cooperative learning. The curriculum, *A World of Difference,* is also useful in promoting these values.

Teachers improve classroom climate by modeling positive, supportive communications skills and teaching these skills to students. The great majority of interactions in classrooms are between students. The teacher can influence these interactions and encourage respect in these interactions by teaching positive skills. Lessons in active listening, using "I" messages, and negotiating conflicts show students how to treat each other with respect. These lessons are desperately needed in our increasingly alienating culture.

Students and teachers encounter stress and anger in their lives. Life in many urban neighborhoods makes one angry. Intergroup conflict is frequent. Physical danger is a reality on the streets and often in schools. This anger and fear must be dealt with—not silenced or ignored. Suppression, or not talking about these problems, diverts and distorts the message, creating an even more dangerous setting.

Teachers and school personnel need to listen to students and to communicate with them. When anger and frustration build, students need to learn to express their feelings nonviolently and to work for positive change. Many schools have successfully taught groups of students and parents to serve as conflict mediators, allowing teachers to invest more time in teaching.

Conflict Resolution

As U.S. society and specific communities have increasingly abandoned their children to urban violence, developments in the area of peace studies and conflict resolution have become increasingly valuable for teachers. Classroom management systems work when the general atmosphere of the school, the neighborhood, and family life is positive, helpful, and supportive. But management alone, even skillfully applied management, will not resolve deeply rooted conflicts of poverty, racism, and schools that rely on authoritarianism to respond to adolescent turmoil.

Until basic needs are met—safety, security, and success—the costs of conflict will continue to escalate, often leading to destructive behavior by young people. The growing alienation of adolescents in our society must be addressed and dealt with—not just managed.

Classroom conflict can be caused by a number of events: an overemphasis on competition, intolerance learned at home or on the streets, teachers and students using poor communication skills, and lack of practice in conflict resolution.

Teachers at times contribute to school violence by overstressing competition. Competition provides motivation only for those who win. In all competition, some students lose. When students consistently lose, they have little reason to study and stay in school. As soon as one group leaves school (some scholars call them "push outs" rather than "dropouts"), a new group of students become the losers in competition.

Teachers who make irrational or impossible demands on students also contribute to classroom violence. The conservative school reform movement advocated raising standards, and certainly standards should be raised in those schools presently failing. But high standards should always be accompanied by support and encouragement.

Simply raising standards and failing more students as advocated by many conservatives without restructuring the curriculum and teaching lead only to failure. It does not serve students and failure does not serve the society. Teachers locked in this narrow perspective abandon their role as teachers and become only evaluators. Humans are required for quality teaching, but not for evaluation. Computers can accomplish this evaluation at reduced costs.

The frustrations, failures, and lack of support in many schools have led some teachers to use forceful management systems, to impose a multitude of inflexible rules, and to resort to authoritarian practices. Such teachers have failed or "burned out." They often confuse teaching with covering the material, rather than stimulating, motivating, and coaching. They should either recover through a sabbatical leave outside of school or leave teaching.

By middle school (grades 6 through 8), many schools have taught positive communication skills and conflict resolution skills to reduce violence, power struggles, and rebellion. This instruction begins with a recognition that feelings are important. Dealing with our feelings in a positive, constructive manner is an important part of schooling.

While all adolescents experience interpersonal conflict, students of color and those who are poor also suffer severe stress and structural oppressions. The level of conflict they experience may reach dangerous and unhealthy levels. One way to lessen the impact of these stresses is for students to learn clear communication skills. In community action projects, they can learn to advocate skillfully for their own interests.

Teachers and students gain from preparation in conflict resolution. Students learn skills of talking through conflicts and mediation. Teachers alone cannot "control" the violence that comes into the schools from outside. They need to enlist students in a cooperative effort to reduce the violence. Students learn alternative, nonviolent strategies for reducing conflict. They learn mediation skills. Most importantly, they learn that even major social problems such as conflict can be faced and dealt with within a cooperative community. It strengthens community to learn to resolve conflicts in a democratic and cooperative manner.

There are several emerging strategies for resolving conflict. One strategy of classroom meetings is described in Chapter 8. In "Teaching Students to Be Peer Mediators," David Johnson, Roger Johnson, and their colleagues (1992) describe successful efforts in Edina, Minnesota, to develop a peer mediation program in the schools. Similar programs are emerging in schools across the country. Some programs focus on improving communication skills, while others prepare specially skilled mediators. Communication skills taught to students include the following:

1. Checking for understanding of the opposing viewpoint,
2. Clearly stating one's own position, and
3. Sharing one's needs, feelings, and interests in the conflict.

Mediators can assist by

1. Recognizing negotiable conflicts and less negotiable conflicts,
2. Helping to restate conflicts in negotiable manners,
3. Reframing the issues (talking about the issues in a new, nonpolarized manner),
4. Stating clear rules for conflict management in schools without threatening the students, and
5. Seeking solutions to conflict rather than suppressing the solutions.

Using these strategies, students can learn to negotiate and to mediate in seeking solutions to common problems.

Curricula have developed to assist classrooms and mediators with training. For more information on conflict resolution efforts, contact

Educators for Social Responsibility
475 Riverside Drive
Room 450
New York, NY 10115

Educators for Social Responsibility
23 Garden Street
Cambridge, MA 02138

International Chapter for Conflict Resolution
Box 53
Teachers College, Columbia University
New York, NY 10027

Teachers using the work of Spencer Kagan (1985) to help students improve their communications skills have posted charts displaying a list of alternative behaviors available to students under stress. Students practice and role-play these alternatives. Then, when conflicts arise, they have a choice of responses. Kagan suggests using and posting the following methods for resolving conflicts on the classroom wall:

- Share,
- Take turns,
- Compromise,
- Change,
- Outside help,
- Postpone,
- Avoid, and
- Humor

The coaching practices described in Chapter 8 describe a useful strategy for helping the increasing number of students with extremely high stress and conflict levels.

Teacher Self-Confidence

Many teachers, particularly during their first year, too often experience the frustration of failure. The feeling that we are failing as a teacher attacks our own self-confidence. Feelings of failure and frustration cause many new teachers to transfer schools or to leave teaching altogether.

Several aspects of teachers' work roles may prevent the development of a positive self-image. Disruptive students, undermotivated students, and demeaning professional work conditions may combine to attack a teacher's self-confidence. Both teachers and students respond to attacks on their self-concepts in a defensive, and at times, hostile manner. Parents may expect that teachers can teach responsibility in a society characterized by self-indulgence, immediate rewards, and consumerism. This expectation is unrealistic and represents an overreliance on schools. A traditional African proverb contends, "It takes an entire village to raise a child."

The clash between teacher role definition and student power struggles often produces an unfortunate, nonproductive, and conflictive environment for both parties in the classroom. Adolescent conflicts are particularly severe in at-risk schools where both the number of students suffering in their home lives and the number of new, inexperienced teachers increase. The quality of the working and learning conditions in many of these schools has deteriorated in the last 20 years.

Teachers Have Power—Students Do Not

Tense conditions and persistent failure for both students and teachers in desperately underfunded schools encourage the development of stereotypes, hostility, and cultural clashes. Teachers, schools, and teacher preparation programs at the universities have sufficient power to defend their cultural domination. But students have less power. Students who refuse to be dominated defend themselves by refusing to go along with school culture or by dropping out. Both resisting and leaving school lead to a long-term economic crisis for the student and the community. Multicultural education offers an alternative to resistance. Students can be incorporated into a cooperative, positive school culture. They can learn to respect communities and cultures. Well-developed parent, peer, and community relationships with the schools can help students learn positive strategies. Successful students contribute to their community's health and safety rather than leave school to join a gang.

Student failure and personal tragedies are so much a part of teaching in communities under stress that, after a few years, many teachers feel inadequate and unsuccessful. Some teachers resort to power-based management strategies in a desperate effort to maintain control. Attempts to dominate, in turn, produce more resistance and more power struggles between the teacher and the students. Overreliance on power strategies in schools produces compliance and a hostile environment instead of a learning environment of trust and cooperation.

In schools all across the country, hundreds of involved, positive teachers of all cultural groups engage and motivate students. Unfortunately, many students also encounter rigid, alienated, resentful teachers who produce troubled, conflict-filled classrooms. New teachers bring a fresh optimism to at-risk schools since they have not yet learned the bitter stereotypes of school failure. But new teachers, teachers who have not yet resolved their own cultural conflicts, or who define "teaching" as "controlling students," get caught in a cycle of power struggle and despair. In positive classrooms, both the teachers and students gain; in negative classrooms, both teachers and students lose.

Building Supportive Relationships

Understanding the position of a cultural mediator helps teachers work with students to establish positive interpersonal relationships. When teachers are comfortable with their own cultural perspectives, they can accept cultural conflicts as normal. Students need instruction in the culture of schools. At-risk students need to learn to negotiate cultural conflicts and to seek positive, respectful resolutions. When formal, hierarchical relationships in schools are rigidly maintained, small conflicts between students become power struggles. Winning, losing, and revenge injure the positive interpersonal relationships needed in the classroom. Culturally competent teachers are able to help to resolve student conflicts. They do not waste their energy in endless struggles for power and control.

Cultural Competence

A teacher's real power to manage a classroom productively comes from cultural competence, experience, and maturity—not from using punishment and physical force. Teachers committed to empowerment for students of color help students to analyze and resolve their own cultural conflicts. Schools have established conflict management teams and teach conflict resolution to improve student safety. Conflict resolution training helps to establish a mutually supportive relationship between the teacher and students.

Teachers are a unique cultural group. Like other cultural groups, teachers tend to communicate well and accept students who share their culture and agree with the norms and values of the school. Most students want to be treated fairly. Training programs such as Teacher Expectations and Student Achievement (TESA) can assist teachers in monitoring and fairly distributing praise, eye contact, and wait time to all students, including those from minority cultures. TESA training has helped to establish a positive relationship with members of racial groups, cultural groups, and with both boys and girls in many schools. Fairness helps to establish an environment in which it becomes easier to teach appropriate school behavior.

Many students learn in school. There are hundreds of success stories as a result of schooling poor and minority students (e.g, Olsen, 1994; Olsen & Mullen, 1990). Students best learn when teachers believe in them. But for teachers to have confidence in the students, teachers must first have confidence in themselves. Teachers must model and teach the value of education and of social service. Encouragement and guidance help students win the difficult struggle to develop a positive, productive life. Schools need good teachers to encourage children to achieve in an often hostile world.

Most middle schools and secondary schools are larger than elementary schools and use more hierarchical, impersonal, and formal control mechanisms. The formality of the schools and rigidity of controls produce more conflict and win-lose situations. Teachers establish personalized and supportive relationships in their classes to work against the problems of size and rigidity. Students and teachers under great stress at times need an accepting, even therapeutic relationship. Young people need the opportunity to belong, to be successful in school life even while they make errors. They are, after all, children or adolescents. For maximum success, middle schools should be broken up into smaller units. To address the many social needs of the students, we need to reestablish teacher guidance and counseling time in addition to subject-matter instruction (McPartland & Slavin, 1990).

Teachers assist students by developing supportive relationships—particularly with those students who are resisting the depersonalization and hierarchical structure of the school. Teachers can talk with the students and explore current crises in their lives. Discussing daily news topics adds intellectual reflection to a chaotic world. The students' own lives should be an important part of the curriculum.

In our current troubled economic system and its lack of resources, no single teacher can reach out to all students who need help. The sheer size of the problem of school failure for at-risk students is overwhelming. Elected officials made the decisions to not provide teachers with adequate resources to reach all young people, but each teacher can make a difference for a few students.

When a School Emphasizes Human Relations

Central Park East School in New York City is one of those rare effective schools serving diverse social classes and multiple ethnic groups. The three Central Park East schools are located in "El Barrio," one of the original Puerto Rican settlement areas of New York City. Large numbers of Dominicans and Mexicans are moving into the area and bringing a distinctly new need for English language acquisition and Spanish language maintenance. In spite of the severe economic poverty of the area, students come from other parts of the city to enroll in the community-based schools of Central Park East. Principal Debbie Meyer and the teachers in CPE have achieved many goals of positive student-teacher relationships. In a report on the school, David Bensman describes the efforts to develop a positive discipline system:

> CPE staff tried to develop an approach to discipline that stressed mutual respect rather than fear and punishment. Teachers spent time explaining to children why certain types of behavior made it impossible for others to do their work, they tried to teach children to empathize with others, to understand the impact of their own actions on other children . . . (p. 13)

A CPE student described the experience:

> I think that kind of open classroom situation was so much better. I liked it because it wasn't formal. When you came from public school to CPE, it was so different because at CPE you could be friends with your teacher. I think you want to learn because you have a friend instead of somebody who's dictating all the time. (Bensman, 1987, p. 12)

Summary

Improving the quality of the human relationships between teachers and students is central to multicultural education. The dominant trend of positivism in education and the behavioral sciences has not been helpful in developing cross-cultural, positive teacher-student relationships. Multicultural education and ethnographic research offer new strategies in developing positive relationships.

The diverse cultures of teachers and students affect their interactions and the classroom climate. Multicultural education encourages teachers to become culturally competent. Dedicated teachers can learn about cultural conflict and improve their skills as cultural mediators. While quality relationships are central, good classroom management, critical thinking, cooperative learning, and teaching for empowerment also provide fundamental building blocks of a new approach to teaching in culturally diverse classrooms. With these skills, teachers guide students toward success in both school and life.

Questions Over the Chapter

1. What are four important goals of the human relations approach?
2. Describe why the poor and some ethnic minorities need a human relations approach in primary grades.
3. How is a teenager's consciousness different from that of a teacher?
4. How can a teacher influence the quality of the student-teacher relationship?
5. List four social skills appropriate to teach in grades 1 and 2.
6. List four communication skills appropriate to teach in grades 6 through 10.
7. How do teachers gain respect from students?
8. What factors do research studies identify as causes of a decline of respect between teachers and students?
9. Define *cultural therapist*.
10. What culture or cultures were you reared in? What cultures have you learned about since age 16? Give examples.
11. Define *alienation*. How can cultural therapy help students cope with alienation?
12. What are characteristics of stress commonly experienced by teachers?
13. How does teacher stress affect a teacher's ability to serve as a cultural therapist?
14. Define *cultural competence*.

Activities for Further Study of Positive Student-Teacher Relationships

1. Interview a student about the teachers who most influenced him or her. What are the characteristics of the influential teacher? What are the characteristics of the noninflu-

ential teacher?

2. Conduct library research on experiential teaching and simulation activities. Then present your findings to the class.

3. Role-play a coaching session between a student and a teacher. Brainstorm a wide range of responses to problems. (See Chapter 7 for more on coaching.)

4. Conduct library research on teacher stress, its symptoms, causes, and consequences. Prepare a written summary of your findings.

5. Conduct library research on learning styles or on the thesis of seven intelligences (Howard Gardner).

6. A group of student teachers can role-play the culture of teachers in school. Create a hypothetical faculty room. What are the concerns and issues discussed? Have observers comment on the behavior as a separate culture. Compare this culture to gang behavior. What are the similarities and differences?

7. Show the video *Beyond Hate* with Bill Moyers. Discuss the viewpoint of the gang members and soldiers on the need to deface or depersonalize the enemy. Discuss ways that schools depersonalize students and describe the consequences of this behavior. Develop a list of alternatives to depersonalization.

Teaching Strategies

1. Ask students to list their favorite three movies or television shows. View these programs for insights into student interests.

2. Record a current music video. Transcribe the words to the song. Play the song in class and read the words. Analyze the themes of the song.

3. Select a student who is not actively involved in your class. Make an effort to talk to this student informally before or after class at least three times per week. If the student finds the experience uncomfortable, change to another student. Analyze the interchange and any change in the student's classroom interaction. Apply your conclusions to other students in the class.

4. Conduct an informal survey of your teaching strengths and weaknesses. Ask your students to list the three best things about your teaching and the three that need improvement. Most students will be generous. (By asking for the best, you give them permission to also tell you some of the worst.) Guarantee the students' anonymity. Consider the students' feedback. Which items do you want to begin to work on? Discuss your ideas with the class or with a small group.

5. Invite a guest speaker to address the issue of gangs. Encourage the speaker to discuss why young people are attracted to gangs. Ask the speaker to compare gangs to other formal groupings in the school (sports teams, cheerleaders, student government). Why do young people join groups? What are the advantages and disadvantages?

6. Assign students to view *American Me* on video. This video is a chilling description of the brutality of gang and prison life among Mexican Americans.

7. Make a list of classroom activities that promote and respect diversity. Perhaps have students make murals or posters of these behaviors, and then display the posters prominently.

8. Have students make a presentation on art posters that are popular. Compare them to the artwork representative of the Chicano movement and the African American movements.

9. Practice clarifying responses and paraphrasing in discussions with students. Consider altering your daily schedule to increase the time available for small-group discussion where these skills best function.

References

African American Male Task Force, Milwaukee Public Schools. (1990, May). *Educating African American males: A dream deferred.*

Bennet, C. (1986). *Comprehensive multicultural education: Theory and practice.* Allyn & Bacon.

Bensman, D. (1987). *Quality education in the inner city: The story of Central Park East schools.* New York Community Trust.

Bowers, C. A., & Flanders, D. J. (1990). *Responsive teaching.* New York: Teachers College Press.

Cintrón, J. (1993). A school in change: The empowerment of minority teachers. In H.T. Trueba, C. Rodriguez, Y. Zou, & J. Cintrón (Eds.), *Healing multicultural America: Mexican immigrants rise to power in rural California.* Washington, DC: Falmer Pess.

Elkind, D. (1988). *The hurried child: Growing up too fast too soon.* Reading, MA: Addison Wesley.

Freire, P. (1972). *Pedagogy of the oppressed.* New York: Continuum.

Freire, P. (1978). *Pedagogy in process.* New York: Seabury Press.

Garcia, E. (1994). Attributes of effective schools for language minority students. In E. Hollins, J. King, & W. Hayman. *Teaching diverse populations: Formulating a knowledge base* (pp. 93–104). State University of New York Press.

Giroux, H. A. (1979, Fall). Schooling and the culture of positivism: Notes on the death of history. *Educational Theory, 29,* 263–284.

Gordon, K. (1991). *When good kids do bad things: A survival guide for parents.* New York: W. W. Norton & Company.

Johnson, D., & Johnson, R. T. (1992, September). Teaching students to be peer mediators. *Educational Leadership,* pp. 10–18.

Kagan, S. (1985). Cooperative learning. 27134 Paseo Espada, Suite 303, San Juan Capistrano, CA 92675.

Ladson-Billings, G. (1994). Who will teach our children? Preparing teachers to successfully teach African American students. In E. Hollins,

J. King, & W. Hayman. (1994). *Teaching diverse populations: Formulating a knowledge base* (pp. 129–15). State University of New York.

Maslow, A. (1954/1987). *Motivation and personality* (3rd ed.). (Rev. ed. by Robert Frager et al.). New York: Harper & Row.

McKenna, G. (1992, March 27). Heartware, not hardware. *Los Angeles Times,* p. A11.

McPartland, J. M., & Slavin, R. E. (1990). *Increasing achievement of at-risk students at each grade level.* Washington, DC: U.S. Office of Education.

Olsen, L., & Mullen, N. (1990). *Embracing diversity.* San Francisco: California Tomorrow.

Olsen, L., et al. (1994). *The unfinished journey: Restructuring schools in a diverse society.* San Francisco: California Tomorrow.

Ramirez, M., III, & Casteñeda, A. (1974). *Cultural democracy: Bicognitive development and education.* New York: Academic Press.

Spindler, G., & Spindler, L. (1991, October). *The process of culture and person: Multicultural classrooms and cultural therapy.* Paper presented at the Cultural Diversity Working Conference, Stanford University, School of Education.

Spindler, L., & Spindler, G. (1992, April). *The enduring and the situated self.* Paper presented at California State University, Sacramento.

Trueba, H. T. (1989). *Raising silent voices: Educating linguistic minorities for the 21st century.* Boston: Heine & Heine Publishers / Wadsworth.

Trueba, H. T., Rodriguez, C., Zou, Y., & Cintrón, J. (1993). *Healing multicultural America: Mexican immigrants rise to power in rural California.* Washington, DC: Falmer Press.

Valdes, G., & Figueroa, R. (1994). *Bilingualism and testing: A special case of bias.* Ablex Publishing.

Weinberg, C., & Reidford, P. (1972). Humanistic educational psychology. *Humanistic foundations of education.* Englewood Cliffs, NJ: Prentice Hall.

West, C. (1993). *Race matters.* Boston: Beacon Press.

Chapter 7

Teaching to Empower Minority Students

If you don't know where you are going, any road will get you there.

—The Cheshire Cat

If you don't know where you are going, no road will get you there.

—Campbell's reply

Each of the approaches to multicultural education has both strengths and weaknesses. Some efforts concentrate on making the curriculum more inclusive, others on raising academic achievement, and still others on improving intergroup relations. Often the discussion of multicultural education becomes confused by mixing references to the different approaches as if they were one program. They are not.

For example, Chapter 2 of this book describes an approach termed "the nature of culture," which incorporates the best of a recent anthropological perspective to overcome the limits of an earlier and very limited educational approach frequently called "teaching the culturally different."

Christine Sleeter and Carl Grant, in *Making Choices for Multicultural Education: Five Approaches to Race, Class, and Gender* (1988), developed a typology of approaches to multicultural education, as did Margaret Gibson (1987). Both of these typologies recognize a human relations approach. Human relations approaches (such as those described in Chapter 6) have been popular among teachers since the 1960s. These approaches include valuable materials and techniques for breaking down habits of thought that lead to prejudice, stereotyping, and discrimination. Human relations and intergroup relations strategies are an important part of a good curriculum, particularly for the primary grades and for students from the macroculture. However, as Chapter 3 demonstrated, the worst damages of racism and sexism are structural or institutional. Human relations strategies of teaching students to eliminate their individual prejudices, though an essential part of an enlightened curriculum, are by themselves inadequate for meeting the crisis of our increasingly divided society.

An approach called "single group studies" or "ethnic studies / women's studies" has led to major debates in the popular media over the appropriate curriculum or "canons" of study in the college curriculum. The timelines and descriptions in Chapter 3 detailing the diversity of U.S. ethnic and cultural experience are a strong argument for the usefulness of single group studies. Students need and deserve to know their own histories and many are empowered by this information. But ethnic studies and women's studies have primarily served the target groups; they have added new specializations but have not recast the macroculture's basic conceptual framework of history, literature, and the social sciences. The great majority of students are still learning the particular worldview of the dominant culture. The single group studies approach has challenged, but not revised, the canons of the academic disciplines.

Choosing Democracy argues for multicultural education in a "strong sense," as a process that engages students in building a more democratic society. Strong-sense multicultural education is similar to the humanist approach but it also emphasizes social responsibility. As Sleeter and Grant (1988) point out, **strong-sense multicultural education** incorporates ideas and strategies from each of the prior traditions and adds the **philosophy of social reconstruction,** or the idea that schools should participate in efforts to create a more just and a more democratic society. The remainder of this chapter will argue that a social reconstructionist position on multicultural education offers the best hope for achieving educational equality of opportunity.

Unlike other approaches, multicultural education that is social reconstructionist deals directly and forcefully with social and structural inequities in our society including racism, sexism, and class prejudice. It prepares students from oppressed groups to succeed in spite of existing inequalities. This approach argues for a bold commitment to democracy in schooling based on a belief in the learning potential of students from all races, classes, and both genders.

In 1990, the National Governors' Conference (co-chaired by then-Governor, Bill Clinton) made a call for equal access to high-quality education. In 1991, President Bush adopted the goals of the Governors' Conference in the report

America 2000: An Education Strategy. The authors of these goals claim a consensus. The goals can serve as a starting point for pursuing high-quality, democratic education. The president's report said:

> American students will leave grades 4, 8, and 12 having demonstrated competency in challenging subject matter including English, mathematics, science, history, and geography; and every school in America will ensure that all students learn to use their minds well, so they may be prepared for responsible citizenship, further learning, and productive employment in our modern economy. (p. 3)

Changing the schools—or **restructuring**—in pursuit of these goals requires ending tracking and rigid ability grouping. Students from all cultural groups deserve the opportunity to learn democratic principles and skills. Violence is done to democratic opportunity when students in "honors" classes and magnet schools receive quality instruction utilizing forums, debates, and critical thinking, while poor, mostly urban kids receive remedial drills and practice sheets. Inadequate school funding, current teacher recruitment practices, and the folk culture of schools encourage teachers to accept the school failure and to select and teach to the "good" students. Multicultural education rejects this process and instead chooses to engage all students in critical analysis and the pursuit of excellence.

Goals for Democratic Schools

The Public Education Information Network (1988), a group of educators interested in developing more democratic schools, offers the following description of appropriate goals for schools:

> In briefest terms, the three aspects of a democratic curriculum are:
> **Critical Literacy:** This goes beyond learning to read and write to include the motivation and capacity to be critical of what one reads, sees, and hears; to probe beyond surface appearances and question the common wisdom.
> **Knowledge and Understanding of the Diverse Intellectual, Cultural, and Scientific Traditions:** We refer not only to the more familiar academic disciplines and traditions of high culture, but to the histories and cultural perspectives of those people, including women and minorities, traditionally excluded from formal study.
> **Ability to Use Knowledge and Skills:** to pursue one's own interests; to make informed personal and political decisions; and to work for the welfare of the community. (p. 3)

Working toward these goals will require substantial changes in the folkways and teaching practices of schools. Chapter 4 details how schools contribute to class stratification when the poor and students of color are pushed out of schools and tracked out of future economic opportunity. Teachers face the choice of continuing the present school system with its 50% dropout rate for many urban students of color, or they can choose alternative teaching strategies based on a multicultural social reconstructionist position that empowers poor and minority students to achieve democratic goals for the society.

Critical Pedagogy

At the turn of the last century, John Dewey (1859–1962) (1966) argued that critical analysis and learning by doing were essential for the preparation of citizens in a democracy. Influenced by the massive European immigration from 1900–1920, Dewey was not an advocate of multicultural education as we presently know it. Like Jefferson before him, Dewey favored having the schools lead the nation in the development of a new, idealized, democratic American. Today, in a parallel period of massive immigration, Dewey's works provide a partial yet incomplete foundation for the ideological position that schools can serve in the cause of social reconstruction.

The Brazilian educator Paulo Freire (1970) contributed to a rebirth and extension of Dewey's ideas in the field of advancing a pluralistic democracy. Freire's work revolves around a socially responsible humanism. Like Dewey, he believed that education had a central role in building a democratic society. But Freire's writings offered a new and fresh view of education's role in liberating the oppressed, which he saw as essential to the process of building a democratic, participatory community (Campbell, 1980).

Freire first gained attention for the methodology he and his colleagues developed to teach literacy to the impoverished people of the Recife area of northeast Brazil. His first major book, *A Pedagogy of the Oppressed* (1970), described a revolutionary educational process and social change process for the poor in Latin America. Freire believed that educational workers could help empower students by engaging in dialogue with them rather than falling into the traditional teacher-student roles. The Brazilian government's official response to his work was to arrest him in 1964. After his imprisonment and eventual deportation, he worked for the World Council of Churches in Geneva. By the early 1970s, *Pedagogy of the Oppressed* was being read and discussed throughout Latin America and among small circles of intellectuals in the United States and Europe (Freire, n.d.; Freire, 1985; McFadden, 1975). In *Pedagogy of the Oppressed*, Freire described the oppressive and colonizing functions served by traditional teacher-dominated education. Freire's ideas have important ramifications for understanding the education of oppressed cultural groups in U.S. schools.

Prior to Freire's work, most published educational research and university work in social science education in the United States had suggested only technical improvements to the existing school curriculum. The "scientific study" of schools, common in the 1970s and 1980s, used positivist research methods (see prior chapter). They generally strengthened the school's role in the domination of oppressed communities. Freire's writings offered new hope and insight to teachers working with alienated and oppressed students in our society. Teachers and activists searched his works and found alternative strategies for immigrant students and oppressed cultural groups. Freire's work proposed solutions to the structural failure of poor children in U.S. schools while the narrow research paradigms of positivism avoided questions of race and class.

Paulo Freire openly acknowledged that his views included a political pedagogy. He revealed the political dimension underlying any educational system. Education and schools could reinforce the domination of the existing elite or they could show citizens how to lead free and self-empowering lives. Following Freire's lead, educational activists in Brazil, Chile, Venezuela, and Nicaragua taught the poor to read by helping community members analyze their life situations. Poor peasants engaged in community organizing to effect social change. Freire used the term *praxis* to describe the process of critical analysis leading to action. The experience of praxis empowers people to participate in democratic struggles. Strong-sense multicultural education applies the principles of cultural action and praxis to U.S. public schools, particularly schools serving students of oppressed classes and cultures.

Conservative scholars accuse advocates of multicultural education of politicizing the curriculum. This charge has often intimidated multicultural education advocates and placed them on the defensive. Yet clearly the writings of John Dewey were profoundly political. Critics attack the political dimension of both Freire's work and multicultural educational theory while refusing to acknowledge that Dewey's major works provide the intellectual foundations of social reconstruction. Dewey argued that the schools should promote immigrant assimilation and build a democratic society. These are political goals. Freire's work, like those of Dewey, recognizes the essentially political nature of education. Both the present Eurocentric curriculum and its multicultural alternatives are highly political. Realistically, the teacher's choice is not between being political or neutral. The conservative's approach of claiming political neutrality actually supports the continuation of the current tracked, starkly unequal school system—a profoundly political position.

The teaching strategies and attitudes described by Freire and adapted for multicultural education in the United States begin by respecting the prior cultural knowledge that all students bring to the classroom. Freire, like Dewey, argued for rooting the educational experience in the real experiences of the students. Freire believed that speech, language, and literacy can be understood only in a social context and that students learn language and literacy best in the context of their social experience. Paulo Freire worked with a number of adult literacy campaigns that have applied this principle and have had enormous impact in societies seeking transition to democracy. Cultural action in literacy contributed to social change in Brazil, Chile, Guinea-Bissau, and Nicaragua. In his writings, Freire also applauded successful efforts in the United States—notably the Foxfire project and Highlander Folk School in Tennessee.

Ethnography

Freire's work occurred at the same time as the field of ethnography developed within anthropology. Both movements were influenced by research efforts in Latin America. Ethnography revised one aspect of positivist scientific methods. Instead of breaking a research problem into parts and subcategories, **ethnography** stresses observing the community, classroom, or school as a complex whole; describing an event in context; and seeking to understand the culture of the participants or a classroom (Trueba, 1989). Both ethnographic research and Freire's work in Latin America considered culture as a field of struggle, not as a fixed or static object. In this view, developing an understanding of their culture helps students to respect themselves, to learn from the past, and to participate in the active creation of a democratic future. The literacy programs designed by Freire and his colleagues used an ethnographic perspective to assist peasants in learning about their culture as a means of empowering them. In a similar manner, students and teachers from oppressed communities of color in the United States need to recover and recognize their own cultures.

Once students recognize their own cultural context, they can learn to think critically about it and make meaningful decisions about their life opportunities. Critical pedagogy, or problem-posing education, seeks to help students understand the world they live in and to critically analyze their real-life situations. Critical analysis, practical skills, and self-confidence lead to empowerment. Participation in community development helps students develop the political courage to work toward the resolution of their real problems. Community action teams working with preliterate peasants in Latin America helped them to learn to read and perhaps to create a labor union or farmer cooperative. For students from oppressed groups in the United States, the goals might be gaining admission to colleges, receiving a good-quality high school preparation for work, or counteracting crime in their communities.

The strong democratic reconstructionist form of multicultural education has adopted the goal of empowerment as central to educational reform. By urging that schools help students build a more democratic society, multicultural education moves away from positivism's stress on being an objective observer of events. Educational projects designed for empowerment help students to take a stand. They provide opportunities for students to intervene in their own families and communities; to analyze situations, decide, act, and then to analyze their actions anew. Empowerment is taught to overcome disempowerment. The problem-posing approach of empowerment gives students reasons to study, to learn, and to stay in school.

The multicultural education movement, incorporating Freire's insights with those of ethnography, argues that because culture is constantly changing, and because cultures adapt through education, then community development is always available as an alternative to oppression. Analysis, social participation, and student action teach skills, confidence, and political courage for community development. While traditional educational strategies dominate students and contribute to the domination of communities, the process of critical analysis leading to positive action (praxis) empowers students and energizes communities.

How the Present Curriculum Fails Students

The present curriculum is often divorced from the reality of youth. Lessons in the social studies should provide a natural starting place for students to engage in multicultural education. However, since the 1970s, the pressure to raise scores on standardized tests, particularly in math and reading, has intensified. As a result, social studies in the primary grades have been practically eliminated. Additional reading, language, and math time have become the priorities.

The conservative school reform movement (1982–1992) successfully convinced textbook buyers and publishers to focus on history and geography—avoiding the more open-ended social sciences of economics and sociology as well as social and controversial issues. In the upper grades, middle schools, and secondary schools, inadequate and unrealistic texts predominate. Instead of engaging students' interests, most history texts offer a sterile, inaccurate, and incomplete view of our society in very boring prose. Teachers resort to grades, tests, and worksheets to motivate students to pay attention. Some teachers have become wardens, forcing rote memorization on reluctant students, adding to the students' growing impression that school, particularly history, is irrelevant to life. Empowerment strategies reverse this debasement of history and reintroduce the social studies (Campbell, 1987; New York States Education Dept., 1988).

Our democracy cannot afford further deterioration in the preparation of its youth. In our schools, too many students are not offered the opportunity to learn the beauty and refinement of their own cultural heritage. Failure to provide children of diverse cultures with knowledge of their heritage leads to low self-esteem, alienation from school, loss of a sense of self-worth, and higher dropout rates.

Students from minority cultures, students of color, and females are routinely presented with two perspectives. On one hand, in school they are given a rather inaccurate and boring history book representing U.S. society as homogeneous and consensus-based. This viewpoint clashes with many students' own worldview, based on their life experience of conflict and oppression. Students are disempowered when the teacher or the textbook negates or ignores their community knowledge, cultural frame of reference and language.

Literature, English, and language arts courses are further arenas of alienation and failure. Too many texts deny the integrity, validity, and even the existence of the students' families and cultures.

In the elementary grades, schools too often rely on haphazard and fragmentary approaches to supplement the textbooks. These intermittent units that touch on cultural holidays, heroes, "foods of other lands," and similar activities may be fun but they hardly amount to multicultural education. Instead of providing an intellectually defensible view of a multicultural society, many middle and secondary schools are even further distanced from the students' reality. They generally follow the canons of establishment history and culture imposed by the universities and textbook publishers and often avoid a rigorous analysis of race, culture, class, and gender even though many students' daily lives are immersed in these conflict areas.

Most teacher preparation programs and the present public school curriculum reflect and promote the majority culture's view of reality. Students of color need empowerment strategies to counteract the pervasive and, for them, dominating influence of disempowerment. These empowerment strategies should include goal clarification and the achievement of clear, measurable progress. For example, immigrant students want to acquire fluent English, but many give up and accept low levels of language learning. Their failure is not from a lack of goals, nor of practice. Failure develops from school experiences that do not provide frequent confirmation of measurable progress toward language mastery. Language acquisition programs fail when they approach lessons as if language were only a skill. Attitudes toward language, toward culture, and toward self all influence language acquisition. Positive experiences with language use and reflective thinking about cultural conflict and assimilation encourage students to stay in school and continue toward graduation.

In addition, the multicultural curriculum must include academic skill development. To succeed in school or to get a better job, students need to improve their reading and writing skills. It is better for students to develop math skills in fourth or even eighth grade rather than struggle with remedial math in high school or college. Practice in reading and writing helps students to experience more school success and to develop a positive attitude toward school. Lesson plans and curricula should include developing improved study skills as attainable, measurable goals appropriate to young people and directly related to economic success and opportunity.

Despite the need for continued improvements in the areas just discussed, our society has changed. There is more equality in 1990 than there was in 1950. Economic opportunities for the well-educated African American, Latino, or Asian have appreciably improved. Instruction that starts with the students' home and community experiences provides the basis for strategies to convert the students' frustration into determination, and prior defeat in school into hope.

Selecting Themes

New teachers often do not know where to begin to find themes that begin in the students' own experiences. A theme can be a topic or subject that reoccurs frequently in the life of a child. The process of studying themes from their own reality validates students' cultures and helps them to recognize the importance of school.

To help students understand that school and lessons are valuable, school lessons should help to explain real life. Teachers err when they assume that the relevance of their lessons is obvious. On the contrary, teachers should explain and re-explain the relevance of lessons to the students' lives and to prior lessons.

Selecting Themes for Kindergarten Through Grade 3

Many good teachers begin the process of discovering their students' interests by observing and listening. What do they do? What do they talk about? Teachers can also ask the parents what the most important things are for their child. In particular, teachers should ask the parents of a child that is mildly off-task or disruptive to share some of the activities and interests the child responds to at home.

If you provide children with a free choice of books, the books they choose will suggest themes. Popular magazines written for their level such as *My Weekly Reader, Highlights for Children,* and *National Geographic World* also cover themes of importance to children. Teachers will find it useful to read the special teacher's editions of these magazines.

Providing students with time to draw and fantasize also reveals their interests and themes of interest to them. During a sharing time, they can explain their drawings to others, revealing even more themes. An excellent series of books has been written and cooperatively published by parents and children in the Literatura Infantil program near Watsonville, California. The books and lesson plans are now available for $8.95 commercially from

Children's Book Press
5925 Doyle Street, Suite U
Emeryville, CA 94608
(415) 655-3395

New teachers often get ideas for themes by watching "Sesame Street" and other children's television shows to observe what interests children. If a district will allow it, there is nothing wrong with regular watching of "Sesame Street," "Square One," and similar educational shows in the classroom. No teacher can compete with the money or skills of a production company, and these programs are excellent. If they are integrated with regular lessons, they can greatly enhance learning. Using computers, hypermedia, and instructional television can also provide the teacher with important time to work with one or two children while other students interact with these excellent programs.

In very poor districts, teachers may have to purchase their own televisions and VCRs, a real burden for underpaid new teachers. This reality shocks many new teachers. Our schools are so underfunded that many teachers spend from $600 to $1,000 per year of their own money to buy classroom materials. This should not be necessary. We seldom ask other professionals to subsidize their work.

Student teachers begin to collect supplementary materials, bulletin board ideas, charts, and other supplies during their practice teaching. It often takes three to four years to collect enough materials to easily conduct classes.

Selecting Themes for Intermediate Grades 4 Through 6

At this level, teachers can start with inventories of student interests. One example, created by Sidney Simon and his colleagues (1972), is the values clarification exercise, "20 Things You Love To Do," shown in Figure 7.1.

In the original values clarification exercise, the list was kept private. The teacher then guided students through the process of values analysis, calculating factors of risk, cost, and parental influence for each item on students' lists (Simon et al., 1972). Changing the exercise and collecting the lists provide the teacher with an excellent source of themes in the students' lives.

A similar exercise has the students list their favorite TV shows. The teacher or the students compile the lists, which the teacher then analyzes. Analysis of television viewing can provide important themes in the curriculum.

Free-choice literature selections often reveal what children are interested in. Many teachers assign students to interview community leaders. When the teacher reads the interviews, new themes emerge from the writing. While students work in groups on interviews, the teacher can circulate around the room and listen to their conversations for additional themes.

New teachers may discover student themes by attending student events and talking to experienced teachers. Teachers can also provide students with imaginary moral dilemmas or other incomplete conflict situations and assign students to describe the most effective responses to the problems. The student scenarios will reveal new themes for the day.

These efforts do not abandon the curriculum in search of student interest. Instead, the teacher is searching for themes in the students' lives that make the curriculum valuable, useful, motivational. As teachers monitor themes, they should respect diversity among the several cultures and both genders.

Lessons should have a context and a sequence. Because students benefit from knowing what teachers are going to teach next and why, teachers should explain their organization of the lessons. Writing the day's agenda on the chalkboard is one way to inform students about what will be covered so they can see the progress they are making.

Selecting Themes for Grades 8 through 12

The examples of student inventories, literature, value clarification lessons, and television described for grades 4 through 6 also apply to grades 8 through 12. However, for grades 8 through 12, teenage students will also need validation of

Figure 7.1. Values Clarification Exercise

The students prepare a paper by listing the numbers 1 through 20 down one side. The exercise calls for students to make a rapid list of their favorite activities. The teacher explains in advance that she will collect the paper. Students should not write intimate items on this paper. Names are not needed on the paper.

When the teacher gives the signal, the students make a rapid list of the items they would most like to do. The items are not listed in any priority.

Example:

Things I Would Most Like To Do

1.
2.
3.
4.
5.
6.
7.
8.
9.
10.
11.
12.
13.
14.
15.
16.
17.
18.
19.
20.

Note. Adapted from *Values Clarification* (p. 30), by S. B. Simon, L. W. Howe, and H. Kirschenbaum, 1972, New York: Hart Publishing.

their own experiences and cultures. Because adolescents often feel as if they are under attack, they may benefit from talking about their frustrations, conflicts, and anxieties. Teachers should listen to the problems of adolescents in a rapidly changing and often dangerous society. Students' own problems constitute important themes for study.

New teachers may have students list their favorite TV shows and movies. A teacher viewing these programs should look for themes that can be connected to classroom lessons. For example, writing the lyrics of a popular song on the chalkboard can stimulate a dynamic discussion. A teacher might pose questions such as these: What is the message? Do you agree with the message? Do your friends agree? To extend the discussion of music lyrics to a homework assignment, the teacher might ask students to explore in an essay one or two of the issues revealed in the lyrics. Some additional topics that encourage valuable discussion include these: What struggles do you have with your parents? Are you prepared for sex? Do you need more information? Where can you get information about drugs?

Analyzing advertising aimed at young people reveals additional themes. For instance, many clothing advertisements encourage teenagers to believe that a certain look will win them access to a desired social group. Some advertisements for clothing encourage conformity, some aggressive sexuality, while others encourage eccentricity. These themes are ever-present in the students' lives. Initially, students may deny the effectiveness of advertising, but a more thoughtful examination usually reveals its function in defining "the good life."

Teenagers particularly respond to stereotypes about teenagers. Often the stereotypes are revealed in name calling and group forming. Gangs for the poor and exploited, and cliques and fraternities for the middle class, are expressions of young people's need to belong to a group. Social studies classes should study the roles and functions of gangs and cliques. The movies *American Me* and *Boyz in the Hood* reveal some of the tragedies of gang life.

Currently violence, sex, drugs, and AIDS are topics of prime concern to young people. Some districts have adopted programs to help teachers discuss these issues. A powerful video, "Still Killing Us Softly," explores the themes of sexuality and violence toward women in the beauty industry. Teachers need and deserve assistance in presenting these controversial topics, but recent financial crises and budget cuts have eliminated many programs. Teachers working in a cash-strapped district often will need to finance their own workshops or take classes at a nearby university that offers preparation programs for these issues. At a minimum, new teachers need to maintain an ongoing dialogue with their fellow teachers, particularly more experienced teachers.

To stay current on themes of importance to their students, teachers can continue to monitor magazines such as *Junior Scholastic* and *Senior Scholastic*, the teen pages of local newspapers, and teen magazines. In New York City, a group of teenagers write their own quality newspaper. *Rethinking Schools*, a Milwaukee-based journal, publishes student writing about important issues.

State education departments and local school districts provide teachers with curriculum guides and even textbooks. These materials reflect adult decisions about what a student should know. These decisions are usually valid, but adolescents must be convinced of the value. We can no longer assume that teenagers accept and participate in the values expressed in the curriculum and the school. One of the roles of school is to introduce students to the real world—the world beyond adolescent movies, music, and fantasy.

Students become bored when learning makes no apparent difference in their lives. Schools need to encourage young people to study, to prepare for adult life, and to talk about what matters to them. The skills of articulate communication are important for professional careers, but the present school system often fails to teach these skills to people of color and poor people, tracking them instead into unemployment and poverty. These skills can be learned. Many migrant farmworkers have learned English to fight their bosses, and African American students learned the discipline of nonviolence to overthrow Jim Crow laws in the South. In these cases, students learned quickly and effectively because they had concrete reasons for developing new skills and acquiring new knowledge. Developing a willingness to analyze problems, formulate plans, and then to act on the plans prepares a people for self-governance.

Reality—Its Place in the Classroom

In spite of the national ideal of promoting pluralism, racism and discrimination remain realities of our society. While human relations approaches may be sufficient for kindergarten through grade 3 and for European American students, students of color need more powerful strategies to prepare them to overcome the institutionalized inequality in our schools and our society. An inaccurate, utopian view of our society and our government invalidates the students' own life experiences as a source of knowledge. An empowerment curriculum should offer the opportunity for students to study racism and pluralism and encourage them to search for new democratic alternatives for our society.

The violence of racism, sexism, and class oppression provide important subjects for study and analysis. By studying oppression in historical settings and analyzing its constituent parts, students develop a perspective that stops placing the blame on the victim. In empowerment classes, this sort of critical analysis leads to planning for social change. By middle school (grades 6 through 8) students should be encouraged to consider empowerment strategies, including seeking individual advancement through education and collective advancement through political struggle.

Current opportunities for schooling are unequal, but educational opportunities are more equal than economic or housing opportunities. From at least 1900 until 1970, schooling was considered a preparation for life and an opportunity to earn a better standard of living. Advocacy groups fought long and hard for educational opportunity culminating in *Brown vs. Board of Education* of Topeka, Kansas (1954), *Lau vs. Nichols* (1971), and the civil rights struggles of the 1950s and 1960s. An empowerment curriculum seeks to bring the results and the orientation of these struggles for equality into the classroom. Present school tracking by "ability groups" promotes the ideology of meritocracy and strengthens discrimination (Oakes, 1985). Students in the upper college-bound tracks have an inherent advantage. At-risk students in the middle and lower tracks need to understand the school system they are subject to and become more mature and more goal oriented in order to gain equal educational opportunity. The study of racism, sexism, and class oppression in schools helps students comprehend this unequal system and to make personal decisions to take advantage of their school experience to prepare for the future.

Television and the youth culture present a competing, less mature, more immediate, self-indulgent life philosophy. The abundance of wealth in our society bestows on middle-class students the luxury of extended adolescence. They can get serious about growing up later in college or after college. But students of color and at-risk students may sacrifice their future educational opportunities when they substitute the value of the commercial youth culture for hard work. These young people especially need adults to present a commonsense, real-world perspective on opportunity.

Social Participation in Schools

Anthropologists refer to two aspects of school curriculum—the formal and the informal. The **formal curriculum** consists of the goals, course outlines, strategies, and materials used to teach and evaluate lessons and skills. The **informal curriculum** includes the messages conveyed by a combination of rules, regulations, procedures, and practices, including the attitudes of teachers, staff, and administrators. The formal and the informal curriculum sometimes conflict. The formal curriculum may encourage students to take a position and to defend that position with argument, but students are seldom coached and supported for taking action on controversial issues in schools such as tracking, alienation, and violence.

Schools have long recognized the value of participation in student councils and student governments, but these structures typically serve a small, select few. It is not an accident that middle-class schools have numerous opportunities for participation while inner-city schools tend to emphasize administrative control of the student population. Such differences betray attitudes that are potentially harmful to many students: A small portion of the middle class is taught to lead while the poor are contained and controlled. The informal curriculum of many schools serving working-class students discourages these students from getting involved in self-governance. The cultural democratic alternative argues that because all students need preparation for democracy, all students should be engaged in the decision-making process.

Humans learn best by doing. Yet schools often seek to teach citizenship to students from dominated cultural groups through passive methods such as readings, discussions, films, and worksheets. To prepare students to participate in our democracy, we must make room in the curriculum for more active strategies that teach democratic participation. Active strategies expose students to meaningful social and political choices and give them opportunities to act as responsible citizens. We know how to reach the "good" students who are already committed to schooling. We need new strategies to reach the isolated, alienated students who are potential dropouts. These reluctant and passive students are in greater need of participatory strategies than are the academically successful.

Schools encourage democratic behavior when students engage in substantial decision making. Some teachers achieve this by having students participate in management decisions and discipline systems in classroom meetings. Many elementary, middle, and secondary schools have engaged student teams in conflict resolution and violence reduction strategies. This strategy of teaching democratic behavior, attitudes, and analysis through encouraging students to participate in social controversy and social movements is called **social participation.** Introducing social participation into the curriculum in the upper grades produces a positive, pro-democratic effect on both formal and informal curricula (Beane, 1990). [1]

Teachers promote social participation by encouraging projects at a level of safety and controversy appropriate to each school community. Social participation projects offer excellent ways to complete thematic units that integrate two or more subjects. For example, fourth-grade students might design a campaign to rid the school of litter. Sixth-grade and older students can participate in conflict resolution training to reduce violence on the school grounds. Tenth-grade students might want to lobby for auto insurance reform or school financing of intermural athletics. Urban students can work to make their school grounds or neighborhood a drug-free and violence-free zone. Students learn academic skills and increase their sense of efficacy and self-worth when they study issues, make decisions, and then take action that helps to eliminate the problems they've identified. Excellent ideas for student-centered educational projects are found in *It's Our World, Too! Stories of Young People Who Are Making a Difference* (1993), by Phillip Hoose.

Through skillful training in decision-making and problem-solving processes, students can learn to accurately predict the possibility of achieving specific changes. Teachers guide students in conducting research on topics and making appropriate selections of targets for their efforts. Later, students analyze the results to measure the accuracy of their predictions and the effectiveness of their chosen strategies.

---

[1] Unfortunately, most of the research on effectiveness of these strategies is limited to its effect on students from the European American majority group. See Leming, J. S. (1985). Research on social studies curriculum instruction: Interventions and outcomes in the socio-moral domain. *Review of Research in Social Studies Education, 1976–1983.* National Council for the Social Studies.

Multicultural curriculum reform often includes civic and community participation projects. Students develop social and work skills along with pro-democratic values through active, guided participation in community service agencies. By working with a wide range of groups such as anti-poverty agencies, political parties, and labor organizations, 11th- and 12th-grade students can gain a realistic and diverse view of the community and of the political process. Social participation develops both the skills and the sense of political courage needed to overcome the present alienation between many students of color and the schools (Quality Education for Minorities Project, 1990).

Too many students from minority cultural groups have been trained for defeat. Sitting in classes completing endless worksheets confirms their cynical belief that schooling and education make little real difference in life. On the other hand, social participation empowers students and provides a means to break out of these defeatist patterns. Work in community agencies teaches students a realistic view of the processes of change. Adult community activists serve as mentors to the students and insist that they complete their education. Students begin their transition to the world of work and return to school more mature and self-disciplined.

Interaction with life, work, and poverty will convince many students of the value of education. Students gain a sense of social responsibility when they participate in projects that actually contribute to the health of the community. It is important to select opportunities for social participation that provide both safety and success. Some schools have fifth-grade students become "buddies" who are responsible for helping first-graders adjust to school. In other schools, 10th-grade students staff tutoring centers to help seventh- and eighth-grade students complete their homework. Students, the school, and the community gain by these efforts. Students learn to work to achieve goals. Social participation teaches that we can accept responsibility and control our own lives, an important step toward believing in the value of education.

In earlier decades, some of the finest traditions of the social studies were built on a conception of curriculum that stressed social participation. Educational philosopher John Dewey stressed the need to create a new society by democratic participation in the construction of such a society. Aronstein and Olsen, in *Action Learning: Student Community Services Projects,* (1974), described how to get students involved in productive community service projects as integral parts of their classroom experiences. James Shaver and others (1977) found a need for further development of the ideas of participation in *Building Rationales for Citizenship Education.* The ideological assault on schools, curriculum, and school boards carried out by conservative forces from the 1970s to the present, however, has eliminated or neutralized social participation efforts in many communities. Conservative forces favor the pattern of presenting often sterile and irrelevant academic lessons even though these lessons teach many students apathy and alienation. They look to the home and the neighborhood to explain school failure, not to the instructional processes of the school. Conservatives often consider social and political participation strategies as radical attempts to "politicize" the schools (Campbell, 1980; Ravitch, 1990).

Social reconstructionism, like other educational philosophies, is political. Multicultural education that is social reconstructionist uses participation as a strategy to politicize students from communities of color to convince them to advance democracy. Future citizens from *all* cultures and classes deserve to learn the skills and acquire the political courage needed to make government work for their interests.

Over 50% of the adults in our nation do not vote in general elections. Even fewer vote in local and school board elections. Nonvoters tend to be poor and are frequently African American, Latino, and Asian (Figure 7.2). By not voting, they participate in their own disenfranchisement. In turn, schools, roads, and social services in their communities are the most neglected, resulting in fewer and fewer resources for their children.

Empowerment Strategies

Empowering students is central to the social reconstructionist philosophy of developing a multicultural curriculum. Many schools empower middle-class students. And even though problems of drugs, suicide, and violence clearly indicate that not all middle-class students are empowered in school, most are taught the skills, attitudes, and behavior patterns needed to succeed in our society.

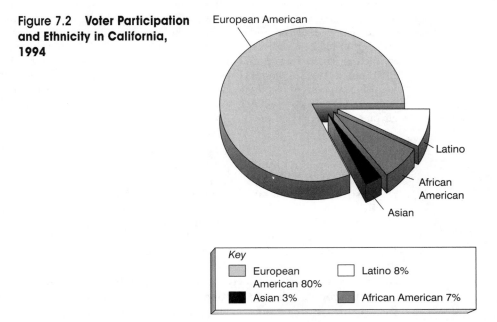

Figure 7.2 Voter Participation and Ethnicity in California, 1994

Key
- European American 80%
- Asian 3%
- Latino 8%
- African American 7%

Schools presently empower students from elite classes and disempower selected cultural, class, and gender groups. As Henry Trueba (1993) explains, empowerment contests with disempowerment. Schools systematically disempower cultural minority groups by silencing students, by denying their culture, or rendering their culture and language useless in school.

Trueba describes the process as follows:

> In this context of cultural contacts between mainstream persons and those from different linguistic and cultural backgrounds (such as between teachers and students), the least conflictive position is taken by those persons who adopt multicultural responses. Yet, cultural therapy, as a means to compare and contrast cultural values and understandings, can enhance communication and resolve conflicts arising from misunderstandings in inter-ethnic and intercultural exchanges. There are at least two main ways in which cultural therapy can help. First, it can help develop a strong personal identity based on a better known and better understood cultural background. Second, cultural therapy can also increase the ability to identify areas of value conflict, differences in interpretations of messages and expectations, range of acceptable etiquette, preferential protocol, and other expected behavioral responses.
>
> A strong personal cultural or ethnic identity is providing the individual with legitimacy and recognition for his or her enduring self. The psychological justification for retaining a personal framework for self-understanding and for self-acceptance, the setting to which we feel attached as children—the quintessence of what we are in our own eyes, our enduring self—remains justified and unchanged regardless of other adjustments. This is the basis for deeper emotional peace and stability. In contrast, being forced to abandon this inner frame of enduring self, especially when the home language is lost, isolates a child from the world of his dreams, the world of his affection. How can a child deal with two different worlds and transfer information from one to the other, if the bridge between the two worlds (the language) is broken? How can a child retain a measure of psychological integrity if he is not allowed to reconcile conflicting values from home and school? How can a child enrich his home learning environment if going home is seen as degrading? How can a child seek emotional and cognitive support from parents who are seen as unworthy and despicable? Sooner or later, a child will comprehend that the rejection of one's own language and culture is ultimately the rejection of one's own self. (pp. 147–149)

In their *Quality of Life Budget, FY 1991*, the Congressional Black Caucus described the crisis for students of color as follows:

> We must recognize that our nation will be ill prepared to enter the 21st century if our children cannot read, write, and calculate mathematics, much less understand the high-tech world they are about to inherit. We must recognize that a nation that condemns its children to hopelessness, and the lure of drug abuse, is a nation that cannot begin to hope to remain economically competitive or morally strong. (p. 3)

For our democracy to survive and prosper, schools serving students of color need a fundamental shift in emphasis. Democratic teachers will design teaching strategies that aim to empower all students. Schools should teach all students to read and provide them with the skills needed for employment, as well as to gain access to both higher education and the knowledge industries of the future. Students from all social classes and ethnic groups deserve to learn the skills of analysis and organization, as well as to develop the self-confidence needed to engage in struggles for political equality (Haycock & Navarro, 1988; Orfield & Jaeger, 1984).

Students from minority cultures and linguistic groups who have been excluded from democratic participation particularly deserve education designed for empowerment (Cummins, 1986). We can summarize the main strategies for empowerment as follows:

1. Study the nature of culture.
2. Study the nature of cultural conflicts and value conflicts.
3. Study the powerful analytic concepts that reveal students' real culture and current status. (See Chapter 2.)
4. Use students' home, school, and community experiences as source material for curriculum and as a basis for analysis.
5. Compare racism and pluralism as options for the individual and the society.
6. Plan lessons to use success as a strategy. All students deserve the opportunity to succeed.
7. Teach critical thinking (reflective thinking). (See Chapter 9.)
8. Use cooperative learning strategies. (See Chapter 10.)
9. Respect the child's home language. (See Chapter 11.)
10. Encourage social participation and praxis as a part of the curriculum.

Subsequent chapters in this book provide practical teacher advice for these empowerment strategies.

The Teacher as Coach

We need not restrict our view of teaching and learning to large-group instruction. Often educational encounters that empower occur between a teacher and one or two students. A teacher question, a comment, or a few words of encouragement sometimes help students to continue their struggle for an education.

Students who experience regular success in school receive affirmation and support from their daily school experiences. Unfortunately, many students simply pass through school. They seldom reflect on their experiences or consider taking charge of their educational and economic future.

When a teacher coaches a student, a simple comment or a student conference can lead the student to reconsider his or skills and behavior and lead to plans for improvements. Good teachers use coaching to conduct conferences on motivation and skill development. A pedagogy for empowerment should make coaching a deliberate, planned series of experiences for all students.

Coaching is begun by teachers analyzing the performance of their students. Students who are performing well should be encouraged to continue. Students who are performing poorly might consider changing their study strategies. Students who are in the middle seldom get noticed. A carefully thought-out strategy of coaching will encourage the success of *all* the students.

The teacher sets a goal of getting to know one student per week by talking with the student and listening to the student's perception of reality. A suggestion, a prompt, a little praise can encourage students to consider themselves important and to make changes in their study habits. Teachers make time for coaching by planning lessons that provide the opportunities for one-on-one interaction (see Chapter 10 on cooperative learning).

Working in Teams

Students and adults in many communities are divided and isolated. They quarrel with each other and are frequently alienated from the government and society. But when residents of poor communities work together on projects ranging from crime control to school improvement, both the community and its members gain power.

Structure activities in group work, decision making, consensus seeking, and group evaluation that can prepare students for community leadership development. Some social action projects should require students to work together in teams. Working in groups helps students learn interpersonal skills and increases their chances of experiencing success. Working in groups helps students learn to practice behavior that supports the values of cooperation, non-competition, sharing of resources, and peer respect.

Sociologist Elizabeth Cohen (1986) argues that there is an urgent need to structure groups purposefully so that cooperation and caring emerge, because American youngsters are so heavily influenced by forces leading to individualism and competitiveness. Students, particularly in the middle school years (grades 6 through 8), want to belong to groups to overcome the alienation and fear of rejection common in their lives. When schools build on group values, they make important and vital connections with the concerns of the students. A curriculum of social participation and empowerment can support group values while redirecting students away from gang fights and crime.

Teams of students can work together to combine analysis and action on the following projects:

1. Changing the classroom environment (such as bulletin boards or seating arrangements).
2. Helping to solve neighborhood problems (such as preventing teenage pregnancy, tutoring, or eliminating litter).
3. Visiting the aged, helping in food lockers and kitchens for the homeless.

4. Volunteering at day care centers and breakfast programs.

5. Participating in political party efforts.

6. Joining union and civil rights organizations.

A detailed description of the process of developing teams and processing their work is provided in Chapter 8.

Critical Theory

The emphasis on empowerment is a part of a broader educational development referred to as **critical theory.** Critical theory developed from Paulo Freire's work, a reconsideration of the work of Dewey, Henry Giroux, Peter McLaren, Lois Weis, Alma Flor Ada, Jim Cummins, Stanley Aronowitz, and others.[2] The following concepts are central to critical theory, and are useful in trying to comprehend and analyze your own teaching experience.

> **Consciousness.** Awareness of yourself and your environment. Consciousness includes self-awareness. Multicultural consciousness refers to a recognition of the ethnic, racial, and social divisions in our society.
>
> **Culture.** The collective knowledge of a group of people, (described extensively in Chapter 2). Please note that critical theorists have tended to rely on European authors for descriptions of culture. The Europeans tend to emphasize class differences and to pay less attention to the differences between cultures and ethnic groups.
>
> **Domination.** The act of controlling a group of people.
>
> **Empowerment.** Educational processes that lead to political courage and political efficacy. Empowerment strategies teach students to analyze and to act on their analyses. Empowerment strategies also help students gain social, political, and economic power, including the power to make their own decisions.
>
> **Ethics.** Normative decisions based on value preferences rather than exclusively on objective research.
>
> **Hegemony.** The overwhelming domination of ideologies or economic systems by a single group. Often ideological hegemony leaves learners unaware of alternative viewpoints. For example, most schools and teachers have an unexamined commitment to competitive grading.

---

[2] See particularly: Aronowitz, S., & Giroux, H. (1985). *Education Under Siege: The Conservative, Liberal, and Radical Debate Over Schooling.* New York: Bergen & Garvey; Giroux, H. (1988). *Teachers as Intellectuals, Toward a Critical Pedagogy of Learning.* New York: Bergen & Garvey; McLaren, P. (1989). *Life in Schools: An Introduction to Critical Pedagogy on the Foundations of Education.* New York: Longman.

Hidden Curriculum. The wide variety of values and ideas taught informally in schools. These attitudes and assumptions permeate the school but rarely reveal themselves in lesson plans or tests. For example, U.S. schools commonly teach individualism, competitiveness, and a European American perspective on our nation's history.

Ideological Domination. The domination of the ideas presented to students by, for example, selecting the content of textbooks.

Ideologies. A series of interrelated ideas, such as racism or cultural pluralism. A dominant ideology is often taught in schools as if it were the only truth. For example, we are taught that the United States has a democratic government. Our system is then presented as the definition of democracy: two competing parties, regular elections, a free press, and limited government intervention in the economy. There are other models of democracy, but our particular system is taught as an ideology. In similar fashion, we are taught an ideology that our schools are neutral, even though they are clearly committed to the maintenance of the present power system.

Social Class. A group identified by its economic position in the society, that is, working class, poor, wealthy owners of production. There are several contending descriptions of classes in the United States.

Social Construction of Knowledge. The observation that most knowledge is created by persons. What we regard as knowledge has a purpose. The concept of the social construction of knowledge treats knowledge as purposeful and serving particular interests rather than as neutral and merely discovered. For example, IQ tests were generated for a particular purpose, to predict school success. They do not define intelligence; rather they measure a specific kind of mental aptitude in relation to a specific purpose. As an alternative, Gardner (1993) proposes that multiple intelligences provide a more useful description of thinking processes.

Summary

It is important for students to learn that study and analysis in school can help them make life decisions. Positive school experiences that make a difference in students' lives lead them to conclude that further schooling can provide an entrance into the dynamic sector of our economy. Empowerment strategies derived from critical theory ideology recognize that public schools have served as an important vehicle for the growth of our democracy and our economy. Analysis, social participation, and social action skills teach confidence and political courage. The process of critical analysis leading to positive action (praxis) teaches students that they can take real steps to improve their lives. Multicultural education that is social reconstructionist encourages students to participate in the long and difficult effort to build a more democratic society.

Questions Over the Chapter

1. What are the differences between literacy and critical literacy?
2. List two of Paulo Freire's pedagogical ideas that are similar to the ideas of U.S. philosopher John Dewey.
3. What are some examples of Freire's idea that all education is political? What are the political dimensions of your current teacher preparation program?
4. Positivism strives for the neutrality or the "objectivity" of the researcher. Critical theory and the work of Freire recognize the political nature of schools and all pedagogy. What are the advantages and disadvantages of objectivity? What are the advantages and disadvantages of political commitment by teachers?
5. Describe the power relationships in your current school or current program. Who has power? Who does not? What is the nature of power in your school site?
6. The basic ideas of critical pedagogy were developed in working with adults. Which ideas would you change when working with young students?
7. Define social reconstructionism.
8. List four ways that the curriculum may not be politically neutral.
9. What are the goals of empowerment?
10. What would be important empowerment goals for a group of five immigrant students?
11. List four examples of social participation projects appropriate to the specific grade level you intend teach.

Activities for Further Study of Empowerment

1. List social participation opportunities that can be related to some element of the curriculum. Work out a strategy with the students for one of these and guide them in implementing it. Evaluate the results.
2. Role-play a coaching session in your university class. Encourage a student to work to improve his or her study skills.
3. Investigate portfolio assessment techniques. They can be powerful tools in evaluating social participation.
4. Write a specific lesson plan for two of the following student objectives. Choose two objectives from each group. For each objective, your student will:

Grades 1–3
a. Assume responsibility for decorating one area of the classroom.
b. Volunteer to assist a limited English-speaking student with his or her lessons.
c. Participate in class meetings about student behavior.

Grades 4–8
a. Work as a volunteer tutor with younger students.
b. Learn negotiation strategies for conflict resolution.
c. Serve as a conflict resolution monitor in school.
d. Make an educational plan to improve their reading and writing skills.
e. Interview school volunteers about their work.
f. Assist the teacher with classroom tasks.

Grades 8–12
a. Work as volunteers feeding the hungry.
b. Describe hopelessness from two or more points of view.

c. Make an educational plan leading toward higher education or a career.

d. Follow through on the first steps of the educational plan.

e. Identify and analyze their own specific academic skills.

f. Plan and practice to overcome a specific skill weakness (for example, writing a paragraph).

g. Conduct research comparing learning conditions between an affluent suburban school and the student's own school.

h. Interview an appropriate elected official concerning the maintenance of unequal funding between school districts.

i. Work as a team within a community service organization. Analyze and improve the team's work.

j. Interview a community activist about what forces prevent community agencies from achieving increased success.

k. Complete a study of conflict resolution strategies. Establish a student-run system of conflict resolution in the school.

Teaching Strategies

1. Present units on culture, cultural conflict, and value conflict.

2. Use students' home, school, and community experiences as sources for the curriculum.

3. Compare racism and pluralism as options for society.

4. Plan community participation and social participation as part of the curriculum.

5. Investigate the present reading and writing levels of your students. Generate plans to advance them at least 1.5 years in one year.

(The goal is to get low-achieving students up to their actual grade level in two years.)

6. Integrate reading, writing, and language development into all aspects of the curriculum.

7. Plan lessons on the value of staying in school, value clarity, and the development of skills to achieve success in school.

8. Provide students with a list of local community agencies accepting volunteers.

References

America 2000: An education strategy. (1991). Washington, DC: The White House.

Aronowitz, S., & Giroux, H. (1985). *Education under siege: The conservative, liberal, and radical debate over schooling.* New York: Bergen & Garvey.

Aronstein, M., & Olsen, E. (1974). *Action learning: Student community services projects.* Washington, DC: Association for Supervision and Curriculum Development.

Beane, J. A. (1990). *Affect in the curriculum: Toward democracy, dignity and diversity.* New York, Columbia University: Teachers College Press.

Campbell, D. E. (1980). *Education for a democratic society: Curriculum ideas for teachers.* Cambridge, MA: Schenkman Publishing.

Campbell, D. (1987). How the grinch stole the social sciences: Moving teaching to the right in California. *Journal of the Association of Mexican American Educators.*

Campbell, D. (1989). *School reform for the few.* (Mimeograph).

Cohen, E. (1986). *Designing groupwork: Strategies for the heterogeneous classroom.* New York, Columbia University: Teachers College Press.

Congressional Black Caucus. (1991). *Quality of life budget, FY 1991.* Executive summary. Washington, DC: Author.

Cummins, J. (1986, February). Empowering minority students: A framework for intervention. *Harvard Educational Review, 56*(1), 18–36.

Dewey, J. (1966). *Democracy and education: An introduction to the philosophy of education.* New York: The Free Press. (Original work published 1916)

Freire, P. (1970). *A Pedagogy of the oppressed.* New York: Continuum Press.

Freire, P. (No date). *Conscienticizing as a way of liberating.* Washington, DC: LADOC, Division for Latin America.

Freire, P. (1985). *The politics of education: Culture, power, and liberation.* New York: Bergen & Garvey.

Gardner, H. (1993). *Multiple intelligences: The theory in practice.* New York: Basic Books / HarperCollins.

Gibson, M. (1987). The school performance of immigrant students: A comparative view. *Anthropology and Education Quarterly, 18*(4), 262–275.

Giroux, H. (1988). *Teachers as intellectuals, Toward a critical pedagogy of learning.* New York: Bergen & Garvey.

Haycock, K., & Navarro, S. (1988). *Unfinished business: Fulfilling our children's promise.* Oakland, CA: The Achievement Council.

Hoose, P. (1993). *It's our world, too! Stories of young people who are making a difference.* Boston: Little, Brown.

McFadden, J. (1975). *Consciousness and social change: The pedagogy of Paulo Freire.* University of California at Santa Cruz: Unpublished dissertation.

McLaren, P. (1989). *Life in Schools: An Introduction to Critical Pedagogy on the Foundations of Education.* New York: Longman.

New York State Education Department. (1988). *A curriculum of inclusion. Report of the Commissioner's Task Force on Minorities: Equality and excellence, July, 1989.* (Mimeograph).

Oakes, J. (1985). *Keeping track: How schools structure inequality.* New Haven, CT: Yale University Press.

Orfield, G., & Jaeger, C. (1984). Minority and low income high schools; Evidence of educational inequality in Los Angeles. *Metropolitan Opportunity Project.* The University of Chicago.

Public Information Network, Washington University, Campus Box 1183, St. Louis, Missouri, 63130.

Quality Education for Minorities Project. (1990). *Education that works: An action plan for the education of minorities.* Cambridge, MA: MIT.

Ravitch, D. (1990, Spring). Diversity and democracy; Multicultural education in America. *American Educator.* American Federation of Teachers.

Shaver, J. (1977). *Building rationales for citizenship education.* Bulletin #52. Arlington, VA: NCSS.

Simon, S. B., Howe, L. W., & Kirschenbaum, H. (1972). *Values clarification.* New York: Hart Publishing.

Sleeter, C., & Grant, C. (1988). *Making choices for multicultural education: Five approaches to race, class, and gender.* Columbus, OH: Merrill Publishing.

Trueba, H. T. (1989). *Raising silent voices: Educating the linguistic minorities for the 21st century.* Boston: Heinle & Heinle / Wadsworth.

Trueba, H. T., Rodriguez, C., Zou, Y., & Cintrón, J. (1993). *Healing multicultural America.* Washington, DC: Falmer Press.

Chapter 8

Democracy and Classroom Management

Discipline Problems in the Schools

For many students, schools are not safe. In California, for example, over 10,000 weapons (including 1,131 guns) were confiscated from students in a single year. Florida witnessed a 40% increase in gun incidents. New York City reported 1,800 weapons violations in 1989. Birmingham, Alabama, suspensions for possession of firearms increased from 30 to 85 incidents in a two-year period.

Such violence in our schools, in our homes, and on our streets is a clear response to the loss of economic prosperity and political opportunities. The economic decline of the last 20 years for working people and the decline of effectiveness of schools in preparing young people for economic success produced a substantial erosion of teacher and school authority.

In the 1970s and 1980s, order declined in our society, particularly in urban areas. Middle school and high school students increasingly challenged the legitimacy of schools and the roles of teachers. An increasingly disorderly environment in many schools demoralized even the most dedicated students.

Increased racial and class divisions between teachers and the communities they serve isolate and divide teachers from effective family and neighborhood control. The increase in street crime parallels the increased disruptions in schools. Both are produced by the growth of poverty, marginal employment, and unemployment, and neither crime nor chaos in the schools can be cured by school practices alone (Jackson, 1993/1994; Miller, 1992).

Often, hostile groups come together in schools. Racial, ethnic, and language divisions from the neighborhoods are brought into the classrooms. The sustained "silent economic depression" of the last 20 years produces ever-increasing violence and hostility among students. Violence teaches violence. Name calling and fighting lead to violence, and the schools stand by, almost paralyzed by the rapidly increasing violence in our society.

Amidst this growing violence, teachers committed to democracy must first attempt to create a positive environment for learning. But some teachers, administrators, and school districts have given up. New York, Chicago, Los Angeles, and other urban districts are forced to divert desperately small instructional funds to buying metal detectors and other hardware.

Children learn best in a safe and orderly environment. Research on "effective schools," common sense, and teacher experience indicate a need for a reasonable and supportive classroom environment. Both teachers and students need order in the classroom (Goodlad, 1984). Teachers want order to encourage learning. Excessive disciplining and lack of classroom order cause extensive wasting of teaching time and learning time. Violence and intergroup conflict, combined with academic failure and the many problems of young people deny many students a classroom environment that is supportive of learning (National Coalition of Advocates for Children, 1991).

When teachers are unable to create a positive atmosphere, when they fail in their attempts to productively manage their classroom, the students lose instructional time. Most off-task student behavior is not dangerous, confrontational, or violent, but it is a frustrating waste of academic learning time. When students are off-task, they tend to become disruptive. The disruptions are cumulative in that talking and other inappropriate behavior spread from student to student. Students who are off-task learn less and they fail more. In many neighborhood schools in poverty areas, a cycle develops of off-task behavior leading to failure, failure leading to discouragement, and discouragement providing a further incentive to get off-task.

Constant discipline and management problems frustrate and discourage teachers. Teachers prefer to teach, but classroom conditions require them to manage disruptive behavior. The teachers pay a price in lowered self-esteem. For many teachers in difficult schools, the price soon becomes intolerable: some transfer, some quit, some give in to student pressure, demanding little from them and expecting even less.

Acquiring the skills of effective classroom management takes first priority for most new teachers. These skills are best acquired in a public classroom with supportive supervision; they are difficult to learn in a college classroom. When cultural differences divide the teacher and the students, or when cultural and ethnic conflict is common among the students, conflict resolution and management skills become even more necessary.

When new teachers fail, they fail more often in their attempts to produce classroom control and motivation than in instruction. This chapter will provide you with detailed and specific ideas for establishing and maintaining positive, democratic, classroom management. The principles and goals of democratic classroom management have long been accepted, but classroom practice suffers from frequent conflict and failure. Too many teachers, particularly new teachers, struggle and are frustrated in their vain attempts to control kids, particularly in "at-risk" schools. Disruptive and rebellious students demand so much of the teacher's time that little time or energy remains for teaching. Teachers can design their classrooms for better democratic control by (a) creating a positive classroom environment, (b) promoting on-task behavior, and (c) promoting positive teacher-student communications.

Reducing Discipline Problems

You probably chose to enter teaching to make positive contributions to students' lives—not to control unruly kids. But when teachers fail to achieve classroom control—and new teachers fail often—a common response is to seek more power, more control. A major problem in this struggle to impose control is that teachers and future teachers have a great deal of experience with authoritarian practices and very little experience with democratic alternatives. They soon discover that their efforts to gain more control through power strategies fail. Endless power struggles exhaust the teacher and remove much of the positive motivation from teaching and from learning. Teachers and students pay an enormous price in lost instructional time and damaged self-esteem for our limited approaches to classroom climate and discipline.

To reverse this unwelcome state of affairs, democratic teachers learn strategies that promote learning and deal effectively with disruptive students. One way teachers can begin effective classroom management and reduce discipline problems is by creating a positive classroom environment in which students feel safe and secure.

Beyond Rewards and Punishment.   The behavior management systems of Fred Jones, Lee Canter, and others may serve a useful purpose to get control of an unruly class. At times, teachers may need to use these techniques (see the section for new teachers on page 203). However, once control and reasonable rules have been established, teachers should move on to systems that teach students to accept the responsibility for their own conduct.

Teachers should decide on their own orientation toward class management by reflecting on their core values as they apply in the specific neighborhood in which they teach. Throughout this book, I have argued that a central value of schools should be to promote democratic behavior and responsibility. Democracy is not anarchy. Nor is it a laissez-faire approach. Democracy includes the development of a series of fair rules and a respect for the rights of all members of the classroom. In a democracy, the citizens (the students) participate in setting up the rules. Then they are made responsible for keeping their own rules and for complying with reasonable class norms. The teacher and the students need to work together to establish norms for acceptable behavior and to develop sanctions for those who do not cooperate.

Creating a Positive Classroom Environment

Choose Instructional Strategies That Encourage Success.   One thing successful teachers do to create a positive environment is to choose instructional strategies that help students to feel confident. Students need to believe that they are acquiring important information and skills. Success builds confidence, whereas failure produces anxiety and hopelessness. The environment and the curriculum should produce success.

One way that teachers can ensure the success of instructional strategies is to demonstrate to students the value and usefulness of the subjects they are studying. An interesting, culturally relevant curriculum assists class management, whereas a boring curriculum invites students to respond with boredom, indifference, and disruption.

Communicate a Belief in the Students' Ability to Succeed.   As Figure 8.1 shows, the failure to reinforce for students the idea that they each can succeed in their own unique ways can sometimes have disastrous results. Students who have poorly developed study skills frequently encounter a failure-filled, tense, anxious environment. Unfortunately, experience has taught many teachers in at-risk schools to *accept* the failure of poor and minority children as normal. But failure seldom helps to achieve instructional objectives with young people. Failure produces tension and anxiety and interferes with learning. The poem in Figure 8.1 illustrates how one child experienced failure in the school environment and points out the vital importance of teachers getting across to students that they believe in the students' ability to succeed.

Give Positive Feedback to Students.   When classrooms are chaotic, full of tension and conflict, and students are fearful that teachers will respond to them with insults, the classroom is not a safe environment. Young people who fear sarcasm and demeaning comments from teachers or other students, respond with anxiety and frustration. Arbitrary enforcement or settlements imposed by power and bullying do not promote democracy. Such classrooms produce failure for both students and teachers.

Figure 8.1 "About School"—Anonymous

About School*

He always wanted to say things. But no one understood. He always wanted to explain things. But no one cared. So he drew.

Sometimes he would just draw and it wasn't anything. He wanted to carve it in stone or write it in the sky.

He would lie out on the grass and look up in the sky and it would be only him and the sky and the things inside that needed saying.

And it was after that, that he drew the picture. It was a beautiful picture. He kept it under the pillow and would let no one see it.

And he would look at it every night and think about it. And when it was dark, and his eyes were closed, he could still see it.

And it was all of him. And he loved it.

When he started school he brought it with him. Not to show to anyone, but just to have with him like a friend.

It was funny about school.

He sat in a square, brown desk like all the other square, brown desks and he thought it should be red.

And his room was a square, brown room. Like all the other rooms. And it was tight and close. And stiff.

He hated to hold the pencil and the chalk, with his arm stiff and his feet flat on the floor, stiff, with the teacher watching and watching.

And then he had to write numbers. And they weren't anything. They were worse than the letters that could be something if you put them together.

And the numbers were tight and square and he hated the whole thing.

The teacher came and spoke to him. She told him to wear a tie like all the other boys. He said he didn't like them and she said it didn't matter.

After that they drew. And he drew all yellow and it was the way he felt about morning. And it was beautiful.

The teacher came and smiled at him. "What's this?" she said. "Why don't you draw something like Ken's drawing? Isn't that beautiful?"

It was all questions.

After that his mother bought him a tie and he always drew airplanes and rocket ships like everyone else. And he threw the old picture away.

And when he lay out alone looking at the sky, it was big and blue and all of everything, but he wasn't anymore.

He was square inside and brown, and his hands were stiff, and he was like anyone else. And the thing inside him that needed saying didn't need saying anymore.

It had stopped pushing. It was crushed. Stiff.

Like everything else.

---

* Anonymous. This poem is said to have been turned in to a teacher in Regina, Saskatchewan, by a senior in high school. Although it is not known if he actually wrote it himself, it is known that he committed suicide a few weeks later.

Communicating positive feedback to students, however, helps both the teacher and students. Students get further confirmation that the teacher is there to help them succeed, they receive feedback on *how* to succeed, and because their needs for success are being met, they are less likely to be abusive and critical of other students. When these conditions are met, the teacher has fewer discipline problems and can spend more time on actual instruction.

Stress-related illnesses are major problems for teachers; therefore, they prefer a positive environment for their own health. The task then is to learn to create a productive environment that is supportive and positive for the lives of both students and teachers. Democratic teachers set up structures and systems that guide students toward positive interpersonal behavior and toward appropriate school behavior.

Arbitrary power and control will not achieve a positive environment. Teachers need to recruit and encourage the students to cooperate in creating a positive classroom environment. (Positive communications between teachers and students are also discussed later in this chapter.)

Promoting On-Task Behavior

Numerous tasks face the new teacher, but few are as frustrating and difficult as classroom management. First, the curriculum must be designed for interest, value, and success. And a classroom social climate must be created that is positive and supportive of students and their diverse cultures. Positive use of classroom time becomes a critical issue.

Students waste a great deal of time. In fact, researchers have reported that they are off-task, not studying, and not learning up to 50% of the time (Charles, 1989; Costa, 1985; Squires & Segars, 1984). Older students are often off-task because what they are being asked to study is boring or irrelevant to their lives. Teachers can promote on-task behavior by demonstrating the relevance of the lessons to students.

Demonstrate the Relevance of Lessons to Students. One way that teachers can show students how schoolwork relates to their lives is by choosing student-centered projects. Excellent ideas for student-centered educational projects are found in *It's Our World, Too! Stories of Young People Who are Making a Difference* (Hoose, 1993). Teachers can also reduce the struggle for control by helping students decide on and pursue some student-centered themes.

Use Positive, Managed Intervention Strategies. Even with the student-centered themes, teachers need to learn skills to assist students to stay on task and to pursue goals. Effective teachers plan for and manage potential conflicts and discipline problems before they even arise. Positive classroom management keeps the students working on interesting, useful, and rewarding tasks.

In the elementary grades, when students are off-task, effective teachers intervene early and frequently to call on students to return to the learning task. In the middle grades (4 through 8), early interventions produce success and can be employed with low levels of power, thus avoiding failure and confrontations.

In the upper grades (6 through 12), some teachers respond to off-task behavior by becoming more authoritarian and more aggressive toward the students. Their efforts may produce control but authoritarian action interferes with efforts to provide the safe and supportive environment students need for success. Often, aggressive teacher behavior is self-defeating because it produces more control problems, exhausts the teachers, and interferes with productive learning—a cycle of frustration, failure, and repression. By fourth grade and throughout adolescence, constant power struggles between student and teacher disrupt the learning environment and encourage more off-task behavior even from those good students interested in learning.

Frequent, low-level, managed intervention provides an alternative. Teachers learn to use eye contact, body language, physical proximity, facial expression, and gestures to structure and manage the class toward on-task learning assignments. These strategies combine commonsense teaching practices with behavioral rewards. Students are rewarded for increased on-task learning time by receiving planned leisure and recreation time. These interventions can be effective and nondisruptive, encouraging students to return to the school task at hand. Once classroom order is established, and at least by sixth grade, democratic management systems should be used.

Try Task Analysis.   Task analysis permits teachers to design a positive environment and to teach students how to succeed. For example, numerous studies have demonstrated that cooperative learning is a helpful strategy, particularly for African American, Latino, and Native American children. Both children and adults need instruction in how to work cooperatively. As teachers begin to use cooperative learning, they teach a series of skills necessary for cooperative work (see Chapter 10).

Task analysis separates the skills of cooperative work into several teachable, learnable skills. Essential skills for a fourth- to eighth-grade class include moving chairs, selecting persons for roles (e.g., monitor, checker, encourager), staying on the subject, listening to one another, taking turns, or supporting the authority of a student leader. Each of these skills is isolated, taught, practiced, and evaluated to improve the quality of cooperative work and classroom relationships.

Promoting Positive Teacher-Student Communications

Teacher behavior either contributes to or detracts from the building of a positive classroom environment. Studies indicate that the average teacher uses negative comments and commands much more often than positive comments. Positive communications strategies are important at all levels. They become increasingly important during adolescence. Violence and domination teach violence and domination, while respect teaches respect. Good teachers contribute to a positive environment by practicing positive comments that guide and structure student behavior (see Figure 8.2).

Learn to Describe Positive Behavior.   Successful teachers learn to describe positive behavior. Consistent repetition of positive directions guide most students to respond without increasing defensiveness. The repetition of positive comments directs student behavior and lowers the anxiety and frustration levels in the classroom. By the middle grades (4 through 8), many students learn to win and lose power struggles. Teachers, on the other hand, produce success through encouragement and cooperation.

Redirect Students' Nonhelpful Behavior.   Effective teachers practice the skill of redirecting students from nonhelpful to helpful behavior by clearly describing precisely *how* to perform a task. Primary teachers often model the task rather than rely on oral instructions. In grades 4 through 8, role playing and physical practice of a task reduce the need for criticism. A clear explanation of how to perform a task provides students with a positive alternative to criticism. Reliance on criticism and correction attacks the students' self-esteem and makes them feel hostile, defeated, alienated, or self-doubting. Since defeat and criticism only rarely lead to intensified effort, strategies built on negative teacher responses are generally best avoided.

Give Clear Directions.   Teachers frequently need to give instructions and commands on how to perform tasks. Giving clear, brief instructions provides a structure within which the student can succeed. When a few students do not carry out the instruction, a repetition of the command is often more effective than criticism (e.g., "Open your books now. Please open your books to page 45").

Giving clear appropriate instructions is essential to the management of classes. But when instructions are demeaning or issued in an attacking manner,

Figure 8.2   Alternatives to Negative Comments

Instead of:	Alternatives:
"Stop talking and get busy."	"Open your book now."
"You haven't started yet?"	"How did you answer question one?"
"Why aren't you working?"	"Can I help you with the first problem?"

they become criticism and are received defensively. Of course, in real classrooms, you will need to criticize. By the middle grades, it often helps to explain your reasoning when offering a critique of a student's response. Effective teachers try to call students' attention to the purpose behind the instructions. When instructions are given with a concern for the welfare of the class, even criticism can be heard in safety and can lead to positive student behavior. "Please stop talking, I want to go on with the lesson" works better than, "Please stop talking."

Use a Supportive, Encouraging Speaking Style.   Democratic teachers seek to give instructions, even commands, without using an aggressive and dominating style. They seek to replace divisive and demeaning communication with encouraging students to cooperate and support one another. Positive communication contributes to the positive social climate in the classroom necessary to promote personal and social growth.

For students beyond grade 6, feedback—or constructive direction—provides a useful instructional strategy. The following guidelines promote positive, nurturing communication.

1. Concentrate on criticizing the act or the idea—not the person. Personalizing criticism is worse than useless because it destroys the possibility of future positive communication.

2. Practice giving feedback and correction when the action occurs and then move on. Repeatedly reminding students of past offenses (nagging) frustrates both teachers and students. No one can change the past. Students cannot undo past mistakes. Concentrate on the present and the future.

3. Feedback and correction should be as specific and concrete as possible. Telling students to be respectful or to behave does not provide the information they need to change their behavior. The best feedback tells students precisely what they can begin doing correctly rather than offering negative evaluations of what they have done.

4. Labeling students and using sarcasm are not helpful. They seldom contribute to behavioral change or instruction.

5. Encouragement always works better than criticism because it helps the student to build self-esteem.

Classroom management systems enable the teacher to design student success. Unfortunately, not all students will respond to the positive environment. In many at-risk schools, teachers spend a great deal of time correcting, directing, and criticizing, hoping to control the class so that some learning takes place. Prior school and home experiences have taught some students to disrupt and to resist learning.

For students from low-status cultural groups experiencing cultural conflict in schools, the intensity of the criticism can reinforce the desire to withdraw from participation and to flee school. Others resist even reasonable school norms. Teenagers frequently experience self-doubt and lack of confidence. The overuse of negative messages by teachers and other students alienates and divorces students from schooling.

Respect Students.   Young people can be cruel and critical of each other. It is a mistake for the adults in the school to enter into the teenage culture of put downs and sarcasm (Kagan, 1986). Even when a specific student appears arrogant or overconfident, public sarcasm is damaging because it intimidates and injures other students. Although students may have developed apparent defenses against sarcasm from other students, too much criticism from teachers can be devastating. The consistent application of positive communication helps students develop a positive attitude. Respect teaches students to respect others. Respect encourages the internalization of new values supportive of the classroom instruction.

Schools were established to instruct youth in information, values, and skills. The teacher has a right and a responsibility to establish a positive classroom atmosphere. Students do not have a right to be disruptive or disrespectful. The school and the classroom need clear, reasonable parameters of appropriate behavior, and effective teachers enforce the rules. Democratic behavior can best be encouraged within a safe environment. When teachers and the school administration fail to consistently enforce a positive, appropriate, fair structure of discipline, peer group pressures will disrupt the school. Young people deserve and need adults in charge who will establish and maintain reasonable standards of school-appropriate behavior (see Figure 8.3).

Isolate Disruptive School Groups and Provide Appropriate Intervention.   Classes tend to have several student-centered groups, some supportive of instruction and a positive school climate, others disruptive. By the middle grades (4 through 8), most students will want to belong to a group. In primary grades, the effective teacher establishes and maintains the classroom environment. By the middle school (grades 6 through 8), peer-group influences become increasingly important. If the peer-group behavior is positive and supportive of instruction, most new students will accommodate the group. A major teacher task is to establish a positive, productive atmosphere and then to encourage and recruit the majority of the students to cooperate. By the teenage years, peer-group and gang pressures can dominate a class. Teachers who encounter difficulties with gang members in classes should seek support and additional resources from the school administration and parent groups.

The individual teacher cannot resolve problems of gangs, resistance, drugs, and violence. In fact, the isolation of teachers from each other and from parents encourages and supports gang behavior in schools. Student groups dedicated to disruptive behavior must first be isolated from influence and then redirected with strong intervention systems including the police if necessary.

Figure 8.3 **Simple and Clear Rules Help to Establish a Safe and Productive Classroom Climate**

1. Everyone affected should have a voice in determining school rules. Language barriers to full participation should be removed.
2. Rules should be clearly stated in behavioral terms.
3. Rules should be reasonable.
4. Rules should be enforceable.
5. Rules should be easily understood.
6. Rules should be taught as part of the curriculum.
7. Rules should be communicated to parents in the language spoken in the home.
8. Rules should be consistently enforced by teachers.
9. Rules should be perceived by students as being fair.
10. Rules that disproportionately impact any one group of students should be changed.

Adapted from suggestions made by the National Coalition of Advocates for Children (1991).

Reteach Appropriate School-Appropriate Behaviors if Necessary. Young students often need to be taught appropriate behavior. Even adolescents at times need reteaching of basic interpersonal skills such as talking to others without making "put downs." Skills of positive behavior are identified and taught just as you would teach the skill of writing a sentence. If you want students to move from a large group into smaller groups, clear directions and rehearsing will help students learn the skills involved. In the primary and intermediate grades, practice of class-appropriate behavior helps students to belong within a positive group and to participate in the creation of a positive environment. In middle schools and secondary classrooms, clear instruction and practice are needed early in each semester to establish the appropriate practice for your class.

Time should be provided for the instruction, practice, and evaluation of social skills. Teaching school-appropriate behavior becomes a part of the curriculum. Teachers and students experience more success from teaching and practicing appropriate behavior than from the teacher having the responsibility to control inappropriate behavior and punishing offenders. Instruction and practice lead to change. Management and punishment lead to control that is always temporary.

Major, lasting changes in student behavior occur slowly. Disruptive behavior in class is the result of years of experience in schools and at home. Producing major changes in classroom behavior for some difficult students often requires months and supplementary counseling resources.

Extending the Teacher's Influence in Managing the Classroom

Coaching

Our society has become increasingly depersonalized in the modern era. Increasing numbers of divorces and the rapid increase in the number of women in the paid workforce since the 1960s have produced children with less positive supervision by parents. Many disruptive children literally need more parenting. While the primary grades provide time for teachers to guide students, school practices after about grade 6 often foster depersonalization.

The upper grades and middle schools adopt a model of instruction that moves away from parenting. Teachers serve primarily as instructors of content and less as parents. While parenting may be an inappropriate role for teachers above grade 6, in our troubled society, many students need guides, coaches, and counselors. The large, often depersonalized school was organized based on a factory model and designed for management control, not to promote a positive, caring environment.

Coaching and conferencing extend the teacher's influence in managing the classroom. Successful democratic teachers use conferencing and coaching with those students who continue disruptive and off-task behavior after instruction and rehearsal of appropriate behavior. Coaching strategies provide monitoring, advisement, and instruction particularly important to students in the middle grades (grades 6 through 8), as well as in high school. Students need positive, adult interaction in school. Setting up coaching and advising sessions helps teachers to guide classroom behavior and build important connections between the students and the school (Comer, 1988).

A coaching process should be planned and implemented when the students need weeks of reinforcement and instruction. Just as planning improves instructional delivery in math, science, and the social studies, systematic planning of coaching will improve most students' behaviors and eventually their attitudes.

A classroom environment of support and success reduces discipline problems. Even when the teacher and the school are positive experiences for most students, some students become discipline problems and interfere with the teacher's efforts to guide the class. Effective teachers need an intervention system to redirect disruptive students toward prosocial and constructive classroom behavior. Dr. James Comer is one of several leading educators who advocate that teachers deserve substantial additional support and assistance to deal with the several children per class who are potentially disruptive of learning, particularly in communities suffering a high degree of economic and social stress (Comer, 1988).

A counseling and coaching strategy provides an intervention system for the teacher. Counseling and coaching work best from a theory of human social behavior. The system of Individual Psychology, as developed by Alfred Adler, Rudolph Dreikurs, and subsequent researchers, provides an effective democratic approach for helping students to move away from disturbing and destructive school behavior.

A Theory of Antisocial Student Behavior

The Dreikurs system (Dreikurs & Stoltz, 1964; Dreikurs, Greenwald, & Pepper, 1971) proposes a theory of how students learn their worldviews and role behavior and assists in developing an intervention system. Dr. Miguel Martinez (1978) has described the theory of Adlerian psychology and of Dreikurs intervention systems as follows:

> From infancy, the individual begins to formulate a cognitive representation, a picture of himself / herself, the world, and the individual's place in that world. This view is like a multi-dimensional puzzle with many sides and levels. The child perceives pieces of data and like a puzzle, he / she puts the pieces into some kind of picture (world view). This picture becomes a map which gives direction and purpose to the child's life. Children observe the environment, evaluate it, and arrive at conclusions about themselves, their worth, their potency, and their place in the environment. They decide on a view of what the world demands of them and how they can acquire a sense of belonging to or a sense of being part of that world. The family is the first social group the child encounters. (p. 59)

Martinez quotes Mosak (1973) to say that through the child's interaction with the family:

> [Each child] . . . stakes out for himself a piece of territory which includes the attributes of abilities that he hopes will give him a feeling of belonging, a feeling of having a place. If, through his evaluation of his own potency (abilities, courage and confidence), he is convinced that he can achieve this place through useful endeavors, he will pursue the useful side of life. Should he feel that he cannot attain the goal of having a place in this fashion, he will become a discouraged child and engage in disturbed or disturbing behavior in his effort to find a place. For the Adlerian, the "maladjusted" child is not a "sick" child, he is a "discouraged" child. Dreikurs classifies the goals of the discouraged child into four groups: attention-getting, power-seeking, revenge-taking, and declaring deficiency or defeat. It should be emphasized that Dreikurs is speaking of immediate, rather than long-range goals. These are the goals of children's "misbehavior," not of all child behavior. (p. 117)

Life, like culture, is dynamic rather than static. The world around the child is continually changing and the child is changing. Students are continually confronted with new information. Some new data are added into the student's existing worldview. Other new information presents a conflict with the student's view of self.

New information that conflicts with previously learned conceptions presents the student with two alternatives. The new data can be incorporated in the worldview in place of the old information, and thus alter the student's view of the role he or she is playing in the classroom. Or the new information can be rejected or distorted so that it is received consistent with the existing self-image.

The worldview and the view of self serve as a cognitive map, guiding each student in his or her actions. This cognitive map provides a guide to the student's worldview. Immaturity, perceptual biases, distortions, and incomplete data make the students' worldview incomplete, but the worldview appears adequate to the student.

Students behave based on their worldviews and their perceptions of reality. A student's cognitive map and worldview guide him or her in comprehending new information. These worldview perceptions are culturally influenced and largely subconscious. Students are aware of their behavior, but usually unaware of the underlying worldview, cultural frame of reference, perceptual set, and motivation.

In his helpful guide to teachers and counselors, Martinez (1978) says that, as students move through life toward adulthood, they encounter three major tasks posed by society. Each student must face social life and the necessity of achieving: (a) cooperative social adjustment, (b) a defined work role, and (c) sex roles. Mosak (1973), an important contributor to the Adlerian theory, argues:

> Since man must live among his fellow man, the individual must come to realize that we live life together, and are responsible for each other. To the extent that the individual assumes this responsibility, he becomes socially contributive, interested in the common welfare. Secondly, the individual must define his sex roles, partly on the basis of cultural definition and stereotypes. He must learn to relate to the other sex, not as the opposite sex, for other people of the opposite sex do not represent the enemy, but rather they are his fellows with whom he must learn to cooperate. Third, since no man can claim self-sufficiency, we are interdependent and division of labor becomes a life requirement. Each of us is dependent upon our contribution. Work, thus, becomes essential for human survival. (Martinez, 1978, p. 118)

Dreikurs and Stoltz (1964) argue that when teachers share these assumptions, they respond to disruptive students as if the students are discouraged. The child's prior life in and out of school may not have provided him or her with either the strategies for successful classroom behavior or the motivation to succeed. Prior experience has taught the student to pursue short-term self-interest, such as attention-getting through disruption or fighting. Children need to learn to pursue their own long-term self-interest by contributing to a positive social environment where they can experience support and success.

Class Meetings

Teachers using the democratic recommendations of Adler and Dreikers and Stoltz (1964) have developed classroom meetings as an important aspect of problem solving to improve behavior. Democratic teachers provide leadership and structure to assist students in taking responsibility for resolving some class problems.

Students as young as first grade are taught to clearly identify the problem-causing disruption. In many classrooms, from grades 1 through 8, students set an agenda for the next classroom meeting by listing a problem behavior on an agenda sheet. At a specified time of the day or week, a classroom meeting is called. Classroom meetings work best when students have been prepared in cooperative learning skills (Chapter 10). The problem behavior is examined, and the students work together to suggest potential solutions. The teacher provides a structure for the meeting by insisting that all solutions must be reasonable, related, and respectful. Suggesting solutions does not resolve problems; students need to agree on the nature of the problem, and they need to agree on the solution.

Class meetings are useful at all grade levels, although the rules for conducting the meetings should change based on the maturity of the students. Typical rules for grades 1 through 3 include these: to give compliments as meeting starters, to use the agenda to keep focused on the problems, and to identify logical consequences for misbehavior rather than punishment (see Figure 8.4).

Classroom meetings work particularly well above grade 4 when combined with training teams of students in mediation and conflict resolution. The meetings alone will not resolve all conflicts in the classroom. When combined with an empowerment curriculum that encourages students to belong, to work cooperatively in groups, to be successful, and to be effective, problem-solving classroom meetings are very effective in improving classroom behavior, encouraging students to develop democratic behavior, and getting students to accept responsibility for their own actions.

Perhaps as a consequence of John Dewey's strong influence of educational theory, most teachers want to assist students in practicing democratic behavior even though they frequently do not know how to advocate for these positions. In classroom meetings, the strategies for empowerment and for cooperative learning combine to provide teachers with powerful strategies for encouraging democratic behavior.

Figure 8.4 Sample Problem-Solving Scenario

> The students in Mrs. G's fourth-grade class have practiced classroom meetings. They know the rules and the skills to facilitate conflict resolution. Mary places Heather's name on the agenda for the next meeting. At meeting time, the students sit in a circle. Mrs. G serves as a facilitator. She asks Mary to explain what is the issue. Mary says that Heather constantly calls her a "dirty Mexican." She wants the name calling stopped.
>
> Several classmates confirm that they have heard this name calling. The class discusses name calling and stereotypes. They decide that children often repeat what they hear from adults. But at school, all children deserve respect. The teacher guides the children in role-playing name-calling events to clarify the issues.
>
> After a time, the subject changes to consequences.

Coaching Using Dreikurs' Ideas

Classroom meetings use the powerful motivations of group cohesion and group belonging to encourage students to learn cooperation, but some students will resist. Many individual students have strong desires to disrupt or to seek control of the classroom agenda. These powerful drives at times are too complex to simply turn the problem over to a problem-solving group; coaching and conferencing are additional strategies for the democratic teacher.

Even though students frequently bring enormous conflicts from their home life and peer lives into school, the teacher's first task is to redirect the behavior to help the student succeed and to function effectively in the classroom. The teacher sets up a coaching / counseling session to redirect the behavior of the consistently disruptive student. The coaching-counseling relationship encourages the student to learn the motivation and strategies necessary to operate positively within the classroom environment.

Harried student teachers may quickly protest that they do not have the time or skills to arrange for counseling and coaching. Only a few schools have adequate counseling and support resources. But teachers have little choice. They must respond. The continued use of power and force for discipline does not resolve the conflicts. Power only suppresses the student's disruptive behavior temporarily. The conflicts will emerge or explode at other times when teachers will be unprepared to manage the problems. If teachers do not develop effective response systems to the problem behavior, such as coaching, the student will continue to disrupt the classroom and the learning environment.

The teacher-coach first schedules a meeting with the student to analyze the problem and to plan for behavioral change. Teachers initiate a positive, therapeutic relationship so that the coaching process can move forward. Typically, the teacher and student can agree on some fundamentals. The teacher is in charge of the class. Disruptive behavior is not acceptable. The teacher wants to set up a system in which the student is not disruptive. After clearly explaining these fundamentals, the teacher and the student analyze the specific behavioral problem displayed in class and attempt to identify the problem's relationship to the student's own goals.

When a safe relationship and a clear goal for coaching have been established, the student can openly examine his or her mistaken goals and select alternative behaviors that will help him or her to belong positively to the group. The teacher-coach and the student work together to give up the disruptive behavior and practice appropriate behavior that will integrate the student positively into the classroom. Successful coaching often requires a number of sessions to help the student gain a more positive and productive control over his or her classroom behavior. Detailed analysis and practice of each step help teachers direct most students toward constructive behavior.

In our violence-prone society, teachers will encounter a few students who, as a result of a dysfunctional family life, drug abuse, or similar trauma, refuse to permit the classroom to function. The school administrator must provide alternative resource classrooms or other resources for such students. Teachers seldom have the time or skills for therapy.

Teachers and counselors working within the Adler-Dreikurs framework have developed strategies of classroom meetings where students engage in analysis, prescription, and helping students to change classroom behavior (Martinez, 1978). Class meetings in grades 4 through 8 provide powerful peer-group pressure and rewards to encourage positive, constructive school behavior.

When children in elementary school are taught self-direction and social cooperation skills, they improve school achievement and develop strong self-esteem. By 10 to 12 years of age, disruptive behavior may become a way of school life, and ever more sophisticated and powerful intervention systems are needed. Fortunately, older students can conceptualize, discuss, and relearn school-appropriate behavior. Respect and safety cannot be assumed, they must be taught. The chaos, crime and violence in many schools, neighborhoods, and homes, along with the general decline in social order, cause many teachers and schools to add formal instruction in respect and appropriate school behavior to the curriculum. Failure of the school to attend to the problem and teach positive social behavior is quite expensive, leading eventually to the student's leaving school and entering the far more expensive criminal justice system.

No one psychotherapeutic theory has proven adequate and useful to teachers in all situations. Nor has adequate quantifiable data validated any one theory's explanation of student behavior. Meanwhile teachers need a strategy to work within on a daily basis. The Adler-Dreikurs theories presented are the theories most connected to the practice and extension of democracy. The promotion of democracy in the classroom is difficult and substantially underdeveloped (Cagan, 1978; Gross & Dynneson, 1991). Democratic teachers seek to change their classroom structures from autocratic practices that fail a great portion of our students in both academic and prosocial development to democratic procedures that achieve both the necessary order and empowerment of the student. Teachers and students, particularly in low-income and poverty areas, need to improve the safety and security of their classrooms and schools (National Coalition of Advocates for Children, 1991). Teachers should use the social studies classes to teach the skills of conflict resolution.

The coaching practices described in the preceeding section describe a useful strategy for working with the increasing number of students suffering from extremely high stress and conflict levels.

A Guide to New Teachers

Schools in minority neighborhoods have a high proportion of new teachers. Many experienced teachers transfer out of such schools to places where they can spend more time teaching and less time managing the classroom. Initially, new teachers experience a difficult time of trial and error. Their teaching skills are learned on the job through practice.

New teachers in difficult schools face a number of hardships, and students inevitably suffer from having less-experienced teachers. The new teacher suffers from having to learn to teach with the most difficult students (Bradley, 1994).

As a new teacher, you will work with children from diverse cultures and can benefit from getting to know the school community. Prior to the first day of school, you should travel around the community, visit its churches, its youth clubs, its neighborhoods. It helps to visit your school early to acquaint yourself with the principal, the secretary, and the resources you will need.

The school is not an island apart from the community. Teachers who arrive at school, spend their time teaching, and leave just after school will misunderstand their children. In the past, prior to the current concern for multicultural education, some teachers displayed an offensive colonial attitude in their relationship to the schools. They entered the community to teach. They received pay from the community but they did not respect the community. They appeared like missionaries bringing the outside culture to the natives. This colonial attitude led to misunderstanding, hostility, and resentment. Most parents know that education and schooling are important to economic success, but a colonial relationship prevents mutual support and respect between the teachers and the parents. When a gap exists between the parents and the school, the younger children suffer. Older students and gangs exploit the communication gap to resist school. To avoid such strained relationships, teachers should think of themselves as employees of the community and make it their responsibility to learn about the community so they can use community resources and culture to support the educational program.

Instruction isolated from the community context too often fails. Quality teaching requires an understanding of the reality of the children, rather than a series of stereotypes. Knowledge of student reality allows the teacher to select experiences in the students' lives to build on.

One of the fundamental differences between successful middle-class schools and failing schools is that middle-class teachers in middle-class schools share the reality of the students. They draw from a common source of experiences for reading, writing, and skill development. When teachers draw from the students' own experiences, this process validates and empowers the students. In contrast, teachers with a colonial attitude seek to impose the content of the curriculum on the student. This imposition of culture invalidates and negates the students' own experiences and culture. Students are made to feel inadequate. They do not learn to have confidence in themselves, their families, or their cultural competencies.

For students to succeed, the classroom must be reasonably orderly. Teachers and students have varying tolerances for disorder. Teaching should start on time and the classroom needs to provide a safe and orderly environment, an environment that encourages learning. You need to provide the students with successful learning experiences, particularly in the first few days of instruction. You should start with a well-organized, firm process of management and discipline. When you have established order and have learned more about the individual characteristics and personalities of the students, you can move toward a more democratic environment.

All teachers benefit from personalizing their teaching. Personal influence, personal knowledge, personal contact provide the teacher with the best instruments of instruction as well as the best instruments of classroom control. When you know students and communicate with them in ways that acknowledge their selfhood, such as learning a few words in their language, the environment of the classroom improves dramatically.

You can be more helpful when you know your students well. Elementary school teachers master this problem with ease, while middle-school and secondary school teachers facing 150+ students per day have difficulty. Instructors who do not learn about individual students are reduced to giving commands and instructions. This command relationship, in turn, produces more student resistance. The structure of depersonalized relationships produces a significant portion of the discipline and conflict management problems of upper-grade teachers. Important school reforms suggested by The Carnegie Foundation for Advancement of Teaching (1988) include breaking middle schools down into smaller schools of 250 students each. Such subschools could personalize and thus provide coaching and guidance.

Small steps such as calling students by name and asking them about their interests personalize the interchanges. You can use transition times between activities and time provided by cooperative learning to make contact with the students about their lives and interests. Students from cultures where interpersonal relations are valued prior to business and task exchanges (e.g., Latinos, Asians, Arabs, and Native Americans) particularly benefit from teachers' efforts to personalize.

Teachers acquire a powerful set of connections when they get to know students individually. You will soon get to know the "good" students. To improve classroom control, make an effort to get to know the potentially disruptive students, the clown, and the resister. Talk to these students. Telephone their parents or guardians. Individual contact provides information useful to direct them toward cooperative rather than disruptive behavior.

Your efforts to personalize interactions in the classroom will help make the classroom a safe environment. Students respond more positively, more respectfully to teachers who treat them with respect.

It is easier for a new teacher to establish a positive environment in the first few days than trying to dominate the class. A tense environment where commands are common and cooperation is minimal produces resistance and disruptions. Beyond grade 6, trying to win consent exclusively with the use of power with students is seldom effective, particularly when some of the students are skilled in resistance.

This is not to argue for a hands-off, libertarian approach. Most students, except for those in kindergarten and first grade, already have experience with school and teachers. Students evaluate new teachers during the first few days to decide what kind of classroom to expect and to determine what they can get away with. It helps to make your goals clear: a safe and orderly classroom, clear and reasonable rules, a high degree of on-task learning time, and a personalized classroom where children are respected by each other and the teacher.

On the first few days of school, establish a few basic rules and post them where all students can read them. Rules commonly used by primary teachers include these:

1. Only one student out of seat at a time.
2. Raise your hand to speak.
3. Keep your hands and feet to yourself.

Rules common to middle school students might include these:

1. Only one student out of seat at a time.
2. No put-downs or negative personal comments.
3. Raise your hand to speak.

Establishing a positive, productive classroom climate is particularly difficult in schools with large numbers of at-risk children. By adolescence, the cultural gaps between the teacher and the student are greater, producing miscommunication and conflicting expectations. Establishing a positive, personal, supportive environment makes important differences between effective and ineffective classrooms.

Teachers have both a right and a responsibility to provide an organized, calm classroom. Once established, rules should be enforced. Students require more than reading the rules and discussing them. The appropriate behavior should be demonstrated, modeled, and practiced. If lack of respect for a particular rule becomes a generalized problem, then the rule should be retaught and the behavior practiced again. Teachers save themselves important time and energy by teaching and reteaching rules instead of trying to manage and control each individual child.

You should identify management problems within the first few days of class. Some teachers have difficulty because six students need to sharpen their pencils just before an assignment, or four students come to the teacher for assistance at the same time, or the noise level becomes intolerable when students are asked to move into groups.

When problem areas appear, the teacher can isolate and analyze the problem. Try to identify the precise behavior that is causing disruption, and then develop a process for teaching the appropriate skill and practicing the appropriate behavior. Learning school-appropriate behavior is like learning to play soccer; it takes practice. Practice improves student performance far more than criticism and demands do.

As a new teacher, you can gain valuable insight by recruiting an experienced teacher as a mentor, someone who can answer the hundreds of simple questions you will have. New teachers also benefit from recruiting an ally, someone with whom you can share frustrations and anxieties. If there are no other new teachers in the school, consider taking a course at a nearby university where you will discuss your concerns with other teachers.

There are a number of good guides for new teachers. For primary teachers, Bonnie Williamson's *A First Year Teacher's Guidebook for Success* (1988) has many useful ideas. Interested readers can find an excellent guide to classroom management in C. M. Charles' *Building Classroom Discipline, From Models to Practice* (1989).

Summary

Teachers need to use classroom management skills with a commitment to cultural and social democracy. Without this commitment, management skills lead to control, not to student empowerment. Neither teacher domination nor chaos and anarchy prepare young people to live responsible, democratic lives. Teachers can use management skills to promote a democratic, trusting, caring environment in the classroom.

Questions Over the Chapter

1. List three classroom rules that would reduce interpersonal violence.
2. What three student behaviors in your classroom produce the most off-task time for students? What steps could you take to prevent these behaviors in the future?
3. Define *coaching*.
4. How can a teacher get enough work time for coaching?
5. What does Dreikurs describe as the four major goals of disruptive behavior by discouraged students?
6. Give two examples of personalizing the interaction between students and teachers.
7. List areas of authority where teachers should assert their adult-teacher responsibilities.
8. What are three areas of responsibility where students should have their primary authority?
9. What are major out-of-school causes for class management problems?
10. What are major in-school causes of class management problems?

Teaching Strategies

1. Decide on your three most important classroom rules. Post them. Teach them. Consistently enforce them.
2. After completing strategy #1, add no more than one new rule per week. Clearly describe and practice appropriate behavior.
3. Isolate off-task behavior and reteach the rule and appropriate behavior to those who are off-task.
4. Step out of power struggles. Go back to strategies #1 through 3 above.

5. Use positive communications whenever possible. (See the suggestions given in this chapter.)
6. Teach and practice appropriate social skills.

7. Plan and implement a coaching strategy.
8. Teach the skills of conflict resolution to students.

References

Bradley, A. (1994, September 14). Education for equality: The story of Ron Rodriguez. *Education Week.*

Cagan, E. (1978, May). Individualism, collectivism, and radical educational reform. *Harvard Educational Review,* pp. 227–266.

Carnegie Foundation for Advancement of Teaching. (1988). *An imperiled generation: Saving urban schools.* Lawrenceville, NJ: Princeton University Press.

Charles, C. M. (1989). *Building classroom discipline: From models to practice* (3rd ed.). New York: Longman.

Comer, J. (1988, January). *Is parenting essential to good teaching?* Washington, DC: National Education Association.

Costa, A. (1985). *Teaching for intelligent behavior.* Orangevale, CA: Search Models Unlimited.

Dreikurs, R., Greenwald, B., & Pepper, F. (1971). *Maintaining sanity in the classroom.* New York: Harper & Row.

Dreikurs, R., & Stoltz, V. (1964). *Children: the challenge.* New York: Hawthorn Books.

Goodlad, J. (1984). *A place called school: Prospects for the future.* New York: McGraw-Hill.

Gross, R. E., & Dynneson, T. L. (1991). *Social science perspectives in citizenship education.* New York / London: Columbia University.

Hoose, P. (1993). *It's our world, too! Stories of young people who are making a difference.* Boston: Little, Brown.

Jackson, T. (1993/1994, Winter). Everyday school violence: How disorder fuels it. *American Educator,* pp. 4–9.

Kagan, S. (1986). Cooperative learning and sociocultural factors in schooling. *Beyond language: Social & cultural factors in schooling language minority students.* Sacramento: California State Department of Education.

Martinez, M. (1978). Unpublished dissertation. Lubbock, TX: Texas Tech University.

Miller, J. (1992, April). Silent depression. *Dollars and Sense Magazine,* p. 6.

Mosak. (1973). Quoted in Martinez (1978).

National Coalition of Advocates for Children. (1991). *The good common school: Making the vision work for all children.* Boston, MA: Author.

Squires, D. A., Huitt, W. G., & Segars, J. K. (1984). *Effective schools and classrooms: A research-based perspective.* Alexandria, VA: Association for Supervision and Curriculum Development.

Williamson, B. (1988). *A first-year teacher's guidebook for success: A step-by-step educational recipe book from September to June.* Sacramento, CA: Dynamic Teaching Co.

Chapter 9

Promoting Critical Thinking

The educational literature is full of terms such as *reflective inquiry, decision making, critical thinking, higher-level cognitive skills,* and *evaluation*. Educational researchers use such terms to describe multiple aspects of complex thought processes. Most educators agree that students gain from instruction in these critical thinking skills. Such instruction teaches students to carefully consider ideas and to examine the assumptions on which they are based. This instruction also teaches students to process evidence, to draw precise conclusions, and to limit the conclusions. There are a variety of instructional strategies that teach students a number of processes for gathering evidence, determining patterns among data, and stating the results of analysis or conclusions.

It is the classroom teacher who makes the most important decisions concerning the teaching of these skills. They choose daily whether to stress equality or inequality, content coverage, skill development, or critical thinking. And teachers choose based on their own view of the students, the students' learning potential, and their view of society.

Teachers dedicated to building a democratic classroom recognize that teaching critical thinking plays a central role in moving away from inequality and toward cultural pluralism. Based on their own values and philosophy of democracy in education, teachers can make the important decision to emphasize critical thinking strategies. Preparation for critical thinking begins with selecting materials and planning lessons.

This chapter provides an overview of what critical thinking skills are and how, in many schools, low expectations for students and an overreliance on drill and practice activities have hindered the development of such skills. Finally, this chapter will describe several strategies for teaching critical thinking skills.

Critical Thinking Defined

Descriptions of the processes of thinking were developed in the modern era by William James (1842–1910) and converted into educational theory by John Dewey (1859–1952), who based their theories on the developing field of psychology and on philosophical works dating back to Plato. Philosophers, beginning with Plato, have argued that quality education should move beyond memorization of facts to teach the processes of learning. An inquiring mind and spirit are admired and promoted. Modern philosophers of education have advanced the idea that development of rational thinking should be a primary goal of schools.

Cognitive psychologists, notably Jerome Bruner and Jean Piaget, used observation as a primary research technique to further advance the theory that cognitive processes develop based on experience. Writings by Vygotsky (1978) have recently amplified and clarified the important relationship of experience, social relationships, and learning.

Most teachers would agree that schools should teach students to solve problems, to make decisions, and to arrive at conclusions based on evidence and reasoning. The formal written goals of most schools, and many curriculum guides, include providing students with experiences in developing critical thinking skills. A central task of multicultural education is to extend the teaching of critical thinking to all of our students so that our several communities can participate in the political process and vote to develop inclusive, democratic public policy for our highly diverse society.

We can begin to define **critical thinking** with Barry Beyer's definition: "Our graduates should be able to make well-reasoned decisions, solve problems skillfully, and make carefully thought out judgments about the worth, accuracy, and value of information, ideas, claims, and propositions" (Beyer, 1988, p. 1). Philosopher Richard Paul further seeks to clarify the field in *Dimensions of Thinking* (ASCD, 1988):

> A passionate drive for clarity, accuracy, and fair-mindedness, a fervor for getting to the bottom of things, to the deepest root issues, for listening, sympathetically to opposite points of view, a compelling drive to seek out evidence, and intense aversion to contradiction, sloppy thinking, inconsistent application of standards, a devotion to truth as against self-interest—these are the essential components of a rational person. (p. 2)

A new group associated with the work of Richard Paul, The National Council for Excellence in Critical Thinking (Scriven & Paul, 1994), defines critical thinking as follows:

> Critical thinking is the intellectually disciplined process of actively and skillfully conceptualizing, applying, analyzing, synthesizing, and evaluating information gathered

from, or generated by, observation, experience, reflection, reasoning, or communication, as a guide to belief and action. In its exemplary form, it is based on universal intellectual values that transcend subject matter divisions: clarity, accuracy, precision, consistency, relevance, sound evidence, good reasons, depth, breadth, and fairness. It entails proficiency in the examination of those structures or elements of thought implicit in all reasoning: purpose, problem or questions-at-issue, assumptions, concepts, empirical grounding, reasoning leading to conclusions, implications and consequences, objections from alternative viewpoints, and frame of reference. Critical thinking—in being responsive to variable subject matter, issues, and purposes—is incorporated in a family of interwoven modes of thinking, among them: scientific thinking, mathematical thinking, historical thinking, anthropological thinking, economic thinking, moral thinking, and philosophical thinking.

Critical thinking can be seen as having two components: 1) a set of information and belief generating and processing skills and abilities; and 2) the habit, based on intellectual commitment, of using those skills and abilities to guide behavior. It is thus to be contrasted with: 1) the mere acquisition and retention of information or beliefs alone, because it involves a particular way in which information and beliefs are attained and held; 2) the mere possession of a set of skills, because it involves the continual use of them; and 3) the mere use of those skills ("as an exercise") without acceptance of their results.

Critical Thinking for All

A recent focus of research on critical thinking has been on how "experts" reason and make judgments in comparison to how "non-experts" reason. When monitored, experts in a field use a variety of testing strategies and intuitive leaps demonstrating more skillful performances than amateurs. A great deal of speculation on critical thinking, however, is egocentric on the part of the educated. Professionals describe and admire their own preferred behavior. What they actually describe is how they prefer to see themselves. Analysis of the behavior of self-described intellectuals (including college professors, philosophers and advocates of critical thinking) in a variety of situations, including university committee work and interpersonal relations, reveals that the traits commonly expressed as positive indicators of intellectual life are not always demonstrated in their lives or the life of the academy (Ryan & Sackrey, 1984).

Evidence has not yet demonstrated that the life of the university demonstrates more rational thought processes than say, the life of a corporation or a professional baseball team. Reflective thought resembles the process scholars admire, write about, and prefer to believe they engage in.

This romanticized egocentric view, coupled with the lack of precise analysis, leads to common folkways of schooling from middle school through the university. If a teacher presents the material and the students learn, then the students are considered capable and intelligent. If the teacher presents the material, and the students fail to learn, then the students are considered limited or not bright. Many teachers respond to students they consider "not bright" by selecting drill, practice, and testing strategies rather than critical thinking strategies.

This inaccurate and simplistic view of learning ignores numerous objective factors including poverty, inadequate school resources, and the important subjective interaction between the instructor's communication and motivation style and the corresponding communication and motivation styles of the students. Since these styles are learned in cultures, conflict between the communication and motivation styles of the teacher and those of the learner frequently produce a failure in learning (Anderson, 1988; Ramirez & Casteñeda, 1974). Because of the power relationship between teacher and learner, the failure to master the material is blamed on the student and too often attributed to limited intellectual capabilities—a usually inaccurate analysis.

Nonacademic Sources of Rational Intelligence

Most authors and teachers assume, without much evidence, that a critical, rational life develops in school. The Italian intellectual Antonio Gramsci (Aronowitz & Giroux, 1985; Giroux, 1988) supplemented the school-based definitions by describing the role of "organic intellectuals" as those in the working class who demonstrate intellect based on their life experience, usually without being subservient to schools or university norms. Gramsci described persons without formal training who often develop the reflective ideal and assist others in reconceptualizing the world-work relationships. Some parent activists and community organizers fit Gramsci's description of "organic intellectuals."

People are expert in a variety of fields. The rice farmer in Africa is an expert in measuring and planting rice. His approach to problem solving offers solutions not available to the novice planter, even if the planter were college educated. The pursuit of intellectual excellence is not an exclusive domain of schools and formal schooling.

If we are cautious to not confuse the lifestyle and culture of professionals for intellect, we can still agree that it is useful to pursue rational analysis and critical awareness. It remains a normative assumption that schools should promote intellectual life and intellectual integrity.

Although philosophers since Plato and U.S. schools since Dewey have been promoting critical thinking and rational processes, researchers do not yet know enough about human brain activity to describe the processes adequately. We operate from a series of hunches. In the last three decades, cognitive psychology has sought to move beyond hunches to define more precisely the intellectual processes that encompass critical thinking.

Overcoming Low Expectations

Schools in poverty areas commonly use more drill and practice and place less emphasis on teaching intellectual processes than do middle-class schools. Teachers make these decisions from the empirically unsupported belief that students from minority cultures are not ready for critical thinking lessons. Some teachers have tried critical thinking lessons as presented in teachers' manuals accompanying textbooks. In working-class schools, lessons were presented and students were not immediately responsive. As a result, teachers adopt a habit of relying on drill and practice. Drill and practice keep the children quiet and they complete their work. These practices tend to support the racially biased view that students of color are unable to perform higher-level thinking or are nonresponsive to such lessons.

Since many of the children score low on standardized exams, a myth has emerged that poor and minority children are incapable of advanced thinking. A series of rationalizations, each based on biased and incompetent research or applications, developed to demonstrate the alleged limited abilities of poor children. Even some well-meaning research on cognitive styles has been abused to reach conclusions not based on evidence. There is no reason to assume that a multicultural school or children from diverse subcultures have any less need for training in critical thinking (DeAvila, 1987; Miller-Jones, 1991; Rist, 1979).

Teachers in multicultural settings face important decisions about what to emphasize in their classrooms. Too often these teachers are forced to choose between compensatory education strategies or critical thinking strategies. This choice is one of the most fundamental decisions in choosing democracy. The power to make the choice lies fundamentally in the hands of each teacher. In this important arena of students' lives, teachers have more power than the legislature, school board members, principals, or unions. The choice for critical thinking is an expression of teacher power. This choice reaffirms basic democratic values and reasons for becoming a teacher.

The pattern of stressing drill and practice over critical thinking in de facto segregated schools has major social consequences. With the slave system, the Africans brought to this country were prohibited from learning to read as a form of social control. In our present schools, social control is further advanced when students living in poverty areas, particularly students of color, are directed away from classes that encourage critical thinking and decision making and into classes that emphasize drill and practice. Promoting the development and practice of critical thinking must be a major concern in school reform. Writers and reports, from the essentialists of Mortimer Adler to the more centrist positions of Goodlad and Beyer, have called for improved teaching of thinking skills (Adler, 1982; Boyer, 1983; Goodlad, 1990).

Critical thinking, or reflective decision making, should be central to the agenda of multicultural educational reform. Whereas many schools have not stressed thinking skills and processes enough, students of color and the poor receive the least training in these areas. Many urban schools have an honors track or a magnet program in which thinking skills and processes are taught and a basic track in which the students are incorrectly assumed to be incapable of abstract thought. Poor and minority students are regularly assigned to the basic track (Goodlad, 1990).

The process at C. Wright Mills High School (situated in a large urban district) illustrates how at-risk minorities are scheduled away from critical thinking classes. Mills is an integrated school: 23% Asian, 22% African American, 20% European American, and 35% Latino. Mills has a "magnet" program emphasizing the humanities and fine arts. Students in the program receive an excellent education stressing critical thinking and college preparation. Visitors to the magnet program are surprised to find 90% of the students are European American and Asian in an otherwise integrated school. Visits to the military science (ROTC) and vocational programs reveal over 80% Latino and African American students. In this manner, a legally integrated school has tracks based on race, and students of color are tracked away from classes likely to stress critical thinking.

We know that effective schools that serve at-risk children emphasize higher cognitive level processes (critical thinking) (Olson, 1986). Yet, in most schools with students from poverty-stricken areas, drill and practice abound. Teachers responded to their failure by turning to behaviorism and away from critical thinking. Worksheets and dittos replaced efforts to motivate and encourage divergent thinking.

Teachers with low expectations of students design their classes in ways that produce students with low achievement (Oaks & Lypton, 1990). Low expectations include not expecting students to excel in reading and writing and not engaging students in tasks that require higher-order thinking. Low expectations are a primary factor in school failure. They are displayed in low cognitive level instruction such as that demonstrated by an overreliance on worksheets, drill, and practice. Combined with other school barriers to success, low expectations on the part of teachers communicate to students not to expect much of themselves or their future.

No significant evidence demonstrates that children from minority cultures have less ability to perform high cognitive demand tasks (critical thinking). Children from all cultures benefit from instruction in critical thinking and the related areas of higher-order thinking. The school and the curriculum need to develop learning experiences in which the child's own repertoire of knowledge is used to stimulate intellectual processes (DeAvila, 1987).

Instead of passively accepting the folkway of low expectations for poor and minority students, teachers need to master skills of sequentially teaching critical thinking processes. Failure in the areas of abstract thinking is most often a result of inappropriate or insufficient clarity in the presentation and practice of skills necessary for the process.

Teachers may ask questions from the textbook or teachers manual and silence follows. Communication barriers are caused by lack of attention to cross-cultural learning and motivational styles. Rather than assume a disability in the students, teachers need to examine the structure and pattern of their questions. When questions seek data from the students' own experiences and are clearly organized on a retrieval chart, students from all racial, cultural, and class groups readily perform higher cognitive functions such as predicting and evaluating. Teaching that blames students for apparent weakness in reasoning is damaging and ineffectual. Rather than blame students, teachers should accept the responsibility to plan questions and lessons that help students to learn critical thinking processes.

The Need for Teaching Strategies to Develop Critical Thinking

The "back to basics" movement of the 1980s most often led poor and minority schools to emphasize skill and rote practice rather than problem solving. Fortunately, many educators and others in the business community now recognize that teaching decision making and critical thinking is the single most important activity for schools. In spite of its importance, schools often pay little attention to critical thinking and seldom evaluate the development of critical thinking skills. There is no conclusive evidence of success in teaching thinking skills (Brant, 1990; Cornbleth, 1985).

There are many reasons for the failure of the schools to focus on teaching critical thinking. The most obvious is that most schools have seldom tried. Teachers are hired and given a job to teach a specific body of content. University professors seldom model critical thinking in their content courses. Few students are trained in teaching critical thinking skills. Further, college courses are usually divided into content areas, and exams largely emphasize content. There is little motivation for teachers to emphasize critical thinking. The growing emphasis on standardized testing influences the curriculum toward content memorization. Few tests exist that measure higher-order thinking skills, and those tests are expensive to employ.

When schools successfully teach critical thinking, students make well-reasoned judgments and solve problems skillfully. They also learn to make evaluative judgments about the worth, accuracy, and value of information. They learn to analyze claims, ideas, and ideologies.

Clearly, learning to think is not the incidental outcome of classroom study directed at subject matter such as history, math, or literature. Rather, development of critical thinking skills can best be approached by a direct study of these skills. In the primary grades, students should learn skills such as sequence, grouping, and categorization. The skills can be taught in one subject matter (reading, social studies) and generalized to another (science).

By fourth grade, critical thinking skills become more specialized by subject field. Each discipline area can teach the skills appropriate to the field with attention to their transferability. For example, the sciences can focus on observation, the use of data, and recognition of cause and effect. History and social studies can focus on identification of bias and propaganda.

The California State Department of Education has delineated by grade level a precise set of critical thinking skills for history and the social sciences (see Figure 9.1). The California model is useful in identifying the subskills needed for criti-

Figure 9.1   Critical Thinking Skill Continuum for History-Social Science—California

3rd Grade	6th Grade	8th Grade

I. Defining and Clarifying Problems
  a. Makes careful observations
  b. Identifies and expresses main ideas, problems, or central issues
  c. Identifies similarities and differences
  d. Organizes items into defined categories
  e. Defines categories for unclassified information
  f. Identifies information relevant to a problem
  g. Formulates questions
  h. Recognizes different points of view
 	
II. Judging Information Related to the Problem
  a. Identifies obvious stereotypes
  b. Distinguishes between fact and opinion
  c. Identifies and explains sequence and prioritizing
  d. Identifies evidence that supports (or is related to) a main idea
  e. Identifies obvious assumptions
  f. Identifies obvious inconsistency and contradiction
  g. Identifies cause-and-effect relationships
 	
III. Solving Problems/Drawing Conclusions
  a. Recognizes the adequacy of data
  b. Identifies cause-and-effect relationships
  c. Draws conclusions from evidence
  d. Puts simple hypotheses into *if, then* sentences
	I. Defining and Clarifying Problems
	  a. Identifies central issues or problems
	  b. Identifies similarities and differences
	  c. Understands the concept of relevance and irrelevance
	  d. Formulates appropriate questions
	  e. Expresses problems and issues
	  f. Recognizes obvious individual and group value orientations and ideologies
	
	II. Judging Information Related to the Problem
	  a. Identifies stereotypes and cliches
	  b. Identifies obvious bias, propaganda, and semantic slanting
	  c. Identifies facts, opinions, and reasoned judgments
	  d. Identifies inconsistency and contradiction
	  e. Identifies assumptions
	  f. Identifies evidence
	
	III. Solving Problems/Drawing Conclusions
	  a. Recognizes the adequacy of data
	  b. Identifies cause-and-effect relationships
	  c. Draws conclusions from evidence
	  d. Predicts consequences
	  e. Hypothesizes
	  f. Reasons with analogies and generalizations
		I. Defining and Clarifying Problems
		  a. Identifies central issues or problems
		  b. Compares similarities and differences
		  c. Determines which information is relevant
		  d. Formulates appropriate questions
		  e. Expresses problems clearly and concisely
		
		II. Judging Information Related to the Problem
		  a. Distinguishes among fact, opinion, and reasoned judgment
		  b. Checks consistency
		  c. Identifies unstated assumptions
		  d. Recognizes stereotypes and cliches
		  e. Recognizes bias, emotional factors, propaganda, and semantic slanting
		  f. Recognizes value orientations and ideologies
		
		III. Solving Problems/Drawing Conclusions
		  a. Recognizes the adequacy of data
		  b. Identifies reasonable alternatives
		  c. Tests conclusions or hypotheses
		  d. Predicts probable consequences

10th Grade	12th Grade

I. Defining and Clarifying Problems
  a. Delineates controversy components
  b. Identifies criteria that serve to organize data
  c. Identifies fallacies of relevance
  d. Formulates appropriate questions
  e. Paraphrases accurately
  f. Distinguishes among diverse viewpoints
 	
II. Judging Information Related to the Problem
  a. Recognizes subtle manifestations of stereotypes and cliches
  b. Recognizes subtle manifestations of emotional factors, propaganda, and semantic slanting
  c. Distinguishes among fact, opinion, and reasoned judgment
  d. Recognizes subtle or indirect inconsistencies
  e. Demonstrates a sensitivity to questionable assumptions
  f. Recognizes subtle differences in judging the sufficiency of data
 	
III. Solving Problems/Drawing Conclusions
  a. Justifies the selection of an alternative
  b. Distinguishes between possible and probable consequences
  c. Concludes only what is justified by the evidence
  d. Understands opposing points of view and reasons with them
  e. Recognizes fundamental problems in causal reasoning, generalizing, and arguing by analogy
  f. Recognizes indirect or extended implications
	I. Defining and Clarifying Problems
	  a. Identifies central issues or problems
	    1. Distinguishes real and stated issues
	  b. Compares similarities and differences
	    1. Analyzes system similarities and differences
	  c. Determines which information is relevant
	    1. Evaluates degrees of relevance
	    2. Assesses different interpretations of data
	    3. Summarizes positions and their supporting evidence
	  d. Formulates appropriate questions
	  e. Expresses problems clearly and concisely
	
	II. Judging Information Related to the Problem
	  a. Distinguishes among fact, opinion, and reasoned judgment
	  b. Checks consistency
	    1. Recognizes subtle consistencies and inconsistencies
	  c. Identifies unstated assumptions
	    1. Recognizes unstated fundamental assumptions
	  d. Recognizes bias
	    1. Identifies emotional factors, propaganda, semantic slanting, stereotypes, and cliches
	    2. Converts biased materials into unbiased form
	  e. Recognizes value orientations and ideologies
	  f. Distinguishes between false and accurate images
	
	III. Solving Problems/Drawing Conclusions
	  a. Recognizes and assesses cause and effect and multiple causation
	  b. Draws warranted conclusions
	  c. Identifies reasonable alternatives
	  d. Tests conclusions or hypotheses
	  e. Predicts probable consequences
	    1. Assesses desirable and undesirable consequences
	  f. Demonstrates the ability to come to a reasoned judgment in reading, writing, and speech

Note. From *Assessment of Critical Thinking in History-social Sciences* by California Assessment Program, 1985, Sacramento, CA: California Assessment Program.

cal thinking. Important elements missing from the California chart, however, include the processes of decision making and the more powerful conceptions of inquiry that move beyond individual skills practice.

Teachers used to assume that by teaching content they were also teaching the operations and skills needed to learn or process the material. There is, however, little evidence to support this assumption. From elementary school to the university, teachers have failed to teach the process of learning. Our citizens do not demonstrate a passion for fair-mindedness and accuracy. Our political processes are not typified by a willingness to explore difficult issues, a propensity for open-mindedness. We have not developed the attitudes of willingness to suspend judgment and to listen sympathetically to opposing points of view. Teachers simply exhort students to work harder. Criticism and exhortation have not served as effective teaching strategies for critical thinking. Instead, teachers deserve assistance in planning their instructional approaches in manners that encourage students to learn the skills of thinking.

Emphasis on content, on processing content, on questions, and on worksheets do not, by themselves, help students improve their thinking. Questions may encourage thinking and, at times, may even provoke thinking, but they do not teach the skills of reflective inquiry.

Direct Instruction in Critical Thinking

The lack of instruction in critical thinking skills is particularly prevalent in classes with cultural and linguistic minority students. Cultural and communication style differences between teacher and students, tracking, low expectations, biased perceptions, and limited reading and writing skills all combine to place these students at risk of failure.

Cultural, linguistic, class minorities, like all students, should receive direct instruction in developing thinking skills. Separating the many facets of critical thinking into clearly identifiable skills allows each skill to be focused on, taught, practiced, and evaluated. The primary structure for **direct instruction** of isolated skill lessons includes the following sequence:

1. Selection of the skill;
2. Clear and precise instruction in the skill;
3. Systematic practice, first by the teacher, and then by the students,
4. Opportunities for practice of a particular skill by the students with the guidance of the teacher;
5. Assessment; and
6. Independent practice of the skill.

Direct instruction is a useful strategy for initial critical thinking, cooperative learning, classroom management, and other lessons. Used in conjunction with other strategies, it provides a good place to teach essential skills. When students have acquired the necessary skills, teachers can vary their strategies. For example, direct instruction can well teach a student to compare. Then, the student should use comparison as a skill within more extended problem-solving tasks. Direct instruction can teach appropriate group roles for cooperative learning, after which the group can explore divergent and imaginative social participation projects. In the midst of an active project of experiential learning, the teacher may want to reteach some basic skill such as writing a paragraph using the direct instruction approach.

Multicultural education designed for empowerment should go beyond teaching isolated critical thinking skills to decision making and what the Brazilian educator, Paulo Freire, calls "problem-posing education" (Freire & Shore, 1987). These powerful forms of intellectual development involve more than the acquisition of a series of isolated skills. Problem-posing education encourages the acquisition of skills and an attitude that supports inquiry, discovery, and decision making. The development of critical thinking skills is an important step forward toward decision making, while problem-posing education takes students several steps beyond. Problem-posing education assumes the radical, democratic stance that all students *and* adults can resolve their own problems and make their own decisions.

Sample Critical Thinking Strategies

Grades K Through 2.   In grades K through 2, we should teach students lessons on grouping and categorizing. You can use the students themselves as participants by categorizing them into groups, such as those with brown hair or red shoes or girls and boys. (Some teachers use ethnic groups as one of several categories for grouping, but it causes much confusion!)

Lessons on sequencing can also be taught. For example, students should recognize the opening, body, and ending of stories. And teachers can direct discussions about the concepts of cause and effect with the students in literature, science, and other subjects.

The following lesson is from a split kindergarten/first-grade bilingual class in Woodland, California. The teacher was Lissette Estrella-Henderson. She describes the events:

> The leg of the reading table which we had been using since the beginning of the year fell off one day without any warning. All of our materials went flying, and by the time we had finished cleaning up the mess, there was no time left to do the activity which the students had been looking forward to. Needless to say, my students were upset and frustrated—not to mention how angry I was, since I had asked the secretary to tell the maintenance department about the problem two weeks before!
>
> I finally realized that the only way I was going to get any action was by illustrating to the administrators how their apathy directly affected my students. I engaged my students in a discussion about what they thought we could do about the problem. (They knew that I had already asked for the leg to be fixed once before.) It was wonder-

ful and enlightening for me to see how their ideas developed and evolved as a result of thinking out loud and putting their ideas together.

The final consensus was to write a class letter explaining our problem and sending it not only to the principal but to the maintenance department and the superintendent as well. The students also drew pictures illustrating the situation and took them home to show their parents as they explained the situation to them. I had the parents and maintenance department at my door the very next day to fix the table, not to mention the visit from the principal and the call from the superintendent. I asked the parents and the maintenance department to let us borrow their tools, and the children fixed the table leg themselves! I could not have come up with a better problem-solving lesson that promoted higher-level thinking skills if I had planned it.

The students really learned that by combining their brains, physical power, and the skills of working cooperatively, they really could make a difference.[1]

Grades 3 Through 6.   To teach critical thinking in grades 3 through 6, teachers integrate lessons on evidence, cause and effect, stereotypes, and similar skills into the curriculum. For example, you can view a portion of the film *Dances With Wolves* and then have one group of students write a description of the westward expansions of the European Americans as explained in their textbooks. Have a second group write a description from the point of view of the Native Americans. Each group should support its point of view with statements of evidence.

Grades 6 Through 8.   Students can build a retrieval chart to compare the experiences of European immigrants with the experiences of Asian and Latino immigrants in the nineteenth century with the present (see Figure 9.2).

By this age you can teach a decision-making process like the following:

1. Identify a problem and clarify the issues.
    - Is the conflict definitional?
    - Is the conflict empirical?
    - Is the conflict value based?
2. Suggest Alternative Solutions.
    a. Have teams evaluate each proposed solution.
        - State the probable outcomes.
    b. Plan a criteria system for the evaluation of each alternative.
3. Implement the preferred alternative.
4. Evaluate the outcomes.
5. Students give an oral or written report on the process of problem solving.

[1] *Note.* From Estrella-Henderson, Woodland, California. Used with permission.

	American Indian	Mexican	African American	European American Northern/Southern
Reason for coming?	Already here.	Already in Southwest when Europeans arrived.	Slavery, brought in chains.	Economic and religious.
To what degree is the group a victim of racism and discrimination?	Faced genocide. Still face some discrimination.	Forced off of their land. Still face some discrimination.	Enslaved until the 19th century. Still face discrimination.	Incidents of discrimination have decreased after one generation.
Present status?	High suicide rate. Many continue to live on reservations.	High school drop out rate is high. Current attempts being made to limit additional immigration.	High unemployment. Some political power.	Assimilated.

Figure 9.2 Sample Retrieval Chart

At these grade levels, students might also develop a plan to assist immigrant students in their classroom or in the school. Then they implement and evaluate the plan.

Grades 10 Through 12.   Provide students with copies of the ethnic and women's history timelines provided in Appendixes A through F of this book. Each team can select a period of U.S. history. Students should compare the treatment of Native Americans, Latinos, Asians, African Americans, and women in their textbooks with the information in the timelines. Ask them to conduct library research to validate their conclusions. Students should consider omissions, assumptions, and the effect of learning a particular point of view in history.

Critical Theory and Critical Thinking

Critical theory is an extension of critical thinking beyond its positivist roots to include empowerment of students and oppressed peoples. Critical theory raises the issues of concern with ideology and the social control of knowledge. When this issue of the ideological loading of education and the curriculum is raised, the political right often counterattacks with vehemence and a vigor, accusing the teacher of politicizing the curriculum.

Those who question ideological control, along with those who advocate bilingualism, must go beyond the limited realms of discussion encouraged by a human rights, human relations, or civil rights viewpoint. These teachers, committed to democracy, go beyond liberalism.

The conservative school reform movement of the last decade displaced the liberal concerns of human relations and civil rights in discussions of schooling and the curriculum. When social reconstructionists and critical theorists discuss the political and ideological content of the current curriculum, and when they emphasize the values of democracy and pluralism, this offends or frightens the conservative forces in education. Many of the most divisive battles over textbooks and the curriculum were provoked by the challenge of multicultural education advocates revealing the ideological control of the present curriculum (Apple & Christian Smith, 1991; Cornbleth & Waugh, 1995).

Social reconstructionists, or proponents of a critical theory view, regard control of access to knowledge as a major form of domination where sexism, racism, and class bias continue to be reproduced in our schools. Critical theories contend that ideological control, such as accepting a melting pot or a human relations point of view while ignoring structural racism, developed from one class, race, gender, and cultural group dominating the production and control of knowledge in universities, schools, and textbooks. The critical theory assumptions and viewpoints have been advocated in Chapters 1 through 7 of this book.

Democratic multicultural education, building on the insights of critical theory, seeks to reveal the ideological domination that keeps political and cultural power in the hands of a small segment of the society. The psychologist David

Perkins developed a critical thinking system termed *Knowledge as Design* that is useful for grades 4 through college to reveal ideological control and domination (Perkins, 1986).

The *Knowledge as Design* system begins by assuming that knowledge is purposeful. Most discoveries were made for a purpose. For example, Galileo described the solar system to explain a pattern he observed. The purpose of Galileo's theories was to explain. The purpose of Louis Pasteur's theories was to find a cure for disease.

After recognizing this general assumption, *Knowledge as Design* sets out to have students discover the purposes of *particular* knowledge. The system is especially useful and helpful with controversial issues and with issues of value conflicts.

The teacher helps students to analyze an issue by pursuing the following questions.

Critical Thinking About the Social Construction of Knowledge.
Knowledge as Design:

1. For what purpose?
2. What is its structure?
3. What are some models or cases of the design?
4. What is the history of the design?
5. What are some of the connected assumptions?
6. What are arguments that explain and evaluate the design?
7. If the design achieved its purpose, how would you know?
8. If the design achieved its purpose, what other purposes would it serve?

You can discover the value of the *Knowledge as Design* system and explore the social construction of knowledge. Simply apply the questions just posed to some of the most controversial issues in your own teacher preparation program or this course. For example, consider the achievement gap between African American, Latino, and European American youth presented in Chapter 2. Now, assume that the achievement gap is not an accident or an error. Assume, for the purpose of analysis, that the achievement gap is deliberate—it is a design. Using this assumption, look for answers to the *Knowledge as Design* questions about the achievement gap.

Follow the same procedure with the preponderance of women in elementary teaching, teachers' salaries, the failure of inner-city schools, the preservation of European American domination of the curriculum to this time, or other value-laden or controversial issues.

To save time, the questions can be divided among different groups. Have the recorder from each group report on the group's findings. That is, if you assume that the achievement gap is purposeful (a design), what purposes could it serve?

You do not need to ask all eight questions about each topic, but it is important to ask at least four. Following this process will allow your class to move beyond mere repetition of opinions and advocacy of previously held positions to analysis.

Summary

In many schools, low expectations and overreliance on drill and practice activities have prevented students in poverty areas and students of color from developing critical thinking skills. It is vitally important that teachers in multicultural settings choose to emphasize direct instruction of critical thinking rather than rely on compensatory education strategies. Teachers committed to establishing democratic classrooms can use several of the sample critical thinking strategies described in this chapter to help their students develop the thinking skills necessary for processing evidence, drawing accurate conclusions, and solving problems skillfully.

Questions Over the Chapter

1. What is the relationship between low expectations and teaching critical thinking?
2. List four critical thinking skills appropriate to your grade level.
3. Researchers have noted that teachers in schools serving low-income areas and people of color frequently rely more on drill and practice and less on critical thinking. How would teachers you know justify this decision? What are some consequences of this decision?
4. Which value positions or value orientations support the teaching of critical thinking in schools?
5. Why would the objectives and strategies of critical thinking lessons be different in grades 1 and 2 and grades 10 through 12?
6. This chapter urges the teaching of separate critical thinking skills in grades K through 6 and then teaching a decision-making process in grades 7 through 12. What are the differences between these two strategies? Do you agree or disagree with this approach? Explain your answer.

Activities for Further Study of Critical Thinking

1. Write objectives for critical thinking skills about topics in multicultural education. (See the example that follows these activities.)
2. Write lesson plans or unit plans that include the teaching of at least one specific critical thinking skill.
3. Plan the evaluation of critical thinking skills.
4. In a small group, research critical thinking. A good starting point is *Developing a Thinking Skills Program* by Barry K. Beyer. This work offers a comprehensive and systematic approach to the topic. The team should report

to the class on the potential integration of critical thinking and multicultural education.

5. A team of students can plan a multicultural education program without including critical thinking. Have the team compare their work with the work of the team that responded to activity #4.

6. In a small group of students, study the system of *Knowledge as Design* as developed and described by David Perkins (p. 395). Then, have each team member respond to the questions from *Knowledge as Design* about several controversial issues in the university classroom. The recorder from your group should report on your group's findings. Teams can answer all questions about some topics. On other topics, teams can respond to specific questions, allowing an intense analysis in a relatively short time period (30 to 40 minutes). For more information on this subject, see *Knowledge as Design* (Perkins, 1986).

7. Prepare lessons for students to analyze their own K through 12 textbooks. Students can compare how the books portray African Americans, Latinos, Asian Americans, or women in literature or history. Write a comprehensive, multicultural, inclusive history of a week or a month in their classroom. They will need to deal with significance, evidence, point of view, and similar problems.

Teaching Strategies

Critical Thinking Lesson Plans

The following list of objectives will help you begin to plan critical thinking lessons. The students will:

1. Cite evidence to support a stereotype.
2. Cite evidence to contradict a stereotype.
3. Form a conclusion about stereotypes.
4. Analyze school inequality from two points of view.
5. Analyze school inequality using the *Knowledge as Design* questions.

You may use a wide variety of lesson plans based on the theories of instruction that you favor. There is no one correct form or format. An actual lesson would include additional objectives and strategies to achieve human relations or empowerment goals in addition to critical thinking.

The following lesson plans are provided to help you as a new teacher get started in planning critical thinking. Your instructor may want to add additional components. For example, many teachers include a component on evaluation.

Sample Lesson Plan for Grades 2 Through 4

The students will:

1. Categorize data as learned or inherited.
2. Group data based on the categories provided.
3. Recognize that students learn both at home and at school.
4. Recognize that culture is learned behavior.
5. Read words on the board.

First list the following categories on butcher paper or the chalkboard:

Things I Learned	Things I Inherited
language	hair color
food preferences	skin color

Then provide students with some clear examples of each category. In class discussion, have students categorize the skills and characteristics as either learned or inherited.

Things I Learned at Home	Things I Learned at School
language	reading

Then have teams of students meet to create lists using this second group of headings. A reporter from each team should share the ideas from that group. You then record the students' ideas on butcher paper or chalkboard.

As you summarize the information generated by the students, provide the conclusion that students learn both at home and at school. This conclusion is important to their understanding lessons on culture. See Chapter 2.

Sample Lesson Plan for Grades 8 Through 12

The students will be able to:
1. State a thesis and support it with evidence.
2. Arrive at a conclusion based on evidence.

First, you should introduce the subject of inequality and review the process of using evidence to support a position. As the teacher, you should provide students with a model by stating a conclusion, supporting it with evidence, and then formulating a thesis. For example, you might use this thesis: Students suffer from unequal funding of schools.

Through class discussion, have students offer evidence to support this thesis. After a

After students have made the first categorization, list the following categories on butcher paper or the chalkboard:

class discussion, have students draft a series of thesis statements on inequality. Record the theses on butcher paper.

Then assign teams of students to collect evidence to support each thesis. Ask students to research responses to the *Knowledge as Design* (p. 223) questions focused on inequality. Allow each team 30 minutes to 3 days to collect evidence to support its position.

Each team should prepare a report on its research responses to the *Knowledge as Design* questions about inequality. Each team report should begin with a statement of thesis followed by the evidence they have gathered to support the thesis. Finally, each team reports its conclusions and the supporting evidence to the class. Provide time in class for feedback.

Each team should write a short essay (1 to 3 paragraphs) using its thesis as its main idea. The supporting evidence will provide the rest of the paragraphs. Each team will edit and improve its paragraphs prior to submission.

Finally, you should offer a summary of the importance of using evidence to support a conclusion.

References

Adler, M. (1982). *The Paideia proposal: An educational manifesto.* New York: Macmillan.

Anderson, J. A. (1988, January-February). Cognitive styles and multicultural populations. *Journal of Teacher Education,* pp. 2–9.

Apple, M., & Christian Smith, L. K. (1991). *The politics of the textbook.* New York: Routledge.

Aronowitz, S., & Giroux, H. A. (1985). *Education under siege: The conservative, liberal, and radical debate over schooling.* Boston: Bergen & Garvey.

Association for Supervision and Curriculum Development. (1988). *Dimensions in thinking.* Alexandria, VA: ASCD.

Association for Supervision and Curriculum Development. (1992, February). The core curriculum conundrum. *Update #2.*

Beyer, B. (1988). *Developing a thinking skills curriculum.* Boston, MA: Allyn & Bacon.

Boyer, E. (1983). *High school: A report on secondary education in America.* Princeton, NJ: Carnegie Foundation for the Advancement of Teaching.

Brant, R. (1990, February). On knowledge and cognitive skills: A conversation with David Perkins. *ASCD Educational Leadership,* pp. 50–54.

Carnoy, M., & Irwin, H. M. (1985). *Schooling and work in the democratic state.* Stanford, CA: Stanford University Press.

Cornbleth, C. (1985). Critical thinking and cognitive process. *Review of Research in Social Studies Education: 1976–1983 Bulletin 75.* Washington, DC: National Council for the Social Studies.

Cornbleth, C., & Waugh, D. (1995). *The great speckled bird: Multicultural politics and education policymaking.* New York: St. Martin's.

DeAvila, E. (1987). *Finding out: Descubrimiento, Teacher's Guide.* Northvale, NJ: Santillana Publishing.

DeAvila, E. (1990, September 10). Assessment of language minority students: Political, technical, practical, and moral imperatives. National Symposium on Limited English Proficient Students. Washington, DC.

Freire, P., & Shore, I. (1987). *A pedagogy for liberation: Dialogues on transforming education.* Boston: Bergen & Garvey.

Giroux, H. (1988). *Teachers as intellectuals.* Boston: Bergen & Garvey.

Goodlad, J. (1983). *A place called school: Prospects for the future.* New York: McGraw-Hill.

Goodlad, J. (1990). Common schools for the common good: Reconciling self-interest with the common good. In J. Goodlad & P. Keating. (Eds.), *Access to knowledge: An agenda for our nation's schools.* New York: The College Entrance Board.

Miller-Jones, D. (1991). Informal reasoning in inner city children. In J. F. Voss, D. N. Perkins, & J. S. Segal. (Eds.), *Informal reasoning and education.* Hillsdale, NJ: Lawrence Erlbaum Associates.

Oaks, J., & Lypton, M. (1990). Tracking and ability grouping: A structural barrier to access and achievement. In J. Goodlad & P. Keating. (Eds.), *Access to knowledge: An agenda for our nation's schools.* New York: The College Entrance Board.

Olson, L. (1986, January). Effective schools. *Education Week.*

Paul, R. (1988). Program for the Fourth International Conference on Critical Thinking and Educational Reform. Sonoma State University, Rohnert Park, CA. In R. J. Marzano et al. (Eds.), *Dimensions of thinking: A framework for curriculum and instruction.* Alexandria, VA: ASCD.

Perkins, D. (1986). *Knowledge as design.* Hillsdale, NJ: Lawrence Erlbaum Associates.

Ramirez, M., & Casteñeda, A. (1974). *Cultural democracy, bicognitive development, and education.* New York: Academic Press.

Rist, R. C. (1970, August). Student social class and teacher expectations: The self-fulfilling prophecy in ghetto education. *Harvard Educational Review,* pp. 411–451.

Ryan, J., & Sackrey, C. (1984). *Strangers in paradise: Academics from the working class.* Boston, MA: South End Press.

Scriven, M., & Paul, R. (1994, Spring). Defining critical thinking: A draft statement for the National Council for Excellence in Critical Thinking Instruction. Sonoma State University.

Spring, J. (1988). *Conflict of interests: The politics of American education.* New York: Longman.

Vygotsky, L. S. (1978). In M. Cole, J. Teiner, S. Scubner, & E. Souberman (Eds.), *Mind in society: The development of higher psychological processes.* Cambridge, MA: Harvard University Press.

Chapter 10

Cooperative Learning and Multicultural Education

Teachers generally have chosen to structure classrooms in a win or lose manner, where competition and individual effort are rewarded or punished. As shown in prior chapters, the urban poor and students of color systematically lose in this system. As a part of the response to the challenge of teaching in the multicultural classroom, some teachers have developed strategies whereby pairs and small groups of students work together, learn from each other, and master the material while building respect, solidarity, and a sense of community. These strategies are called **cooperative learning.**

Cooperative learning strategies engage students from diverse cultures who may be alienated from the macroculture. This high-energy approach also has shown success with students across social classes whose interest in learning may have been dulled by rapid changes in society and an increasing dependence on television. Teachers can no longer assume that the home has nurtured in the student positive attitudes toward school and toward working with others. Using the cooperative learning approach, we can teach students how to build positive relationships with other students and with adults.

Cooperative learning takes advantage of the complex relationship dynamics that exist in all classrooms—teachers instructing students and students interacting with each other. Students learn more when they talk about a subject, explain an idea to another student, even argue about an idea, than when they hear a lecture or read a book. Rather than trying to suppress student-to-student interaction in the interest of "classroom order," teachers who use cooperative learning regard such interaction as an important learning resource, and they plan strategies to capture this energy to support and strengthen the learning process. The total amount of teacher talk is reduced, and the amount of teacher-directed student-to-student interaction, and thus student learning, is increased.

Cooperative learning provides both elementary and secondary teachers with strategies to teach positive social skills, such as listening, sharing, and working together. These lessons are particularly needed in depressed neighborhoods where economic and social stress combine to thwart student achievement. The process of improving group interaction is enormously interesting to young people, and they soon become engaged in creating a positive supporting classroom environment. They learn from one another.

Groupwork conducted within multicultural classes encourages students to exchange viewpoints, check the validity of those viewpoints, and gradually engage in dialogue. Groupwork can move the class away from seatwork and ditto sheets to high cognitive demand instruction. Cooperative learning also encourages students to take responsibility for their own education.

Teachers use cooperative groups to break down the effects of ability grouping and to establish high expectations for all. Cooperative strategies counter traditional tracking and ability-grouping strategies, which undercut student perceptions about equality of opportunity and democratic principles. Spencer Kagan (1986) cites evidence to suggest that cooperative learning can equalize the achievement between certain at-risk students and majority group students in subjects such as math and science. It provides a needed step toward equal educational opportunity.

The use of cooperative learning results in improved academic achievement for many underachieving students. While cooperative strategies are valuable in all schools, they are particularly important in a multicultural environment because they produce high achievement levels for all, promote equal-status interaction among students, and teach students to work together to resolve problems (Johnson & Johnson, 1991). Cooperative learning is a direct way to teach positive intergroup relations. Kagan's research (1986) indicates that when students are taught how to cooperate and are placed in teams, student friendship and respect across racial lines increase.

The Tracking Debate

A sharp debate has developed around the nation over ability grouping and tracking. Most multicultural education advocates oppose tracking. They see classes for the gifted and for low-track students as contributing to the problems of unequal access to the curriculum. There is significant evidence to support this view. Advocates of programs for the gifted and talented argue that heterogeneous classes prohibit "bright" students from seeking educational excellence. They too have substantial research to support their position.

While excellent work is being done by a small group of teachers to oppose tracking, most teachers take ability grouping for granted. High school teachers accept that some students are college bound, and others terminal. Teachers avoid low-track classes, and principals assign these classes to the newest faculty. Teachers in low-track classes find it difficult to establish positive, productive learning environments because many of the students recognize their low status and conform to the low expectations of the schools. Students exhibit defeatism, alienation, and resistance to academic work. There is more authoritarian teacher behavior and more student-to-student violence in these classes. In racially integrated schools, low-track classes have an overrepresentation of African American, Latino, and Native American students. Soon both teachers and students develop low expectations of these classes.

In developing a professional view on tracking and ability grouping, several important issues must be considered. Substantial evidence indicates that identification and placement of students into ability groups are frequently based on poor measures and inadequate placement decisions. Jeannie Oakes (1985) and others have demonstrated that race and social class strongly influence the placement of individuals. High-track programs are available in middle-class schools, whereas urban schools have a preponderance of low-track, remedial, and terminal programs. The placement process itself is unequal and unfair.

A second problem is that placement in low-track classes or low-ability groups is unnecessarily and inappropriately rigid. Students change and mature. Schools help students to learn. But initial placements too often remain rigid, punishing students for poorly informed or immature decisions made by students and faculty in prior years. The rigidity of ability grouping reduces the value of hard work. A fixed conception of ability and intelligence has long been abandoned by most serious researchers.

Being placed in a low track contributes to the several attacks on self-esteem that devastate many students—particularly adolescents, girls, and students of color. Ability grouping, as presently practiced, frequently contributes to racial, ethnic, and class isolation. Law suits are presently in the courts challenging this new and sloppy form of segregation by IQ scores that leads to segregation by income and race.

If all these criticisms of tracking are true, then what about the arguments of the advocates for gifted and talented programs? Aren't bright students bored and held back in "regular" classes? Haven't magnet schools and programs for the "gifted" kept European-American students in urban public schools when they would have otherwise fled? These arguments also have merit. Changing to homogenous classes will not, by itself, overcome the failure to motivate and interest students as is common in too many classrooms. Without other significant improvements in the quality of education, ending ability grouping might simply bore all students equally.

In real-world classrooms, the two positions on ability grouping should not be treated as only polar opposites. A concern for equality of opportunity leads to the conclusion that students should be primarily taught in homogenous classes. Teachers can change their teaching strategies to encourage all students to learn. Cooperative learning strategies are some of the fundamental strategies for teaching in homogenous classes.

In a few subjects that are highly sequential, such as math, students can be grouped based on their demonstrated abilities. That is, some students can study math while others study calculus. But these groupings are less harmful if they are not rigid. That is, while the students may be placed in a "gifted" class for math, they should be in a homogenous class for social studies, physical education, and other less sequential courses. There should be advanced classes in art, music, and other subjects where other students might also be "gifted." Also, students with special needs sometimes require special services to gain access to the mainstream curriculum. For example, limited-English-speaking students might be separated for part of the day to give them increased opportunity to learn and practice English. At other times, students might be in a class that studies literature or some other appropriate subject in Spanish.

A change to a less-tracked curriculum requires teachers to adjust their strategies. And most importantly, teachers need to consider multiple definitions of intelligence (Gardner, 1993) and abandon current fixed and static views.

Language-Minority Students

Groupwork is particularly helpful in a classroom where some students have limited English skills. Placing students in teams increases the amount of English they hear and increases their opportunities to practice the language. Those learning a second language usually understand student-to-student exchanges better than they comprehend teacher-to-student talk. Dialogue between students provides context cues and opportunities for comprehension checking missing from most formal teacher presentations. Working in groups also provides the second language learner with a significantly improved learning environment because cooperative learning strategies dramatically increase the number of student-to-student exchanges. Increased oral language usage and one-to-one dialogue help students from many cultural groups who need additional language practice. (The following chapter, "Teaching Language-Minority Children," offers additional strategies for extensive oral language usage through cooperative learning.)

Not only does groupwork stimulate the development of better language skills, but it also increases learning across all subject matter. A teacher's professional vocabulary and interests often create a gap between the material presented and students' prior knowledge. This gap interferes with learning. The student-to-student exchanges common in cooperative learning help to close the gap by allowing students to discuss presented material using terms and contextual clues that are meaningful to them (Vygotsky, 1978).

As the reader knows, traditional strategies of competition do encourage some students to work. Cooperative learning does not replace the competitive approach, but it does add additional strategies to encourage the participation of students who may not flourish under individual, competitive practices. There is no evidence to show that time spent on cooperative interaction slows down academically talented students. These students actually learn more—not less—as they interact with the material in group discussions and explain difficult sections to others.

When students have practiced cooperative learning and have learned a few basic rules and roles (see Figure 10.2), groupwork resolves many classroom management problems. For example, students can learn to work independently on clearly defined tasks. One student per team serves as a task monitor to assist the teacher in keeping students involved in their team project. The teacher serves as a monitor, a helper, and a coach.

Teachers in the middle grades (4 through 8) particularly benefit because they can spend less time trying to control the class and more time working with individuals. Well-run cooperative groups allow teachers the time and freedom to build the positive human relationships required for effective teaching.

Preparing a Class for Cooperative Learning

There are four initial steps in preparing a class for cooperative learning. The teacher must

1. Design the environment,
2. Select appropriate tasks,
3. Teach appropriate roles, and then
4. Encourage positive interdependence.

Designing the Environment

Students need to be *taught* to work together. Learning how to work in groups requires instruction and practice. In preparation for teamwork, practice sessions should be designed so students can learn new roles and new social skills. Long-range projects covering a week or two are appropriate only after skills of cooperation and processing have been developed.

For very young students and for students new to cooperation, instruction often begins with extended practice working in pairs. In these early stages of cooperative learning, tasks should be selected which can be completed within 5 to 10 minutes. Later, the pairs are combined to create teams of four to six students, small enough so each student can participate.

Team membership should be reorganized and rotated every two to four weeks. Separate teams should be formed for different subjects to avoid the perception by students that the teams are ability groups.

The teacher should require frequent oral progress reports from each team. These reports encourage high expectations. Any member of the team can be given the recorder's notes and make a report for the team. The teacher can say, "The person to the left of the recorder will make the report." The distribution of the reporting function helps to keep the entire team responsible for quality work. The teacher can encourage and monitor student participation by regularly collecting and reviewing team notes.

Teaching students how to engage in cooperative learning takes time, but there are no shortcuts. A lecture on role behavior is no substitute for practicing role behavior. The teacher must define the roles, help students practice those roles, evaluate the practice, and then help students improve their role behavior. Some teachers may be reluctant to divert valuable class time to this training, but class time used in learning and practicing role behavior will result in time saved over the school year. Students who have learned on-task behavior and know how to work in teams to pursue independent study projects will more than make up the time spent in learning these skills.

Teachers have developed a variety of team-building exercises to begin instruction in cooperative learning. Guides to these exercises can be found in the work of Spencer Kagan (1989), in the video by Heredia-Arriaga and Campbell (1991), and in the lesson plans shown at the end of this chapter.

Selecting Appropriate Tasks

Cooperative assignments work best when they provide intrinsic and immediate rewards based on successful completion of appropriately challenging tasks. These tasks should require multiple skills and encourage students to take diverse viewpoints. Whenever possible the teacher should draw on students' personal experiences as subjects for study.

Effective tasks for cooperative learning should involve conceptual thinking rather than a group search for a single right answer (see Figure 10.1). Creative problem solving also works well.

Not all tasks are appropriate to group investigation. Groupwork lends itself to problem solving rather than to rote memorization of predetermined material. A group structure can be used for memorizing the definitions of adverbs and nouns, but it is more useful in helping students to edit their own writing. Groupwork is of marginal value in memorizing historical or geographical facts, but it is very useful for teaching critical thinking in the course of a history or social science investigation.

Figure 10.1 Suggested Cooperative Tasks

Primary
Share feelings
Language practice

Upper Elementary Grades 3–5
Math problems
Language practice
Science projects

Middle Grades 6-8
Process writing
Language practice

Secondary Grades 9–12
Discussion of controversial issues
Process writing
Student governance
Social participation projects

Teaching Appropriate Roles

Teachers begin cooperative learning by teaching appropriate role behavior. The roles suggested in Figure 10.2 have proven useful in many classrooms.

The several tasks of group maintenance are too complex to assign to a single individual. Assigning multiple roles allows all students to learn and practice leadership skills. The teacher should rotate role assignments within the group to ensure that each student acquires the skills necessary for each role.

Science and math projects often involve handling materials and objects, and it is helpful to assign some additional roles to group members. The Finding Out/Descubrimiento Project described on page 241 uses a "go-fer," a safety mon-

Figure 10.2 Suggested Roles for Cooperative Learning

Checker: This student checks for agreement in the group and makes certain all students understand the answers.

Praiser: This student praises the students' efforts, ideas, and role behavior.

Recorder: This student records ideas and decisions and shares the final product with the class.

Task Monitor: This student keeps the group on the assigned task and monitors time.

Gate Keeper: This student encourages all students to participate and keeps any one person from dominating.

itor, and a cleanup director (Cohen, 1986). The go-fer has the task of getting all materials to the work area. Assigning this role discourages dozens of students from getting out of their seats to get materials. The safety monitor remains alert for sharp objects, spills, and other safety concerns. The cleanup director supervises and monitors the cleanup activities for all team members. Once established, these roles assist the teacher and reduce stress.

Encouraging Positive Interdependence

The teacher using cooperative learning seeks to establish positive interdependence among the students. Tasks and evaluation are arranged so the group does better when it cooperates. The task of broken circles is a good example (see Figure 10.3). Students in a group are supplied with a series of parts to circles. Each group has all the parts necessary for all members to make complete circles. Group members are expected to assist their teammates in completing their circles. How-

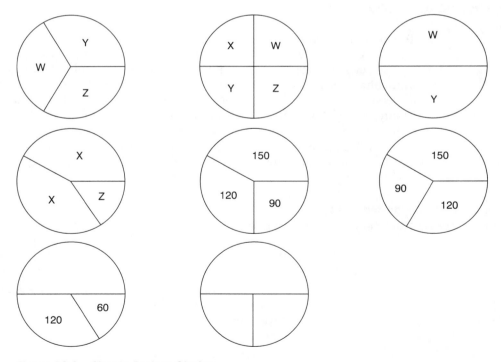

Figure 10.3   Simple Broken Circles

Note. From *Designing groupwork: Strategies for the heterogeneous classroom* (p. 162) by E. Cohen, 1986, New York: Teachers College Press.

ever, if a few students seek only their own success and ignore the needs of others, they will complete their circles using parts that their teammates need to complete theirs, thus preventing the group as a whole from completing the task.

Projects in which the entire group receives a common grade engender positive interdependence. Teams are encouraged to look for ways in which the artistic or mechanical aptitude of an apparent underachiever can be used to the team's advantage. Spencer Kagan (1989) describes ways teachers encourage positive interdependence by establishing a grading system in which bonus points go to the team that has the fewest members with low scores. Helping a teammate to review basic multiplication and division improves the teammate's score, the team score, and all students' math competence (Kagan, 1989).

Traditionally, the grading system and curricula of most schools have emphasized competition and the resultant sorting of students into winners and losers. Cooperative learning, and particularly group grading, counteract these school folkways (see Figure 10.4) (Johnson & Johnson, 1991).

Teamwork serves particularly well for social action projects in the middle grades and high schools. The ideas and diversity of a four- to six-member student team bring originality, intellect, and creativity to bear on resolving the real-life problems of classrooms, agencies, service organizations, and community groups. Teamwork skills developed in social action projects, like development of critical thinking, prepare students for employment in the growing world of knowledge-based industries. Team projects provide a bridge from the passive-receptive behavior common to students in teacher-centered classrooms to the active and responsible behavior required in the adult world of work.

Periodic evaluation of the teamwork is critical. Teams should regularly monitor their processes and work on improving team skills. A sample evaluation sheet is shown in Figure 10.5.

Figure 10.4   Differences Between Typical Groups and Cooperative Groups

Cooperative Learning Groups	Traditional Learning Groups
Positive interdependence	Little interdependence
Group accountability	Individual accountability
Heterogeneous	Homogeneous
Shared leadership	One appointed leader
Shared responsibility for each other	Responsibility only for self
Task and group maintenance emphasized	Task emphasized
Social skills directly taught	Social skills assumed
Teacher observes and intervenes	Focus on task
Groups process their effectiveness	Little or no focus on group processes

Note. From *Circles of Learning*, by D. W. Johnson, R. T. Johnson, E. J. Holabec, and P. Roy, 1984, Alexandria, VA: ASCD.

Figure 10.5 Evaluation of Small-Group Work

In addition to the information and ideas discussed, you should be learning to improve the processes of group work. The questions below were selected to assist you in evaluating your progress.

A. How well is the group working toward solving the problem?	Very Far		Not Far
defining the task?			
gathering information?			
sharing information from several sources?			
making a decision?			

B. What issues were discussed?
Was agreement reached on any issues?

C. What strategies or behaviors helped to move the discussion along toward your goal?
What strategies or behaviors interfered with progress?

D. How well are members of the group helping each other? Are members:	Very Well		Poorly
sharing?			
expressing different points of view?			
seeking solutions to problems?			
encouraging each other?			

A Classroom Example

Miguel Hernandez teaches eighth-grade social studies in Merced, California, a medium-sized city in California's Central Valley. He wants his students to think about the world of work and their own future job prospects, to recognize the advantages of staying in school, and to improve their writing skills.

Miguel initiates the project by first discussing these issues and sharing a short autobiographical paper he wrote on schooling and his own job. The students are encouraged to comment on the paper and to critically evaluate its ideas.

Miguel directs students to move into their prearranged small groups. Each group spends about 8 minutes reacting to Miguel's paper and recording suggestions for improvement. Then Miguel refocuses the discussion. He tells each group to brainstorm ideas and issues the members could use in papers of their own. Each group delegates a recorder to write down all of the ideas. This brainstorming might last 10 to 15 minutes. Each team member makes a copy of the ideas from the recorder.

After brainstorming, group members write a draft of an outline for their individual papers. Each student must record three to five ideas. Students are allowed to share and discuss their ideas during this time. If one student has difficulty, the team helps that person to draft his or her initial ideas. Miguel monitors progress during this time, visiting each group and offering his assistance if needed.

Once the rough outlines are done, each student writes an opening paragraph based on the outline. The paragraph is improved for spelling and sentence structure.

Back in their groups, team members read their opening paragraphs aloud. This is called a read-around. The other team members comment and make helpful suggestions. They are encouraged to offer ideas on content, clarity, and style. Team members may also make "me too" comments to affirm the writer's themes. Team members suggest additional ideas that might illustrate or support the themes of the writer. The writer takes notes and considers the teammates' ideas.

After all opening paragraphs have been discussed in the teams, each writer prepares an initial draft of the paper. Usually the drafts are short, one to two pages. The writer prepares the draft for further discussion by correcting spelling and sentences. If a photocopier is available, each author makes four copies of the paper.

The team now takes the time to read the paper and to make marginal notes. The members hold a discussion of the paper focusing on the main ideas, clarity of expression, and communication, while the author takes notes. At times, Miguel assigns tasks such as having one student provide feedback on sentences or paragraphs, while another is assigned feedback on clarity.

At this point, Miguel groups the writers in pairs to rewrite, proofread, and edit a final copy of each paper. Once that is done, the papers are "published" on a copy machine. Finally, Miguel reads the papers, grades them, and confers with each student on how he or she is developing as a writer. Miguel's strategy for conducting a cooperative learning writing project is shown in Figure 10.6 in outline form.

After the project is completed, Miguel further guides his students in processing the experience and in selecting social skills for future development.

Figure 10.6 **Outline for Cooperative Learning Writing Project in Miguel Hernandez's Class**

1. Brainstorm on themes	(Small group, 2–4 students)
2. Build an outline	(Cooperative)
3. Write first draft	(Individual)
4. Read-around	(Small group, 2–4 students)
5. Critique draft	(Small group, 2–4 students)
6. Redraft	(Individual)
7. Edit	(Pairs—Writer and team member)
8. Rewrite	(Individual)
9. Second read-around	(Cooperative)
10. Edit or rewrite	(Individual)
11. Publish/print	(Cooperative)
12. Distribute	(Cooperative)

Confronting Racism and Sexism Through Equal-Status Interaction

Cooperative learning helps teachers to deal with the societal problems of racism and sexism. It provides excellent strategies for directly working against different forms of prejudice.

Children Learn Prejudice

In a society like ours, which is structured by racial, sexual, and homophobic ideology, prejudice is easy to learn. Children learn prejudice, often at an early age from their parents and peers.

For students from stressed and disrupted families, where safety and security are often missing, misinformation and prejudice are often projected onto groups who serve as convenient targets to blame for the problems in the family, the neighborhood, or the economy. In other families, the burden of learned racism is passed down from generation to generation.

Teaching students positive human relations helps to reduce prejudice by providing the support and self-esteem they need. Teachers must themselves provide a consistent model of behavior that respects the diverse cultures and abilities in the classroom. Your modeling will contend against the other examples in the society. Teachers can bring up these issues by presenting accurate information, rather than stereotypes, about all cultural groups. The empowerment strategies described in Chapter 7 reduce prejudice by moving the potential victim out of the position of oppression. When students achieve equality, it is very difficult for oppressors to maintain their prejudices except by the most distorted logic.

Cooperation and mutual respect are central goals of the multicultural curriculum. Teachers should plan for and work toward these goals rather than only hope that they will emerge in the classroom. Gordon Allport, in his classic work *The*

Nature of Prejudice (1979), says, "Prejudice (unless deeply rooted in the character structure of the individual) may be reduced by equal status contact between majority and minority group members in pursuit of common goals" (p. 281).

Cooperative learning that includes equal-status interaction strategies works against prejudice by providing students with regular experiences of mutual support, dependence, and caring. The teacher consciously plans the control of status in the class. To achieve this interaction, the roles of group behavior are carefully taught (page 235). The teacher selects the group members and integrates each group to the degree possible by race, ethnicity, gender, observed talents, and perceived ability. Once learned, the role positions are rotated so that all students have an important function in helping the group achieve its common goals.

Students who initially do not perform well or who lack academic or cooperation skills are given extra instruction and assistance rather than criticism and avoidance. Students who might be low status are placed in high-status positions for group projects and are assisted in performing there. Teachers design cooperative groups in ways that ensure the distribution of high status to all, particularly to those who might otherwise be left out. Further, group work is evaluated and consistently improved. Students are expected and helped to function well. This activity requires caring and support for all group members rather than rejection and avoidance (Cohen, Lotan, & Whitcomb, 1992).

Consistent planning of role-playing simulation games and rotating roles within cooperative learning, along with planning status interventions, significantly reduce the stereotyping, prejudice, and social distance between students in the class.

Students with strong acquired prejudices may resist working cooperatively in groups, but the teacher should exercise leadership and insist on positive, democratic behavior in the classroom and the school. Prejudices brought from outside are not permitted to structure the classroom interaction. If some students resist even more, the teacher may want to use coaching (page 198) behavior to increase the demands on students to behave cooperatively and respectfully.

Certain cooperative learning programs have developed a sophisticated approach to equal-status interaction among ethnic groups and between the genders. Through careful planning and monitoring, students participate in equal-status role relationships rather than hierarchical or oppressive relationships. Prejudices tend to be reduced when students working cooperatively succeed at a mutual task (Cohen, 1986).

One of these programs was developed by Elizabeth Cohen, Ed De Avilla, and associates at Stanford University. Called Finding Out/Descubrimiento, this program combines curricula, teaching strategies, and evaluations to effectively establish equal-status interaction. This bilingual math/science curriculum project provides numerous insights into critical thinking, classroom management, and group processes (De Avilla, 1987).

By rotating the students through roles, all the students practice and develop the skills of leading and assisting others. Students learn to participate with and depend on students from diverse ethnic and cultural backgrounds. The teacher arranges tasks so students must turn to all of their peers, not just the ones they may feel most comfortable with.

Planned cooperative learning encourages the students to use the multiple talents in the group. Some cooperative learning tasks may require a good artist, some a good negotiator, and others a bilingual advocate. Cooperative projects demonstrate the slogan, "All of us together know more than any of us apart."

In classes with two to six children with limited English skills, teachers should design role relationships that place bilingual children in roles as experts. For example, a bilingual child could serve as a translator from English to the target language and from Spanish, Chinese, or Russian to English for the group allowing all the students to learn. The bilingual child gains status by using two languages to communicate, while the student learning English in the group is assisted in comprehending and participating in the tasks. Using bilingual translators in cooperative groups creates a win-win situation for students.

Most countries use the metric system and many immigrant children can excel in tasks related to metric measurement. Teachers can enlist the assistance of immigrant children as experts when teaching this system. The English-dominant students on a team reciprocate by helping immigrant students with their English language development.

During the Civil Rights Movement (1954–1968), young people working together to solve problems of segregation and injustice learned to believe in their own worth and to make demands on the government for redress of grievances. Today students from poverty areas and people of color seldom encounter opportunities to work successfully together for positive, constructive purposes. Teamwork in schools that focuses on social service and participation tasks provides the instruction in morals and values necessary to extend our democracy to include, rather than exclude, the lower class and ethnic minorities from public participation. Teamwork also involves students in social issues vital to their own future by helping them learn to respect diversity of skills, talents, perspectives, and the values essential to community building.

Cooperative learning empowers both teachers and students. Students learn problem-solving strategies. Student teams identify problems, draft solutions, consider the possible outcomes of each proposed solution, implement a solution, and then work to overcome any barriers. Teams working toward problem resolution provide excellent preparation for participation in a democratic society.

Classroom Management

Teaching cooperative learning in an increasingly individualistic and competitive society is difficult. Many children are not prepared to cooperate. The skills of cooperation and the attitudes supportive of cooperation must be taught. Teachers will need to use the classroom management strategies described in Chapter 8 to teach and promote cooperation.

Two groups of students are particularly resistant to adopting cooperative learning: those who consistently win in the competitive classroom and those who have mastered the art of avoiding teacher attention and scrutiny. Teachers should use a balance of cooperative learning and individualized learning to provide both competitive and cooperative students with an environment where they can succeed.

When a small number of students fail at cooperation, the teacher should carefully reteach the skills and roles of cooperative learning. Teaching and insisting on role behavior sometimes need to be done assertively, especially in the early stages of learning cooperation. Later, once the groups are functioning well, new students can receive orientation and skill training from other students in the group (Johnson & Johnson, 1991).

Major problems of management alienation or nonparticipation by a few students should be addressed by the teacher, not assigned to the group. When one student refuses to work, it frustrates other group members. The task of correcting student behavior is potentially very divisive to the group since most students have little or no experience in conflict resolution. They may resort to brutal and severe strategies. After several weeks of cooperative learning, these problems will decrease as groupwork becomes rewarding.

Heterogenous grouping works best for most cooperative learning. After practicing roles, teachers structure the groups for integration of ethnic, gender, class, and perceived ability levels within the teams. When cooperative work is initiated prior to second grade, inter-ethnic tensions are quickly reduced. Inter-ethnic cooperation may take time with older children.

In communities where racial hostility is significant, weeks of student preparation and extended social skill practice will enhance the success of cooperative groups. For example, in a recently integrated school or in a school to which children of different ethnicities are bussed long distances, students need clear goals and rules of conduct for working together. They need to practice social skills as a part of preparation for cooperative work. Team-building activities can contribute to the creation of an equal status, integrated environment. The systematic development of cooperative learning in the classroom will reduce ethnic divisions in the classroom and contribute to the reduction of violence at the school.

Cooperative learning produces a change in classroom management. The noise level often increases in classrooms using groupwork. Teachers and administrators learn to distinguish between productive, on-task noise and idle chatter. As students develop increasing skills in cooperation, the teacher's role changes from one of struggling for control to one of giving direction and guidance. The teacher spends more time establishing the cooperative environment and designing tasks for it and less time criticizing students for their behavior. Initially, designing appropriate tasks takes a great deal of time and ingenuity. Fortunately, once designed, the tasks are useful year after year. Teachers gain time, ideas, and support by working with other teachers—cooperating—in project design.

Summary

Schools and teachers need additional strategies to respond to the growing diversity of our society and the growing alienation of some our students from that society. The recent development of cooperative teaching strategies provides a direct and interesting approach to democratic, multicultural education. Cooperative learning empowers students and teaches self-confidence as well as a sense of responsibility to the welfare of others. It also teaches students to listen, to share, and to advocate for their own interests. Cooperative learning strategies change the relationship between teacher and student to promote person-to-person dialogue and a sharing community in the classroom.

Questions Over the Chapter

1. What are some skills for grades K through 3 that are taught through cooperative learning?
2. Define *tracking*. Are there examples of tracking in your school?
3. What are the results of tracking?
4. Give examples of groupings that are not tracking.
5. Why do many teachers assume that tracking is beneficial?
6. As a student teacher, would you rather work in a high-tracked class or a mixed-ability class?
7. How would you prepare differently for teaching the two different classes?
8. Do you support special classes for the gifted? Explain.
9. Do you support "magnet" programs? Explain.
10. How can cooperative learning provide an alternative to tracking?
11. What new social skills do students need to learn as a teacher "de-tracks" a class?
12. What are some advantages of heterogeneous grouping?

Teaching Strategies

Sample Objectives for Cooperative Learning Lessons

The students will:

1. Work cooperatively in a group.
2. Share materials with others.
3. Stay on the subject while working in the group.
4. Listen to other members of the group.
5. Gather information by listening to others.
6. Contribute ideas to others in the group.
7. Accurately report on the group's progress.
8. Assist other members of the group.
9. Serve in a specific role (for example, checker, task master, etc.).
10. Contribute to improving the process of the group.
11. Select a skill for the group to work on next.
12. Evaluate the effectiveness of the group.
13. Plan and practice group improvement.

Sample Lesson Plans for Cooperative Learning

Lessons in cooperative learning teach values, skills, content, and critical thinking, while using cooperative strategies. The following lessons focus only on the cooperative strategies. Teachers should add content, values, and skills to these preliminary lessons.

Grades 1 Through 3
The students will:
1. Listen to others.
2. Work in a group (or pairs).
3. Get to know other students in the class.

Have students line up based on height (from shortest to tallest). Other variables for lineups might include number of brothers and sisters, birth dates, etc. Once lined up, the person at one end steps forward and walks to the opposite end. The persons second from the end will follow in a line.

The students are now facing a partner. The teacher designates which line of students should share their ideas first. Select some easy-to-answer question, such as What is your favorite ice cream, food, television show, sport, or game? or What do you like to do after school?

Students in the first line share their responses to the teacher's questions. Then students in the second line share their responses to the same questions.

Have students return to their seats and pose to them sample discussion questions such as these: What is one thing you learned about your classmate? What did you do to show you were a good listener? You should praise students who exhibit specific examples of positive social and academic skills during the activity.

Video examples and lesson plans of this and nine other cooperative learning lessons are available from Superior Learning Programs, *How to Integrate Cooperative Learning for the Elementary Teacher* by Sue Heredia-Arriaga and Duane Campbell, P.O. Box 2194, Carson City, NV 89702.

Grades 4 Through 8
The students will:
1. Work cooperatively in a group.
2. Stay on the subject while working in a group.
3. Practice specific role behavior (checker, task master, etc.).
4. Contribute to improving the group's functioning.

Present the specific roles provided in Figure 10.2. Describe and discuss each role.

Then provide the task. Each group will discuss cooperation. Each group should make a list of the advantages and disadvantages of cooperation. The assigned persons will practice their roles within each group.

After an eight-minute work session, each group reports on their list. Each member of the group gives one evaluative remark to the checker. The group plans to improve the practice of working as a team. The roles are rotated one person to the right. Each group member now has a new role to practice.

The group discusses improved group functioning, with each student practicing the new role. Provide an evaluation system in advance. Have the students evaluate how well the group members are sharing opinions and how well they respect the points of view of others.

Evaluate the discussion. Then summarize the skills practiced this day. These skills should be used with discussions again the next day.

Grades 8 Through 12
The students will:
1. Work cooperatively in a group.
2. Define the task prior to beginning work.
3. Consider the points of view of others.
4. Give feedback to each other.
5. Decide to reduce the name calling in the class.

Divide the class into small groups and assign appropriate roles. Then instruct students on the importance of clearly defining the task prior to initiating group discussion.

Provide the task. Each group is to decide on three suggestions for reducing the use of derogatory names in the class. In a small-group discussion, each group member should suggest ideas.

Each person should practice their assigned role. Have the reporter from each group report on the group's ideas. Record the ideas on the chalkboard. Later, students could make charts of these ideas for posting in the class.

Select the three to five most common or most interesting suggestions provided by the reporters. Then assign two groups this task: Describe the positive and negative consequences of these suggestions.

Assign two other groups this task: List the influences that will work against or prevent students from following these suggestions.

Have the recorder in each group report for the group.

The groups should process their work. The groups can complete the group processing exercise found in Figure 10.5.

As the teacher, you should comment on positive and helpful behavior observed while the groups were working. Remind students of the importance of having a clear definition of the task prior to beginning work.

References

Allport, G. W. (1979). *The nature of prejudice.* Reading, MA: Addison-Wesley.

Cohen, E. (1986). *Designing groupwork: Strategies for the heterogeneous classroom.* New York: Teachers College Press.

Cohen, E., Lotan, R. A., & Whitcomb, J. A. (1992). Complex instruction in the social studies classroom. In R. J. Stahl & R. L. Van Sickle (Eds.), *Cooperative learning in the social studies, 87.* Washington, DC: National Council for the Social Studies.

De Avilla, E. A. (1987). Three questions: Three circles. *Finding out: Descubrimiento, Teachers guide.* Northvale, NJ: Santillana Publishing.

Gardner, H. (1993). *Multiple intelligences: The theory in practice.* New York: Basic Books/HarperCollins.

Heredia-Arriaga, S., & Campbell, D. (1991). *How to integrate cooperative learning for the elementary teacher: Video and training program.* Carson City, NV: Superior Learning Programs.

Johnson, D. W., & Johnson, R. T. (1991). *Learning together and alone: Cooperative competitive and individualistic learning* (3rd Ed.). Englewood Cliffs, NJ: Prentice Hall.

Johnson, D. W., Johnson, R. T., Holabec, E. J., & Roy, P. (1984). *Circles of learning: Cooperation in the classroom.* Alexandria, VA: ASCD.

Kagan, S. (1986). Cooperative learning and sociocultural factors in schooling. *Beyond Language: Social and Cultural Factors in Schooling Language Minority Students,* p. 245. Los Angeles, CA: Evaluation, Dissemination, and Assessment Center, CSU Los Angeles.

Kagan, S. (1989). *Cooperative learning, resources for teachers.* San Juan Capistrano, CA: Resources for Teachers.

Oakes, J. (1985). *Keeping track: How schools structure inequality.* New Haven, CT: Yale University Press.

Vygotsky, L. S. (1978). *Mind in society: The development of higher psychological processes.* Cambridge, MA: Harvard University Press.

Chapter 11

Teaching Language-Minority Populations

Do you think "English is under attack?" If so, from whom?

And what should you as a teacher do if you have three to four students in your class who do not speak English well? Whose job is it to serve these students?

Many teachers in the 1990s must face new questions such as these: What languages will your students speak? What is your own position on language acquisition? How do your own feelings on the issue differ from your classroom policy on language acquisition? This chapter will help you to develop responses to these questions.

Defining Minority Status

Considerable misunderstanding occurs among teachers about the differences between groups of minority students as they seek to improve school achievement. Teachers and educational critics tend to believe in legends that Asian students and earlier European immigrants seemed to do well in school without special programs such as bilingual education. Such analysis is misleading. In this legend, several distinct Asian cultures—Chinese, Japanese, Korean, Filipino, Hawaiian, Vietnamese and others—are inaccurately grouped together into one generalization. Some have been successful—others not. And most European

Figure 11.1 **Success Stories**

Miguel Perez

After fleeing with his mother from the war in El Salvador, Miguel Perez entered the United States illegally. He struggled for years to learn English and to stay in this country. Soon after he came to the United States, his mother died. Once he was even ordered deported by the Immigration and Naturalization Service. However, in 1992 he graduated as valedictorian of his class from California State University–Dominguez Hills and is currently studying health education in Pennsylvania. He won his case with the INS and received permanent resident status. When eligible, he wants to become a U.S. citizen.

Moa Vang

At age nine, Moa and his family walked three weeks to flee the invasion of their village in Laos. Half of his family died en route to the refugee camps in Thailand. After four years in the camps, Moa and one brother were allowed to come to the United States. A sponsor took him in and helped him to succeed in school. As a refugee, he did not have the fear of deportation experienced by Miguel. Now 34, Moa has spent over a decade getting permission for other family members to immigrate. The war, the refugee camps, the difficulty of immigration and adjustment have devastated his family and much of his community. After working for three years as a teacher assistant, Moa began the long, difficult task of becoming a teacher.

Ann Ngo Tran

As a young girl, Ann remembers life in Vietnam. Then, she and her family had to flee. Because her father worked in the military, they were able to fly out of Saigon. Many members of her family were left behind. When she arrived in Portland, Oregon, Ann spoke only a few words of English, but she was able to attend school and struggled to learn English. The stresses of migration and learning to live in this country have produced great divisions in her family. One brother is a gang member. But Ann is a respectful daughter. She has watched her generation achieve and has watched her parents' generation struggle with their loss. She has now graduated from college and become a bilingual teacher, hoping to assist other immigrant students with their difficult transitions.

The descriptions of William and Ann are composites drawn from the experiences of several students in the bilingual program at California State University, Sacramento.

immigrants entered an economy where manual labor was needed and moderately rewarded. It was the *children* of the immigrants who succeeded in school, as many children of immigrants do today (see Figure 11.1). The legend that schools served as the gateway to societal integration for European immigrants persists in spite of the data to the contrary and leads directly to several destructive viewpoints about cultural pluralism and bilingualism.

The work of John Ogbu (1978, 1990; Ogbu & Matute-Bianchi, 1986) contributes to our understanding of minority status in schools by describing three distinct kinds of minorities: autonomous, caste-like minorities, and immigrant minorities. Ogbu defines **minority status** as when the population occupies a subordinate power relationship in the society. Sometimes even majorities, such as women in U.S. business or blacks in South Africa, can occupy subordinate power relations. In the United States, these groups are treated as minorities. Each of Ogbu's three types of minorities has dramatically different experiences in schools.

Autonomous Minorities

Groups that have a distinctive culture and language but are not politically, socially, or economically subordinated are **autonomous minorities.** Jews, Mormons, and some other religious groups largely fit into this category of minority status. In Hawaii, the Chinese American and Japanese American communities function as relatively autonomous minorities. Autonomous minorities may experience prejudice and discrimination, but they are not systematically kept in subordinate positions. These students do not have a pattern of systematic failure in schools. Human relations lessons responsive to reducing stereotyping and encouraging respect are helpful in promoting respect for and among autonomous minorities.

Caste-Like Minorities

A second group of minorities are subordinate or **caste-like minorities.** Ogbu argues these groups were originally brought into the country involuntarily (African Americans), by conquest (Native Americans and Chicanos), or colonization (Puerto Ricans, Hawaiians). Caste-like minorities are racially identifiable and usually relegated to low-status positions in the society. Assimilation is barred by the racial structure of the society. Light-skinned Hispanics can assimilate more easily than dark-skinned Mexicans or Puerto Ricans. Racially distinct children of immigrant minorities often become subordinated or caste-like minorities (Chicanos and Puerto Ricans). For these students, racial prejudice, low expectations, discrimination, and tracking combine with poverty to produce failure. It is these subordinated minority groups that experience the most severe problems in school.

Not everyone agrees with Ogbu's work in this area. Henry Trueba, Forrest Davis, and others have criticized the usefulness and descriptiveness of this category (Trueba, 1991). They argue that Ogbu has overgeneralized in grouping these peoples together.

Immigrant Minorities

For Ogbu, a third category of minorities is immigrant minorities. Immigrant students clearly have distinctly different school needs and experiences. Most of these immigrants have chosen to come to the United States more or less voluntarily. Groups such as the Hmong, Vietnamese, Salvadorans, and Guatemalans may have fled war, starvation, or poverty in their homeland, but their choice to come to the United States was primarily voluntary. They could have become refugees in a number of other societies. **Immigrant minorities** choose to come here for the social, economic, and political opportunities offered in this society. Recently, large numbers of Poles, Russians, Rumanians, and some Israelis have also made this choice. Immigrant students have diverse school conflicts and experiences often distinctly different from the experiences of African American, Mexican American, Native American, and Puerto Rican students. This chapter deals with the distinct language and cultural conflicts experienced by immigrant minority students in our schools.

The New Immigration

Since 1970, the United States has experienced massive immigration similar to the levels that occurred from 1890 through 1910—at least 10 million new people have come to live in this country. This phenomenon has brought some 2.5 million new language-minority students to our schools from a wide variety of cultures. Probably best known are the Southeast Asian children: Vietnamese, Cambodian (Khmer), Laotian, Hmong, Mien, and ethnic Chinese. Since the mid 1980s, schools in several cities have also experienced massive arrivals of students from the former Soviet Union and Eastern Europe speaking Russian, Polish, and other Slavic languages. Since the 1970s, well over 70% of all new immigrants are Latinos.

The experiences of immigrant Latinos provide an all too common example of the problems faced by the new immigrants. Poverty and the violence in Mexico and wars in Central and South America have sent millions of hungry and desperate people across our southern border. Some bring their families, including school-age children. As a consequence of the extended civil wars in Central America between 1979 and 1992, which were fueled by U.S. tax dollars, over 300,000 Salvadorans and an unknown number of Salvadoran Guatemalans fled to Los Angeles, Washington, New York and other major cities.

In December 1994, the Clinton administration ordered Salvadoran refugees to return to their native country, but many families have children who are now U.S. citizens and want to remain in our country.

Most countries in Latin America are experiencing massive economic changes and disruptions of their societies as their industries are incorporated into global, competitive markets for investment and production. The crisis for the poor in Latin America is several times worse than the crisis for the poor in the U.S.

In 1994, in *The State of the World's Children*, the United Nations Children Fund reported:

In the last 10 years, in particular, falling commodity prices, rising military expenditures, poor returns on investment, the debt crisis, and structural adjustment programs, have reduced the real incomes of approximately 800 million people in some 40 developing countries. In Latin America, the fall in incomes has been as much as 20%. In sub-Saharan Africa, it has often been more. At the same time, cuts in essential services have meant health centers without drugs and doctors, schools without books and teachers, family planning clinics without staff and supplies.

For many millions of families in the poorest villages and urban slums of the developing world, the daily consequence of these economic forces, over which they have no control, is that they are unable to put enough food on the table, unable to maintain a home fit to live in, unable to dress and present themselves decently, unable to protect health and strength, unable to keep their children in school.

Through such processes, millions have become destitute and desperate. (p. 11)

Most of the larger countries in Latin America have adopted economic policies of neo-liberalism that reduce government investments in health, food production, and education.

The global economy is restructuring the world, and millions of people are forced to move in search of food and work. Many nations in Latin America, Africa, and Asia suffer extreme poverty and destitution for the majority of their people. Latin America is a primary market for U.S. goods. Future U.S. economic growth depends on resolving the chronic economic crises of Latin America. But the major economies in the region have turned to loans and foreign investment in search of economic growth. Mexico, like most countries in Latin America, has adopted the economic "liberalization" policies favored by the International Monetary Fund (IMF). These policies force governments to reduce state ownership and state intervention in the economy and cut back on health, education, and other social services. When Mexico raises the price of tortillas, sells its national airlines and telephone system, and raises taxes charged to farmers, all to pay interest on bank loans, Mexicans do not have money to buy tractors, autos, computers, or other U.S.-produced goods. As a result, the majority of the people in Latin America get poorer and poorer.

The continuous economic decline in the standard of living for large majorities in Latin America produces a massive migration to the United States. The 1994 adoption of a new "free trade" policy—first with Mexico and then with other countries in Latin America—has increased income for the upper classes, but not for the vast majority. In 1995, the Mexican economy entered another economic crisis, devalued its peso by up to 30%, and disrupted investment and development plans for much of Latin America. Free-trade policies and unequal economic growth will increase the migration of poor people to the United States looking for work.

Schools and Immigration

Schools and employment are the entrance points into our society for all new immigrants. Some immigrants bring families with them. The children born here of immigrant parents are immediately citizens of the United States and are eligible for all school services. The recent immigrant populations, particularly Latino and Asian, are young people and usually have a higher number of children than do older, European American groups. Each year thousands of new immigrant children enter the schools speaking a home language other than English.

For almost 100 years, schools served as the primary vehicle to "Americanize" immigrants. They taught the children of immigrants to speak English. From the 1870s until the 1940s, many—even most—immigrants failed in school and left school prior to eighth grade. In an industrializing economy, there were jobs for unskilled labor. Today, the rapid change toward a new technology-based economy has eliminated many jobs and lowered the wage scale of unskilled labor. School dropouts no longer have access to good-paying industrial jobs. Therefore, schools must now prepare immigrant students for entrance into the new, high technology economy. Numerous business reports recognize that our economy needs these students as skilled graduates—not low-skilled dropouts (National Center on Education and the Economy, 1990).

Immigrant students and language-minority students have unique educational needs that, when met, result in successful integration into the rapidly changing economy. Immigrant students primarily learn the structure and rules of the dominant culture—particularly the language—in school. These students are particularly concentrated in a few states—New York, Florida, Illinois, Massachusetts, California, and Texas. Schools in these states are heavily impacted by the rapid growth of the limited English-speaking population. Recent linguistic research indicates that instruction provided by bilingual teachers and sheltered English programs offer the best way to encourage students toward school success and employment (Ramirez, Yuen, & Ramey, 1991). However, none of the states with large concentrations of immigrants has an adequate number of bilingual teachers to serve the rapidly growing immigrant populations.

It is difficult for teachers to understand the diverse realities of their students. Each immigrant group, each language group, has its own culture and experiences.[1] They are not the same. Schools must not rely on research drawn from the school experiences of African American and English-speaking Latino students (subordinated groups) to understand the immigrant students' reality. For example, a Salvadoran, Cambodian, or Croatian student who has experienced and witnessed the trauma of war, death, and family destruction has unique problems. Punjabi-speaking Sikh immigrants and Hmong students arrive at schools accustomed to arranged marriages and a subordinated status for women. For example, in 1994, a California court ruled that Sikh students should be allowed to wear a small, religious ceremonial knife to school, while all other weapons were banned. Language, background experiences, traditions, and cultures all vary dramatically. Even within a cultural group, children who have spent most of their lives in the United States have experiences substantially different from those of recent immigrant students.

---

[1] For important insights into the differences, see the works of H. Trueba, his colleagues and students (Trueba, Jacobs, & Kirton, 1990; Trueba, Rodriguez, Zou, & Cintrón, 1993), and the work of M. M. Suarez-Orozco (1989).

The Need to Learn English

Contrary to popular stereotyping promoted by groups dedicated to reducing U.S. immigration, most immigrant students recognize the need to learn English immediately. Children want to learn English to fit into their new society. Students who were educated in their homeland and acquired school skills there readily transfer their academic skills to U.S. schools. The first wave of Vietnamese immigrants from 1977 to 1982 were primarily middle-class successful students in Vietnam. They quickly became successful here. Such students need an opportunity to learn English and the ways of the macroculture. A three- to four-year transitional English program provides these students access to school success.

English competence facilitates the inclusion of the student into the school and the inclusion of the student's family into the society. Despite the clearly recognized need and the district's legal obligations, almost 1 in 4 students who enter our schools with limited English, receive *no* special instruction. They are placed in classes with teachers who lack preparation for English acquisition skills. These students are expected to sink or swim. Only acquisition of English offers the student access to the rest of the curriculum.

Teachers should not simply turn to their own language arts preparation and theories to assist them in dealing with students acquiring English as a second language. Shirley Brice-Heath (1986), a researcher in the field, argues:

> Educators know relatively little about how children from families and communities of language minorities learn to use language. It is not possible to generalize to these children the findings of current research on children from middle-class, English-speaking families which posit a unilinear developmental path of language acquisition for all children. Yet behind the language arts curriculum in schools stands an image of a "natural" path of development in language learning for all children. . . . I argue that all language learning is cultural learning: Children do not learn merely the building blocks of their mother tongue—its sounds, words, and order; they learn also how to use language to get what they want, protect themselves, express their wonderings and worries, and ask questions about the world. The learning of language takes place within the political, economic, social, ideological, religious, and aesthetic web of relationships of each community whose members see themselves as belonging to a particular culture. (pp. 145–146)

The Natural Approach to Language Acquisition

Language acquisition theory offers guidance to teachers working with language-minority children. Early second-language teaching strategies, such as the audio-lingual approach, were based on the limited behaviorist view of language learning. In the early 1960s, linguist Noam Chomsky argued that language ability in young children is too complex to explain by the simple accumulation of learned responses as reported by prior behaviorist researchers. Chomsky (1965) noted that children in all societies learn and use the complex underlying structures of their native languages without learning formal rules. Children learn their home language prior to attending school or formally studying language. In Chomsky's view, language is acquired by children as they attempt to communicate. Children learn a language by negotiating comprehension as they use the language.

Prior to Chomsky's work, second-language courses stressed learning rules, grammar, and vocabulary. Students in these programs learned about language, but they seldom acquired advanced communication skills in the second language. Yet immigrant students need advanced English competence to succeed in school.

The Work of Stephen Krashen

By the mid-1970s, Stephen Krashen and others sought to apply Chomsky's language theses to the design of effective second-language programs. Krashen (1981) argued that language needs to be acquired rather than learned. In acquiring a language, students follow much of the same pattern and strategies as used in learning a first language (California State Department of Education, 1986; Crawford, 1989; Krashen, 1981). Tracy Terrel termed this alternative process of fostering second-language acquisition the **natural approach,** since it sought to follow seemingly "natural" language acquisition patterns of children (Krashen & Terrel, 1983). Students acquire language when they understand the language. The focus in language acquisition must be on communication, not rules of grammar.

Krashen also suggested an "input" hypothesis. He argued that only comprehensible "input," or comprehensible language would help students acquire a second language. The **input hypothesis** suggests that language fluency in students emerges naturally, over time, as a result of communication. Fluency emerges under conditions of comprehensible input and low anxiety. Teachers promote a low-anxiety environment by avoiding overcorrection of language errors. Constant correction impedes and frustrates communication in the classroom. Soon many students are reluctant to volunteer and to speak. Overcorrection actually slows down language acquisition. Students learning English or any second language, like children learning a first language, will hear and correct many of their own errors as they seek improved communication.

The work of L. S. Vygotsky and his students studying linguistic minority student achievement in the Soviet Union, although long suppressed and ignored, added important additional insights to second-language acquisition theory (Trueba, 1989; Vygotsky, 1978). Vygotsky described a **proximal zone of development,** an area of knowledge the student was ready to learn. The student was ready to learn the new language in part because the student could comprehend the input.

Social Relationships

Psychological and attitudinal factors, or what Vygotsky termed "social relationships," greatly influence the pace and rate of language acquisition. When students want to learn a new language, they can. When second-language acquisition brings prestige and new opportunities, students learn quickly. But when learning a second language is mixed with criticism, ridicule, cultural conflict, and self-doubt, language acquisition is slowed. When students are overcorrected, a negative environment is established. Overcorrection strains the social relationship, thereby increasing anxiety and interfering with language learning.

Krashen termed this social component of language acquisition the **affective filter.** Most immigrant students are from low-income families, and they first learn the social and cultural patterns of low-income schools and neighborhoods. Immigrant students may suffer low self-confidence and low status in school, which combine to impede language progress. The immigrant student may begin to exhibit anti-school and anti-social behavior similar to some of the behavior of students from subordinate or caste-like minority groups.

Teachers can encourage language acquisition by stressing communication in the native language and in English and by not stressing correction of pronunciation and grammatical errors. Bilingual education—and bilingual teachers, when available—lowers the anxiety levels (affective filter) and encourage second-language acquisition by respecting the home culture and promoting positive self-esteem. Bilingual instruction includes the student in the curriculum, providing an important source of status and self-esteem.

English Language Development

When students first enter school speaking a second language, and a bilingual program is not available, the teacher needs to begin instruction with regular, well-organized instruction in English. (Direct-English-language-only instruction, without native language support, is an inadequate approach particularly for young students in grades K through 4.) The approaches for teaching English are frequently called **English as a Second Language (ESL)** or **English Language Development (ELD).** The basic ELD strategies require a teacher with special preparation who usually follows an organized curriculum. The ELD lessons might last from 25 to 45 minutes per day in grades 1 through 4, or could expand to 2 hours per day in the middle school years. Some parts of these lessons can be delivered by well-prepared teaching assistants.

ELD lessons teach students first to comprehend and then to speak English. These lessons require a low-anxiety, supportive environment and usually are done in small groups. Even though immigrant students want to learn English, they frequently respond to initial instruction with a quiet period. Observation of children's natural process of acquiring their first language helps to explain this "silent" period. They must hear the language and comprehend the language for some time before they are ready to produce the language. The teacher should respect this silent period and allow students time to develop language confidence. Often the ELD instructors use the strategies termed *total physical response* during this period so that the student can see, comprehend, and respond to English prior to speech. **Total physical response** involves saying phrases such as "stand up" while the teacher stands up. The students respond physically to the instruction. In early stages of language, this combination of language with movement and action promotes communication and comprehension. Students can learn several important phrases prior to trying to say words, which helps them to begin to comprehend without waiting until they have learned proper pronunciation of the new language.

ELD teachers strive for comprehensible input, using a wide variety of activities, role playing, pictures, and modeling to encourage comprehension. The emphasis in the first 6 to 12 months is to teach the student to communicate in English in order to survive in school. Communication is enhanced by the teacher or an aide accepting errors. We all speak a language poorly before we speak it well. A series of specific strategies has been developed for instructors to use to strive for comprehension and dialogue. The teacher achieves comprehension by carefully developing the context of language through interactive, experiential lessons (see Figure 11.2).

Even after students achieve an ability to communicate and perform in English, planned and organized English Language Development (ELD) lessons must continue for up to 5 years (4 for secondary students) to provide the students with a constantly improving access to the mainstream curriculum.

Sheltered English

After 6 to 12 months of ELD instruction, students will begin to use English in the classroom. The school can then begin to add the strategies of sheltered instruction in context-rich subject fields such as art, music, and physical education. **Sheltered instruction** is the teaching of grade-level content (such as art and music) in specially designed English so that students learning English can comprehend the instruction. Sheltered instruction must be used only after students have learned to comprehend English.

Sheltered instruction strategies include language simplification, avoidance of idiomatic expressions, frequent clarification and comprehension checks, use of

Figure 11.2 Guidelines for English Language Development Lessons

1. Low-anxiety environment,
2. Comprehensible input (role playing, modeling, pictures),
3. Focus on communication,
4. Error acceptance, and
5. Amplifying the context of language use through interactive teaching strategies and dialog.

simplified and direct sentences, and focusing on very important and reusable vocabulary.

Teachers expand sheltered lessons whenever possible by bridging or being clear about how the new concepts being presented connect with the information and skills the students already have (often learned in their native language). Sheltered lessons also incorporate many strategies from ELD instruction that stress providing students with contexts for ideas, using pictures, videos, field trips, and numerous ways for the students to understand the context of an idea.

After one or two semesters of sheltered instruction in highly context-rich subjects such as art, physical education, and music, students can begin to achieve success through sheltered instruction in intermediate subjects such as math and science where demonstrations, modeling, and experiential learning are common in the elementary grades (see Figure 11.3).

Sheltered instruction has as its goals achievement in the subject field (art, music, and physical education at first) and improved usage of English. Sheltered instruction does not consist of watered-down courses made easy. Rather, quality sheltered instruction requires teachers to enrich instruction so that they amplify and extend lessons to encourage more comprehension. Unfortunately, counselors who have in the past placed second-language students in simplified, watered-down, or low-track classes have contributed to the degradation and destruction of opportunities for these students.

After one or two years in school, immigrant students generally learn the social English necessary for basic interpersonal communication. If the students have not received instruction in their native language, they may be two to four years behind in subjects such as math or history. Many continue to fall behind in school. This problem is explained by considering two types of language competence—communicative language and academic language. When a student learns basic interpersonal language, teachers may mistakenly assume the student is ready for the regular English language curriculum. The counselor inappropriately transfers the student into regular classes. But the cognitive academic English language ability needed for success in learning to read, write, and participate in critical thinking, takes up to seven years to develop. Abstract concepts such as those presented in history, social studies, literature, math, and science are difficult to learn in a second language. The student must first obtain an advanced ability in English.

Figure 11.3 Sheltered Instructional Strategies

1. Frequent clarification,	5. Modeling,
2. Comprehension checks,	6. Bridging,
3. Language simplification,	7. Contextualization,
4. Reusable vocabulary,	8. Schema building, and
	9. Cooperative learning.

Bilingual Education

Bilingual education was defined in 1970 by the U.S. Office of Education as:

> The use of two languages, one of which is English, as mediums of instruction for the same pupil population in a well-organized program that encompasses part or all of the curriculum and includes the study of the history and culture associated with the mother tongue; a complete program develops and maintains the children's self-esteem and legitimate pride in both cultures. (Carter & Segura, 1979, p. 334)

Simply put, bilingual education is a series of instructional strategies to teach students school subjects (some in their home language) and to teach English. In bilingual classes, the instruction might be in Spanish or another language for part of the day and English for another part. In this manner, the student learns math, reading, and other subjects while acquiring English. **Bilingual education** uses ELD strategies to help students acquire English and teach them to communicate in English. Bilingual education teaches English and encourages the development of bilingual and biliteracy skills in both languages—valuable assets in our increasingly international economy.

Many of the 5 million children in U.S. public schools have serious language limitations in English and have proficiency in another language. In California and the Southwest, 73% of those who do not speak English speak Spanish (Olsen, 1988). Bilingual education provides appropriate strategies in situations where a group of 10 or more students speak a single second language (e.g., Chinese, Navajo, Spanish).

All children acquire a language and a vast amount of knowledge prior to entering school. The first years of schooling are a time of transition when the young child learns how to adapt within a social institution (e.g., school). Effective primary teachers build on the concepts the children have acquired at home, such as communication and social skills. When the teacher and the child do not speak the same language, it is difficult for the teacher to build on the vast base of learning provided by the home. The teacher has no access to the child's conceptual base and, frequently, the child is terrified.

In these first years of school, children are taught a series of complex subjects such as reading, math, and social studies. It is difficult for the child to learn when the instruction is in a language the child barely understands. Too many second-language children fail to learn to read and fall behind in their studies. Bilingual education teaches the academic subjects as it teaches English. While children are learning English, they are also taught the difficult tasks of reading, math, and science in the language they best understand. After two or more years of instruction and practice in English (preferably five to seven years), instruction in most subject areas gradually changes to English. Because of an acute shortage of bilingual teachers, less than 20% of all the children needing bilingual instruction receive a quality bilingual education.

Bilingual education requires the teacher or a teacher assistant to instruct in two or more languages. Most states have been unable to provide a sufficient number of bilingual teachers to provide native language instruction for students who need this instruction. In areas of a high concentration of a specific language group (such as Chinese, Navajo, Spanish), school districts can organize classrooms to provide bilingual instruction. Young children in grades K through 4 particularly need bilingual education. They need education in a language they can comprehend. They deserve an environment that encourages their enthusiasm, an environment that makes them independent and autonomous learners. Young people can communicate with the teacher and with each other to make this possible.

The U.S. Office of Education estimated in 1992 that only 11% of the students who have a legal right to bilingual education actually receive bilingual services (McKeon, 1994).

Many urban schools have a mixture of several language groups—perhaps Lao, Spanish, Korean, Polish, Russian, and Chinese—in a single class. When a mixture of several languages confronts the teacher or when bilingual teachers are not available, structured classes in English or English as a second language provide the more common strategy. ELD and sheltered English strategies are most appropriate for students in middle schools and high schools who have mastered their native language prior to learning English.

Bilingual instruction is preferred over English language development whenever the conditions permit. Acquiring English is first priority in our schools, but bilingual education allows students to learn math, science, and other subjects while learning English. The schools should not delay instruction in math, science, and other academic areas for the necessary two to three years while students learn English. Students deserve and have a legal right to academic instruction in each of these disciplines in a language that they can comprehend (*Lau vs. Nichols,* 1974). Exclusive reliance on English for instruction, even modified and simplified English, forces students to fall unnecessarily behind in academic subjects.

Both bilingual instruction and English language development respond to the needs of the student to learn English. By law and by practice, well over 80% of all bilingual programs are **transitional,** that is, they use the home language for only a few years while the student learns English. A few bilingual programs also maintain and develop academic skill in the home language as well as English. Rarely do language skills get preserved and developed in the sheltered English programs, ignoring and negating tremendous language skills these students bring to school. In an increasingly international economy, our society needs to preserve and develop language skills in Spanish, Korean, Vietnamese, and a number of other languages.

Bilingual education and extended use of sheltered English allow the student time for transition to English. Fortunately, the student can later "catch up." A common underlying language proficiency and common learning skills facilitate rapid progress once English has been acquired. Students may have learned important concepts in school in their home country. For example, children need to learn to read or learn math only once. When reading and math have been learned in the native language, the skills readily transfer to English.

Native language instruction is vital for young children. By 1990, the Bush administration was advocating policies that encouraged preschoolers to learn only English. These policies divide the children from their parents. As children seek to speak only English, too little communication about life, respect, and the family occurs. Lack of adult communication, even in the home language, impedes the child's mastery of English and the native language.

In some families, a misguided emphasis on English results in little talk between parents and children, for example, between Korean-speaking parents and their English-speaking, Korean American children. Children and adolescents need parenting. When school pressure for speaking only English in the home divides the family, children lose their major source of guidance for cooperation, fairness, personal responsibility, and attitudes about work and effort. They become alienated and isolated from their family, and alienated and isolated from their school by failure. Failure to communicate produces a dangerous breakdown in family support and guidance. In the turbulent years of adolescence, this lack of guidance and communication invites disrespect, lawlessness, and crime.

A Short History of Bilingualism

Bilingualism has a long history in our nation of immigrants. Forms of bilingual education were common practice in the early years of the nation. German language rights were considered for a special guarantee in the writing of the Constitution. Spanish language rights were implied in the Treaty of Guadalupe Hidalgo (by which the United States took the Southwest from Mexico) and were explicit in California's and New Mexico's first state constitutions.

From 1880 to 1910, the United States experienced massive migration from Europe and Mexico. A two-party political system had emerged, as well as a strong populist movement in response to dramatic shifts in the nation's economic system. The populists demanded more democracy in the political system and supported universal public education as a means to promote economic opportunity.

At the same time, fraternal and social organizations were formed to limit immigration and to insist on the dominance of English in the nation. During World War I, government-sponsored anti-German pressures led to the cancellation of German language schools, and several states passed laws restricting schools to English language usage. Public schools were charged to promote rapid assimilation of immigrants and to encourage the use of the "American" language.

Policies to eliminate ethnic enclaves and use of foreign languages were advocated as good for the students. Crude and inaccurate racial theories developed, based on early Darwinism, to argue for the superiority of Anglo-Saxon culture against Greeks, Slavs, Italians, Mexicans, and immigrants (Crawford, 1989; Omi & Winant, 1986).

Language submersion strategies and other non-theory-based versions of language teaching developed into folkways in schools. A legend was created that U.S. schools served as the vehicle for immigrant opportunity in spite of significant evidence to the contrary (Aronowitz, 1973; Boyer & Morais, 1955; Colin, 1975; Davis, 1986). In this period, leaving school early was not viewed as a crisis since a young person could get a job in industry with little formal schooling or preparation.

In a diverse, fragmented, and at times, divisive society, language uniformity became an important political movement advocated by conservative business groups. If immigrants used Polish, Yiddish, or Finnish to organize radical unions, conservatives used their control of government to promote "Americanism" by developing language uniformity. Insistence on speaking English was an important mechanism for weakening ethnic group loyalty and support for labor unions. Speaking English became the approved way for immigrants to "Americanize" their families.

During the 1920s, in response to these pressures and World War I, prior academic interest in "foreign languages" declined and English became the exclusive language of the educated in the United States. Speaking a second or third language lost status and value. Instead of considering the language abilities of immigrants as an important resource, teachers urged immigrant children to speak English and to forget the language of their parents and family. Greek immigrants were discouraged from teaching their native language to their children while university doctoral candidates struggled to learn Greek to read the Bible, Plato, and Aristotle. The Bureau of Indian Affairs used boarding schools and harsh measures to promote English over tribal languages.

Language domination became closely connected with "Americanism" in the popular culture until the 1950s. Only the competition with the Soviets in the Cold War finally called into question these English-only and English-first policies. In 1959, a rebel army led by Fidel Castro liberated Cuba from the corrupt, U.S.-backed, Batista regime. The new Castro government turned to the Soviet Union for support and adopted a Soviet-style authoritarian government. Over 100,000 Cubans fled to the United States. The Central Intelligence Agency armed, trained, and prepared these Cuban refugees for a reinvasion of Cuba. The U.S. government provided substantial resettlement costs to Cuban refugees and their families including provisions for temporary bilingual schools in Florida. Spanish-speaking Cuban refugees were recruited to work for the Department of State and for the Central Intelligence Agency in these agencies' efforts to stop the "Cuban communist expansion" in Latin America. Federal policy recognized and benefited from the language resources of thousands of Cuban refugees.

In the same era as the Cuban exodus, the U.S. Civil Rights Movement (1956–1968) emphasized educational reform as a strategy to gain equal economic opportunity for minorities in the United States. Mexican American political activists argued that if 100,000 Cuban refugees received preferential treatment for their Spanish bilingualism (and their anti-communism), why should 5 million Mexican American children in the Southwest be relegated to educational wastelands of a second-class school system because they spoke Spanish? Why should students be punished and held back for speaking Spanish? A Mexican American political movement and an emerging Chicano student movement in the Southwest (1958–1980) demanded bilingual education programs to overcome the educational barriers faced by Spanish-speaking children. Legislators were convinced to include provisions prohibiting the denial of state services and voting rights on the basis of language in the 1964 Civil Rights Act. The language provisions of this act became the legal basis for bilingual education in the United States.

In 1974, in the *Lau vs. Nichols* case, a federal judge ruled that the San Francisco School District violated the 1964 Civil Rights Act. The judge ordered the district to provide instruction that Chinese-speaking children could understand. The Lau case established the principle that children have a right to instruction that they can understand in the public schools. The court ordered the district to develop remedies to overcome existing inequalities of opportunity. Bilingual education was one of several strategies included as a possible remedy to the Lau court order.

The Lau decision did not require a school district to implement any specific remedy, such as bilingual education. It listed bilingual education as one of several available legal options. Subsequent federal court decisions (*Castañeda*, (1981) and *Keyes*, 1983) further insisted that districts provide a quality program, with trained teachers, that would provide the student with equal access to the regular curriculum, and that the program collect data to demonstrate its adequacy. Quality bilingual education programs meet these court established criteria, while other programs may or may not do so.

State laws were established to guide school districts in providing special programs for limited English proficient (LEP) students.

By 1976, California had one of the strongest bilingual education laws in the nation. Even with a strong law, some 50% of the children legally eligible for bilingual assistance received only **Individualized Learning Programs (ILP).** These individualized programs pulled the child from the regular classroom for approximately 45 minutes, twice a week, for a special class in English as a second language. For the rest of the day, the child was submersed in an English-only environment. Some of these programs were federally funded and self-described as bilingual education. ILPs were a totally inadequate response to the child's need to acquire English in a safe and motivating environment. Under such conditions, little of the instruction was understood and the children continued to fail.

Of the children in "bilingual programs," few had a consistent and organized approach to language acquisition. Frequently, schools with large numbers of limited English-speaking children were also at-risk schools that failed to educate their English-speaking students. The California legislature passed a bilingual education law in 1976 that included a "sunset" provision. **Sunset provisions** established a law for a limited time—in this case, 10 years. If the law was not passed again, it would go out of existence. In 1986, the required reauthorization bill passed both houses of the California legislature and then was vetoed by the Republican governor. The present legal status of bilingual education in California relies on federal court decisions; there is no state law guiding the program. Federal court decisions determine the legal minimums required of all states and school districts.

The California experience is representative of the attacks on bilingual education in several states. Bilingual education laws vary considerably. No state and few districts provide quality programs for all the students who need bilingual instruction. A 1994 report, *The Unfinished Journey: Restructuring Schools in a Diverse Society*, by California Tomorrow, concluded that the field of bilingual education remains largely marginalized from current popular efforts of school restructuring.

The new immigration waves of the last two decades, particularly with the wars in Indochina and then in Central America, changed bilingual programs. Now schools often face five to six different language groups rather than two. California alone has over 90 different language groups. Schools seldom finance bilingual education for language groups when only a few students speak a specific language. Most bilingual programs are Spanish-English bilingual classes. In some areas, Cantonese-speaking and Navajo-speaking groups are sufficiently concentrated to justify classes.

Basic Principles of Bilingual Education

The following summary of principles for quality bilingual instruction, developed for California's Case Studies project, (cited in Crawford, 1989) provides an overview of bilingual program elements.

> [These] principles, along with their practical implications in the classroom, . . . are adapted from *Basic Principles for the Education of Language-Minority Students: An Overview*, a 1983 publication of the California State Department of Education.
>
> 1. For bilingual students, the development of proficiencies in both the native language and English has a positive effect on academic achievement.
> 2. Language proficiency is the ability to use language for both basic communicative tasks and academic purposes.
> 3. For limited-English-proficient students, reaching the "threshold" of native-language skills necessary to complete academic tasks forms the basis for similar proficiency in English. Implications:
>   - Students are provided substantial amounts of instruction in and through the native language.
>   - Initial reading classes and other cognitively demanding subjects are taught in the native language.
>   - Sufficient texts and supplementary materials are available in the native language.
>   - A sufficient number of well-trained teachers with high levels of native-language proficiency are available to provide instruction.

- Teachers avoid mixing English and the native language during instruction.
- Teachers accept regional and nonstandard varieties of the native language.

4. Acquisition of basic communicative competency in a second language is a function of comprehensible second-language instruction and a supportive environment. Implications:

   - Comprehensible second-language input is provided through both English-as-a-second-language (ESL) classes and sheltered English instruction in academic content areas.
   - When content areas are used to provide comprehensible English input, subjects are selected in which the cognitive demands are low to moderate.
   - ESL instruction is communication-based rather than grammar-based and is characterized by the following: (a) content is based on the students' communicative needs; (b) instruction makes extensive use of contextual clues; (c) the teacher uses only English, but modifies speech to students' level and confirms their comprehension; (d) students are permitted to respond in their native language when necessary; (e) the focus is on language function or content, rather than grammatical form; (f) grammatical accuracy is promoted not by correcting errors overtly, but by providing more comprehensible input; and (g) students are encouraged to respond spontaneously and creatively.
   - Opportunities for comprehensible English input are provided for LEP students when grouped by language proficiency and when interacting with fluent English-speaking peers.

5. The perceived status of students affects the interaction between teachers and students and among students themselves. In turn, student outcomes are affected. Implications:

   - Teachers use positive interactions in an equitable manner with both language-majority and language-minority students.
   - Language-majority and language-minority students are enrolled in content area classes in which cooperative learning strategies are used.
   - Whenever possible, language-majority students are enrolled in classes designed to develop second-language proficiency in the minority language(s) represented in the school.
   - Administrators, teachers, and students use the minority language(s) represented in the school for noninstructional purposes. (p. 129)

Culture Conflict and Language Acquisition

The frustration experienced by children trying to learn a new language is evident in the following excerpts from a book entitled *Immigrant Students and the California Public Schools: Crossing the Schoolhouse Border* (California Tomorrow, 1988):

> "I just sat in my classes and didn't understand anything. Sometimes I would try to look like I knew what was going on; sometimes I would just try to think about a happy time when I didn't feel stupid. My teachers never called on me or talked to me. I think they either forgot I was there or else wished I wasn't. I waited and waited, thinking that some-day I will know English." (Ninth-grade Mexican girl who immigrated at age 13, p. 62)

"You don't know anything. You don't even know what to eat when you go to the lunch room. The day I started school, all the kids stared at me like I was from a different planet. I wanted to go home with my Dad, but he said I had to stay. I was very shy and scared. I didn't know where to sit or eat or where the bathroom was or how to eat the food . . . I felt so out of place that I felt sick. Now I know more, but I still sit and watch and try to understand. I want to know what is this place and how must I act?" (Eighth-grade Vietnamese girl who immigrated at age 9, p. 71)

For young people and adolescents, learning English for school survival requires learning about a new culture. For students from immigrant communities treated as low status, acquiring English requires redefining their own cultural frame of reference or worldview. When immigrant students are older than about 10 years of age, competent and confident in their own culture, they can learn a second language and adapt to a second culture with relative ease. If, however, the instruction in English is presented as an attack on their own culture, then English acquisition becomes intertwined with cultural conflict. Parental talk and guidance, usually in the home language, are essential to understand and to adjust to cultural conflict. Teachers should encourage rather than discourage bilingualism and continued development of the home language.

For students above the fourth grade, difficulty in learning English is often a result of cultural conflict, not a failure of the language teaching strategies. Second-language students at times group together in a defensive manner to avoid ridicule and to belong to a group. Teachers can assume the students are experiencing cultural conflict if they observe that students tend to associate only with students who speak the same language. Students also indicate cultural stress when they seek to speak only English or appear embarrassed about their parents' use of the home language. When students find their cultures and home languages under attack, some resist and defend their parents' ways. The anxiety produced by cultural conflicts impedes English acquisition.

Success for the language-minority student in school depends on both academic language mastery and the student's comprehension of the cultural systems of the schools. Self-confident immigrant students make great progress. They can direct and influence their own language acquisition process. The teacher can reduce conflict and anxiety by providing conditions that facilitate learning and by studying cultural conflict as described in Chapter 6.

Language lessons can explore:

- Why do I want to learn this language?
- What is the value of learning the language?
- How will other people who are important to me perceive me if I study, practice, and learn this language?
- How do I feel when I fail to use English properly?
- What steps can I take to acquire English without giving up my language, culture, family and friends?

Cross-cultural respect is intricately tied with language usage. Respectful multicultural education provides an important component of a quality English-language acquisition program. Schools should not insist on the use of English in the home. Such suggestions contribute to cultural conflict and increase language frustration. The attempt to restrict home communication to English by parents who do not speak English well results in reducing the amount of time they talk to their children. Parental talk, in any language, models the use and value of language for effective communication. Children need to see language modeling and they need to talk freely to their parents.

Submersion—A Failed Strategy

Young children from Mexico, Vietnam, Laos, and Korea are often simply immersed or submerged in English. Since schools lack bilingual teachers, the students are thrown into an English environment. They quickly learn to prefer English. They learn that English is the high-status language, the language valued by the school. Many children learn to avoid their home language, even to the extreme of avoiding talking with their own parents in public. In spite of this great division and great pain, the language submersion strategy does not lead quickly to accomplished English. The combination of negative attitudes and failure leads the child to use both languages poorly.

Some children, in their haste to Americanize, adopt the status system of the United States and regard their home language of Spanish, Cantonese, or Vietnamese spoken by their grandparents as inferior or less important. Such attitudes engender disrespect for elders. The adoption of such attitudes divides the family against the school, raises the affective filter, and slows English acquisition.

It is important for children to continue to develop their first language while acquiring English. Home language usage adds to the common, underlying bank of concepts, knowledge, and skills students need. Schools can help reduce cultural conflict by respecting, supporting, and reinforcing the value of the language spoken at home. Teaching strategies and assignments should recognize, respect, and use the students' previous experience and home culture.

Bilingualism Plus

Students in sheltered English, ELD, and bilingual classrooms deserve a nourishing, enriched environment as they become bilingual and biliterate. Erminda Garcia and Nadeen Ruiz (1995), recognized leaders in language acquisition, list the following ways that teachers can provide effective language instruction for their students:

1. Students should have continuous experiences with whole and authentic texts.
2. Create places where children can exercise choice in their language and literacy lessons.

3. Connect lessons with students' personal experiences and background knowledge.
4. Focus first on constructing meaning in literacy lessons, then on the mechanics of print.
5. Create social organizations (such as cooperative learning) for active, collaborative learning.
6. Teachers should immediately respond to students' work in ways that acknowledge their personal interpretations and stories. (p. vii–x)

The strategies suggested by these principles include shared reading, literature circles, interactive journals, writers workshops, cooperative learning, and publication of student work using computer publishing systems.

Ruiz and Garcia use a constructivist approach to language and literacy. Kathryn Au (1993) has described this approach and given examples of the development of literacy as a part of language acquisition. Particularly for older students, there is no need to restrict and inhibit reading and writing during efforts to develop the second language (usually English).

Languages and Empowerment

Most of the major strategies described in Chapters 6 through 10 also apply to language-minority children. The Canadian scholar, Jim Cummins, has combined the insights of critical theory in the sociology of education with current theories of second-language acquisition. In an important book, *Empowering Language Minority Students* (1989), Cummins lists the major components of a language empowerment strategy as:

1. A genuine dialogue between student and teacher in both oral and written modalities,
2. Guidance and facilitation rather than control of student learning by the teacher,
3. Encouragement of student-student talk in a collaborative learning context,
4. Encouragement of meaningful language use by students rather than correctness of surface forms,
5. Conscious integration of language use and development with all curricular content rather than teaching language and other content as isolated subjects,
6. A focus on developing higher level cognitive skills rather than factual recall, and
7. Task presentation that generates intrinsic rather than extrinsic motivation. (p. 64)

When a Bilingual Program Is Not Available

Most teachers do not have the benefits of organized bilingual instruction. Increasingly, teachers face the problem of how to organize their classroom to help their three to five second-language students while continuing instruction for the English-speaking students.

Teachers with students learning English as a second language deserve assistance. You should ask for it. Most schools and districts have programs, resource specialists, and materials for the limited-English-speaking student. Federal law requires, and many state laws encourage, that limited-English-proficient students receive instruction in an appropriate program with properly prepared professional staff (*Castañeda vs. Pickard*, 1981).[2]

Teachers deserve the assistance of an adult who can help them translate. The children need assistance to comprehend instruction, and federal law guarantees that assistance. School districts with federal or state-funded programs may provide bilingual aides to assist in instruction. Teachers can also use the assistance of a parent or other students. Some teachers recruit assistance from church or ethnic associations. Schools in low-income areas often use their federal Chapter I funding to secure bilingual teacher assistants and community aides.

The use of cooperative learning (Chapter 8) in the classroom provides substantial assistance and language practice for the student learning English. Students learn social skills, psychology, and civic responsibility while they help each other. The students learning English need to hear comprehensible English.

In classrooms organized for cooperative learning, students have opportunities to practice English. Groups can include a limited-English student, a bilingual student, and other English speakers all working on a task. The limited-English-proficient student will gain language practice from cooperative groups while the bilingual student will gain status for the ability to communicate in two languages. The English-dominant students will not only learn about culture, language, and respect, but they will also gain academically by actively explaining concepts to others.

Whole Language

In elementary and middle schools, second-language students seem to gain from classes where teachers use the language experience or whole language approaches to literature. Whole language strategies allow limited-English speakers to gain comprehension while their classmates are working at more advanced stages of written and oral production. In the intermediate grades and middle schools, sheltered English classes are helpful in academic subjects. The use of whole language and natural approaches requires active teacher intervention, not simply dumping the student in the traditional curriculum and ignoring their particular language needs (De La Luz Reyes, 1992).

Schools often use scarce resources for second-language students in a "pull-out" program. Students are "pulled out" of their classrooms and sent to a separate room to practice English with a language specialist, an aide, or a student teacher. Teachers can assist these students by working closely with the pull-out teacher to integrate the students' lessons. The teacher extends the lessons cov-

---

[2] For legal guidelines, see Office of Civil Rights Memorandum, U.S. Department of Education, September 27, 1991.

ered in the pull-out program. Or, the language specialist can review and build on the concepts previously taught by the teacher. A bilingual aide can explain the central concepts in the student's native language. Integration of lessons between the classroom and the language specialist provides students with time to hear and practice the new language.

Older students and students with several years of formal schooling in their native country benefit from structured programs in English as a second language for a part of the day (perhaps two hours). When students have acquired basic social English, they can be mainstreamed into two or three classes per day. Music, physical education, and other hands-on classes are particularly appropriate places for mainstreaming, as are classrooms using cooperative learning. Civil rights laws require that these students be provided with access to the general curriculum, including gifted and talented and college preparatory programs.

Language Buddies

Teachers assist language-minority students in their classrooms by taking the time to find an English-speaking friend or buddy for the new student. Often the students who themselves have struggled to learn English as a second language are particularly helpful. Teachers should stress that the buddy is helping the teacher, so that the new student is not perceived as a burden. If one student is reluctant to assist the new student, find someone else. A positive association—not a reluctant association—promotes communication.

It is particularly important to recruit a buddy or a teacher assistant for the initial few weeks of school. These assistants provide extra opportunities to explain rules and procedures to the new student. Language comprehension is enhanced by a careful explanation, modeling, and review of new vocabulary. The teacher can introduce and pronounce a few new key words each day. The student assistant reviews the new words and practices their use with the new student. The teacher and the assistant can help the new student with assignments or listen to the student read during independent study times.

Teachers promote understanding and cooperation by taking the time to talk and to listen to the new student. In the first few weeks, it is important to check in with the new student each day. Talk to new students before school, during recess, or at lunch. Teacher assistants can help the new student with the most basic information: how to buy lunch, where to buy pencils, etc. Teachers gain insight into the students' viewpoints and culture by dialogue and listening to the students' views of how well they are adjusting to the new language and the new school.

A Communication Focus

Communication provides a lifeline for new students. It helps them to become members of the class. Even before the students speak English, the teacher can use hand motions, a dictionary, and eye contact to make new students feel welcome in class. Some teachers learn 10 or 20 words in the student's home language to show respect for their language and culture and as a recognition of how difficult it is to learn a second language. Other teachers choose to have the class learn a few introductory greetings and phrases to open the possibility of student-to-student exchange.

As students make progress, they need support in efforts to speak English, not criticism. Talk should focus on themes and concepts rather than on grammar and sentence structures. Effective language teachers learn to accept errors while encouraging language exploration and communication. Substantial evidence indicates that students will naturally correct mispronunciations and sentence structures as they become more proficient. When a student is interrupted to correct a word or phrase, the student's thinking pattern is disrupted and the disruption causes more errors and frustrations.

Students in the process of acquiring English need extra thinking time when asked to perform abstract, critical thinking tasks. Second-language students typically translate abstract tasks into their native language and then evaluate the task. These students are able to perform critical thinking tasks as well as English speakers; they simply need time and practice to translate these skills into English.

The language needs of older immigrant students are somewhat different from those of younger students. After several months of working in a positive climate, older students want to say things correctly. Pattern drills and choral practice are useful to teach specific language usages. Students want to master basic greetings, sentence structure, and slang so they can fit in within the school. Songs, commercials, and chants are useful for such lessons.

Attacks on Bilingual Education

The political mobilization of conservative forces throughout the nation in the 1970s and 1980s attacked taxes, schools, and bilingual education. In the 1990s, these same groups frequently attack multicultural education as divisive to national unity. English speakers were offended that immigrant children were taught in their native tongue for part of the day. Conservative political activist Al Shanker, the President of the American Federation of Teachers, and others alleged that second-language children were receiving special "privileges." Political leaders argued that bilingualism handicapped the children. Conservative business and educational activists tried to reverse the move toward cultural and linguistic diversity. They sought to reestablish the dominance of the viewpoints of the English-first movements of the early twentieth century. Their arguments ignored the data on immigrants' school performance and the need for educational remedies to respond to students' need to learn English.

Bilingual education became one of the most controversial issues in education. Columnist Noel Epstein (1989) argued that bilingualism was a government-financed program to foster positive ethnic identity. He alleged that such efforts were ineffective and inappropriate to public education.

As in the case of "evidence" about IQ differentials, dubious research was marshalled to criticize bilingual education. Like the debates on affirmative action, conservatives created the deception that minorities were gaining an advantage, that bilingual education was discrimination against European Americans. The attacks on bilingualism continue today with voters in several states voting for "English as the Official Language" bills.

Political advocacy groups, such as U.S. English, perceive a threat to English language hegemony in this country. Conservatives argued that bilingual education was an affirmative action program for Latinos. These critics distort the issue and refuse to acknowledge that bilingual education is a process of teaching English to school children.

All sides to the vehement debate have opinions, many of them poorly informed. Former President Ronald Reagan, Education Secretaries Bennett and Cavozos, and writer Arthur Schlesinger, Jr., opposed bilingual education based more on ideology than on language theory. Political consultants distorted the issues to galvanize public support and solicit campaign funds from conservative financial donors and favor from Republican administrations.

The public debate on bilingual education often deals with a false dichotomy of choosing either English or the home language. Both languages are valuable. Almost all educators agree that children, except in Puerto Rico, should learn English to succeed in school. Bilingual advocates urge that the nation should gain from the language resources of its immigrant communities. There is no necessary contradiction between these goals. The contending sides seldom recognize the classroom realities facing teachers. Former Education Secretary Cavozos argued that all children should come to school speaking English. Given the large immigrant population, this simply does not occur. Parents should be encouraged to talk to and read to their children in the language parents know best. The argument put forward during the Bush administration that children should learn English early to avoid the bilingual "problem" in school is unsound family policy and an anti-democratic denial of the value of the language and the home culture.

Teachers can also recognize that the attacks on bilingual education lead directly to the generalized attacks on public schooling promoted in some school choice and voucher initiatives and other efforts to defund public schools. Conservatives seek to strip teachers and public schools of their legitimacy. This attack on teachers and public education was at the heart of Secretary Bennett's efforts, and it continues in a variety of forms within the conservative wing of the Republican Party. When it is popular, these attacks single out bilingual education. In 1993 and 1994, a California campaign led by Republican Governor Pete Wilson alleged that immigrants were abusing the social welfare system and causing a slow down in the economy. Then Governor Wilson proposed that immigrant students be banned from public schools or charged high tuitions—a practice prohibited by *Plyer vs. Doe* (102S. Ct. 2382) and the U.S. Supreme Court Hull decision.

Targeting immigrants becomes popular in times of economic recession. An interconnected conservative network cooperated on the English-only efforts, the immigrant-bashing efforts, and the school voucher initiatives. The antibilingual efforts work closely with anti-immigrant campaigns, particularly anti-Latino immigration. Groups such as FAIR (Federation for American Immigration Reform) have little criticism of Irish, Canadian, Russian, and other "white" immigrants (Crawford, 1992; Filmore, 1991). The precise nature of the bilingual programs is not the real target. These public campaigns of scapegoating create an ideological space for conservatives to organize, to raise money, and build a political agenda for winning elections. They do not provide improved school services for children.

In spite of the successful conservative political mobilization against bilingualism, the rapidly growing language-minority populations require schools to respond to the needs of children. Professional groups such as the National Association for Bilingual Education and the California Association for Bilingual Education have become a part of important coalitions and teachers unions presenting the case for educational equity for second-language students.

Teachers can accomplish a great deal within the present limitations of law and funding. First, they can learn the language of their students. It is not difficult to arrange for a 12-week, intensive Spanish language course in Mexico, Guatemala, or El Salvador. Teachers already spend four to five years studying to become a teacher. Some may recognize the value of spending 12 weeks to be able to talk with their students. When teachers acquire a second language, they also learn language acquisition strategies. In intensive language programs, they frequently experience cultural conflict. The experience helps them to empathize with and understand the struggles of their students.

Effective Bilingual Programs

Bilingual education, like other forms of multicultural education, requires a commitment to cultural democracy. Only a portion of the educational community shares that commitment. Bilingual education challenges the English-only worldview and conflicts with the "folk wisdom" of language acquisition. As a result, bilingual education faces unusual and rigorous demands for evidence to support its claims. Substantial and adequate research has been collected in the last two decades to support bilingual strategies. The study by Ramirez, Yuen, and Ramey (1991) is but the latest in a long series of research reports supporting bilingual strategies. Resistance to bilingualism is now a political issue, not an educational research issue.

Because schools are complex environments with hundreds of variables, researchers have problems in measuring bilingual education or any other major intervention such as cooperative learning. The new program by itself will not change schools. During the last decade, a body of research has demonstrated that certain schools, called **Effective Schools,** successfully educate at-risk children. In this small group of select schools—less than 2% of the total—students of color and economically disadvantaged students perform academically in ways similar to middle-class students (Carter & Chatfield, 1986; Olsen, 1986; Squires, Huitt, & Segars, 1985).

Not all of the schools in poverty areas are educational wastelands. There are schools that work. Effective schools research has particular importance for second-language students. Students in effective bilingual programs become achievers rather than dropouts or school casualties. Bilingual education works to teach English and school success when a bilingual program exists within a well-functioning school (Carter & Chatfield, 1986; Ramirez, Yuen, & Ramey, 1991).

Summary

Schools have developed a wide variety of strategies, including English as a second language, sheltered English, and bilingual education, in response to the needs of immigrant students. Virtually all bilingual programs are designed to help students make a transition to speaking English. Few encourage the development of a bilingual, biliterate student. Most programs were established as a compensatory measure to help students learn English more effectively. These transitional programs offer one-way bilingualism. For example, Spanish-speaking children learn English, but few English-speaking children are encouraged to learn Spanish. Few programs encourage the development of the language resources of immigrant populations. Our schools have yet to recognize the advantages of bilingualism.

Developing new strategies for language acquisition and bilingual education is a part of the complex task of reforming schools. Language struggles, like struggles for racial and social justice, have been a consistent aspect of our history. In each decade, parents and teachers have struggled for equality. Currently, bilingual education and other language development strategies provide the immigrant student with access to the educational community. They offer access to a democratic society.

Language acquisition and a multicultural curriculum should provide students with school opportunities that are meaningful, comprehensible, challenging, and substantive. Bilingual education and sheltered English teach students from cultural and linguistic minorities the macrocultural values and language necessary for survival in the public schools.

Schools are complex and interdependent societies. They change slowly. Teachers can mitigate some of the pain and damage done to second-language students by designing safe and supportive classrooms where students can learn the linguistic rules as well as the social and cultural rules of our society.

To help you review some of the important issues discussed in this chapter, you should be familiar with the terms in the following glossary.

Glossary

Bilingual education, bilingual teaching: Teaching strategies that provide both English instruction and subject-matter instruction for limited-English-speaking students in the students' native languages. Bilingual instruction is based on second-language acquisition research that demonstrates that development of a student's home language provides the best background for learning a second language (English). Bilingual education is the preferred approach to language acquisition.

English language development (ELD) and English as a second language (ESL): Teaching strategies to teach English to speakers of other languages. The instruction is in English and the subject is acquiring the English language. These strategies are generally used in classes with several mixed languages and where bilingual education is not provided.

Limited English proficient (LEP): Students who are presently acquiring English and deserve assistance to gain access to the school curriculum.

Maintenance bilingual program: A bilingual education approach that continues instruction in the native language during and after English has been learned. The goal is to ensure that students become bilingual and biliterate.

Transitional bilingual education: An approach to bilingual education that uses the native language only as long as necessary to encourage English language instruction. The goal is to use this instruction as a transition to English. Students generally become English dominant, not bilingual.

Sheltered English: An instructional approach used in English-as-a-second-language classes. English is used as the language of instruction. The teacher uses strategies to encourage comprehension by the student such as illustrating, role playing, modeling, contextualizing, and checking for understanding. Sheltering can be used for older students, after grade 4, when bilingual education is not available.

Questions Over the Chapter

1. Study the graph on page 68. How is the current era of immigration like that from 1809 to 1910? How is it different?

2. Do you find that Mexican Americans, Puerto Ricans, and African Americans have so much in common that they can be classified together as "caste-like minorities"? What usefulness does this category serve?

3. How are immigrant minorities different from autonomous minorities and "caste-like minorities"? What is the significance of these differences?

4. What are the major differences between immigrants and refugees?

5. Schools often "Americanize" immigrants. In what ways is this "Americanization" appropriate?

6. What examples are there of inappropriate "Americanization"?

7. In what ways is learning a second language like learning a first language?

8. Which strategies help teachers stress communication rather than formal language rules?

9. What are some advantages to teachers of becoming bilingual?

10. The Lau decision requires that all students be provided with access to the mainstream curriculum. Which teaching strategies help provide immigrant students with access to the curriculum?

Activities for the Further Study of Language Acquisition

1. Make a list of the advantages to an adult of becoming bilingual.
2. If you have studied a second language, describe to a classmate your experiences in trying to learn this second language. How did you respond to your teacher's correction of language errors? Based on your own language experiences, what strategies would you employ as a teacher to help your students learn a second language?

References

Aronowitz, S. (1973). *False promises: The shaping of American working class consciousness.* New York: McGraw-Hill.

Au, K. H. (1993). *Literacy instruction in multicultural settings.* New York: Holt, Rinehart, & Winston.

Boyer, R. O., & Morais, H. M. (1955). *Labor's untold story.* New York: United Electrical Workers.

Brice-Heath, S. (1986). Sociocultural contexts of language development. *Beyond language: Social and cultural factors in schooling language minority students.* Sacramento, CA: Bilingual Education Office, California State Department of Education.

California State Department of Education. (1981). *Schooling and language minority students: A theoretical framework.* Los Angeles, CA: Evaluation and Assessment Center.

California Tomorrow. (1994). *The unfinished journey: Restructuring schools in a diverse society.* San Francisco, CA: Author.

Carter, T. P., & Chatfield, M. (1986, November). Effective bilingual schools: Implications for policy and practice. *American Journal of Education,* pp. 200–231.

Carter, T. P., & Segura, R. (1979). *Mexican Americans in school: A decade of change.* College Entrance Exam Board, U.S. Office of Education. A more detailed and less comprehensible definition is found in Public Law 93-380 (1974).

Chomsky, N. (1965). *Aspects of a theory of syntax.* Cambridge, MA: MIT Press.

Colin, G. (1975). *The great school legend: A revisionist interpretation of American public education.* New York: Basic Books, Inc.

Crawford, J. (1989). *Bilingual education: History, politics, theory and practice.* Trenton, NJ: Crane Publishing.

Crawford, J. (1992). Hispanophobia (Ch. 6). *Hold your tongue: Bilingualism and the politics of English only.* Reading, MA: Addison-Wesley Publishing Company.

Cummins, J. (1989). *Empowering language minority students.* Sacramento, CA: California Association for Bilingual Education.

Davis, M. (1986). *Prisoners of the American dream.* London, England: Verso Press.

De la Luz Reyes, M. (1992, Winter). Challenging venerable assumptions: Literacy instruction for linguistically different students. *Harvard Educational Review,* pp. 427–446.

Epstein, N. (1989). Quoted in J. Crawford, *Bilingual education: History, politics, theory, and practice* (p. 39). Trenton, NJ: Crane Publishing.

Filmore, L. W. (1991, June). A question for early childhood programs: English first or families first? *Education Week,* pp. 32–34.

Garcia, E., & Ruiz, N. T. (1995). *Guia para las bibliotecas en Español.* Washington, DC: Heath.

Krashen, S. D. (1981). *Second language acquisition and second language learning.* New York: Pergamon Press.

Krashen, S. D., & Terrel, T. D. (1983). *The natural approach: Language acquisition in the classroom.* Hayward, CA: Alemany Press.

McKeon, D. (1994, May). When meeting 'common' standards is uncommonly difficult. *Educational Leadership*, pp. 45–49.

National Center on Education and the Economy. (1990). *America's choice: High skills in low wages*. Rochester, NY: Author.

Ogbu, J. (1978). *Minority education and caste*. New York: Academic Press.

Ogbu, J. (1990). Overcoming racial barriers to equal access. In J. Goodlad, & P. Keating. *Access to knowledge: An agenda for our nation's schools*. New York: The College Entrance Exam Board.

Ogbu, J., & Matute-Bianchi, M. E. (1986). Understanding cultural factors: Knowledge, identity and school adjustment. *Beyond language*. Sacramento, CA: Bilingual Education Office, California State Department of Education.

Olsen, L. (1986, January). Effective schools. *Education Week*, pp. 11–21.

Olsen, L. (1988). *Crossing the schoolhouse border: Immigrant students and the California public schools*. San Francisco, CA: California Tomorrow.

Omi, M., & Winant, H. (1986). *Racial formation in the United States*. New York and London: Routledge & Kegan Paul.

Ramirez, J. D., Yuen, S. D., & Ramey, D. R. (1991, February). *Final report: Longitudinal study of structured English immersion strategy, early-exit and late-exit transitional bilingual education programs for language-minority children*. Washington, DC: U.S. Department of Education.

Squires, D. A., Huitt, W. G., & Segars, J. K. (1985). *Effective schools and classrooms: A research based perspective*. Washington, DC: Association for Supervision and Curriculum Development.

Suarez-Orozco, M. M. (1989). *Central American refugees and U.S. high schools: A psychological study of motivation and achievement*. Stanford, CA: Stanford University Press.

Trueba, H. (1991, March). Comments on Foley's "Reconsidering anthropological explanation." *Anthropology and Education Quarterly, 22*(1), 89–94.

Trueba, H. T. (1989). *Raising silent voices: Educating linguistic minorities in the 21st century*. Cambridge, NY: Newbury House Publishers.

Trueba, H. T., Jacobs, L., & Kirton, E. (1990). *Cultural conflict and adaptation: The case of the Hmong children in American society*. London, England: Falmer Press.

Trueba, H. T., Rodriguez, C., Zou, Y., & Cintrón, J. (1993). *Healing multicultural America: Mexican immigrants rise to power in rural California*. London, England: The Falmer Press.

United Nations Children Fund. (1995). *State of the world's children*. New York: Oxford University Press.

Vygotsky, L. S. (1978). *Mind in society: The development of higher psychological processes*. M. Cole, V. John-Teiner, S. Scribner, & E. Sauberman (Eds.). Cambridge, MA: Harvard University Press.

Part 3

The Dialogue Between Democracy and Multicultural Education

Chapter 12

Curriculum and Multicultural Education

When we are really honest with ourselves, we must admit that our lives are all that really belongs to us. So it is how we use our lives that determines what kind of people we are. It is my deepest belief that only by giving our lives do we find life. I am convinced that the truest act of courage . . . is to sacrifice ourselves for others in a totally nonviolent struggle for justice.[1]

—César Chávez (1927–1993)

Multicultural education is part of an ideological movement whose aim is to make schools more democratically inclusive. Its intellectual roots lie in the civil rights struggles of the 1960s, the ethnic studies movements of the 1970s, and in the struggles for bilingual education (Banks, 1992). Multicultural education responds to a rising militancy among some students and an increased alienation, failure, and school leaving among others.

---

[1] Statement made at the termination of a 25-day fast for nonviolence, March 10, 1968, in Delano, California.

Conservatives distort the debate by raising an "alarm" concerning writings arguing for an Afrocentric curriculum. The debate over Afrocentrism has only begun, but multicultural education is not the same as Afrocentrism. Racism in the United States is inadequately described with a Black-White paradigm. There are multiple races and even more cultures, each of which deserves study. A part of the effort of multicultural education is to rewrite the curriculum and textbooks so that all students—members of the United States' diverse communities—recognize their own role in building the society and the economy.

The content of the curriculum and of textbooks is very important. These materials direct and shape what students read and often outline the teaching strategies to be employed. Most school systems assume that teachers will follow a curriculum provided to them by the district or by a text publisher. Lacking sufficient preparation time and support services, teachers simply do not have the time to write new curricula. Additionally, many teachers feel they do not have the expertise to design a math or science curriculum, so they rely on the textbook and curriculum guides to organize their lessons. Throughout our school system, most teachers accept the decisions of distant writers and publishers for many curriculum and teaching decisions.

This reliance on textbooks makes the content and structure of these books very important. In some school districts, teachers enjoy a great deal of latitude in selecting and using materials. In these districts, principals and other administrators consider the teachers professionals and hesitate to impose decisions from outside the classroom. In other schools and districts, administrators closely monitor the curriculum. Schools and districts where test scores are low often insist on a uniform curriculum and a blanket set of rules governing homework and tests because they lack other strategies to measure and promote quality teaching.

The increased diversity of our society requires multicultural curriculum reform. The following guidelines for reform are suggested by the National Coalition of Advocates for Students (1991) and Olsen and Mullen (1990). Textbooks and curriculum should be changed to:

1. Eliminate bias and stereotypes in instructional material.
2. Eliminate tracking.
3. Reduce overreliance on worksheets and other materials of questionable educational merit.
4. Reduce reliance on materials and strategies that focus primarily on direct teacher instruction.
5. Include higher-order thinking skills (critical thinking) in the curriculum of all students.
6. Provide time for teachers to prepare enriching instructional material.
7. Revise the texts and materials for all students to tell a comprehensive, complete, and inclusive view of society and its history.
8. Encourage cooperative learning, sharing, and helping each other.

9. Base materials in the life experiences of the children.
10. Emphasize the development of language and communication skills.
11. Develop materials that explore cultural and national differences and that teach students to analyze diverse viewpoints.
12. Provide all students with introductions to the rich contributions of many cultures.
13. Build on and extend the experiences of the students.
14. Build on and extend the languages of the students.
15. Promote dialogue between teachers and students.
16. Help students analyze and comprehend their real-life situations; that is, peer groups, gangs, drugs, violence, romance, youth culture, and music.

Existing textbooks do not meet these minimum criteria.

The Debate Over Textbooks

Harvard Professor Nathan Glazer (1993) points out that multicultural school wars are far from new. Battles over the place of ethnic groups, history, and culture in the curriculum date back at least to 1840. Further, he notes:

> [N]one of the leading critics of a multicultural curriculum—neither Arthur Schlesinger, Jr., author of *The Disuniting of America*, nor Diane Ravitch, the educational historian and former assistant secretary of education, nor Albert Shanker, president of the American Federation of Teachers—argues against a healthy diversity that acknowledges the varied sources of the American people and its culture. Still, all see a multicultural curriculum as a threat to the way we live together in a common nation. ("Forum," p. 1)

Diane Ravitch, a leading critic of multicultural education, documents the battles in the New York City schools in her own book, *The Great Schools Wars* (1974). Prior generations battled over the role of Irish Catholics, of Germans and German languages, and the appropriate manner in which to accomplish the "Americanization" of immigrant groups. The past 20 years have witnessed a resumption of these battles over textbooks, state curriculum adoptions, and the appropriate inclusion of multicultural and gay and lesbian lifestyles in literature. (For a good description of the educational agenda of the political right, see Apple, 1989; Carlson, 1992.)

Critic Ravitch describes the conflict as follows:

> Questions of race, ethnicity and religion have been a perennial source of conflict in American education. The schools have often attracted the zealous attention of those who wish to influence the future, as well as those who wish to change the way we view the past . . .

> The rising tide of particularism (multicultural education) encourages the politiciza-
> tion of all curricula in the schools. If education bureaucrats bend to the political and
> ideological winds, as is their wont, we can anticipate a generation of struggle over the
> content of the curriculum in mathematics, science, literature and history . . .
>
> The spread of particularism throws into question the very idea of American public
> education. (pp. 331, 357)

In her writings, Professor Ravitch supports the inclusion of a limited amount of
multiracial history within U.S. history, but she uses a narrow and restrictive
framework for considering what is important or significant history.

In recent years, even the popular press has given a voice to such critics. For
example, in July 1991, *Time* magazine raised an alarm over textbook wars when
it featured the following on its cover: "Who are We? American kids are getting a
new-and-divisive view of Thomas Jefferson, Thanksgiving, and the Fourth of
July" (July 8).

Textbook battles frequently occur over religious issues, sexual preference, and
women's issues as well as multicultural education. Texas, for example, has a
long history of struggles by a group of religious conservatives to edit, censor, and
ban specific references in textbooks. Groups such as Citizens for Excellence in
Education have supported local religious evangelists in challenging curriculum
materials in Pennsylvania, Michigan, Colorado, and California. In 1993, religious conservatives organized along with many working-class Latino and African
American parents to force the dismissal of New York School Chancellor, Joe Fernandez, and they sought control of the school board to prevent use of a "Rainbow Curriculum," which they alleged included children's stories about families
with gay and lesbian parents.

Efforts to achieve comprehensive representation of diverse cultures often are
rancorous and frequently is opposed by commercial publishers. The conflicts
reveal the underlying struggle for power in education. When long-hidden issues
are unmasked, persons who have enjoyed undeserved and unwarranted privileges of defining "history" and literature react with alarm. Presently, textbook
publishers control the selection of common knowledge. And control of knowledge determines who controls the future. Changing the control of knowledge is
central to school reform (Glazer, 1991; Goodlad & Keating, 1990; Taskforce on
Minorities, 1989).

Michael Apple, in *Teachers and Texts: A Political Economy of Class and Gender Relations in Education* (1988), and Martin Carnoy and Henry Levin, in
Schooling and Work in the Democratic State (1985), discuss the importance of
control of knowledge. Apple contends that control of knowledge has been a primary factor in controlling women and devaluing women's work in the field of
education. The field known as **critical theory** has paid particular attention to
ideological control and domination within education. Critical theorists argue
there has been a persistent slanting of the historical record to support ideological
control and institutional racism (Apple, 1993). When scholars use a multicultural perspective to reveal historical biases, when they criticize narrow defini-

tions and perspectives on history, they frequently encounter hostile responses and a vigorous defense of a European American-centered viewpoint as the only truth (Schlesinger, 1991; Sewell, 1991).

Recent textbook struggles in California and New York reveal the opposing viewpoints. The view that won out in California was crafted by neoconservative historian Diane Ravitch and supported by Paul Gagnon and former California State Superintendent Bill Honig, among others. This view argues that textbooks and a common history should provide the glue that unites our society. Historical themes and interpretations are selected in books to create unity in a diverse and divided society.

This viewpoint assigns to schools the task of creating a common culture. In reality, television and military service may do more to create a common culture than schools and books. Neoconservatives assign the task of cultural assimilation to schools, with particular emphasis on the history, social science, and literature curriculum. Historians advocating consensus write textbooks that downplay the role of slavery, genocide, and imperialism in our history. They focus on the success of achieving political reform, representative government, and economic opportunity for European American workers and immigrants.

In arguing for this unity, the authors consistently tell one viewpoint of the historical events. They select heroes that champion unity and events that support their theses while ignoring heroes that championed diversity (see Figure 12.1).

Figure 12.1 Common History Textbook Heroes

Unity Heroes	*Diversity Heroes*
Alexander Hamilton	Daniel Shay
	Patrick Henry
Andrew Jackson	Chief Pontiac
	Chief Tecumseh
Stephen F. Austin	Gregorio Cortez
Abraham Lincoln	John Brown
General Custer	Sojourner Truth
	Sitting Bull
Samuel Gompers	Eugene Debs
Teddy Roosevelt	Big Bill Haywood
	Emma Goldman
George Washington Carver	W. E. B. DuBois
	Elizabeth Cady Stanton
	Jane Addams
	Alice Paul
	Lucia Gonzales Parsons
Martin Luther King, Jr.	Malcolm X
	M. L. King, 1967–1968

Ravitch, Schlesinger, Shanker, and other opponents of most multicultural curriculum reform contend that teaching a common history—albeit an incomplete history—has served to build unity out of diversity. The **consensus viewpoint** dominates textbook publishing, and these partial and incomplete histories do not empower students of color. By recounting primarily a consensual, European American view, history and literature extend current racist, sexist, and class biases in our society. When texts or teachers tell only part of the story, schools foster intellectual colonialism, an ideological domination that contributes to the subjugation and oppression of communities of color.

A 1991 New York social studies review committee argued against continued ideological domination and for diversity in the curriculum:

> If the United States is to continue to prosper in the 21st century, then all of its citizens, whatever their race or ethnicity, must believe that they and their ancestors have shared in the building of the country and have a stake in its success. (p. 1)

The New York committee included articulate advocates of the position that history should be selected to create a consensus, but they did not win out. Consensus advocate and historian, Arthur Schlesinger (1991), wrote a strong dissent from the committee position.

The differences between these two positions are profound. These two views differ both on what happened and whose knowledge gets validated. Young people have their own background knowledge. They have a worldview based on their experiences each day in their homes, among their friends, and on the streets. If the curriculum reaches out to build on and extend their background knowledge, then they feel validated as part of the larger society. Students need to see themselves and their lives as a part of history. A curriculum of diversity and inclusion treats them as members of the community. Inclusion encourages students of color to participate in building a more tolerant and a more democratic community.

Students of color encountering the neoconservative consensus view find their own history discounted or ignored. When their background knowledge is ignored, they are invalidated. The discounting of working-class students and students of color, combined with economic subjugation, leads to the pain and rage that periodically explode in crime, in violence on school grounds, and occasionally in urban riots.

The struggle between the two viewpoints is a struggle over worldviews. The new multicultural worldview contends against the existing Eurocentric consensus view. Both sides can marshal evidence, and both sides have competent historians. Both sides have advocates who refuse to give a fair rendition or just consideration to the viewpoints and evidence of their opponents. The interpretation and analysis of history and the social sciences are a continuous project in which students can participate. There is not historical consensus on a single viewpoint. To present only the conclusions of the unity advocates in textbooks encourages poor scholarship and limits students' freedom of thought.

Each worldview selects specific concepts to present and specific content to cover. Power relationships, along with research, are expressed in the defining and selecting of categories (Popkewitz, 1987). Teachers need to know about several views and their nuances in order to present materials that provide academic balance.

Democratic multicultural education works to transform the curriculum to achieve the goals previously listed and to present an inclusive curriculum. For example, most U.S. and state histories use the concept of the frontier in telling the story of the conquering of the Middle West and the West. Textbooks portray the European settlers as bringing civilization to a previously uncivilized land and people. Any reasonable analysis of the lifestyle of gold miners, cattlemen, and others, in comparison to Native American lives, reveals that the European American settlers were not "more civilized" and the Native Americans "less civilized" even though textbooks frequently perpetuate these views. The Europeans were not less violent, more family oriented, or more respectful of life, social mores, and other community values. They were better armed and more numerous. And they won. Most public school texts present a romanticized, Eurocentric view of the frontier and civilization (Foner & Werner, 1991). A similar misapplication of the concepts of frontiers and civilization occurred in the recording of the Europeans' conquering of Africa and initiating the transatlantic slave trade. Textbooks often portray the expansion of European culture as a historical inevitability, as natural. The resultant destruction of peaceful societies and the deaths of millions are dismissed as historically insignificant.

When parents and others seek to revise the textbooks to offer a less Eurocentric view of territorial expansion, they can expect to be attacked by neoconservatives in education, government, and private foundations. Although neoconservatives do not totally control the public discussion, their network of institutes and foundations is effective in getting media attention (Asante, 1991; Ravitch, 1991; Sowell, 1991; "Whose America?," 1991). The vehemence of the attacks on efforts to revise textbooks and the use of distorted evidence as a primary rhetorical device reveal the volatility of issues surrounding multicultural education.

The conservative attack on multicultural education often mixes criticisms of the university and public school curriculum in a way that distracts public attention from the most important issues. The university debate has been about proposals to require an ethnic studies or women's studies course or revising the "canon" of survey courses in history, humanities, and literature. This debate is interesting. More vital to the survival of our democratic society is the call for a radical improvement in the quality of public school education for students of color and students living in poverty. While the university debate rages in the journals and press, another generation of African American, Latino, and Native American children has entered grades K through 3 in inadequate, underfunded, failing schools. And another generation of students in our major cities has entered ninth grade where over half of them will drop out prior to graduation.

Beyond the Melting Pot

Most educational leaders continue to accept the "melting pot" point of view. They believe in a legend of how the public schools served European immigrant groups (Banks, 1992; Greer, 1972). The view of history presented in books conflicts with the multiethnic reality students see around them.

In 1992, California's school population was made up of European Americans (44.5%), Latinos (35.3%), African Americans (8.6%), and Asians (8%). In Mississippi, a majority of the students are African American. In New Mexico, Hispanics and Native Americans together constitute the majority of students. In Hawaii, Japanese and Chinese Americans make up the majority while European Americans and Hawaiians are minorities. These diverse populations scarcely exist in some books and appear as "problems" in others.

The **melting pot thesis,** dominant until the 1990s, held that these "new" populations should melt into the majority group, becoming as much like the European American majority as possible. The dominant culture was assumed to be superior and worth the pain of assimilation. Many European immigrants chose this path to "Americanism."

Now times and populations have changed. Even advocates of the melting pot seldom argue that European American students should melt into the new majority of non-European Americans and cultures. While all groups clearly accept the school goal of mastery of the English language and work skills, the prior functions of schools forcing cultural assimilation are rejected by advocates of multicultural education. A multicultural worldview insists on the development of a more comprehensive and inclusive view of history, the social sciences, and the humanities than has been presented in the past.

When a people's history is absent from coverage in the curriculum, this absence is usually a product of lack of power, a lack of political and educational capital. It is not a product of having contributed little to the development of our communities and nations. Many of the several cultures found in the United States with their distinct viewpoints have been with us all along. The melting pot worldview excluded them from textbooks, but not from the economy and society. Now these diverse communities have achieved political and economic recognition; these communities insist that their children and their histories, cultures, and languages be respected in the curriculum.

The domination of the language and literacy curriculum by researchers familiar only with the macroculture leads to teaching strategies that fail many students. Shirley Brice-Heath (1986) argues:

> The school expects children to follow a single developmental model in acquiring uses of language. Yet, educators' developmental models have, in large part, come from psychologists or linguists who have either studied their own children or children of similar primary group membership. Much of the research of those who have described language acquisition and posited universals has been carried out with what we term "mainstream children," whose families are school-oriented, nuclear, and open to numerous types of involvement with secondary groups such as Boy Scouts, Sunday School, camps, swimming clubs, and nursery schools. (p. 150)

The clear majority of strategies and materials used for language arts instruction were developed based on assumptions of working with English-dominant students. Kathryn H. Au, in *Literacy Instruction in Multicultural Settings* (1993), provides detailed descriptions of how to use constructivist strategies and materials for multilingual classrooms.

Knowledge is required for self-identity (Tetreault, 1989). The existing male-dominated, Eurocentered curriculum rests on the false assumption that experiences of the European American male adequately represent all of our history and culture. It assumes that the European American male experience provides sufficient basis for generalizing about society as a whole. Today several communities refuse to be rendered invisible in textbooks as if they had not contributed to the development of this nation.

The battle over what history and literature to study in the university has been hotly contested and shamelessly distorted. The standard curriculum of the universities provides future teachers with the canons of "appropriate" knowledge. Under the Reagan Administration (1980–1988), Secretary of Education William Bennett and then Director of the National Endowment for the Humanities, Lynne Cheney, charged that the curriculum was being diluted by "tenured radicals" because, after two years of debate, Stanford University decided to add one book from a non-Western viewpoint to the 10 books required in a freshman world civilization course. This token level of curriculum change fails to address the growing racial polarization in our society and on campuses.

The struggles over the content of public school curriculum are of far greater significance. Interest groups arguing for multicultural education must contend with the established and preferential political power of the publishers and many educators. The case of history and social science textbook adoptions in California in 1990 illustrates the complexities of the struggle.

Writing the California Framework for History and Social Science

Upon election as California Superintendent of Public Instruction in 1982, Bill Honig agreed with the *Paideia Proposals* (Adler, 1982)—that a classical academic curriculum, such as that taught in elite academies, was appropriate for all students. This position neglected the academic and vocational interests of a majority of the students in inner-city schools. The classical, Eurocentered curriculum was an inaccurate representation of history and the humanities. It discounted or ignored the contributions of people of color. Honig proceeded to direct the redrafting of the *History-Social Science Framework for Public Schools*, the guidelines for social studies teaching and textbook selections. Legal regulations required a broadly representative committee of teachers, scholars, and professionals to draft the framework and submit their draft to the Board of Education.

Members of the framework committee struggled for an agreement that would balance their existing concerns for historical accuracy, ethnic diversity, and valid curriculum principles with the pressures for change in the neoconservative directions insisted on by Superintendent Honig and his staff. The committee agreed to shift away from the interdisciplinary study of the social studies, including economics, political science, and sociology, toward an emphasis on history and geography. In January 1987, the committee wrote a compromise draft. The staff of the Department of Education found it totally unacceptable.

Three persons then separated themselves from the legally constituted drafting committee and rewrote the document for submission to the State Curriculum Commission. They were Diane Brooks (a Honig staff person), curriculum commission member Charlotte Crabtree (an Early Childhood Education professor), and historian Diane Ravitch. These three wrote a major revision without substantive participation of the other members of the framework committee (Cornbleth & Waugh, 1995).

Their draft, which followed the consensus, Eurocentric viewpoint, excluded an accurate history of Latino and Native American settlement of the Southwest and neglected coverage of the substantial Asian history in the West. By electing to concentrate on a melting pot and consensus point of view, the *Framework* assumes that telling the history of European immigrants adequately explains the experiences of Mexicans, Native Americans, and Asians.

The *Framework* does not describe the displacement and destruction of Native American, Mexican, and Mexican American communities from 1850 to 1930 throughout the Southwest including Los Angeles and San Diego. The *Framework* ignores how American settlers used land laws to steal land from Californios and Mexican settlers and reduce them to day laborers. The authors, including historian Ravitch, failed to note that the present mosaic of Southwest culture was created by the subjugation and domination of previously existing groups, both Native American and Mexican American. To tell only the European American side of the story is dishonest.

The California document won the praise of conservative educators. Diane Ravitch and Superintendent Honig cited the document as a positive example of multicultural inclusion in their writings and speeches. The *History-Social Science Framework for California's Public Schools* was one of several documents that pushed forward the neoconservative position on school reform in the 1980s and engaged in a broad ideological battle to define the direction of curriculum reform. Ideological conservatives joined forces with other popular movements opposed to multicultural education in an effort to align the curriculum more closely with the interests of big business (National Center for Education and the Economy, 1990). California law requires that textbook selections be based on the *Framework*. Major publishers who want to win a part of the lucrative California market write textbooks to meet the *Framework*'s criteria. There were, however, some problems.

The California *Framework* requires that material be presented within a new chronological structure, making the courses, and thus, the books, incompatible with those of other states. For example, the 1987 *Framework* requires the fifth-grade U.S. history course to cover the period from the early Native Americans through the colonial era, the founding of the United States, and up to the Civil War. In the eighth grade, the main emphasis is on the Civil War period through

World War I. Emphasis on the modern era is left until grade 11. In most states, an eighth-grade U.S. history course would include the modern era.

After studying the *Framework*'s unique new chronological divisions, several publishers chose not to compete in the California textbook market because California's peculiar *Framework* would make the books less marketable in other states.

Much worse than the problems that the *California Framework* has created for publishers are the problems it has created for teachers, particularly at the middle-school level. By requiring that the study of the modern era be put off until grade 11, the plan essentially instructs fifth-, seventh-, and eighth-grade students to study only ancient history. This has contributed to making history instruction unnecessarily distant and irrelevant to the lives of these young people. Before these students can become interested in the broader historical picture, they need to have their own more immediate history explored. The *Framework* discourages this. Further, Asian and Latino students—some 44% of the total school population—are essentially absent from history as presented in the *California Framework*.

The U.S. history books submitted for the 1990 California adoption expanded the African American, Native American, and women's history coverage, but were totally inadequate in the coverage of Latinos and Asians—both significant population groups in the development of western history and among the California student populations. The coverage of Native Americans in the fourth-grade books was embarrassingly Eurocentric. The proposed seventh- and eighth-grade texts treated the history and cultures of Africa and the U.S. slave system in ways that were promptly challenged by members of the African American community (King, 1992). The history of African Americans was portrayed in an add-on manner, as if their story was not central to understanding U.S. history. The books failed to accurately describe the interactive and interdependent nature of the African, European, Native American, Latino, and Asian communities.

African American legislators as well as Latino and Asian groups criticized the texts and asked for a delay in adoption to insist on revisions. Superintendent Honig decided not to attend the hearings. He displayed his intolerant views on the inclusion of multicultural history and the demands of non-European groups when he said: "A lot is at stake here. . . . Do we try to keep this society together or do we split up into *tribal warfare?*" [emphasis added] (Trombley, 1990). Ignoring written testimony and the protests of a wide range of scholars, teachers, and community activists, the conservative-controlled California Board of Education unanimously approved the books (Olsen, 1991). The books adopted were distributed to all schools, although Oakland schools and a few other districts declined to use them. Curriculum Commissioner Charlotte Crabtree and textbook series author Dr. Gary Nash subsequently received a $1.5 million grant to establish a National Center for History in the Schools at the University of California at Los Angeles. This center has taken the lead in writing proposed national standards for U.S. and World History. The proposed standards are under attack as using a too inclusive, too multicultural approach (Olson, 1995).

The New York Curriculum of Inclusion

Similar textbook and curriculum struggles have occurred elsewhere in the United States. In 1987, the New York Commissioner of Education, Thomas Sobol, convened a task force, "Minorities: Equity and Excellence," to evaluate the progress of New York's schools toward meeting a series of state requirements on inclusiveness. In July 1989, the task force published *A Curriculum of Inclusion*, a report calling for substantial revision of the New York state curriculum. The report began as follows:

> African Americans, Asian Americans, Puerto Ricans / Latinos, and Native Americans have all been the victims of intellectual and educational oppression that has characterized the culture and institutions of the United States and the European American world for centuries. (p. iii)

The report was quickly attacked and criticized as extreme by the neoconservative network of education advocates, as well as several major newspaper columnists.

After considering the criticism in 1992, the New York Commissioner's office drew together a new commission composed of several eminent scholars. This second commission wrote *One Nation, Many People: A Declaration of Cultural Interdependence*. This document offers extensive guides and suggestions to teachers to supplement the inadequate textbooks available. Once again, the report was attacked as extremist. Arthur Schlesinger, Jr., resigned from the committee in protest while historian Oscar Handlin and others defended the report. In their attacks on the New York efforts, the network of conservative scholars repeatedly cited the *California Framework* as a preferred example of curriculum response to the demands of inclusive history. The California State Board of Education had adopted a "consensus" view, and the New York Board of Regents had adopted an inclusion view.

Unfortunately, to date, an integrated, comprehensive U.S. history suitable for public school use has not been published. Nor do adequate supplementary materials exist for teachers. This gap between the current scholarship and available textbooks contributes significantly to alienation of students from history and social science courses (Tyson-Bernstein, 1988).

The problems of textbooks and the problems revealed in the battles over texts are not accidental; nor are the relentless political attacks to restrict and de-fund bilingual education. These struggles are the product of past choices by people in power to use the teaching of history to promote a specific worldview. This worldview is being challenged by both the evangelical Christian right and from the left by the multicultural education movement. The views that pass for a consensus history have been developed in history departments in universities and influenced by the current distribution of political and ideological power. Both university departments and the political power structure are dominated by a conservative stratum of our society.

Cornbleth and Waugh, in their excellent book, *The Great Speckled Bird* (1995), describe the process of opinion shaping and media control as follows:

> Also noteworthy is the organizational location of individual members (of the conservative network) which lent status and authority to their pronouncements. One speaks not for oneself but for a committee, commission, council or center or a university or federal government agency. Network members supported one another and their reform cause by praising each other's work in public statements and journal articles, appointing one another to advisory boards, hiring one another as consultants for their various projects, and helping to fund these projects.

These institutions and networks resist the emerging multicultural reality. In many cases, members of this political stratum choose to remain unaware of the dramatic changes occurring in our economy and society. They are holding on to the past because in the past they were "leaders," respected, and financially successful. The emerging multicultural society challenges the traditional distribution of power (Apple, 1993).

The curriculum should help students understand the society and their place in the society, and it should prepare them for a positive, productive future. To achieve these goals, a democratic multicultural perspective argues that students should not be left out of the curriculum. All students need to learn that they belong, that they are participants in the democratic project. The curriculum should help students to learn that they are important. They need to learn the skills, information, and attitudes that will protect and extend democracy and allow them to participate in the economy.

Clearly, U.S. society is more democratic today than it was in 1776. Textbooks and curricula should tell the stories of struggles for democracy: the right to vote for women, the struggle against slavery, the struggle for labor unions, the civil rights struggles, and the struggle for economic justice. The curriculum can help empower students by teaching them that past struggles have made our society more democratic. In studying these events, students learn that conflict is a normal and natural way to make change and that progress is the result of hard work.

Beyond the Text

A universally acceptable, ideologically neutral body of knowledge that all students should learn does not exist. Nor can a teacher be an expert in all areas. Textbooks serve as a guide. They are a particular selection of knowledge. This selection delivers power to some people—those who are in charge of writing, publishing, and selecting textbooks.

Teachers interested in promoting democratic multicultural education seldom have textbooks on their side. But the existing texts can be used. Teachers can help students to study the texts for what they are—a particular point of view on history, literature, and language. One good way is to analyze and compare two or more texts on the same issue. This strategy requires that you skip some material and cover other material in more depth. Teachers and students can bring in current news reports from multiple perspectives and compare them with the texts. After acquiring critical thinking skills (see Chapter 9), students can analyze these textbook presentations.

Using texts as critical thinking subjects demystifies the books. Students interact actively with the books rather than read and repeat the ideas of others.

Since current books are usually inept in presenting the histories and cultures of minority groups, teachers must become resources for the children. Teachers engage in an endless gathering of materials and ideas for students. The curriculum, *A World of Difference,* made available by B'nai B'rith (1986), provides some interesting human relations lessons. Teachers will need to locate and use Latino, African American, and Asian bookstores in the community to gather additional material. Regular reading of newspapers and magazines written for each community will provide students with substantial resources. Teachers can gain the necessary background by taking ethnic studies classes at nearby universities. Cooperation among teachers also provides useful materials. Professional associations such as the National Association of Bilingual Education and its state affiliates hold conferences that provide a ready source of materials. In the last decade, new materials have emerged. Teachers now face the formidable task of locating and using those materials.

Creating Your Own Materials

Some of the most effective materials are produced by teachers and students. Although not achieving the graphic quality and professional look of commercial materials, students writing their own curriculum empowers them and their community.

Young students can research and record the history of their classroom. Middle-grade students (grades 6 through 8) can interview neighborhood residents and research local communities. With the help of computer programs, students can now write their conclusions and leave their studies for next year's class. Then the following year, students can read the material and add new chapters to the stories. In North Sacramento, immigrant students from Cambodia, Laos, and El Salvador have written textbooks of their own stories of migration and adjustment to U.S. life. These tales, researched, written, edited, and published by students, provide preparation, writing, and language practice. They also provide far more accurate analyses of the society of young people than the material offered by most textbooks.

Students can write multiple perspectives on an event and compare their conclusions to those provided in their textbooks. Soon students question who wrote these books. They begin to understand the process that has left their own history out of the texts.

The *Foxfire* project and books and the Highlander Folk School in Tennessee both have a long history of validating culture while supporting young people in the recording of the history and culture of Appalachian areas. These projective history and cultural recovery efforts offer outstanding guides to the creation of dynamic, living history. Students develop cultural knowledge and perspective, reading and writing skills, and self-confidence by producing their own curriculum. Often this material is of higher intellectual quality than that of commercial textbooks. Through this kind of participatory curriculum development, multicultural education can make a racially divided nation more united (Popkewitz, 1987).

Stages of Improvement in Instructional Materials

Changing textbooks and curriculums for gender, racial, and cultural equity requires a long-range struggle. The chart in Figure 12.2, by James Banks (1988), describes the levels of curriculum reform necessary for integrating the curriculum.

The Contributions Approach

A few books have taken the first step—a contributions approach. In the **contributions approach,** publishers and teachers add a few ethnic heroes and subjects to the present curriculum. The primary grades use biographies, literature, and holidays to "integrate" the curriculum.

Typically the school selects a few important dates, such as El Cinco de Mayo and Martin Luther King Jr.'s birthday. Students participate in lessons, pageants, and celebrations of the events. The contributions approach, combined with human relations strategies such as those described in Chapter 6, is the most common approach to multicultural education.

The contributions approach, however, has several limitations. It leaves the existing curriculum unchanged and unchallenged. Children are first taught the main story, history, and literature of society from a mainstream European American point of view. Then a few interesting stories are added. The authors of New York's *A Curriculum of Inclusion* criticize this approach as "multiculturalism . . . [that] is additive and not at the center of the endeavors." The contributions approach does little to validate the students' culture and background knowledge. Since the students do not look at society from several perspectives, they fail to learn the concept of multiple perspectives. The contributions approach declines to recognize that the mainstream curriculum carries a fundamental ideological slanting.

Heroes and holidays of the contributions approach tend to isolate the story of people of color from inclusion in the development of our society. The Houghton Mifflin history texts authored by Gary Nash and adopted for use in California are particularly limited by the contributions approach. While dances, music, and celebrations are interesting, this focus tends to present the non-European cul-

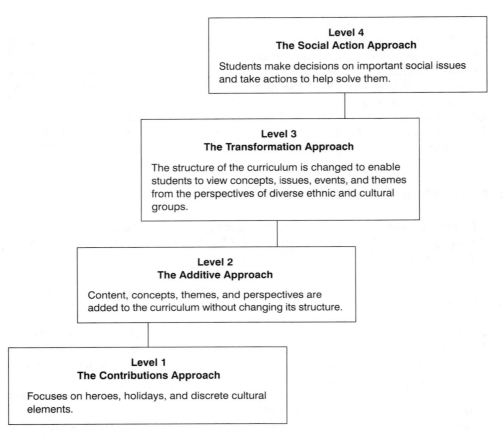

Figure 12.2 Levels of Curriculum Reform

Note. From *An Introduction to Multicultural Education* by James Banks, 1994, Boston: Allyn & Bacon. Used with permission.

tures as exotic or unusual. Usually the dances, foods, and dress are of a romanticized, idealized culture from another country. Of course, recognition of ideal culture is important to all students. The stories of historical figures such as Abe Lincoln, George Washington, and Betsy Ross describe ideal culture for the dominant European American culture. But ideal culture should be clearly distinguished from dynamic, real culture. For students in the middle grades and high school, the history of African American, Latino, Asian, and indigenous cultures would more accurately be presented in a context of the struggle against racism and the struggle for decent jobs in society, rather than through a heroes and holidays approach.

The conflict over the *History-Social Science Framework for California's Public Schools* and the California textbook adoption battles illustrate some of the limitations of the contributions approach. The *English-Language Arts Framework for*

California's Public Schools uses a similarly limited contributions approach while California's *Bilingual Education Handbook* recognizes the need to restructure the curriculum for language-minority students.

Ethnic Additive Approach

Several textbooks, school districts, and curriculum guides now offer units and materials on specific ethnic groups—the **ethnic additive approach.** While moving one step beyond the contributions approach, the ethnic additive approach continues to isolate ethnic history and society from the mainstream curriculum. School districts using this approach add ethnic content and units to the curriculum, but without restructuring the curriculum.

The ethnic additive approach assumes that the present conceptual framework and viewpoints of society are accurate but incomplete. Teachers or curriculum guides add some African American or Chicano history or literature. Like the contributions approach, the ethnic additive approach views the history and culture of the United States from the mainstream perspective. Writers select heroes and contributions to supplement and support the mainstream views. For example, students will study the Civil Rights Movement and Martin Luther King, Jr., but they will seldom study the separatist challenge of Malcolm X or the radicalization of King's own ideas from civil rights to economic justice in the last three years of his life.

Native nations and African slaves certainly had a different view of history than those presented in most textbooks. For example, Native Americans were not considered citizens of the United States until 1924. They were residents of domestic, occupied, defeated nations. The Native American viewpoint of the expansion of European America could not be adequately presented in a single chapter or reference. From Jamestown to Hawaii, native peoples and cultures were displaced and destroyed by the advancing "Christian civilization." The ethnic additive approach rarely helps students to understand the diverse perspectives of native peoples. Minority groups and minority languages become a problem, an unexplained opposition to majority "progress."

The New York efforts on *A Curriculum of Inclusion* and *One Nation, Many Peoples: A Declaration of Cultural Interdependence* were based on the ethnic additive approach. This move beyond the California contributions approach was vehemently attacked by established European American historians and advocates of the melting pot thesis of consensus history.

The Transformative Approach

Just as European American power established the Eurocentered curriculum, the political shift to democratic empowerment of all peoples in this multiethnic nation requires a shift to multicultural perspectives in the curriculum. The **transformative approach** to multicultural curriculum recognizes that present textbooks are a product of past power, not a reflection of "truth" or neutral or "objective" analysis. The transformation of the curriculum involves the reconsideration of basic themes, units, and courses.

The transformative approach to curriculum, based on critical theory, becomes appropriate and even necessary for the educational survival of many students of color. Studies in history, social sciences, language, and the humanities would break with current content coverage to assist students in defining themselves and their own worldview.

Popkewitz (1987) describes the issue well:

> The social sciences are social productions, being neither neutral, disinterested, nor unrelated to their political context. . . . The methods and procedures of science are produced often in response to particular social agendas. The modern testing and measurement industry has its origins in a political movement of eugenics to improve the quality of racial stock. . . . The values underlying our science help us to understand that there is no one notion of science but multiple traditions for understanding and interpreting. Our social sciences contain paradigms or different constellations of value, commitment, methods and procedures. (pp. 338–339)

In a transformative curriculum, students study the relationship of knowledge to power. They learn that there is a strong relationship between whose knowledge gets validated and whose power is respected. The transformative curriculum involves students in considering the social, cultural, and political interests of those who select "school" knowledge and who define success.

Teachers require a great deal of assistance in transforming the curriculum. Their university coursework prepares them for admission into the field of teaching but seldom provides them with an adequate background for curriculum revision. New books and new course outlines are needed. To transform the curriculum, teachers must have taken a number of ethnic studies courses and become cross-culturally competent in their disciplines. Such a transformation requires teachers to work with students to continually reconstruct the curriculum.

The Portland, Oregon, African-American Baseline Essays are the best-known examples of a transformative curriculum. These essays provide one of the few applications of African centrism as advocated by Molefi Kete Asante (Asante, 1991). Conservatives insist that these essays, organized by Asa Hilliard, include some problems of historical accuracy. The *California Bilingual Education Handbook* calls for a transformation of the curriculum to provide parallel Spanish, Cantonese, and other literature and textbooks to students who need them. The few efforts at maintenance bilingualism are based on a transformative approach. The special magazine *Rethinking Columbus*, published by the Milwaukee-based Rethinking Schools, provides excellent and interesting models of transformative education about the experience of European colonization of the Americas. (For a debate on the practical implication of this approach, see "Whose Culture?" [1992] and African American Task Force of Milwaukee Public Schools, [1990].)

The Social Action Approach

The **social action approach** applies the ideas of social participation and uses the empowerment strategies described in Chapters 7 and 11. Only a few teachers, programs, and schools have attempted social action approaches to reconstruct the curriculum. The best known is the *Foxfire* curriculum development projects for Appalachian students. (See Foxfire Fund, P.O. Box 541, Mountain City, Georgia 30562.) Many English-as-a-second-language (ESL) classes for immigrant students have used a whole language and social action approach to record the students' own histories of immigration. The Writers' Workshops and the computer program *Bilingual Writers' Workshop* (1993) teach students to write, edit, and publish their own stories. These materials add transformative elements to the curriculum.

The social action approach goes further than the other approaches to include the important issues of critical thinking and decision-making processes. Critical thinking processes are essential to multicultural curriculum reform.

The social action approach recognizes and confronts the political nature of the mainstream curriculum. Public school officials rarely acknowledge openly the degree to which ideology shapes the curriculum. The social action approach often develops from local curriculum development efforts such as Ojibwa in Northern Wisconsin and the SNCC (Student Nonviolent Coordinating Committee) Freedom Schools in 1965.

Social action curriculum reform happens when teachers move outside of textbooks. The economics of textbook publishing dictate that commercial texts will be slow to respond to social change. Emerging computer technology already permits high-quality, low-cost printing of student-created materials. Students learn from well-organized class discussions of the current and vital issues in their communities. Particularly by middle school (grades 6 through 8), students need places to discuss their concerns about race, violence, fear, sex, power, and drugs. Rather than simply relying on textbooks, teachers can use the numerous materials already available to promote an authentic and hopeful dialogue.

What Can Teachers Do with Eurocentric Texts?

The battle over textbooks continues. Despite more than 20 years of struggle, few districts have a pluralistic curriculum. New teachers frequently encounter terrible texts selected by a state or district committee. In your first year of teaching, you will probably not have an opportunity to influence textbook selections. But in your classroom you can go beyond the texts to pursue critical thinking, cooperative learning, and a transformative pedagogy.

The single most important curriculum reform of all is for the teacher to help students succeed with whatever materials are used. Some imaginative teachers design their curriculum around the life experiences of the students, using newspapers, magazines, literature, and other sources to supplement the textbooks.

Teachers also select and provide, sometimes at great personal expense, reading materials of interest to the students. With the advent of the video recorder, teachers can copy and analyze programs from television to supplement bland, boring, and inadequate textbooks.

By working together, teachers can produce their own curriculum materials. Teacher teams select empowering themes that bridge across the disciplines. For example, in the study of discrimination, teams of students can use reading skills to learn the history of discrimination, writing skills to compose essays and letters, and math skills to calculate and demonstrate tracking, voting patterns, and income inequalities. They can make presentations and video recordings of their work. Focusing on themes and student production helps teachers to emphasize quality and useful English and social studies.

Teachers can work in teams to share planning and read samples of students' work in other classes. Teachers, not textbooks or curriculum, establish high expectation levels. Effective teachers combine their skills and experience to establish a curriculum that stresses success for all.

Summary

We face a massive challenge—to create a new curriculum based on the full participation of all students. Creating schools that are equitable across race, class, and gender, and that provide high quality education appropriate to a rapidly changing economy requires a fundamental rewriting of the curriculum.

There are two distinct curriculum reform movements. The neoconservative school reform of the 1980s stressed raising standards, increasing testing, and creating a common culture through textbook selection and publication. Neoconservative reform stressed aligning schools and the curriculum more clearly with business interests and corporate productivity. The multicultural curriculum reform movement developed from a different worldview and thus a different theory of the appropriate role of schooling in our society. Multicultural reform seeks to make the curriculum more inclusive. Multicultural education advocates seek to transform the curriculum to empower all students for economic and political participation. School reform and curriculum reform can play a role in uniting—in healing—a divided nation.

The differences between these two viewpoints have produced a sustained conflict over textbooks and the curriculum.

Questions Over the Chapter

1. What do you believe are the differences between "particularism" and a multicultural approach to curriculum?
2. Under what conditions is it appropriate for a group of European American children to study African American history? Under what conditions should an African American student study European American history?
3. Explain why there have been major conflicts between scholars over history and literature books, but fewer conflicts about multicultural content in math and science texts?
4. Define the melting pot thesis. What are the goals of assimilation?
5. Many advocates of multicultural education reject the melting pot thesis. What are their arguments?
6. Describe your own experiences in reading history and literature. Were the textbooks inclusive and pluralistic? Do you now comprehend the basic historical narrative of the nation's major cultural groups? Of women?
7. How are textbooks selected or adopted in your school, district, and state?
8. Using a transformative approach to textbooks, how would you change this textbook?

Activities for Further Study of Curriculum

1. How accurate and complete do you think the textbooks you used in school were? Compare your views with those of a person from another cultural group.
2. Conduct historical research on one of the diversity heroes listed in this chapter. Do you conclude that this person should have been included in a general U.S. history text? Why do you think the person was left out?
3. Read James Loewen's book *Lies My Teacher Told Me: Everything Your American History Text Got Wrong* (1995, New York: The New Press). Write a short essay on the significance of omissions from history books.
4. List three ways you could use a textbook in the classroom even if the textbook had inadequate coverage.
5. Design two examples of a transformative approach to curriculum. Share your ideas with a classmate. What obstacles will prevent you from using a transformative approach?
6. Create a list of social action projects appropriate to the grade level you are working with. Share your list with other students. (Be cautious about the safety level of any project.)

References

Adler, M. (1982). *Paideia proposals: An educational manifesto.* New York: Macmillan.

African American Task Force of Milwaukee Public Schools. (1990). *Educating African American Males: A Dream Deferred.* Milwaukee Public Schools.

Apple, M. (1988). *Teachers and texts: A political economy of class and gender relations in education.* New York: Routledge & Kegan Paul.

Apple, M. (1989). The politics of common sense: Schooling, populism, and the new right. In H. A. Giroux & P. McClaren (Eds.), *Critical Pedagogy, the State, and Cultural Struggle.* State University of New York Press.

Apple, M. (1993). *Official knowledge: Democratic education in a conservative age.* New York: Routledge & Kegan Paul.

Asante, M. K. (1991, Spring). Multiculturalism: An exchange. *American Scholar,* pp. 267–272.

Au, K. H. (1993). *Literacy instruction in multicultural settings.* New York: Harcourt Brace Jovanovich.

Banks, J. A. (1988, Spring). Approaches to multicultural reform. *Multicultural Leader, 1*(2), 1–3.

Banks, J. (1992). African American scholarship and the evolution of multicultural education. *Journal of Negro Education, 61*(3), 273–285.

Banks, J. A. (1994). *An introduction to multicultural education.* Boston: Allyn & Bacon.

Bilingual Writing Center. (1993). [Computer program]. The Learning Company.

B'nai B'rith Antidefamation League. (1986). *The wonderful world of difference: A human relations program for grades K–8.* New York: Author.

Brice-Heath, S. (1986). Sociocultural contexts of language development. *Beyond language: Social & cultural factors in schooling language minority students.* Sacramento, CA: Bilingual Education Office, California State Department of Education.

Carlson, D. (1992). *Teachers and crisis: Urban school reform and teachers work culture.* New York and London: Routledge.

Carnoy, M., & Levin, H. (1985). *Schooling and work in the democratic state.* Stanford, CA: Stanford University Press.

Cornbleth, C., & Waugh, D. (1995). *The great speckled bird: Multicultural policies and educational policymaking.* New York: St. Martin's.

A curriculum of inclusion: Commissioner's Task Force on Minorities: Equity and excellence. (1989, July). New York State Education Department.

Foner, E., & Werner, J. (1991, July). Fighting for the West. *The Nation,* pp. 163–166.

Glazer, N. (1991, September). In defense of multiculturalism. *The New Republic,* pp. 18–20.

Glazer, N. (1993, November 28). Multicultural school wars. In *Sacramento Bee,* from *Values and Public Policy* (forthcoming). The Brookings Institute.

Goodlad, J. I., & Keating, P. (Eds.). (1990). *Access to knowledge: An agenda for our nation's schools.* New York: College Entrance Examination Board.

Greer, C. (1972). *The great school legend: A revisionist interpretation of American public education.* New York: Basic Books.

Grey, P. (1991, July 8). Whose America? *Time.*

King, J. E. (1992). Diaspora literacy and consciousness in the struggle against miseducation in the black community. *Journal of Negro Education, 61*(3), 317–335. Washington, DC: Howard University.

National Center for Education and the Economy. *America's choice: High skills or low wages.* (1990). Rochester, NY: Author.

National Coalition of Advocates for Students. (1991). *The good common school: Making the vision work for all students.*

New York State Social Studies Review and Development Committee. (1991, June). *One nation, many peoples: A declaration of cultural interdependence.* New York: State Education Department.

Olsen, L. (1991). Whose curriculum is this? Whose curriculum will it be? *California Perspectives, California Tomorrow.* San Francisco: California Tomorrow.

Olson, L. (1995, January 11). Looks cloudy for standards certification. *Education Week,* p. 12.

Olson, L., & Mullen, N. (1990). Embracing diversity: Teachers' voices from California's classrooms. *California Tomorrow.* San Francisco: California Tomorrow.

Popkewitz, T. S. (1987). Knowledge and interest in the curriculum. *Critical studies in teacher education: Its folklore, theory, and practice.* London, New York, and Philadelphia: The Falmer Press.

Ravitch, D. (1974). *The Great Schools Wars.* New York: Basic Books.

Ravitch, D. (1991, Spring). Multiculturalism: E. pluribus plures. *American Scholar*, 337–354.

Schlesinger, A. (1991, Winter). The disuniting of America. *American Educator*, pp. 57–61.

Schlesinger, A. (1991, May). A dissenting opinion. *One nation, many peoples: A declaration of cultural interdependence. A report of the New York State Social Studies Review and Development Committee*. New York: State Education Department.

Sewell, G. T. (1991, Winter). *Social Studies Review*. New York: American Textbook Council.

Sowell, T. (1991, May / June). Cultural diversity: A world view. *The American Enterprise*, 45–54.

Task Force on Minorities. (1989). *A curriculum of inclusion*. New York: State Education Department.

Tetreault, M. K. T. (1989). Integrating content about women and gender into the curriculum. In J. Banks, & C. Banks (Eds.), *Multicultural education: Issues & perspectives*. New York: Allyn & Bacon.

Trombly, W. (1990, September, 13). Honig defends textbooks of real history. *Los Angeles Times*, p. A3.

Tyson-Bernstein, H. (1988). *A conspiracy of good intentions*. Washington, DC: Council on Basic Education.

"Whose Culture?" (1992, January). *Educational Leadership*. [Entire issue]

Chapter 13

Democratic School Reform: How Do We Get from Here to There?

Power concedes nothing without demand.
It never did, and it never will.

—Frederick Douglass

The Context for School Improvement

In *An Imperiled Generation: Saving Urban Schools* (1988), the Carnegie Foundation for the Advancement of Teaching stated the central issue of school improvement:

Without good schools none of America's hopes can be fulfilled. The quality of our education will determine the strength of our democracy, the vitality of our economy, and the promise of our ideals. It is through schools that this nation has chosen to pursue enlightened ends for all its people. And it is here that the battle for the future of America will be won or lost. (p. xi)

303

For many years this battle for the future has been waged in the courts—through the landmark Supreme Court decision in *Brown vs. Board of Education* (1954), the Civil Rights Act (1964), and other legislation brought about by the Civil Rights movement. All of these efforts made providing equal educational opportunity a national goal (Coleman, 1990). In spite of these admirable goals, progress has been slow for students of schools in poverty areas.

By the standards set by the Carnegie Foundation, we are losing the battle for America's future, at least in the cities. Why are urban schools (and rural poor schools) failing? Because for the majority of voters, for elected officials, and for the political and economic elites of this country, it is okay for these schools and these students to fail. These schools are brimming with immigrants and students of color. Some of our elected officials accept the assumption—the fundamentally racist assumption—that these students can't be taught. Or that it would cost too much to educate these students. It will, in fact, cost far more to *not* educate them.

One of the reasons for this poor progress was the nature of the school reform cycle that occurred in the United States from 1982 to 1992, a time in which reformers and critics were more concerned with furthering their own professional careers and winning elections than fostering genuine reform efforts.

The 1982 report *A Nation At Risk* initiated this reform cycle, which was based on conservative ideological passion and frequently poor research. The reform rhetoric of this period taught the public and the media to accept a set of conventional wisdoms: Today's graduates don't have the skills needed for a technologically advanced society; academic achievement is stagnant or declining; the nation is at risk due to a "rising tide of mediocrity"; and—crucial to this conservative strategy—none of these problems can be solved by putting more money into schools. The reformers deceptively blamed schools for the nation's economic decline, and the media pounced on the story with great enthusiasm.

The facts, however, precisely contradict the conservative ideology assault. In fact, the average U.S. high school student does as well today as the average student in the 1930s or the 1950s; in the 1990s, only 12.1% of total students do not complete high school or its equivalent. Students in the United States do almost as well as their counterparts in Japan, Korea, and Europe. Schools in middle-class areas are improving, not getting worse (Bracy, 1991, 1992).

It is important to note, though, that in spite of this progress for middle-class students, in the 1980s and 1990s, schools continued to fail most students from dominated and marginalized cultures. Although this reform received much attention from the press and elected officials, by 1992, little genuine reform had taken place in these students' schools.

Many educators and researchers are developing powerful intervention strategies, however. For example, the efforts by James Comer to integrate schools and their communities into a cooperative, supportive endeavor began in New Haven, Connecticut, and have spread around the nation. Henry Levin, a professor of economics and education at Stanford University, has helped to initiate a program of accelerated learning that is being tried in over 700 schools. This program seeks to treat all children as if they were gifted and immerse them in enrichment activities. Levin's strategy (1994) proposes "powerful learning" in accelerated environments based on the principles of:

1. building on the strengths of children and the staff;
2. empowerment combined with responsibility; and
3. unity of purpose at the school site. (pp. 2–3)

A number of schools used the conclusions of the "effective schools" literature as a catalyst to reform with notable results in Lozano Elementary School in Corpus Christie, Texas, and Lauderbauch Community School in San Diego, California. The Coalition for Essential Schools, associated with the work of Theodore Sizer, has created a loose coalition of schools working together for reform, although most of these schools serve an overwhelmingly European American suburban population.

In Kentucky, South Carolina, and a few other states, the reform dialogue helped to pass legislation bringing new monies and new standards to rural schools. In 1991, California implemented SB 1274, an initiative to encourage restructuring and experimentation in schools. In spite of a lack of funding, groups of teachers and parents in a number of schools have organized their own renewal efforts.

Richard Rothstein, in *The Myth of Public School Failure* (1983), says that:

[D]espite relatively modest increases in regular education funding, real progress is reflected in reduced dropout rates, higher test scores for whites and especially minority students, improved minority college attendance, and more students going into science and engineering. (p. 20)

However, while the average student in the average school is doing well, many inner-city and poverty-stricken rural schools are disaster areas. For the vast majority of poor and minority schools, there has been no substantial improvement. At the beginning of the decade, schools failed African American, Latino, and poor students; at the end of the decade, schools continued to fail these students.

The Carnegie Foundation for the Advancement of Teaching summarized the crisis this way:

[W]e are deeply troubled that a reform movement launched to upgrade the education of all students is irrelevant to many children—largely black and Hispanic—in our urban schools. In almost every big city, dropout rates are high, morale is low, facilities often are old and unattractive, and school leadership is crippled by a web of regulations. There is, in short, a disturbing gap between reform rhetoric and results.

The failure to educate adequately urban children is a shortcoming of such magnitude that many people have simply written off city schools as little more than human storehouses to keep young people off the streets. We find it disgraceful that in the most affluent country in the world so many of our children are so poorly served. (p. xi)

While middle-class students of all ethnic groups are doing reasonably well, a persistent crisis of race and poverty affects those schools serving poor people and people of color. The educational crisis is not generalized—it is specific. Underfunded and dysfunctional schools are destroying educational opportunity for some students and destroying some communities. These specific schools need substantial reform and substantially more money.

Few of the efforts of the conservative reform movement focus specifically on schools failing to meet the needs of poor and cultural minority students. A recent California report, *The Unfinished Journey: Restructuring Schools in a Diverse Society* (Olson, 1994), finds that

> Based on our look at schools, multicultural curriculum is not a feature of the school restructuring movement, despite the presence of an increasingly diverse population. . . . The bilingual education field remains largely marginalized from the school restructuring field. (pp. 182, 218)

And in *Resolving a Crisis in Education: Latino Teachers for Tomorrow's Classrooms* (1993), the Tomas Rivera Center staff states:

> Teacher education programs have failed to meet two crucial challenges: the need to produce more Latino teachers and the need to improve the way they prepare all teachers to work with Latino students. The problem is clear: the culture, language, race, and social status of the student population has changed radically over the past 20 years, while those of the teaching force have not. (p. 8)

The same could well be said for African American and most new immigrant students.

Increasing numbers of parents are giving up on schools. Some place their children in "safe" church schools, others initiate home schooling, some support school "choice" plans, and still others support the establishment of all-male or predominantly black academies. These are the responses of a population that doubts the effectiveness of public schools for their children. Middle-class parents achieve the same ends by moving to the suburbs, "better" neighborhoods, and by establishing "magnet" schools for their children.

School improvement efforts benefit from an ideological commitment to schools serving as vehicles for social mobility. Although schools generally fail this challenge, the ideological commitment itself gives reformers an opportunity to promote change. Like the Civil Rights Movement, a campaign for radical democratic school improvement can call on political leaders to live up to the promise of equal schooling.

The Failure of Conservative School Reform

If the conservative agenda of the period from 1982 to 1992 was to improve the quality of schools, then it failed. If the agenda was to preserve and extend the privileges of the well-off sector of society, to justify underinvestment in education in poverty areas, and to prevent schools from serving to advance political and economic democracy, then conservative school reform was successful.

Dennis Carlson, in *Teachers and Crisis: Urban School Reform and Teachers' Work Culture* (1992), offers a comprehensive assessment of the conservative school reform effort. Reform was presented as a management issue. New school bureaucracies were created. Business management ideas were advocated and applied. School failure was presented as a technical issue, subject to a new science. These directions for school reform suppressed the ideological issues of equality of opportunity. Conservative school reform advocates portrayed bilingual and multicultural education as divisive and a distraction from important issues. Carlson asserts that the reformers argued that new management and control systems, along with an emphasis on remedial drills and skill development, would improve schools for all students (Carlson, 1992).

During the reform decade, political advocates such as William Bennett blamed teachers for poor instruction. They continually argued that more money was not needed to improve schools—a patently false claim. By arguing based on the ideological position that all schools were in a crisis of mediocrity, legislators and antitax advocates in many states avoided consideration of basic issues such as class size, per-pupil expenditures, and unequal funding. The reality is that some middle-class schools could benefit from reform, but most middle-class schools work. But the educational system as a whole—especially schools in our cities and schools serving poor and minority children—is terribly underfunded. In many cities such as New York, Newark, Chicago, and Los Angeles, political mismanagement and educational bureaucracies strangle the schools and consume funds intended for classrooms.

Let us be clear. Most schools in urban areas are unable to provide the equal educational opportunity called for by our national ideals and constitutional law. There will be no substantial change in the quality of urban education without substantial new funds allocated to these schools. The children in these schools need and deserve the same quality of buildings, teachers, materials, and resources as the affluent neighborhoods.

While conservatives blamed teachers and ethnic minorities for school failure, Joe Fernandez, formerly the Chancellor of New York City's public schools, argues in *Tales Out of School* (1993) that we must begin a serious analysis of school reform by looking at our federal priorities. He notes that in 1991 U.S. Government expenditures were as follows:

- $9 billion for education
- $45 billion for the Persian Gulf War
- $160 billion for savings and loan bailout
- $294 billion proposed military budget for 1992 (p. 6)

Clearly, urban schools fail in large part because our nation refuses to invest in its children.

The 1982–1992 school reform movement had little positive impact on the quality of education for students in urban America. In some states, such as California, and in most major cities, all real reform has stopped—crushed by an endless series of budget crises for state and local governments. In this cycle of school reform, discussion was dominated by professional school managers, consultants, and managerial and business representatives. While they presided over another decade of urban school failure, they studiously avoided discussion of democratic goals and imperatives.

Seymour Sarason, an authority on school change, correctly noted that this reform movement refused to consider schools as an interconnected system of actors. Instead it worked from a management production model in which the students were supposed to be the products. And it failed (Sarason, 1990). In looking at schools as a series of unconnected parts, reformers ignored the perspectives of teachers, students, and the parents of the disenfranchised students who were failing to learn. Rather, the business-class reformers took care of their own short-term self-interests and developed reform proposals that scapegoated schools for the problems of society and the deteriorating economy.

Conservatives and their allies in the business community successfully passed legislation in over half of the states, including California and Kentucky, that called for reform. California's SB 1274 and similar efforts at "restructuring" offer hope of breaking the stranglehold on education held by several entrenched administrative bureaucracies. But conservative efforts, based as they are on the myth that nearly all schools are in crisis, have not generated sufficient new funds for reform and have not concentrated the funds provided in neighborhoods and schools with the most needs. Struggles for equal funding in New Jersey, Texas, Ohio, and Michigan have raised the basic and central issue of unequal funding between districts. Unfortunately, equalizing funding does not necessarily lead to an improvement in education. California, in both *Serrano vs. Priest* and Proposition 13, leveled funding to almost equal, yet inadequate, levels for all public school children.

National Goals for The Year 2000

Although the conservative reform effort failed to improve schools, the themes from this effort continue to dominate governmental discussion. In 1989, the nation's governors, co-chaired by then-Governor Bill Clinton, announced goals for U.S. education. The governors' goals were accepted by President Bush in April of 1991 and are listed here:

By the year 2000:

1. All children in America will start school ready to learn.
2. The high school graduation rate will increase to at least 90 percent.
3. American students will leave grades four, eight, and twelve having demonstrated competence in challenging subject matter including English, mathematics, science, history and geography; and every school in America will ensure that all students

learn to use their minds well, so they may be prepared for responsible citizenship, further learning, and productive employment in a modern economy.

4. U.S. students will be first in the world in science and mathematics achievement.
5. Every adult American will be literate and will possess the knowledge and skills necessary to compete in a global economy and exercise the rights and responsibilities of citizenship.
6. Every school in America will be free of drugs and violence and will offer a disciplined environment conducive to learning. (p. 3)

After the May 1992 riots and rebellion in Los Angeles, President Bush said that these plans for school reform were the cornerstone of the government's response to poverty and a racially divided society.

The Clinton administration, elected in 1992, interrupted the conservative reign and took a positive step toward improving schools by reversing a decade of blaming teachers for the school crisis. Conservatives, such as Secretaries of Education Bill Bennett and Lamar Alexander and Director of the National Endowment of the Humanities Lynne Cheney, had used their positions to support the conservative network of consultants and think tanks and to advance conservative ideas in the media.

President Clinton interrupted this network, but did not create a positive alternative that focused on bringing an equal opportunity agenda to school reform. He chose to focus on the bipartisan efforts of Goals 2000 rather than respond to the Los Angeles riots and the growing crises in our cities.

Unfortunately, in March 1993, Congress chose to continue the failed emphasis of recent conservative reform efforts by passing the *Goals 2000: Educate America Act* (Public Law 103-227). Setting goals and standards allows members of Congress to appear to respond to the school crisis while making few real changes in schools that systematically fail a substantial portion of our children, particularly poor students and students of color. By passing goals and not allocating new money, elected officials avoid the issues of raising taxes and spending money that any serious effort to provide equal opportunity would require. Efforts by Congressman Major Owens and the members of the Congressional Black Caucus to include language making it national policy for students to have an "opportunity to learn" were defeated in the U.S. Senate. A small but well-organized conservative voting block relies on the Senate's undemocratic method of apportionment (two Senators from each state) to stop democratic initiatives at the national level. In passing Public Law 103-227, Congress said that its purpose was to provide a framework for meeting the National Education Goals by "promoting coherent, nationwide, systemic education reform."

Congress added the following additional provisions to the original goals as drafted by the governors:

- The Nation's teaching force will have access to programs for the continued improvement of their professional skills and the opportunity to acquire the knowledge and skills needed to instruct and prepare all American students for the next century.

- Every school will promote partnerships that will increase parental involvement and participation in promoting the social, emotional, and academic growth of children.

Congress further declared that "the gap in high school graduation rates between American students from minority backgrounds and their non-minority counterparts will be eliminated."

Professor Allan Odden (1992) cites the document *America 2000: An Education Strategy* (U.S. Department of Education, 1991) to assert that there is an emerging consensus on a macrostrategy for accomplishing school reform.

- Set clear student learning outcomes.
- Have a high quality curriculum program.
- Implement site-based management, allowing teachers to have a major influence and power over implementation.
- Have an assessment or monitoring system calibrated to world class standards that indicates the degree to which objectives are being accomplished.
- Have a sharp-edged accountability system with rewards and sanctions. (Odden, 1992, p. 12)

National standards, accountability, and testing efforts continue the failed emphasis of the conservative reformers. The nation's schools went through a similar accountability phase in the 1970s that produced little measured school improvement. New York, California, Iowa, and other states have used standardized testing for over 20 years with no measured improvement in the quality of schools. Along with school choice efforts, standards and accountability are conservative ideological projects that substitute rhetoric for school reform on these topics.

Elliot Eisner, Professor of Education at Stanford University and an authority on school reform, says "focusing on standards is a 'superficial distraction' from the real work of making schools better places for teachers and students. . . . What do you do if the children do not achieve the standards?" (Eisner, 1994, p. 6).

Conservative efforts to substitute testing and standards for school reform and adequate school funding illustrate well Senator Daniel Patrick Moynihan's cryptic comment: "There is good money to be made out of bad schools" (1993–1994, p. 14). Specifically targeted reform is required to improve schools that are presently failing.

Conservatives Return to Power

The basic federal legislation on education, the Elementary and Secondary Education Act, was reauthorized by Congress in the fall of 1994. The legislation set the major directions for federal school policy, including the Goals 2000 efforts.

The fall elections of 1994 brought conservative Republicans to power in the House and reopened questions about the direction of school reform. The Republican conservatives won a 26-vote majority in the House, the first time in 20 years that they had lead that chamber, and they won a 5-vote majority in the Senate. Republicans won this election after receiving only 17% of the total potential vote, while the Democrats received 16%. Nearly 67% of adults either chose not to vote or were prevented from voting by state registration laws.

Central themes to the new Republican leaders of the Congress included severe budget cuts for social programs and re-allocating power and decision making to the states. In drafting their budget, they cut $1.6 billion dollars in current spending by the education department. Thus, Republicans are using their budget powers to reduce and reverse the emphasis on school reform of the Goals 2000 project.

A favorite legislative strategy is to propose block grants or direct funding transfers to the states rather than to fund "categorical" programs such as Head Start or desegregation assistance. The block grant approach eliminates the past achievements of gaining funding for programs for language minorities, the economically disadvantaged, and the disabled.

The 10 additional Republican victories at the state levels in 1994, along with the new Congressional policy of allocating more power to the states, have changed the focus of much school reform debate. Republicans have adopted "voucher systems" in Minnesota and have proposed voucher systems in Pennsylvania, New Jersey, Ohio, Texas, and California. Vouchers are checks that are given directly to parents to allow them to pay tuition and to select a school for their children. Parents use these vouchers to shop for a school of their choice, including religious and private schools. Advocates of voucher systems assume that competition among schools for parental dollars will improve the quality of schools.

Throughout the nation, low-budget school districts—urban and rural—have been left behind by structural changes in the economy and by school reform rhetoric. Only a small portion of the children in these districts are prepared for jobs in a high-technology, high-wage future. In California, over a decade of school budget cuts has led to class sizes of 35 to 40 students and low-quality schooling for over half of all Latino and African American students. In large classes, only the bright and the aggressive receive a high-quality education. The average and the below average simply pass through school.

This nation spends about $200 billion per year on education in kindergarten through grade 12. We spend less per student than 16 other modern, industrialized countries. Our economy needs well-educated workers. We cannot permit schools to continue to fail students of color. When schools succeed for the middle class and fail for working-class students and students of color, schools contribute to a crippling division along economic and racial lines in our society. Schools, as public institutions, must find ways to offer all children equal educational opportunity. Yet reformed schools are more exceptions than the common pattern, particularly in urban America.

School Reform Networks

Working with networks or consortiums of schools helps to sustain efforts for systemic change. Leading networks with some focus on education for cultural diversity and equity include:

1. *Accelerated School Project.* Henry M. Levin, Director, Stanford University, Ceras 109, Stanford, CA 94305-3084. Telephone: (415) 725-1676.
2. *Association for Effective Schools.* 8250 Sharpton Road, R.D. Box 143, Stuyvesant, NY 12173. Telephone: (518) 758-9828.
3. *California Tomorrow.* Fort Mason Center, Building B, San Francisco, CA 94123. Telephone: (415) 441-7631.
4. *Coalition of Essential Schools.* Brown University, Box 1969, Providence, RI 02912. Telephone: (401) 863-3384.
5. *Foxfire Fund.* P.O. Box 541, Mountain City, GA 30562. Telephone: (706) 746-5318.
6. *Success for All.* Robert Slavin, Director, Center on Research on Effective Schools for Disadvantaged Students, Johns Hopkins University, 3505 N. Charles Street, Baltimore, MD 21218. Telephone: (410) 516-8809.

Teacher Unions and School Reform

Anyone serious about democratic educational reform should address their concerns first to teachers. Teachers are the major resource available improving education. Teachers' salaries are the largest part of any school budget. It is the teachers—not administrators—who conduct the basic educational process. Most teachers want to do better and would welcome an opportunity to help more students to succeed. Reformers interested in improving the educational opportunities for poor kids should first look to help teachers perform their jobs better. On the other hand, the conservative school reform movement criticized, demeaned, and commanded teachers. It seldom listened to them.

Over 75% of teachers are represented by unions. Teachers responded to the growth of educational management and bureaucracy in the 1960s and 1970s by organizing increasingly militant unions. A serious effort at school reform must engage teachers through their unions. Teachers interested in school reform need to bring their unions with them. Unions have the organization and political capital that can assist or defeat efforts to democratize public schools.

Teachers' unions have learned to use political organization and money to protect their members' interests. Organized teachers' unions often protected school funding in the midst of a public fiscal crisis.

In the wake of the California tax revolt of 1978, which limited the growth of the state budget, California teachers' unions in 1988 led a successful campaign to pass a ballot proposition protecting school funding from cuts. But the 1990–1993 recession produced an unprecedented budget crisis in California and 25 other states. Policy paralysis in national and state governments led to severe cuts in many school budgets. This financial crisis froze teachers' salaries and demoralized teachers. In major cities such as Los Angeles, school boards attempted to cut teachers' salaries by up to 14%.

The California Teachers Association (NEA) used its powerful organization, political skills, and money to successfully limit attempts to cut state educational funds in grades K through 12, while the California Federation of Teachers (AFT, AFL-CIO) worked for the same goal by using its ability to bring together coalitions of other trade unions. Union political power forced an undisciplined and weak Democratic party to defend school funding.

In California, Michigan, Illinois, Massachusetts, and many other states, the prolonged economic crisis stopped most efforts at school reform. In 1992, teachers' unions and particularly the NEA devoted substantial staff and money to the successful effort to defeat George Bush and elect Bill Clinton. They judged the changing of a president as a top priority.

In 1993, conservative organizations in several states campaigned for school "choice" systems. After more than a decade of federal budget deficits and state budget crises, schools were underfunded. Achievement scores were declining as new immigrant populations entered schools. Since some schools were failing, conservatives argued for "breaking the monopoly" of public education. They wanted to use tax monies to finance private, even religious schools. Minnesota and Wisconsin adopted limited "choice" programs. With strong union financial and volunteer efforts, Colorado and California voters defeated similar proposals that would have challenged the current system of public education.

Vouchers

The effectiveness of voucher systems has not yet been tested or evaluated. Voucher advocates, usually conservatives, argue that competitive markets will improve schools and that schools need more competition, not more money. Voucher systems seek to make formerly public schools more competitive and more private. Advocates contend that, as parents shop for the best schools, competition will force changes in public education and will eliminate the current bureaucratic waste of resources.

Both teachers' unions oppose vouchers as attacking the very essence of public schools and for taking desperately needed funds from public schools to be used in private ones. In addition, voucher proposals do not address the particular failure of schools to educate the poor and students of color extensively discussed in prior chapters. There is ample evidence of bureaucratic administrative mismanagement of school systems particularly in New York, Chicago, Philadelphia, Boston, and other major cities.

Campaigns for voucher systems particularly seek support from African American and Latino parents, pointing to the failure of public schools to provide quality education in these neighborhoods. Additional major support comes from supporters of religious-based parochial and private schools. The approach of voucher systems in emphasizing competition and ignoring the serious issues of race, class, tracking, and low expectations, rather than providing more funding, offers little hope for real school improvement. Voucher efforts seek to privatize schools rather than to reform schools for the democratic common good.

Massachusetts, California, and other states have experimented with "charter schools" as a step toward providing more parental choice. State laws vary, but in essence, schools are given a "charter" to operate the school outside of the many restrictions, rules, and constraints of state laws, textbooks, and union contracts. Charter school advocates argue that charter schools give parents a wide variety of choices on kinds of schools.

While unions have led the efforts to protect school funding and to elect pro-education legislators and a new president, they have not provided substantial leadership in the struggle to improve the quality of education in our urban educational wastelands.

In their struggles for adequate funding, the unions usually do not challenge inequality of funding among districts and schools. Some districts are adequately funded, others are not. Poor districts often receive limited funding and have poor schools. Taxpayers in well-funded districts are reluctant to pay more taxes to educate children in inner-city and rural areas. Battles over property taxes, directly tied to inequality of school funding, have been the major educational battleground in New Jersey, Ohio, Michigan, and Texas. Teachers' unions have not been leaders in the fights for equal redistribution of state school funds. Suburban taxpayers see their schools as adequate and assume that the chaos of inner-city education must be related to the ethnicity of the students, not unequal funding (Fernandez & Underwood, 1993).

When schools in general are under attack, unions provide a vital and vigorous defense. But when only poor schools suffer ruinous underfunding, unions have been unwilling to commit their resources to the struggle for equality of opportunity.

Union protection of teacher salaries while school conditions in many urban areas become intolerable makes them ineffective leaders for today and unstable coalition partners in the struggle for equity-based school reform. As a group, teachers are overwhelmingly European American and middle class, and their unions are tenuous allies in the effort to restructure schools to serve poor and working-class students. It does not appear to be in their short-term self-interest to change (Carlson, 1992). When parents in New York, Chicago, and Los Angeles unite to demand school reform, the teachers' unions often end up defending the existing schools, funding, and even administration.

Teachers' unions can be expected to continue to protect the jobs of their members and fight for increased funding. They can be expected to resist new demands such as requiring teachers to become bilingual, and they will deny any allegation that teachers are to blame for school failure.

Democratic school reform will require the creation of a new coalition of teachers, parents, and new political forces. Many excellent and devoted teachers become union activists in hopes of affecting educational policy. These union activists must be involved in school improvement agendas. Teacher-activists can insist that their unions work in partnership with parents to pursue substantial school reform.

Activists concerned with producing equal educational opportunity for children from urban districts will have to reconceptualize the roles of their unions. Negotiations with an entrenched management may produce improved benefits, but it will not produce educational improvement. Management-preferred solutions lead to process reforms and more teacher involvement, not to substantial school improvement for teachers and students.

Carnoy and Levin (1985) describe solutions as coming from a different direction: "By contrast, the push for greater student and teacher rights, for social mobility through education, for educational expansion, and for programs to improve educational equity have come from the political and social movements" (p. 110).

The ideas of the Accelerated Schools' efforts to build on the teachers' and students' strengths, initiated by Henry Levin, along with building positive and humanizing relationships within schools, promote change. Teachers must struggle within their unions to improve their own work lives *and* the lives of their students. Unions must be forced to recognize the need for both humanizing struggles.

A beginning was made toward union activism on educational reform in August 1994, in Portland, Oregon, at the meeting of the National Coalition of Educational Activists. A group of union teachers wrote a document, "Social Justice Unionism," reprinted in the Autumn, 1994, issue of *Rethinking Schools*. They said, in part:

> Public education is at a crossroads and so, too, are our unions. Our society's children face deepening poverty and social dislocation, challenges and higher expectations with declining resources. . . . As the organized core of the teaching profession, education unions remain central to resolving these crises. (p. 12)

Parent Participation

U.S. schools work best for middle-class children. For the poor, for African Americans, Latinos, Native Americans, and European Americans in low-income districts, education is often a disaster. The failure of urban education should not surprise us. Cities fail to offer decent living conditions for the poor. They fail in police protection, health, fire, housing, and jobs. Living conditions for the working poor have deteriorated for more than 20 years. The streets in many areas are not safe from crime and violence.

Federal policies have exacerbated the problems of urban areas. A U.S. House of Representatives study (Moynihan, 1992) said:

> Between 1970 and 1991, the value of AFDC (Aid to Families with Dependent Children) benefits declined by 41%. In spite of the proven success of Head Start, only 28% of the eligible children are being served. As of 1990, more than 18 billion dollars in child support went uncollected. At the same time, the poverty rate among single-parent families with children under 18 was 44%. Between 1980 and 1990 the rate of growth of the total federal budget was four times greater than the rate of growth of children's programs. (p. 13)

At times, the legitimate pent-up anger and resentment of people focus on schools. Many parents are angry. They have paid a heavy price to raise and protect their children in a hostile and often violent society. Few understand how the economic crisis and the structural fiscal crisis of government reproduce school failure. Parents are frustrated by the decay in our society and our schools. Some blame their children for their failure at school. Others, frustrated and without voice, resent schools. Underfunded, understaffed schools steal their children's best hopes for the future. Parents get angry. They do not know a way to stop schools from damaging their children's future (see Figure 13.1).

Our communities want and deserve better schools, particularly in urban areas. Parent participation in school reform can produce significant change. In Chicago from 1986–1990, an aroused public took control of schools, cutting the power of the central administration and of the educational bureaucracy and reestablishing local control of their schools.

Decentralized decision making and school site-based management assist parental participation. Although some parents are aggressive, others are not. Effective teachers and principals eliminate policies and barriers that keep parents out of schools. Unfortunately some experienced teachers have learned to view parents as pushy or aggressive, difficult to contact, and resistant to the teachers' recommendations (National Coalition of Education Advocates, 1991). Faced with rebellious students, teachers may blame parents for failing to teach students proper behavior and respect. This often hostile or distant relationship between teachers and parents is the result of long and complex histories of miscommunication and school failure. Only frequent and positive contacts between the school and parents will improve these relationships, and a close working relationship is required for school reform.

Developing an effective home-school communication system is the first step toward positive parent participation. Individual teachers can reach out to community agencies and initiate frequent and respectful communication with parents. Students in our difficult neighborhoods need the coordinated and cooperative support and guidance of neighborhood support agencies. Working together, teachers and parents can create new advocacy systems for students. Teachers and parents can create tutoring, counseling, and conflict resolution systems to improve school conditions. Local community organizations can assist schools by offering parents classes on discipline, team building, group dynamics, and advocacy skills.

Figure 13.1   Example of an Effective School Site Council

When a School Site Council Works

While raising six children, Ella sat on her share of school/parent advisory groups. She soon learned that parents usually don't have much power; paid professionals dominate decision making. Ella is relieved that parents are the majority on this council. Some folks have reservations about parents having the most votes, but not Ella. In her mind, numbers aren't the real issue. The real issue is parity.

Ella knows—and others are learning—that although the council sets policies, principals and teachers run the school all day long, day in and day out. For professional educators, running a school is both a career and a full-time job. They needn't worry about staying well informed; they are automatically inside the information loop. And information is power.

For real negotiations to occur between the community and the school, a more equitable sharing of power is necessary. Even very active parents spend relatively little time at the school—almost always after meeting the demands of their own employment. Parents' involvement with school is usually limited to the amount of time their children attend it. Having a majority of parents on the council is one way to offset this inherent power imbalance.

In addition to Ella, council membership includes five other parents, two community representatives, two teachers, and the principal. Ella knows educating children requires a strong partnership between parents and professional educators, and she works hard to build it. Because Ella deeply values a true partnership, she is determined that the shared decision making of the council not play itself out as "anti-teacher." She knows this would sabotage the school's ability to support the academic success of its students.

She always perseveres until consensus can be reached at council meetings—even when the agenda is full and meetings run overtime. In fact, the council has agreed to not adjourn until all disagreements are settled. She is also very clear about the council's role. It sets policy. It hires the principal. It develops a plan that sets priorities for school improvement. It prepares and approves a budget supporting the school improvement plan.

The school's professional staff has a strong voice in helping to shape policy and is responsible for its implementation. A professional advisory committee works closely with elected teacher members of the council who carry staff views on various issues to council meetings. The professional advisory committee plays a large role in determining the content of curriculum and rethinking teaching methods.

Note. From *The Good Common School: Making the Vision Work for All Children* (pp. 12–14) by National Coalition of Education Advocates, 1991, Boston: Author. Reprinted by permission.

Parents should be involved in setting clear goals for school reform. The vague, informal goals of education presently in use in many school districts do not adequately serve the more than 13 million poor, alienated, and disenfranchised. These goals were established long ago and passed on from generation to generation. They lack a current analysis of society by educational professionals. Advocates for change need to develop new goals that will help to overcome the particular failure and isolation of oppressed communities. These new goals should concentrate on preparing students for the realities of life in an urban society and a rapidly changing economy.

New Goals for Democratic School Reform

Parents and teachers working together can plan curriculum and strategies to teach the following ideas:

1. In a changing economy, education in specific skills and work habits is necessary for a decent standard of living. These skills, habits, and knowledge are learned through the students' own efforts.

2. The essentials of education for economic survival include basic numeracy and literacy skills, computer fluency, bilingualism (in Spanish, Japanese, or Chinese, for example), and the skills of working in a collaborative team.

3. The real results of not getting a good education and dropping out of school are poverty, family disintegration, and lost opportunity.

4. Schools and other institutions can organize to help students move out of poverty toward work and democratic participation.

5. Crime, drugs, gangs, teenage pregnancy, and dropping out of school are destructive to students' opportunity for quality education.

6. Through democracy, people can fashion a political-economic system of good jobs, a decent standard of living, provisions for good health, and education for everyone in society.

7. Individual students can choose to work for an education and against crime, social destructiveness, and poverty.

8. Students and adults have a right to seek an improved standard of living—and to change structures that prevent the development of a decent standard of living.

9. Not all school failure is due to the individual's lack of effort or ability. School practices can be examined and changed to promote success and equal opportunity.

10. Our comprehensive secondary schools, including community colleges, should allow students to make career decisions, change their directions, and work toward economic opportunity.

Few people will disagree with goals 1 through 5. However, goals 6 through 10 are controversial because they challenge the existing distribution of power and wealth. They are congruent with the values expressed in the United States' Declaration of Independence but are contrary to the conservative ideological position that government and economics are separate spheres of life.

While teaching these new goals, reformers need to recognize—not romanticize—the destructive nature of aspects of life among the poor and growing urban underclass in our society. Poorly informed middle-class writers and conservative ideologues have distorted and abused the concept of underclass. They substitute their own stereotypes and criticisms of the poor for analysis. Social forces in our society, such as racism, job ceilings, class bias, and poor schooling, create a culture of school failure for the poor. Individual children are the victims of this oppression. These children deserve educational opportunities to work their way out of this oppression. Tragically, while conservatives and their allies spent the last decade attacking teachers and schools, another generation of Latino, African American, and Native American young people was abused, neglected, and tracked toward poverty.

Elected Officials Continue a Separate and Unequal System

Refusal to invest substantial money in poverty-area schools damages the educational and economic opportunities of one out of every four children—at least two out of four Latino, African American, and immigrant children. As parents, teachers, and political leaders, we must stop the destruction of school opportunities before it creates yet another generation of crime and violence.

Elected officials generally represent the existing political balance of power. They regularly call on schools to solve the growing problems of unemployment and economic restructuring in our society. But the evidence is not convincing that either elected officials or corporate leaders want substantial democratic reform of schools. The middle-class majority of voters have reasonably good schools. The poor seldom vote. Few political leaders respond to the needs of nonvoters.

In the macroeconomic sector of school funding, little has changed during the school reform cycle. Federal dollars for education are limited. Most states receive between 6% and 12% of their total school budget from the federal government, while the larger portions of budgets are provided by states or local governments. New Jersey, a high school-funding state, receives only 3.3% of its school funds from federal sources. It receives 43% from state sources and 53.7% from local sources. California, a very low school-funding state, receives 8.6% of its budget from federal sources, 61.4% from state sources, and 30% from local sources. Alaska receives 12.6%, Mississippi 17%, and Massachusetts 6.1% from federal sources. Federal dollars are important, but totally inadequate to the crisis.

Advocates of democratic school reform unfortunately cannot rely on federal funding to assist them significantly to gain monies for the presently inadequate schools. Federal funds typically are distributed politically, not necessarily based on need. And there is little likelihood that federal funding priorities will change. The 1995 budget increase for Goals 2000: The Educate America Act, reflecting the Bush-Clinton efforts to promote new standards and assessment-based "reform" increased funds from $105 million in 1994 to $403 million in 1995. Meanwhile the Chapter 1 grants, the basic financial aid for impoverished children, rose from $6.4 billion to $6.7 billion dollars for the nation. Efforts to reform Chapter 1 by concentrating these anti-poverty funds in poor schools and districts were blocked by powerful Congressional representatives who preferred to gain a share of the dollars for their own districts.

Since 1984, both major political parties have received a majority of their campaign funding from corporate interests. A majority in both parties consistently voted to lower corporate taxes and to pass the resulting budget deficits along to the states and to working taxpayers. William Greider (1992) has well described how these well-established interests promote gridlock in government and prevent any substantial change of national priorities toward funding education. The Reagan-Bush era also impoverished the states by shifting tax burdens for health and welfare programs onto the state budgets so that few states could afford to invest substantial new dollars in schools.

Political leaders hold hearings, publish reports, and fund research projects and pilot projects, but they are unwilling to tax the privileged and unwilling to reform education for the poor. Corporate interests dominate the state governments at least as well as they control the national agenda.

A few states, notably New Jersey, New York, and to a lesser extent, Kentucky and North Carolina, are attempting to tax themselves to finance a high-quality school system based on the theory that high skills lead to high wages and economic growth. Such attempts to raise real substantial monies for public education are often vigorously opposed by conservative and antitax groups.

The several antitax crusades of the last 20 years have produced a devastating funding crisis for schools and other human services. Antitax groups and conservative school reform advocates combine to ensure that legislators and other elected officials seldom consider substantial new taxes for schools or funding equalization. In Texas, California, New Jersey, Michigan, and other states, legislative stalemates on this issue are endemic. Advocates for equal school funding have had to turn to the courts to even get a hearing on the need for equity of funding.

Over 14 states, lately including Michigan, Ohio, and Texas, have been forced by the courts to provide more equality in funding between districts, challenging a disgraceful practice of economic segregation. These struggles for equal funding offer hope to low-budget and low-funded districts. But this effort does not always lead to improvement. California responded to the Serrano Court decisions by substantially equalizing funding. The state now pays 61% of its education costs. But a series of state budget crises caused by recessions and antitax crusades has resulted in the per-pupil funding falling rapidly. California, once a state proud of its schools, now ranks about 41st out of the 50 states in per-pupil funding, and 50th out of 50 in providing counselors, librarians, or even computers for its students. The 1994 scores on the National Assessment of Educational Progress show that California's fourth graders rank 48 out of the 50 states in reading and last of the states in math. Underfunding schools destroys children's opportunities.

Separate, unequal, and inadequate schools and classrooms for African American and Latino students and for residents of urban ghettos and rural poverty pockets continue to be the primary characteristics of our educational system. Conditions such as these make a mockery of our constitutional ideals about creating a just, healthy, democratic society.

In 1954, the U.S. Supreme Court decided in *Brown vs. Board of Education of Topeka, Kansas* that seven-year-old Linda Brown could attend an integrated school because separate schools were never equal. Today Topeka schools remain segregated. In 1968, Demetrio P. Rodriguez sued the Edgewood School District in San Antonio, Texas, seeking equal educational funding for his children. The federal district court found Texas in violation of the equal protection clause of the U.S. Constitution, but this decision was overturned by the U.S. Supreme Court in 1973. In 1994, parents in Texas are still in court trying to get equal and adequate funding for their children and grandchildren.

There is a great deal that teachers and educational leaders can do to improve existing schools. But until the separate and unequal system of education is dismantled, the United States will not have high-quality education for all of our children and we will not have a healthy society.

In California and several other states, relatively equal state funding was mandated by the courts. In the California Serrano case, parents have applied three times to the courts for redress. However, the power of political privilege proved so strong that elected officials chose to comply by reducing public school funding across the board, even for middle-class students. Instead of increasing taxes to improve schools for all children, these politicians passed voter-pleasing tax reductions and tax limitations.

In the 40 years since *Brown vs. Board of Education*, both race and class privilege have been protected. Those in power consistently chose not to raise taxes, choosing rather to preside over the decline and destruction of a good part of the publicly funded school system. Separate, unequal, and inadequate schools continue to contribute to an even more divided society.

It is unlikely that federal or state funding will dramatically increase. And the important efforts to equalize funding within a state may lead to equal but totally inadequate funding, such as occurred in California. In our major cities—including, but not limited to New York, Chicago, Philadelphia, and Los Angeles—the school system bureaucracies are substantially inefficient, ineffective, and often corrupt, wasting desperately needed education funds intended for children. Our current corporate-dominated political and tax system, and both of our major political parties fail the test of school reform for the oppressed in our society.

Class privilege produces the slow and steady destruction of both educational opportunity and economic opportunity for those living in or near to poverty. The question is political. Do we or do we not choose to teach the children of the poor?

A traditional African proverb says, "It takes an entire village to raise a child." In the United States, we assign the task of raising children to teachers. Corporate America says we will educate the children of our executives in our affluent suburbs. Corporate leaders demand tax exemptions and low tax rates for their business properties and profits. Political leaders say there is no additional money for schools and ignore the glaring inequalities between schools in poverty areas and schools in affluent neighborhoods. Police forces, prisons, and entitlement programs demand ever-increasing portions of state budgets. Political interest groups (such as teachers' unions, administrators' unions, and business associations) each seek to protect their own privileged special interest positions in state budgets. Many parents are too busy struggling for a living to struggle for school reform. Other parents abandon their responsibilities to guide their children or even to vote in the interests of their children.

It may take an entire village to raise a child, but most of the adults in our village are too busy protecting their own privileges. Children in poverty schools are left to fend for themselves. In the streets and alleys of our urban ghettos, in hospital emergency wards, and in the prisons, our society is now reaping the results of not helping or encouraging our children to grow.

These problems are recognized by many. Donaldo P. Macedo (1993) summarized some of the results of continuing the present school system in the *Harvard Educational Review* (1993):

> It is indeed ironic that in the United States, a country that prides itself on being the first and most advanced within the so-called 'first-world,' over sixty million people are illiterate or functionally illiterate. . . . To the sixty million illiterates we should add the sizable groups who learn to read but are, by and large, incapable of developing independent and critical thought.
>
> . . . I believe that, instead of the democratic education we claim to have, what we really have in place is a sophisticated colonial model of education designed primarily to train state functionaries and commissars while denying access to millions, a situation which further exacerbates the equity gap already victimizing a great number of so-called "minority" students. Even the education provided to those with class rights and privileges is devoid of the intellectual dimension of true teaching, since the major objective of a colonial education is to further deskill teachers and students so as to reduce them to mere technical agents who are destined to walk unreflectively through a labyrinth of procedures. What we have in the United States is not a system to encourage independent thought and critical thinking. Our colonial literacy model is designed to domesticate so as to enable the "manufacture of consent." (p. 203)

Political struggles for changes in funding and school structures are important to creating new, more equal school opportunity. Unfortunately, political struggle takes time. Individual students and families need a strategy for the present. Under present political conditions, there are few additional resources to fund major educational reform.

Nevertheless, a realistic strategy for school reform must draw on resources presently available. Schooling is one of the few institutions in our society where parents and teachers can pursue democratic opportunity. Even with present limitations and weaknesses in our economy, individual schools and districts can make a positive contribution to the future for millions of children. Teachers and parents deserve vastly improved schools. In the poor school districts of Socorro and Ysletta, Texas, for example, voters have kept average class size to under 25, while California has allowed its average class size to surge to over 35.

Parents and teachers can influence school policies through organized political effort. In New Mexico, 19 Indian pueblo tribes and the Navajo (Dineh) nation now have control of their own schools. Black colleges have long provided high-quality education and produced professionals ready to compete with anyone in the American job market. Chicanos now serve as superintendents and run school boards in cities and towns in Texas and California.

The educational bureaucracy creates a constantly changing series of terms to describe programs for school change—for example, "restructuring," "school-site management," and "reform." Community control of schools and the more current trend of "restructuring" do not always improve educational opportunity. New York is presently moving away from community control while Chicago, Miami, San Diego, and other cities are experimenting with local site management.

Affirmative action in hiring is a strategy that results in limited changes. In New York, Chicago, Oakland, Los Angeles, and El Paso, hiring and patronage systems have passed into the hands of Latinos, Native Americans, and African Americans with little improvement for the children in schools. None of the essential elements of change—democratic control, affirmative action, parental participation, teaching reform, good teacher preparation, and improved bilingual and multicultural curriculum—is by itself enough. All are important for substantial school reform.

School Reform Is Political

We face a massive challenge in our society: to create a new educational system that fulfills the American ideal of equal educational opportunity for all students. Restructuring schools and creating new schools that are equitable across race, class, and gender, and that provide quality genuine citizenship preparation and job skills for our dynamic economy require fundamental changes in the structures and practices of those schools presently failing. Multicultural school reform seeks to create equal opportunity in schools as a step toward democratic opportunity in the economy and society.

First, democratic educators must recognize the value-laden nature of present curriculum and school-funding decisions, which support the current unequal distribution of wealth, power, and authority in our society—they are anti-democratic.

The National Coalition of Educational Activists (1994) reveal the value-laden nature of the reform struggle when they argue:

> Conditions of teaching and learning must dramatically improve. Class sizes need to be much smaller, bureaucracy reduced, preparation and planning time increased. Teachers

need more time to personalize instruction, to assist their students, to plan with their colleagues, and to evaluate what works.

We must address the negative impact of racism—both on U.S. education and within the educational reform movement. Schools must give a high priority to confronting the long history of racism that has shaped our education system. (pp. 12–13)

To strengthen our democracy, we must defeat racism, sexism, and class bias. Schools, because they are public institutions, have an obligation to provide equal educational opportunity and to promote pro-democratic values. Whenever and wherever schools or school districts fail the test of equal opportunity, they must be changed.

Michael Apple and others have described how schools and the curriculum serve as arenas in the struggle for democracy (Apple, 1993; Bowers & Flinders, 1990; Sarason, 1990). A pro-democracy school reform movement must emerge. Persons with a self-interest in change—teachers, students, parents, community organizations, and unions—must work together to eliminate failure, tracking, educational discrimination, and inequality.

Our professional and political challenge is to build a new civil rights movement in education. Multicultural education in democratically run schools is central to this struggle. Should we fail, we may lose our best hope for building a democratic society.

The following brief examination of six reform ideas will illustrate how the new coalition could directly pursue democratic reform.

1. *Problem.* A crisis exists in most urban schools. The cumulative effect of problems in society and in many urban neighborhoods has led to disorder in schools, failure, and dropping out of over half of all Latino and African American students. Urban schools are different than suburban schools. They must respond to different political forces. In our large urban centers, the economically and politically powerful do not have their children in the public schools.

   Reform. In schools with dangerously low scores, the class size should be reduced to fewer than 22 students per teacher. The state and federal governments should concentrate resources on education in poverty areas not just for the sake of education but as a strategy for preventing unemployment, crime, and future economic crises. Several states already have adopted programs to provide small classes.

2. *Problem.* Under present conditions, teachers are exhausted, burned out, and leaving the profession. The exit of teachers brings a constant flow of inexperienced, new teachers. New teachers are assigned to the most difficult schools.

   Reform. Teachers in difficult schools should receive two hours of paid preparation time per day. The time would be used to read more student papers, plan improved instruction, and coach individual students. New teachers in difficult schools particularly need mentoring and support from experienced teachers. Experienced teachers and site administrators in these schools also need time, coaching, and support for renewal.

3. *Problem.* Many students are not learning sufficient content and skills. Teachers' unions and legislatures believe, perhaps inaccurately, that improved salaries will attract "more qualified" teachers.

   Reform. Provide year-round schools for all students who fall behind in grade-level standards. Teachers could elect to work 11 or 11.5 months per year for a 20 percent increase in pay. Fewer students would fall behind in skills since they would receive supplementary instruction to catch up each summer.

4. *Problem.* Large, impersonal secondary schools lead to alienation and isolation of the students. They permit violence.

   Reform. Break up existing large schools into smaller campus communities of 250 to 300 students each. Teams of teachers would work with the same students for at least two consecutive years. Schools would become more personalized and responsive to students' emotional needs.

5. *Problem.* Many schools are unable to provide the safe and orderly environment necessary to learning. Schools in many communities are plagued by violence, gangs, drugs, and other abuses brought in from the deteriorating neighborhoods. Teachers in these schools are forced to spend a great deal of time on control and management, areas in which they have limited success and expertise. The disruption and disorder prevent teaching and learning. (See Toby, 1993–1994.)

   Reform. Prepare and train students as conflict resolution negotiators. Hire social workers, drug counselors, parents, and others to improve campus discipline. Through mediation and conflict resolution, students exhibiting serious disruptive behavior should be sent immediately to a social worker or counselor with the time and skill to deal with the problem. Teachers could spend their time teaching. Increased teaching time will help all of the students.

6. *Problem.* Many non-college-bound teenagers find high school boring and irrelevant. They leave school poorly prepared for work.

   Reform. Redesign the secondary education programs to promote a school-to-work transition similar to those in Japan and Europe. Provide high-quality, job-related education by age 16. Apprenticeship programs should bridge the gap between school and work. Early entrance into the world of work will encourage a more responsible, mature approach to work.

These six reform proposals illustrate that real, substantive reform is available. The real problem is that the distribution of political power in our society and in our schools prevents communities from moving in the direction of reform.

School Reform: One School at a Time

We know how to improve our schools. The report *Making Schools Work for Children in Poverty*, prepared by the Commission on Chapter 1 (1993), said:

> The fact is that we know how to educate poor and minority children of all kinds—racial, ethnic, and language—to high levels. Some teachers and entire schools do it every day, year in and year out with outstanding results. But the nation as a whole has not yet acted on that knowledge, even though we need each and every one of our young people to master high-level knowledge and skills. (pp. 46–47)

The essentials of teacher-initiated reforms are:

- Building on the strengths of students in bilingual and cross-cultural classes,
- Positive human relations,
- Cooperative learning,
- Critical thinking,
- Coaching and encouragement, and
- Democratic empowerment.

Active parental participation, a multicultural curriculum, a focus on critical thinking, teachers serving as cultural mediators, cooperative learning, the untracking of classrooms, special programs for students who speak limited English—all are necessary to reform a school. In addition, research into "effective schools" undertaken between 1976 and 1987, some of it problematic, led to the following summary of characteristics of schools where working-class students and students of color perform at national and state averages (see Figure 13.2).

Effective schools research offered great hope in that it demonstrated that some schools (about 1.6%) in impacted areas worked well to promote student achievement.

In *Teachers and Crisis* (1992), Dennis Carlson argued that effective schools research was unfortunately often used to strengthen state and school district bureaucracies rather than to improve schools. Well-paid administrators and consultants used a reductionist, and somewhat inaccurate, view of the research to support their own ideological commitment to drill and low-level skills development (Carlson, 1992). By using this research to further the processes of control, school managers maintained their own positions and salaries while not improving schools.

Figure 13.2   Summary of Characteristics of Effective Schools

A. A well-functioning total system producing a school social climate that promotes positive student outcomes

B. Specific characteristics crucial to the development of effectiveness and thus to a positive school social climate

    1. A safe and orderly school environment

    2. Positive leadership, usually from the formal leaders

    3. Common agreement on a strong academic orientation
        a. Clearly stated academic goals, objectives, and plans
        b. Well-organized classrooms

    4. Well-functioning methods to monitor school inputs and student outputs

C. A positive school social climate

    1. High staff expectations for children and the instructional program

    2. Strong demand for academic performance

    3. High staff morale
        a. Strong internal support
        b. Consensus building
        c. Job satisfaction
        d. Sense of personal efficacy
        e. Sense that the system works
        f. Sense of ownership
        g. Well-defined roles and responsibilities
        h. Belief and practice that resources are best expended on people rather than on education software and hardware

Note. From "Effective Bilingual Schools: Implications for Theory and Practice" by T. Carter & M. Chatfield, 1986, November, *American Journal of Education,* pp. 200–231. Reprinted with permission.

Many school sites have demonstrated that quality education can be produced in a neighborhood by focusing on the essentials of effective schools and encouraging the dynamic intervention of parents, teachers, and administrators. The Coalition of Essential Schools, organized by Theodore Sizer, has continued this effort. Unfortunately, only a few members of the coalition represent urban, multicultural schools, notably the Central Park East Schools in New York City. Other coalition members tend to be suburban schools where reform has a substantially different character.

One of the positive results of effective schools research is that parents and teachers armed with this evidence can demand high-quality schooling for their children. They can break the pattern of schools and teachers accepting low levels of performance.

Unfortunately, to date there is little evidence of maintaining effective schools serving minority populations for a sustained period. Budgets get slashed, schools lose faculty, principals get promoted, and schools too often revert to recycling the present inequality of educational opportunity.

A Process of School Change

Individual schools and school systems are difficult to change. Popkewitz, Tabachnick, and Wehlage (1982) describe some of the formal regularities that keep schools from changing:

> Like all institutions, schools function according to rules and procedures which give coherence and meaning to everyday activities and interactions. Such rules and proce- dures are embodied in regularized patterns of behavior, specific vocabularies and par- ticular roles (teacher, pupil or administrator). So potent are institutionalized patterns that the social structuring experienced in schools, channels the thought and action of the participants, giving definition and meaning to both school reform and pedagogical practice. Institutionalized patterns, for example, evoke various theories, folk knowl- edge, myths and common sense ideas which make a school's activities and the roles and relationships of its personnel appear normal and reasonable within their setting. Theories of teaching, learning, or administration are believed to be sensible because they are consonant with the background information people have about schools and classrooms. Similarly, the focus of and questions asked in current educational theories are seen as reasonable because they fit in with our beliefs about existing patterns of interaction. (pp. 8–9)

James Banks (1994) has noted three major approaches to school reform: cur- riculum efforts (Chapter 12), achievement-oriented approaches (Chapters 8 to 11), and intergroup or prejudice reduction approaches (Chapters 6 and 8). Chap- ters 7 and 13 argue for an additional approach, the empowerment of families and communities to take control of their own future. School reform strategies require new skills for teachers and parents if they are to become advocates for change in large, complex organizations like schools.

Chapter 2 focused on the concept of culture. Understanding culture and the skills of a cultural mediator are essential for those who are to become the agents of educational change. Consider the school as a community or a culture. School com- munities are dynamic and changing. Schools may be in the process of becoming either more educational or less educational, more democratic or less democratic.

The school community, like a culture, has a variety of participants. It is not homogeneous. The faculty, students, parents, and other school participants have diverse points of view and orientations toward change. Inertia and resistance to change are constants in most schools. Teachers, students, and staff tend to con- tinue conducting business in the ways they have always done. Each member of the community has his or her own strengths, goals, and expectations. Some teachers are excellent instructors, some are skilled at nourishing and support, while only a few demonstrate political clarity about the social regularities of schooling in our society. Members of the community have a variety of networks they work within and to which they respond. Each member of the community also has his or her weaknesses. For some, it might be lack of instructional skills, for others too much ego, and still others too little self-confidence. Some teachers listen to others and seek to support their colleagues, some perennially complain, while still others teach their classes and choose not to interact with parents and the community.

While some members of the school community may desire school improvement, others have accepted the present school functioning as natural. Most teachers have learned an individualist perspective. They see successful teaching and learning as primarily a product of individual effort. The social constraints to learning are seldom analyzed or responded to in a planned manner. Individual teachers respond to their own priorities and agendas. For example, an excellent teacher might want to become a principal. Another may be planning to leave teaching. These individual agendas interact within the school community. When a school reform effort responds to an individual's agenda, the person will participate. If these private agendas are not addressed, some teachers pursue their individual goals with little regard for the needs of the school community and thus thwart school reform.

Teachers committed to democracy need to work in teams within the school community. They share common goals: to improve the educational opportunities of their students and to improve their own work environment in a manner that enhances creativity, strengthens support mechanisms, and promotes democratic decision making. The teachers and parents interested in democratic reform can begin the process by recruiting members of the community to develop a common vision of what constitutes a good school. The parents, teachers, and administrators should come to agree on a vision for their school and a plan for how to achieve the necessary changes. This book has argued that the appropriate agenda is multicultural democracy. The students in an impoverished neighborhood school should have at least the same resources, the same class size, and receive the same quality of instruction as students in the district, the county, or the state. The conservative movement has never addressed this commitment to equal opportunity. The multicultural democratic reform movement must make equality of resources a central value, along with excellence.

Other members of the school community may well prefer to continue the school culture as it presently functions. Efforts at change will challenge the existing systems of rewards, privileges, authority, and definitions of self-worth. The lives of teachers and parents are full and busy with personal and family priorities. Busy parents and exhausted, stressed teachers may be reluctant to invest the substantial effort needed to create and sustain school reform. Over a period of two to three years, reluctant participants must either be convinced to join the school improvement effort or be asked to step aside.

Positive experiences of planning and improving the school culture can lead to nourishing experiences for teachers and to a healthier work life (Cintrón, 1993). Positive experiences with community or parent councils improve communication and develop trust and respect. Development of mutual respect contributes to a safe environment for children and teachers and dispels and reduces destructive personal conflicts.

Most school administrations know how to manage the school; few know how to *improve* a school. New leadership skills are needed for teachers, administrators, and parents. Change occurs best in a cooperative setting. The recent efforts at administration-led reform illustrate that when adults are pressured and managed, they resist or avoid participation. But when teachers and parents engage in the decision making, control, and direction of significant aspects of the students' lives, they become imaginative and responsible. Cooperative leadership helps teachers and parents find new solutions to old problems.

Conditions Under Which Change Occurs

The implementation of multicultural education, like any complex process of change, requires certain conditions. Dr. Tom Carter (1990), long a facilitator of school-site renewal, lists the conditions that facilitate change as follows:

1. Participants must first recognize a need to change.
2. Participants must understand the change.
3. The change must offer more rewards or less pain than would continuing the present practices.

For serious school improvement to begin, the participants in the school community must acknowledge that a problem exists that requires a response. Although individual teachers and parents recognize that there are problems, the dominant conservative ideology encourages them to treat the symptoms, such as a high dropout rate, in isolation, rather than building the broad-based coalition needed for structural school reform. Teachers, fully engaged and often overworked by the pressures of their daily lives, may regard fundamental school improvement as unrealistic. The stress of teaching under current conditions leaves little time to reflect on improving or changing the school environment. Teachers have learned to accept the cruel reality of the current tracked and unequal school system as normal or natural, even though they would not send their own children to low-tracked schools.

Seymour Sarason, in *The Predictable Failure of Educational Reform* (1990), argues that change efforts fail when considered primarily in isolated fragments. A teacher may decide to change a book, a course, or a strategy, but not a school. The isolation of teachers and the fragmentation of change efforts produce limited results. Most isolated change efforts depend on teachers' working harder. Since good teachers already invest 60 to 70 hours per week in teaching, grading, and preparation, strategies based on teachers' devoting more time to their work are not likely to succeed.

For example, consider a project where a group of teachers want to change the curriculum to build on the diverse cultural heritages and languages of their students. Faculty promoting the change first need to help the other teachers recognize that a problem exists that requires attention or a resolution. Some teachers believe that the school is doing fine or that celebrations of holidays like Cinco de Mayo or Martin Luther King, Jr.'s birthday are sufficient for multicultural education. Other teachers are exhausted by stress in their personal lives or from previous efforts at school improvement. Tired teachers often respond that the school is doing as well as can be expected considering the home lives of the students. Yet other teachers are frustrated from efforts to teach students who read poorly or students who suffer from stress in their homes and communities. This group of teachers wants change, but not a change that requires more work from them.

Democratic reform requires a new vision of school (see Figure 13.3). Teachers and parents need to work together to set new goals. Working together with parents to develop a vision of the possible provides an important initial step toward school improvement. Unfortunately, most teachers have never observed an effective school serving students of color. They may have seen individual inspiring teachers, but not an effective school. Teachers and parents may want to take a field trip to observe high-quality schools while working on their own vision statement.

A second step is to describe the initial changes so that members of the faculty and the school community understand the proposal. Unclear proposals for change increase resistance by parents and teachers. For example, most teachers and parents misunderstand and fear bilingual education. Because teachers hold a

Figure 13.3 The Interactive Change Process

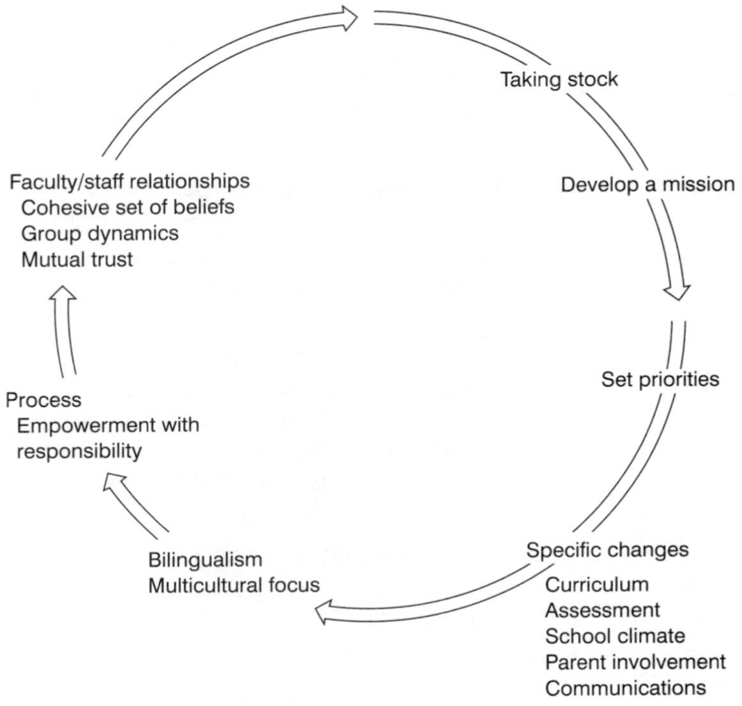

Taking stock

Develop a mission

Set priorities

Specific changes
Curriculum
Assessment
School climate
Parent involvement
Communications

Bilingualism
Multicultural focus

Process
Empowerment with
responsibility

Faculty/staff relationships
Cohesive set of beliefs
Group dynamics
Mutual trust

wide variety of definitions and opinions on multicultural education, a clear description of the changes needed and the resources needed to bring them about can reduce the resistance of skeptical teachers.

Thirdly, proposed changes must offer more rewards or cause less stress than continuing the current practices. For example, many teachers respond positively to changes that allow them to be successful with the rapidly increasing number of limited-English-speaking students. Programs such as cooperative learning or conflict resolution give the teacher an opportunity to observe, to listen, and to coach students. The teacher gains rewards and benefits from such school improvement efforts and will usually support them.

Undoubtedly most change will occur at the local school site level, not on the state or national level. Teachers interested in democratic school reform need to work closely with their unions to avoid unnecessary and destructive confrontations. The National Coalition of Educational Activists records efforts of where the teachers and parents have developed valuable mutually supportive relations with local union organizations. Rochester, San Francisco, and numerous other cities have experimental projects of union participation in school-site management and reform (see Figure 13.4).

Reforming the School System for Multicultural Democracy

Could the major systems of schools throughout the nation be reformed? Of course they could. It would cost money, billions of dollars, money that would be returned as savings in the employment, criminal justice, and welfare systems. But substantive reform is possible only if and when a major redivision of power occurs. Frederick Douglass spoke to this issue in 1849 when he said:

Figure 13.4   Elements of a Change Process

1. Align with one of the intervention systems (Success for All Accelerated Schools, Comer Schools, Coalition for Essential Schools, California Tomorrow).
2. Select a coach knowledgeable about the change process.
3. Separate the data on achievement (desegregate the data) to be certain to monitor the achievement of all groups (language minority, ethnic minority, social class, and gender).
4. Plan your interventions based on the culture of the school.
5. Involve teachers and their unions in the planning.
6. Plan parent participation at the center of the planning and change.
7. Make specific curricular, assessment, and faculty recruitment plans for language acquisition and multicultural education.

The whole history of the progress of human liberty shows that all concessions yet made to her august claims have been born of earnest struggle. The conflict has been exciting, agitating, all absorbing, and for the time being putting all other tumults to silence. It must do this or it does nothing. If there is no struggle there is no progress. Those who profess to favor freedom, and yet depreciate agitation, are men who want crops without plowing up the ground. They want rain without thunder and lightning. They want the ocean without the awful roar of its many waters. This struggle may be a moral one; or it may be a physical one; or it may be both moral and physical; but it must be a struggle. Power concedes nothing without demand. It never did and it never will. (p. vii)

Bilingual education has helped the immigrant student to succeed. Multicultural education is a necessary response to the growing diversity in the nation. It teaches students to respect and value diversity, to value and to empower their own communities.

The current administrative and educational leadership approaches to school reform are exhausted. They seek to improve the efficiency of the current system, leaving sexism, racism, and class privilege intact. To achieve more fundamental reforms, progressive teachers need to add the skills of community organizing (Bobo, Kendall, & Max, 1991; Lowe, Peterson, & Tenorio, 1993). We need to build trust and solidarity with the parents, the students, and the communities across antagonistic racial, class, and cultural boundaries. We need to join with other social movements to build a progressive majority to adequately fund schools and other social programs.

Teachers enter the school improvement struggle by analyzing the realities of racism, sexism, and class inequality in their own schools. Democratic, anti-racist teachers seek to restructure the teacher-student relationship. Teachers are needed to assist students in finding their own identities and achieving success in this often violent and unfair world.

While waiting for systemic reform, we can recognize our schools as sites of cultural struggles. When students respond to control with silence or sullen resistance, democracy and education both lose. Within the context of our individual school, we can participate in cultural struggles, educational solidarity, mutual support, and shared decision making.

Existing schools can enter into dialogue with their students and their communities. Teachers need to re-convince the village to help them educate their children. Only when communities come together for positive goals can we stop the gang violence and gang recruitment presently destroying our schools.

A Choice Between Two Futures

Two possible scenarios present themselves. William Greider describes the political deadlock and economic crises facing our nation in *Who Will Tell the People?* (1992). In this deadlock, schools can continue as they are. A segment of our society will be well-educated, and a another segment will continue to fail. The economic crisis for working people and people of color will continue to grow (Coleman, 1987; Lowe & Miner, 1993).

In *Thinking for a Living: Education and the Wealth of Nations* (1992), Ray Marshall and Marc Tucker contend:

> . . . [T]here is every reason to believe that if we continue on our current path, our national prosperity will evaporate. A rising portion of our people will sink into poverty and the well being of our middle class will slowly decline, thereby rending the political fabric of America, perhaps beyond repair. . . . (p. xiv)

Within this scenario there will continue to be a few effective schools serving poor and minority students and a few effective classrooms created by dedicated teachers and administrators.

As an alternative, teachers, parents, and activists could organize a political coalition of conscience and caring that revitalizes our communities. Nonvoters and disenfranchised voters would begin to participate politically as advocates for their children, their schools, and their communities. A progressive agenda for school reform would insist on equality of opportunity.

A bold democratic agenda raises the fundamental political issue of providing equal funding. Our commitment to democracy permits nothing less. This second democratic scenario would develop one community at a time. Some neighborhoods and some schools in San Antonio, El Paso, Los Angeles, Oakland, Chicago, New York, Corpus Christi, Santa Fe, and others are already making progress.

The possibility for change exists. Democratic reform is unlikely to emerge from the cynical intellectualism prevalent among faculty of our universities and colleges. Higher education serves primarily to maintain the present system. The present class- and race-stratified system of publicly funded higher education transfers significant resources from the working poor to a professional elite. Currently popular proposals such as school choice and using public monies to fund private education will not lead to democratic reform (Chubb & Moe, 1989). Rather than continue these privileges, a reform movement must build on the American working people's beliefs in progress and equality of opportunity. These traditional values can triumph over the hostility and violence produced by racism, sexism, and class bias presently accepted as "normal" and natural in our schools.

The growth of the African American, Asian, and Latino middle class—a direct result of the civil rights movements' use of political power to reduce discrimination based on race—provides direct evidence that racism can be combatted through education and public policy.

Summary

Schools cannot bring an end to the economic restructuring and the growing inequality in our society. Schools are not an independent social force that shapes the society. Rather, unchallenged, they reflect the political and economic forces in the society.

Advocates for democratic multicultural education challenge these forces. We consider schools as sites for the struggle for or against more democracy in our society. In schools, teachers and parents can participate in creating a more democratic society. Carnoy and Levin (1985) describe it in this way:

> Democratic struggles (by parents and teachers) are important for achieving the types of schools and economy that serve the broadest needs of our society and our citizenry. Even under the present circumstances—when the quest for improved educational services for minorities, the poor, and the handicapped is under attack by conservative interests—it is the marshaling of social movements and the democratic forces that places limits on the retrenchment and makes the battle costly for the other side. But beyond this resistance, the struggle enables the tide of hegemony of the narrow interests of the wealthy to be countered in the courts, at the polls, in the media, and on the streets. Continuing struggle, together with the failures of existing policies to meet the larger concerns of democracy, will increase the power of democratic coalitions for fairness, equity, and participation. (p. 267)

Paulo Freire has revealed the essentially political nature of education. The struggle for educational improvement and educational equality is a struggle for or against democratic participation. The struggle for multicultural education, based in democratic theory, is an important part of the general struggle against race, class, and gender oppression.

Schools serving urban and impoverished populations need fundamental change. These schools do not open the doors to economic opportunity. They do not promote equality. Instead, they recycle inequality. They prepare less than 50% of their students for entrance into the economy and society. A democratic agenda for school reform includes insisting on fair taxation and equal funding for all children. Schools must be de-tracked, and the territorial tracking revealed between suburban and urban districts redistributed in favor of equality.

Schools exist in a political/economic context. A new movement for democratic multicultural school reform must be based on the well-established equal opportunity ideals of *Brown vs. Board of Education* and public education. Teachers and parents have a common self-interest in improving their schools. Quality schools, safe schools, equal schools, can serve as a unifying force in our society and provide hope for our children.

We cannot build a safe, just, and prosperous society while we leave behind 20% or more of our students in urban ghettos, barrios, and rural poverty. We know which schools need improvement, and we know how to improve them. Teachers can pursue democracy with instruction in multicultural education, critical thinking, cooperative learning, language acquisition, and empowerment. Teachers and parents together face a political choice. Shall we continue providing high-quality schools only for the middle and upper classes, and underfunded, understaffed schools for the poor? Or, shall we work together to improve schools that are presently failing? Without justice there will be no peace.

Questions Over the Chapter

1. Define equal educational opportunity. What are the legal bases for this goal?
2. Why do you think there are so many diverse reform efforts rather than one agreed upon reform plan?
3. Most school reform reports recognize a need for new skills. What skills are needed for entrance into the emerging economy? What attitudes and values are most urgently in need of clarification among our young people (for example, violence, drugs, and crime)?
4. According to the reports and research cited, which kinds of schools are doing well? Which schools are in a crisis?
5. In 1991, President Bush declared National Goals for the Year 2000. What evidence can you cite to indicate that we are closer to achieving any of these goals today? How has the legislation passed in 1994 advanced these goals?
6. Examine the Goals for the Year 2000. Which goals have we made little or no progress on?

Activities for Further Study of School Reform

1. Explain what is the federal role in education. What percentage of the local school budget comes from the federal government?
2. List three reasons that some parents are frustrated with the schools. Share your list with other students.
3. If you are working in a school, would you be pleased to have your own child attend this school? Share your answer with other students.
4. List three activities parents could assist with at your school site.
5. If you are a resident of one of the states struggling with equal funding (such as Kentucky, Ohio, New Jersey, and Texas), investigate how the conflict over equal funding is affecting school budgets. What difference does this make?
6. Decide on the three most urgent reforms you could initiate as a student teacher (such as language support, coaching, or conflict resolution, for example). Make a plan for initiating one of these efforts.
7. Decide on three urgent reforms you would initiate as a tenured, experienced teacher. What are the differences between the answers to questions 6 and 7?
8. Do you plan to join a teachers' union? Explain your choice. What are the advantages and disadvantages of each choice?

References

Apple, M. W. (1993). *Official knowledge: Democratic education in a conservative era.* New York: Routledge & Kegan Paul.

Banks, J. A. (1994). *An introduction to multicultural education.* Boston: Allyn & Bacon.

Bobo, K., Kendall, J., & Max, S. (1991). *Organizing for social change: A manual for activity in the 1990s.* Washington, DC: Seven Locks Press.

Bowers, C. A., & Flinders, D. J. (1990). *Responsive teaching: An ecological approach to class-*

room patterns of language, culture, and thought. New York: Teachers College Press.

Bracy, G. W. (1991, October). Why can't they be like we were? *Phi Delta Kappan*, pp. 105–117.

Bracey, G. W. (1992, October). The condition of public education. *Phi Delta Kappan*, pp. 104–117.

Carlson, D. (1992). *Teachers and crisis: Urban school reform and the teachers' work culture.* New York and London: Routledge.

Carnegie Foundation for the Advancement of Teaching. (1988). *An imperiled generation: Saving urban schools.* Princeton, NJ: Author.

Carnoy, M., & Levin, H. M. (1985). *Schooling and work in the democratic state.* Stanford, CA: Stanford University Press.

Carter, T. P. (1990). Effective schools and the process of change. Unpublished manuscript. Sacramento, CA: California State University-Sacramento.

Carter, T., & Chatfield, M. (1986, November). Effective bilingual schools: Implications for theory and practice. *American Journal of Education*, pp. 200–231.

Chubb, J. E., & Moe, T. M. (1989). *Politics, markets and America's schools.* Washington, DC: Brookings Institute.

Cintrón, J. (1993). A school in change: The empowerment of minority teachers. In H. T. Trueba, et al. *Healing Multicultural America* (pp. 115–132). Washington, DC: The Falmer Press.

Coleman, J. (1987). *Public and private high schools: The impact of communities.* New York: Basic Books.

Coleman, J. S. (1990). *Equality and achievement in education.* Boulder, CO: Westview Press.

Commission on Chapter One. (1993, January). Making schools work for children in poverty. *Education Week*, pp. 47–51.

Douglass, F. (1849). Letter to an abolitionist associate. In K. Bobo, J. Kendall, and S. Max. (1991). *Organizing for Social Change: A Manual for Activity in the 1990s.* Washington, D.C.: Seven Locks Press.

Eisner, E. (1994, January). *Update.* Alexandria, VA: Association for Supervision and Curriculum Development.

Fernandez, J., & Underwood, J. (1993). *Tales out of school: Joseph Fernandez's crusade to rescue American education.* Little, Brown & Co.

Greider, W. (1992). *Who will tell the people? The betrayal of American democracy.* New York: Simon & Schuster

Hopfenberg, W. S., Levin, H. M., & Associates. (1993). *The accelerated schools resource guide.* San Francisco: Jossey-Bass.

Levin, H. (1994, Spring). Powerful learning in accelerated schools. *Accelerated Schools Project.* Stanford, CA: Stanford University.

Lowe, R., & Miner, B. (Eds.). (1993). False choices: Why school vouchers threaten our children's future. *Rethinking Schools: An Urban Education Journal* Milwaukee, WI: Rethinking Schools, Ltd.

Lowe, R., Peterson, B., & Tenorio, R. (Eds.). (1993, Spring). *Rethinking schools: An Urban Education Journal*, 7(3). Milwaukee, WI: Rethinking Schools, Ltd.

Macedo, D. P. (1993, Summer). Literacy for stupification: The pedagogy of big lies. *Harvard Educational Review*, pp. 183–204.

Marshall, R., & Tucker, M. (1992). *Thinking for a living.* New York: Basic Books.

Moynihan, D. P. (Winter, 1993–1994). Defining deviancy down. *American Educator*, pp. 10–18.

National Coalition of Education Advocates. (1991). *The good common school: Making the vision work for all children.* Boston, MA: Author.

National Coalition of Educational Activists. (1994, Autumn). Social justice unionism. *Rethinking Schools*, 9(1), 8, 12–13.

Odden, A. (1992). School finance and educational reform. *Rethinking School Finance: An Agenda for the 1990s.* San Francisco, CA: Jossey-Bass.

Olson, L., et al. (1994). *The unfinished journey: Restructuring schools in a diverse society.* San Francisco, CA: California Tomorrow.

Popkewitz, T. S., Tabachnick, B. R., & Wehlage, G. (1982). *The myth of educational reform.* University of Wisconsin Press.

Resolving a Crisis in Education: Latino Teachers for Tomorrow's Classrooms (1993). Claremont, CA: The Tomas Rivera Center.

Rothstein, R. (1983, Spring). The myth of public school failure. *The American Prospect.*

Sarason, S. B. (1990). *The predictable failure of educational reform: Can we change course before it is too late?* San Francisco, CA: Jossey-Bass.

Toby, J. (Winter, 1993–94). Everyday school violence: How disorder fuels it. *American Educator*, pp. 4–9, 44–48.

U.S. Department of Education. (1991). *America 2000: An Education Strategy.* Washington, DC: Author.

Appendix A

A Brief Guide to African American History

Prior to 1500	Africans live in diverse cultures and communities in Africa. Several societies are as advanced as their European counterparts, except they do not have firearms.
1619	The first Africans arrive in the English colonies of North America.
1619–1800	African endure massive slave trade and forced migration to North, Central, and South America and the Caribbean.
1783	Slavery is recognized in the U.S. Constitution.
1808	Slave trade legally ends, but illegal slave trade continues. Societies made up of former slaves dominate parts of the Caribbean and coastal areas of Central and South America.
1817	Frederick Douglass is born.
1831	Nat Turner leads a slave rebellion.
1857	Dred Scott decision is made in the U.S. Supreme Court; racist and anti-African violence common in the North.
1861–1865	U.S. Civil War.
1863	January 1, 1863—President Abraham Lincoln issues the Emancipation Proclamation. All slaves in the states fighting against the Union forces are declared free.
1865	Thirteenth Amendment to the U.S. Constitution abolishes slavery.
1866	Fourteenth Amendment to the U.S. Constitution recognizes all persons born in the United States or those who are naturalized as citizens of the country.
1866–1876	Reconstructionist state governments develop populist cooperation for public schools and other reforms.
1870	Fifteenth Amendment to the U.S. Constitution allows most African American males to vote.
1875–1880	Reconstructionist governments in the South are overthrown by racial conflicts, intimidation, and economic pressure. African American col-

	leges are established (Tuskegee, Fisk, Morehouse, and Howard) to prepare Black leadership.
1887	Marcus Garvey is born on August 17, 1887.
1896	*Plessy vs. Ferguson*, the Supreme Court rules that "separate but equal" facilities are constitutional.
1905	W. E. B. DuBois and others establish an African American scholarly tradition.
1909	The National Association for the Advancement of Colored People (NAACP) and other major civil rights organizations are formed in response to anti-Black violence, lynchings, and intimidations.
1914	Marcus Garvey organizes the Universal Negro Improvement Association, establishing a Black nationalism position.
1916–1919	African American troops participate in the invasion of Mexico and in World War I.
1919	W. E. B. DuBois organizes the First Pan-African Congress. Race riots against Negroes occur in Washington, DC, Chicago, and Arkansas.
1921	The Harlem Renaissance, a cultural, literary movement flourishes in New York.
1929	Martin Luther King, Jr., is born.
1942	Congress of Racial Equality (CORE) is founded.
1943–1946	Violence against African Americans leads to a series of "race riots" in Texas, Detroit, Harlem, Athens, and Philadelphia.
1950	Ralph Bunche awarded Nobel Peace Prize for service to the United Nations.
1954	On May 17, 1954, the U.S. Supreme Court rules in *Brown vs. Board of Education* that school segregation is illegal.
1955	Rosa Parks' refusal to yield her seat on a bus ignites the Montgomery Bus Boycott in Alabama.
1957	The Southern Christian Leadership Conference (SCLC) is organized by Dr. Martin Luther King, Jr., and other clergy. President sends U.S. troops to Little Rock, Arkansas, to prevent interference with school integration.
1960	Sit-in movement starts in Greensboro, North Carolina, and spreads quickly. Over 1,000 arrested throughout the South.
1961	CORE organizes Freedom Riders to integrate bus facilities throughout the South.
1963	More than 250,000 persons participate in march on Washington, DC. Civil rights demonstrators are attacked by police in Birmingham. Dr. Martin Luther King, Jr., and hundreds of others are arrested. A landmark civil rights bill passes.
1964	Malcolm X (Malcolm Little) leads a complex movement of cultural integrity and independent Black political action. Civil Rights Act signed on July 2, 1964.

1964–1971	The rise of Black nationalist forces and culture redefine the Civil Rights Movement.
1965	Malcolm X is assassinated. Campaigns of nonviolent direct action lead to the passing of a Voting Rights Bill, allowing African Americans to register and vote in the South. Later court decisions based on the bill encourage voting by Latinos and other minorities.
1966	Dr. Martin Luther King, Jr., leads a protest demonstration of 125,000 in New York against the war in Vietnam.
1968	Dr. Martin Luther King, Jr., is assassinated assisting striking sanitation workers in Memphis, Tennessee. Riots follow in many major cities. Poor Peoples Campaign creates a Resurrection City in front of the White House to protest poverty in the United States. Black and Latino parents struggle for community control of schools in Oceanhill-Brownsville district of New York. Community control defeated by a citywide teachers' union strike in New York City.
1969	Assassination of Fred Hampton in Chicago. Destruction of the Black Panther Party by police infiltration and violence. COINTELPRO program of FBI.
1970–1979	Major growth of Black elected officials. Black college enrollment expands from 92,200 in 1960 to 341,000 in 1975. Emergence of Black feminist movement.
1971	Black and Afro-American Studies programs established on predominantly White university campuses.
1972	National Black Political Assembly in Gary, Indiana. Shirley Chisholm is a candidate for Vice President in the Democratic Party Primary. Coalition of Black Trade Unionists founded. Federal judge orders integration of Boston Public Schools against strong resistance.
1976	Democratic Party Convention has 508 elected Black delegates; 310 of them are women. Jimmy Carter elected, appoints Andrew Young to Ambassador to the United Nations.
1978	William Julius Wilson publishes *The Declining Significance of Race* seeking to establish a policy focus on the Black underclass. The Association of Black Sociologists denounces the thesis of *The Declining Significance of Race* for inadequate comprehension of the complexity of the Black experience in the United States.
1980	Miami Riots, a repetition of Black revolts in earlier decades, occur. Changing federal policies place traditionally Black colleges at risk for survival. Election of Ronald Reagan ends a decade of Black political progress. Black industrial working class impacted by economic shift away from heavy manufacturing to service industries. Black Congressional Caucus provides a unified electoral agenda.
1982	Economic recession accelerates loss of good-paying jobs for African American industrial workers.
1983	After years of pressure, Dr. Martin Luther King, Jr.'s birthday becomes a national holiday. Harold Washington elected mayor of Chicago.

1984	Rev. Jesse Jackson organizes a National Rainbow Coalition within the Democratic Party. Alphonse Pinkney publishes *The Myth of Black Progress*.
1988	Rev. Jesse Jackson becomes a leading contender in the Democratic Primaries.
1989	Ron Brown becomes Chairperson of National Democratic Party. Continued dramatic growth of numbers of Black elected officials.
1990	Michael Wilder elected governor of Virginia. African Americans elected as mayors of New York, Seattle, and Denver. National economic policies take funds from anti-poverty programs. The society becomes increasingly divided. "Curriculum of Inclusion" debate emerges in New York. Afrocentric views of curriculum reform are proposed by Leonard Jeffries and Molefi Kete Asante. Inner-city schools become increasingly segregated. Disparities of funding between urban and suburban districts reach crisis proportions. In a voter rebellion, Chicago residents gain community control of their schools.
1991	Clarence Thomas replaces Thurgood Marshall on the U.S. Supreme Court. Black conservatives gain substantial media attention. The nation becomes increasingly racially polarized. Ku Klux Klan, Skinheads, and other White racist groups gain membership. Ex-Klan leader, David Duke, runs for governor of Louisiana in the Republican Party and receives 40% of the vote. Ron Daniels, former National Director of the Rainbow Coalition, runs for President as an independent candidate. Detroit, New York, Milwaukee, and other large school districts experiment with all-African male elementary schools in grades 1 through 3 to reduce the crisis of Black males.
1992	April 28–May 3: Lack of hope and economic opportunity combine with police brutality and lead to urban riots and rebellion in Los Angeles and is soon followed by other cities. At least 56 people are killed and thousands arrested. Fifty percent of dead and 35% of those arrested are African Americans. These were the most violent and costly civil disturbances since 1863. No systematic or structural response is made by either political party. Carol Moseley Braun becomes the first African American woman elected to the U.S. Senate.
1993	Benjamin Chavez becomes head of the NAACP. A new generation of African American intellectuals and leaders emerges. Cornel West publishes *Race Matters*. African Americans serve in the President's cabinet. U.S. Congressman, Ron Dellums, chairs the powerful Armed Services Committee.
1994	Benjamin Chavis is dismissed as head of NAACP. This major civil rights organization is divided and in turmoil.
	A book, *The Bell Curve*, by Charles Murray and Richard Herrnstein, is published and widely discussed. The book cites data that its authors allege demonstrate the old and often disproved thesis that African Americans tend to have lower IQ scores than the national average.

While Democrats lose heavily in the fall elections, African Americans continue to hold 38 seats in Congress, 19% of the total Democratic party vote.

1995   Myrle Evers Williams, wife of slain civil rights leader Medgar Evers, is elected as Chair of the Board of the NAACP.

Affirmative action programs come under attack in many states and at the national level. This program, central to the progress of African Americans and women, becomes a target of conservatives and the center of political debate. African American conservatives continue to receive increasing media coverage.

Appendix B

A Brief Guide to Mexican American (Chicano) History

200–800 A.D.	Mayan civilization flourishes with advanced agriculture and cities.
1400	Aztec civilization conquers the several major civilizations of present-day Mexico. All societies forced to pay tribute.
1521	Hernán Cortés, leading the Spaniards with thousands of Indian allies, defeats the Aztecs.
1598	Juan de Onante establishes a Spanish city near present-day Santa Fe, New Mexico. First European settlement of the area.
1610	First Catholic Church is established in land presently part of the United States at Santa Fe, New Spain.
1630	Some 30 small settlements and missions are established along the trail to Santa Fe.
1680	The poet, Sor Juana Ines de la Cruz, becomes the Americas' first published feminist writer in Mexico City. Pueblo Indians revolt against brutality and slavery imposed by the Spanish. Pueblos drive the Spanish from the Southwest. Pueblos maintain their cultures and societies in the area. Some members of the Isleta Pueblo forced to retreat and serve the Spanish.
1692	The Spanish return with superior military power and occupy Santa Fe. Resistance continues to Spanish conquest. The Spanish are able to control cities and a few missions. They survive, at times, by raiding and stealing from pueblos.
1718	Missions and presidios are established in San Antonio, Texas.
1769	Fray Junipero Serra and the Franciscans establish the San Diego Mission and Presidio and later 21 California missions.
1810	Father Miguel Hidalgo is major leader of the Mexican War of Independence from Spain.
1821	Mexico bans slavery in Mexican territory including present-day Texas and the Southwest.

1836	Anglo Texas settlers seeking to maintain and extend slavery, rebel against Mexican rule. Anglo-Texans win the battles and declare Texas an independent republic. Eight Mexicans die in the Alamo on the side of the Texans.
1845	The United States annexes Texas.
1846	The United States invades Mexican territory and begins the Mexican American War. Mexico is deeply divided by internal strife. The United States seizes California with the assistance of Californio leaders.
1848	The Treaty of Guadalupe Hidalgo ends the war. Mexico is forced to give up one third of its territory. The Southwest becomes a part of the United States by conquest. The treaty promises that Mexican culture, language, and property rights will be respected.
1850	California becomes a state. The first constitution promises a bilingual California. Eight leading Californios, descendants of Spanish settlers, sign the constitution.
1850–1880	Mexican citizens in the Southwest are systematically deprived of their property and political participation by terrorism and court decisions.
1853	The United States purchases 45,532 square miles of Mexican land through the Gadsden Purchase.
1859	Juan N. Cortina leads a rebellion against Anglo domination in the Rio Grande Valley of South Texas.
1862	Battle of Puebla. Mexican forces defeat the French. Independence reestablished on Cinco de Mayo.
1870–1920	Texas Rangers control and harass Mexicans and keep them from civic participation. Poll taxes and other devices exclude Mexicans from voting.
1877	Mexicans rebel against Anglo privatization of the salt beds in the El Paso Salt War.
1886–1889	A series of armed resistance efforts against Anglo land seizures occurs in Northern New Mexico.
1910	Revolution in Mexico causes extreme hardship. Over a million people migrate to the Southwest. Revolutionary leadership surfaces in the Southwest, particularly the brothers Ricardo and Enrique Flores-Magon.
1912	New Mexico is granted statehood. Status is delayed by Congress in objection to New Mexico's official bilingualism and large Spanish-speaking population.
1916	The United States invades Mexico at Vera Cruz. U.S. policy helps determine the winning side of the Mexican Revolution.
1924	The U.S. Border Patrol is established along the Mexican border to control immigration.
1929	League of United Latin American Citizens (LULAC) is formed to defend civil rights of Mexican Americans.
1929–1935	Thousands of Mexican immigrants and U.S. citizens of Mexican descent are deported to Mexico during the Great Depression.

1930	Mexicans are forced to attend segregated schools in Texas and California. Emma Tenayuca Brooks leads pecan shellers strike in Texas.
1932	Extensive Mexican labor union activity occurs in agriculture and mining.
1938	El Congreso de Pueblos de Habla Español organized. Luisa Morena, leader of the California Congress of Industrial Organization (UCA-PAWA), is elected as Chair.
1942	The United States and Mexico sign an agreement to import temporary workers for wartime labor—Braceros.
1943	The "Sleepy Lagoon Case" leads to anti-Mexican attacks in Los Angeles (Zoot Suit riots). Sailors and others attack Mexican American residents of Los Angeles area.
1946–1950	Luisa Morena and hundreds of Mexican labor leaders are purged and deported, often accused of being communists.
1950–1960	Numerous attempts are made to organize farmworkers.
1954	Immigration Service begins "Operation Wetback," a massive program to deport Mexican laborers.
1965	Grape strike initiated by Filipinos, combines with Mexican union to create the United Farmworkers Union (AFL-CIO). Multiracial organizing is a critical element for success. Rodolfo "Corky" Gonzales forms the Crusade for Justice in Denver.
1966	Reies Tijerina and others are arrested for seeking to reclaim land in New Mexico taken from their ancestors at Tierra Amarilla. Mexican American Political Association (MAPA) is founded to contend for respect within the Democratic Party.
1966–1972	United Farmworkers Union uses consumer boycott to win contracts. UFW trains generations of union organizers. César Chávez and Dolores Huerta are leaders of U.F.W.
1968	Over 1,000 high school students walk out of classes in Los Angeles protesting inadequate educational opportunities. Protests spread to other cities in the Southwest.
1969	El Plan de Santa Barbara sets out a program for the development of Chicano self-determination in education. Chicanos participate in Third World Strike in San Francisco. Over 20,000 Chicanos participate in a march in Los Angeles protesting the deaths of Chicanos in the war in Vietnam. Police attack the march resulting in a three-day battle between police and the community; three persons are killed.
1970	La Raza Unida Party organized in Crystal City, Texas, by Jose Angel Gutierrez and others. Chicano nationalism becomes prominent. U.S. Census begins using the term *Hispanic origin*. Chicano studies programs are established on university campuses. Chicana feminist movement is organized.
1971–1972	Community organizations seize buildings and public property to establish Chicano community organizations in Seattle and Santa Barbara.

1976   After years of boycott pressure, a farm labor law is signed in California providing free, supervised elections in the fields. This is the first legal protection of farmworkers' rights. Jerry Apodaca and Raul Castro are elected as governors of New Mexico and Arizona. Meaningful Bilingual Education law passed in California. Mexican immigrants and Chicanos work together to protect the rights of undocumented immigrants.

1980   After Republican electoral victories, Mexican and Chicano programs are assaulted. Previous legislative gains were reversed (e.g., farmworkers' rights, bilingual education). A Decade of the Hispanic is declared by conservative organizations. Henry Cisneros is elected Mayor of San Antonio, Texas.

1982   Severe economic recession particularly impacts Latino families. A two-tiered economy develops—one prosperous, the other in crisis. Texas authorities try to deny admission to school for children of some immigrant parents. The U.S. Supreme Court decides in *Plyler vs. Doe* that Texas must allow all children to attend school.

1984   Latino votes are critical to the election of Harold Washington in Chicago. Enrollment in Chicano Studies declines.

1986   Albar Pena is elected Mayor of Denver, Colorado. Latino organizations participate in the Rainbow Coalition. In Sacramento, California, a march of a coalition of Third World students (over 5,000 in number) demands educational reform. Major growth occurs in new organizations, National Association for Bilingual Education (NABE) and CABE, to extend and protect bilingual education. Growing Latino population remains excluded from political offices by gerrymandering.

1987   Growth of Hispanic conservative forces with Richard Rodriguez and Linda Chavez as prominent spokespersons.

1988   A series of states with large Latino populations pass English as an Official Language statutes. MALDEF serves as a major litigant.

1989   Latino votes are critical to the election of Mayor David Dinkins of New York. Federal courts make decisions overturning prejudicial voting districts in Texas and Watsonville, California.

1990   A federal judge rules that the Los Angeles County Board of Supervisors have deliberately drawn electoral districts that discriminate against Latinos. The decision affects 8.5 million residents. Los Angeles is forced to redistrict. National economic policies shift funds from anti-poverty programs to the protection of corporate interests. Poverty increases, and the society becomes increasingly divided by class and by race.

1992   Neighborhood violence, lack of hope, economic decline, and police brutality toward an African American ignite an urban insurrection and riot in Los Angeles. Twenty of the 55 killed were Latinos; over 50% of all those arrested were Latinos—mostly from immigrant neighborhoods. Governmental policy response is minimal. The Latino participation in the rebellion is ignored by policy makers. Hispanic Congressional Caucus grows to 16 members. The Mexican Government (PRI) and the Bush administration propose a free trade agreement between the

United States, Mexico, and Canada. The NAFTA agreement, signed in 1993, accelerates the integration of these economics.

1993   Lucille Roybal-Allard, a Chicana, is elected Vice Chair of the Congressional Hispanic Caucus.

1993   May, 1993—César Chávez, President of the United Farmworkers of America (AFL-CIO), dies. California Governor Pete Wilson, U.S. Attorney General Janet Reno, and others declare a crisis of immigration. Over 1 million immigrants arrive. Major concerns are raised about "illegal" immigration. Over 40 people are killed along the U.S. Mexican Border. Latinos are assaulted in race-based incidents in Davis, Chico, and San Diego, California. Over 31 restrictive pieces of legislation are introduced in California and the U.S. Congress. Proposals are made to amend the U.S. Constitution to restrict rights of immigrant children.

1994   California Governor Pete Wilson leads an anti-immigrant initiative seeking to deny education to children without legal documents. Anti-immigrant, anti-Mexican campaign reaches intense animosity—the worst since the 1950s.

By a margin of 62% to 38%, California voters support Proposition 187, a measure to restrict and punish illegal immigration. California Governor Pete Wilson focuses his reelection efforts on this anti-immigrant campaign. California's population is 56.3% European American, 26.3% Latino, 9.4% Asian, 7.4% African American, and 0.6% other (including Native Americans). However, because of age, citizenship, and differences in voter participation rates, the actual voters in the 1994 election, according to exit polls, were 80% European American, 9% Latino, 7% African American, and 4% Asian. The electorate of California is significantly different from its general population.

In the election, the electorate divides along racial and ethnic lines. Latinos voted against the measure 3 to 1; African Americans and Asians voted against by about 52% each, and European American voters (80% of the total) supported the measure by 60%.

Anti-immigrant campaigns spread from California to other states.

All but one provision of Proposition 187 is blocked from enforcement by the federal courts, citing U.S. constitutional protections.

While Republicans win a major electoral victory, the actual number of Latino elected officials increases at both state and federal levels. The Hispanic Caucus in Congress increases to 19 members.

Court decisions forcing equalization of school funding in Texas promise increased funding for the heavily Mexican American areas along the Rio Grande Valley.

1995   The New Mexico legislature passes a resolution denouncing anti-immigrant campaigns similar to California Proposition 187. In Texas, similar campaigns have little support.

Mexico's economy suffers a major financial crisis. The U.S. government guarantees loans of $40 billion to its NAFTA partner. The effectiveness of economic integration and foreign investment-led growth is questioned. The crisis in the Mexican economy produces increased pressure on immigration in the United States.

In the public schools, high rates of failure and drop outs / push outs continue for Latino students. In Texas, the Industrial Areas Foundation, led by Ernesto Cortes, organizes parents into a potent political force demanding school improvement.

California Governor Pete Wilson decides to run for President of the United States, in part based on the success of his anti-immigrant campaign in California. Anti-immigrant positions become important parts of the Republican party platforms and programs.

Appendix C

A Multicultural History of Women in the United States

1500	Iroquois Confederation women participate in substantial decision making. Women select the leaders of the nations.
1680	Mestizo culture comes to the Southwest (New Mexico, Texas, California) bringing ideas of community property and protects the legal status of women to own property.
1690	Sor Juana Inez de La Cruz—poet and feminist—receives education, publishes, and advocates for education of women and teachers.
1700	In English colonies, women are excluded from voting and political participation. African American women, as slaves, have substantial responsibilities as heads of families.
1776	Women help plan the Boston Tea Party. Women participate in American Revolution (War of Independence). European American women's legal and social states are not affected by the revolution. There are few records of protest, with exceptions of Abigail Adams and Mercy Otis Warren. Abigail Adams warns her husband, John Adams, to grant women's rights in the drafting of the U.S. Constitution. Settlement of colonial population destroys Iroquois Confederation and their tradition of women's active participation.
1820	Large New England textile mills begin factory system. Women organize strikes to improve working conditions. In Mexico (current U.S. Southwest), women enjoy community property rights and legal status. Women in the West endure hard and difficult lives. Women participate and lead anti-slavery agitation (L. Mott, the Grimke sisters, Sojourner Truth, and others). Women and children become dominant work force in factories. Difficult working conditions and long hours are normal.
1833	Oberlin College is founded as coeducational institution.
1837	First college for women at Mt. Holyoke, Maine.
1840	Chinese immigration begins. Chinese women specifically excluded from immigration as a form of labor and social control.

1845	First women form trade unions such as the Lowell Female Reform Association.
1848	Seneca Falls Women Rights Convention. First national organization of women. Women demand right to vote and other reforms.
1850	Coeducational public elementary schools are developed. U.S. forces conquer the Southwest: Texas, California, New Mexico, and Arizona. Traditional community property laws and legal status for women weaken as a result.
1850–1860	Women's Rights Conventions continue. Several women's colleges are established to promote education: Smith, Mt. Holyoke, Vassar.
1860	Upper-class women begin to gain leisure time through domestic help and labor-saving devices. Women are admitted to higher education institutions. More women's colleges are established. Oneida Society seeks to establish communitarian life where women are treated more equally. Charlotte Perkins Gilman develops feminist economics ideas. Elizabeth Gurley Flynn and Mother Jones work as labor organizers.
1886	Establishment of Hull House by Jane Addams. Lucy Gonzales Parson gains fame as organizer of Haymarket Square Defense Committee. Later, she founds Industrial Workers of the World.
1890	Women in most states achieve the legal status and property rights equal to men. This is an era of intense reform and development of settlement houses. Socialists and populists lead demands for expansion of democracy. Helen Keller leads anti-imperialist movement. Clara Zitkin becomes a leader of Garment Workers Union. May Elizabeth Lease organizes the Populist Party.
1910	Eighty percent of elementary and secondary teachers are women. Women found and lead several peace organizations. Flores Magonistas provide substantial feminist perspective and feminist leadership in Mexican Revolution and the Southwest. Sara Estela Ramirez is a writer and activist in Partido Liberal Mexicano.
1920	Outstanding women such as Emma Goldman and Alice Paul serve as leaders of radical politics. Ida Wells Barnet leads anti-lynching campaign. National Women's Political Party is founded. Nineteenth Amendment to the U.S. Constitution is approved, giving women the right to vote. Southern male senators are assured by suffrage advocates that this doesn't mean Black women can vote.
1928	Emma Tennayuca organizes pecan shellers strike in San Antonio, Texas.
1930	This is an intense period of union activity and organizing for women. CIO increases its membership of women to 800,000.
1936	Luisa Morena serves as President of UCAPAWA (CIO). Frances Perkins becomes the first female member of the Cabinet as Secretary of Labor. Women provide critical support for the Flint Sit Down Strike, establishing the United Auto Workers Union. Women such as Stella Novicki serve as union organizers. Eleanor Roosevelt uses her position as First Lady to advocate for women's rights.

1940	Masses of women enter war industries and unions. After the war, they are "encouraged" to return to home. Programs for child care, national health, and other "women's issues" get pushed off of national agenda.
1948	Margaret Chase Smith becomes first woman to serve in both houses of Congress.
1950	One out of three women works outside of the home.
1955	Rosa Parks initiates Montgomery Bus Boycott. Ella Baker organizes for SNCC and Congress of Racial Equality.
1960	Dolores Huerta becomes a leader of National Farm Workers Association, and later, Vice President of United Farmworkers Union (AFL-CIO).
1963	*Feminine Mystique* is published. New forms of gender oppression are identified and articulated. Equal Pay Act is passed.
1964	Fannie Lou Hammar leads the Mississippi Freedom Democratic party to challenge White control of Democratic Party. Patsy Takemoto Mink of Hawaii (D) is the first Japanese American (Nisei) woman elected to U.S. House of Representatives.
	Title VII of the Civil Rights Act prohibits discrimination.
1965	Executive Order 11246, signed into law by President Johnson, bars discrimination on the basis of race, color, religion, or national origin by federal contractors.
1966	National Organization for Women (NOW) is founded.
1967	Executive Order 11375 expands the definition of nondiscrimination to include women. These orders are the basis for affirmative action.
1969	Shirley Chisholm becomes first African American woman to serve in Congress.
1970	Third major women's movement grows. Women's studies become established as university courses. Fifty thousand women march for equal rights in New York City.
1971	National Women Political Caucus (NWPC) is established.
1972	*Ms.* magazine is established as forum for new women's movement. Shirley Chisholm runs for president.
1973	Equal Rights Amendment to the U.S. Constitution passes Congress, but fails to get two thirds of state legislature to ratify. U.S. Supreme Court *(Roe v. Wade)* rules that a woman may choose to terminate a pregnancy, based on her constitutional right to privacy from government intervention. *Our Bodies/Our Selves* is published.
1974	Women form the Coalition of Labor Union Women (CLUW). Ella Grasso is elected governor of Connecticut.
1975	International Woman's Year proclaimed by the United Nations.
1980s	The Pill and other forms of birth control give women more choices. Anti-feminist political forces organize in the Republican Party under the name of pro-family. Women become 40% of all union members. Clerical and government services become unionized. Mary Furtrell leads the

	National Education Association as major spokesperson for liberal causes.
1981	Sandra Day O'Connor becomes first woman in the U.S. Supreme Court. Rose Bird is appointed Chief Justice of California Supreme Court.
1983	Sally Ride is the first woman in space shuttle.
1984	Geraldine Ferraro receives Democratic nomination for Vice President of the United States.
1986	Wilma Mankiller is the first female Chief of Cherokee nation.
1990	*Ms.* magazine reborn. Between 1970 and 1990, the number of women physicians doubled from 7.6% to 16.9% of the total, a result, in part, of affirmative action.
1991	Sexual harassment becomes national issue in the confirmation hearings for Supreme Court Justice Clarence Thomas. NOW commission recommends exploration of a third political party after concluding that neither major political party is responsive to women's needs.
1992	Carol Moseley Braun becomes the first African American female elected to the U.S. Senate. A total of five women become Senators. Women's Caucus in the House of Representatives and U.S. Senate are increasingly effective. Congressperson Patricia Schroeder leads criticism of the Navy for sexual harassment. Marian Wright Edelman, founder and President of the Children's Defense Fund, publishes *The Measure of Our Success.* The American Association of University Women publishes the report *How Schools Shortchange Girls,* initiating a new dialogue on gender equity in classrooms.
1993	Issues of gender equity increasingly are studied as a component of multicultural education programs for teachers.
1994	Affirmative action programs come under serious attack in California and in other states. Opposition to affirmative action programs becomes increasingly a campaign issue in the Republican party. Organizations opposed to choice on abortion rights become increasingly militant and aggressive in their demonstration. Women's health clinics are bombed and shut down. Two doctors and health workers are killed by terrorists. Conservative leaders, such as Diane Ravitch, oppose funding for gender-equity efforts in the federal education budget.
1995	After significant congressional victories by Republicans, federal budgets are cut for children's programs, school lunches, and AFDC. Since over 60% of all welfare recipients are women or their children, the assault on welfare is interpreted by major organizations such as NOW (National Organization for Women) as an assault on women . A women's perspective on economic development emerges at the United Nations world social summit. The National Women's History Project continues to produce excellent books and videos to support the inclusion of women's history in the curriculum.

Appendix D

A Brief History of Japanese Americans

1868	Over 100 Japanese contract laborers begin to work in Hawaii. Japanese are recruited to break the power of Chinese workers.
1869	Japanese immigrants arrive in California and establish a colony at Gold Hill (Coloma, California—near present-day Sacramento).
1882	Chinese Exclusion Act passes Congress.
1884	Japan permits legal emigration.
1885	Men, women, and children immigrate to Hawaii.
1894	*Nishimura vs. U.S.* leads to an agreement that the United States shall protect the rights of Japanese living in this country.
1900	San Francisco School Board establishes segregated schools for 93 Japanese school children. The order is rescinded in 1907. The United States and Japan agree to restrict Japanese immigration to the United States.
1910	Japanese are banned from marrying non-Orientals. Practice of arranging for picture brides begins.
1913	California legislature makes it difficult for Japanese to own land.
1922	The U.S. Supreme Court declares Asian immigrants ineligible for naturalization *(Ozawa vs. U.S.)*.
1924	Asian Exclusion Act prohibits most Japanese immigration.
1930s	Anti-Japanese propaganda common in United States.
1930	Japanese American Citizens League founded.
1940s	U.S. soldiers of Japanese descent fight valiantly in World War II in a segregated unit. Three hundred and ten Nisei women serve in the Armed Forces.
1941	Japanese bomb Pearl Harbor in Hawaii. The United States enters war with Japan.
1942	President Roosevelt signs Executive Order #9066 establishing forced relocation camps (concentration camps) for all Japanese Americans on the mainland.

1944	The U.S. Supreme Court rules that the removal and detentions are legal (Korematsu case).
1945	The United States drops atomic bomb on Hiroshima and Nagasaki, ending World War II. On December 28, President Truman signs War Brides Act allowing G.I.'s to bring wives back to United States.
1946	Four hundred thirty-six persons of Japanese ancestry are repatriated or deported to Japan. Internment camps are closed.
1948	The U.S. Supreme Court declares the California law banning interracial marriages unconstitutional.
1952	McCarren-Walter Immigration Act permits new immigration and naturalization.
1964	Patsy Takemoto Mink of Hawaii (D) becomes first Nisei woman elected to U.S. House of Representatives.
1970s	Robert Matsui, Patricia Saiki, and Norm Mineta—all Japanese Americans—are elected to Congress. Daniel Inowe is elected to U.S. Senate from Hawaii. Japanese American (Nisei) and Chinese American politics become majority politics in state of Hawaii.
1980	Commission on Wartime Relocation is created by President Carter. It recommends a formal apology, monetary redress, and educational funds for Japanese Americans interned during World War II. Anti-Japan feeling is revived in United States based on economic dislocation and competition. Vincent Chinn is murdered because Detroit auto workers thought he was Japanese.
1988	President Reagan signs redress bill for Japanese Americans who had been interned.
1990	Japanese Americans are granted reparations for World War II incarceration. Asian Americans dramatically improve their rates of participation in higher education.
1992	Urban riot and rebellion in Los Angeles include an anti-Korean component. Poor African American communities are, at times, polarized against Koreans and other Asians. Six Asian Americans are elected to Congress.

Appendix E

A Brief History of Chinese Americans

1640	Chinese immigrants go to Philippines, Mexico, Brazil, Peru, and the United States.
1839	British troops occupy Canton and create oppression in China, resulting in the Anglo-Chinese War.
1840	Chinese immigrate to Hawaii as contract labor. Yankee missionaries and traders live in China.
1849	Gold Rush spurs Chinese workers, like many others, to move to California.
1851	Cantonese immigrants form Chinese Association.
1852	Anti-Chinese activism is common in California.
1854	A Chinese worker rejected as a witness in court against a White person in *People vs. Hall.*
1855	California passes tax on Chinese workers. Twenty-four thousand Chinese work in the mines.
1864	Chinese workers provide the labor for the Union Pacific Railroad/Central Pacific.
1866	Chinese workers work through winter building railroads through the Sierra Mountains. Chinese workers strike for higher wages.
1868	Businesses seek Chinese immigrants as cheap labor.
1869	Chinese farmers develop the San Joaquin and Sacramento River delta. Chinese are the primary agricultural laborers in California. Chinese become workers in southern United States. Anti-Chinese riots occur in San Francisco.
1870	Sixty-three thousand Chinese live in United States, 50,000 in California. California prohibits immigration of most Chinese women.
1871	Anti-Chinese attacks in Los Angeles by more than 500 Whites.
1877	Anti-Chinese "riots" in San Francisco.

1880	California law prohibits intermarriage between Whites and Chinese.
1882	Chinese Exclusion Act, the first openly racial U.S. immigration law, prohibits further immigration.
1885	In Rock Springs, Wyoming, miners murder 28 Chinese American miners.
1893	Anti-Chinese violence and ethnic conflicts occur in labor force.
1906	Earthquake in San Francisco destroys most immigration records. After 1907, thousands of new immigrants arrive.
1910	Chinese move to cities to resist oppression and violence. Chinatowns are established in San Francisco and Sacramento. Anti-Chinese violence drives Chinese from agriculture to Los Angeles, Oakland, Chicago, Seattle, and Portland.
1920	Chinese develop urban professions such as laundry services. Urban ghettos develop.
1923	Education becomes a major process for Chinese American advancement for second- and third-generation Chinese Americans.
1935	Chinatown develops into tourist attraction in San Francisco. Higher education leads to few job opportunities.
1939	Chinese, as World War II allies, improve U.S. attitudes toward Chinese Americans.
1943	Chinese Exclusionary Laws are repealed. Chinese again are admitted as immigrants to the United States.
1949	Communists win control of mainland China. Political divisions are deep in Chinese American community.
1959	Hiram L. Fong becomes first U.S. Senator of Asian ancestry (D-Hawaii).
1970s	Asian Americans build some political ties between Japanese and Chinese communities. Chinese Americans establish successful positions in higher education.
1974	Nationalist Chinese government seeks to influence U.S. Chinese communities. In *Lau vs. Nichols,* the U.S. Courts found that San Francisco Unified Schools were denying Chinese American students a "meaningful opportunity to participate in public educational programs." This court case established the legal foundations for most bilingual education programs. Hong Kong, Taiwan, and Singapore become major commercial centers in Asia.
1976	Ethnic Chinese from Vietnam immigrate to the United States as refugees. Existing bilingual education programs assist their assimilation into the society.
1980	A reforming China allows extensive travel and study. U.S. government establishes closer relationships with Chinese government.
1989	Chinese government crushes the "pro-democracy" movement in Tiananmen Square, China. Chinese Americans respond with support for the dissidents.

1993   Hundreds of Chinese seek to enter the United States illegally, fleeing poverty in their homeland. A crisis of "illegal immigration" targets Latinos, Chinese, and Arabs. Eight Chinese drown trying to reach the United States from boats.

1994   Anti-immigrant campaigns in California affect the Chinese community. Attempts to build Asian support for immigration and bilingual education struggle to deal with the diversity of the Asian population: Chinese, Korean, Japanese, Vietnamese, Khmer, Hmong, and others.

1995   Campaigns against affirmative action divide the Chinese community by generation, and at times divide the community from other immigrant groups. Chinese, and some other Asian groups, have more representation in the Republican party while other immigrant communities are traditionally Democratic.

Appendix F

A Brief History of Puerto Ricans

	Arawak and Taino people live on the Island of Puerto Rico.
1493	Columbus lands on Puerto Rico.
1508	Juan Ponce de León becomes Spanish Governor of Puerto Rico.
1511	The Taino people rebel against forced labor and are defeated.
1513	African slaves are brought to work on plantations in the United States.
1868	El Grito de Lares—Puerto Rican revolutionaries—attempt a revolt for independence.
1873	Slavery is abolished in Puerto Rico.
1898	The United States invades Puerto Rico as a battle in the Spanish-Cuban-American War. In the Treaty of Paris, Spain cedes Puerto Rico to the United States.
1899	League of Patriots of Puerto Rico seeks a plebiscite on the island to test if the people accept the U.S. control.
1900	The U.S. Congress passes Foraker Organic Act, bringing Puerto Rico under the administrative control of the United States. The President of the United States appoints the Governor and Executive Council. The people are allowed to elect a House of Delegates.
1917	In March, the Jones Organic Act is passed. Puerto Ricans are given U.S. citizenship. The government of Puerto Rico, imposed by the United States, allows some local self-government. Presidential appointees control the major posts. Puerto Ricans are subject to U.S. Selective Service (the draft) in World War I.
1918	President Woodrow Wilson proclaims that natural self-determination is "an imperative principle of action." Wilson prevents the plebiscite in Puerto Rico and invades Mexico, Nicaragua, and Haiti.
1920	Eleven thousand, eight hundred Puerto Ricans live on mainland United States.

1930–1937	The Nationalist Party demands immediate U.S. withdrawal from Puerto Rico.
1933	President Roosevelt transfers jurisdiction over Puerto Rico from the War Department to the Department of the Interior.
1935	Fifty-eight thousand Puerto Ricans now live on U.S. mainland.
1936	The United States suppresses the Nationalist Party and jails its leaders.
1945	The Puerto Rican legislature proposes that the people be given a free choice of independence, statehood, or dominion status. The U.S. military opposed the plan "for national security reasons."
1947	U.S. Congress approves an Elective Governor Act for Puerto Rico. Luis Muñoz Marin, a Puerto Rican, is elected governor.
1950	Nationalists attempt a revolution on Puerto Rico.
1951	A plebiscite is held; the voters of Puerto Rico choose a commonwealth status.
1952	Puerto Rico becomes a commonwealth, defined as "an Associated Free State."
1953	The United States is challenged in the United Nations for its continued colonial relationship with Puerto Rico. Rapid urbanization and light industrialization change Puerto Rico. Hundreds of thousands of displaced workers migrate to the U.S. mainland in search of employment.
1959	Puerto Rico presents the Fernó-Murray Bill in the U.S. Congress, requesting a clearer definition of the status of a commonwealth.
1960	Puerto Ricans do not fit into the racial categories of *White* or *Black* that are commonly used in United States.
1962	The United Nations considers the case of decolonizing Puerto Rico.
1965	The U.S. Civil Rights Act allows Puerto Ricans living in the United States to vote without passing an English literacy test.
1967	Puerto Ricans vote in a plebiscite to maintain their commonwealth status.
1969	The Oceanhill-Brownsville dispute in New York divides Puerto Rican and Black parents from the leadership of the American Federation of Teachers.
1972	The United Nations Committee in Decolonization approves a resolution supporting the self-determination and independence of Puerto Rico. Bilingual education programs offer improved educational opportunities for Puerto Rican children.
1973–1975	A "New Pact of Association" is drafted and presented to the U.S. Congress. Puerto Ricans begin to hold important posts in labor unions.
1978	President Jimmy Carter promises to respect the principle of self-determination and to support a referendum for the Puerto Rican people to decide on their status.
1980	Over 2,000,000 Puerto Ricans live in the United States; 3,187,000 live in Puerto Rico.

1982	Puerto Rican votes are critical to the election of Harold Washington in Chicago.
1989	Puerto Rican votes and community organizations are determining factor in the election of David Dinkins in New York. The U.S. Senate Committee on Natural Resources prepares a bill for a plebiscite to establish a plebiscite on statehood or independence (S-172).
1992	A Puerto Rican woman, Nydia Velasquez, is elected to the U.S. Congress.
1993	Puerto Ricans on the island vote to become a state in a preference poll. José E. Serrano (D-New York) is elected chair of the Congressional Hispanic Caucus.

Index